Activity Math

Using
Manipulatives
in the
Classroom

Anne M. Bloomer
Phyllis A. T. Carlson

Addison-Wesley Publishing Company

Menlo Park, California • Reading, Massachusetts • New York
Don Mills, Ontario • Wokingham, England • Amsterdam • Bonn
Sydney • Singapore • Tokyo • Madrid • San Juan • Paris
Seoul, Korea • Milan • Mexico City • Taipei, Taiwan

This book is dedicated to all those students who inspired us to create these lessons and who helped us refine them.

We would like to thank the following people from Minnetonka Public Schools, Excelsior, Minnesota, for their support and assistance: Dr. Dale Rusch, Dr. Lorraine Boyle, Charles Andrews, Shirley Bierma, Mark Broten, Kris Grimstad, Pamela Orr, and Eileen Poul.

Our appreciation to Barbra Spiess for her technical assistance, and to Mali Apple and Michael Kane of Addison-Wesley Innovative Division for their expertise.

Managing Editor: Michael Kane
Project Editor: Mali Apple
Production: Karen Edmonds
Design: Vicki Philp
Cover Art: Rachel Gage

ISBN 0-201-45506-4

6 7 8 9-DR-97 96 95

Contents

Symbol Key

■   Manipulative introduction of a key skill or subskill.

☐   Procedure includes writing. Reinforcement of a concept at a connecting or more abstract level.

Introduction

The National Council of Teachers of Mathematics (NCTM) made specific recommendations in the *Curriculum and Evaluation Standards for School Mathematics*. One recommendation was to increase the use of manipulative materials.

The use of manipulatives enhances concept formation when both the concrete and connecting stages are fully understood before moving to the abstract. This way of instructing students promotes understanding of the "why" as well as the "how" of mathematics. The fundamental concepts developed in this way enable the student to build on "old" knowledge and adapt it to new tasks and situations.

Although many books about using manipulatives have been written, most cover one particular material and its uses. Teachers, however, need to teach the skills covered in their texts, and it is often too time-consuming to check each book to see which might apply to the current skill.

We therefore developed skill-based lessons that include several kinds of appropriate manipulatives for each skill and that are easily adaptable to any text. Since activities are for both concrete and connecting levels, these lessons provide ample opportunity for students to see relationships and to develop understanding, along with a high level of confidence. This multi-sensory way of instruction is ideal for students of all abilities. Cooperative learning is also a key element.

Lessons cover most skills. Some skills and materials, however, such as calculators, that are usually covered adequately in regular textbooks are not treated in this book, as it is intended to be supplemental to a basal math program.

Lessons are divided into the following strands:

1. Number Skills
2. Place Value
3. Addition
4. Subtraction
5. Multiplication
6. Division
7. Fractions
8. Decimals
9. Ratio and Percent
10. Geometry
11. Measurement

Book features include

1. Scope and Sequence with sub-skills and appropriate grade levels listed
2. Lessons correlated with NCTM Standards
3. Section on making and using manipulatives
4. Materials needed listed by grade level
5. Reproducible pages
6. Organized by strands—specific lessons easily found

7. Perforated pages, punched for a binder
8. Labels for strand and chapter dividers

Lessons are written in a step-by-step way to make the teacher's initial job easier. Features include

1. Skill, boxed near the top of the page
2. Key sub-skills identified
3. Approximate time
4. Materials, listed and explained
5. Anticipatory Set—motivating introductory activities
6. At least two manipulatives for each skill
7. Identification of, and procedures for, both concrete and connecting stages
8. Practice and Extension—activities tying skills to problem solving and real-life uses.

Rationale for Using Manipulatives

Putting Theory into Practice

Children construct, test, and change ideas as they integrate them into their structure of understanding. As they explore and interact with their environment, they build understanding at the concrete, then the semiconcrete or representational level, and finally at the abstract level. Appropriate experiences need to be provided to facilitate each stage of this process. Merely providing blocks to work with—the concrete level—will not necessarily ensure that a student will be able to multiply a 3-digit number by a 1-digit number on paper.

Doris H. Gluck (*Arithmetic Teacher*, vol. 138, no. 7 [March, 1991], p. 13) offers the following paradigm for helping students make connections between the concrete and the abstract:

Blocks
Blocks and teacher writes
Blocks and student partner writes
Blocks and write
Writing only
Repeat with another physical model

We urge you never to shorten the connecting stage of both using materials and writing the process at the same time. Otherwise, many students will never make the connection between the concrete and abstract. They will have built few bridges. Even if they have learned the sequence of steps in an algorithm, they may not be able to use this knowledge in a meaningful way.

The use of manipulatives not only aids with specific skills, but helps students discover the connections between operations and different areas of mathematics. We have included such connections in our lessons, tying new skills to previously experienced ones. Students who have made these connections using manipulatives, especially when these are presented in a problem-solving or real-life format, will know better which operation to use in solving a new problem. They can often work out an answer even if their paper-and-pencil skills are still at a lower level.

Communication

Because of students' natural interest in using materials and discovering new ideas, working with manipulatives leads to discussion, whether you want it or not! Since communication about math is important as students construct, evaluate, and integrate their ideas, each lesson includes opportunities for discussion. You can guide students toward fuller understanding by using such questions as the following reprinted with permission from *Professional Standards for Teaching Mathematics*, copyright 1991 by the National Council of Teachers of Mathematics.

- Helping students work together to make sense of mathematics

    "What do others think about what Janine said?"
    "Do you agree? Disagree?"
    "Does anyone else have the same answer but a different way to explain it?"
    "Would you ask the rest of the class that question?"
    "Do you understand what they are saying?"
    "Can you convince the rest of us that that makes sense?"

- Helping students to rely more on themselves to determine whether something is mathematically correct

    "Why do you think that?"
    "Why is that true?"
    "How did you reach that conclusion?"
    "Does that make sense?"
    "Can you make a model to show that?"

- Helping students learn to reason mathematically

    "Does that always work?"
    "Is that true for all cases?"
    "Can you think of a counterexample?"
    "How could you prove that?"
    "What assumptions are you making?"

- Helping students learn to conjecture, invent, and solve problems

    "What would happen if . . . ? What if not?"
    "Do you see a pattern?"
    "What are some possibilities here?"
    "Can you predict the next one? What about the last one?"
    "How did you think about the problem?"
    "What decision do you think he should make?"
    "What is alike and what is different about your method of solution and hers?"

- Helping students to connect mathematics, its ideas, and its applications

    "How does this relate to . . . ?"
    "What ideas that we have learned before were useful in solving this problem?"
    "Have we ever solved a problem like this one before?"
    "What uses of mathematics did you find in the newspaper last night?"
    "Can you give me an example of . . . ?"

Students also need to communicate about math in writing. Journals are a good way to do this, helping students integrate their knowledge and you to assess their understanding. Some possible topics for journal entries:

- what I learned in class today
- what helped me understand it
- why would it be important to know it

Even just asking "Why?" after student responses is a good way to begin to improve communication. Eliciting answers and conjectures from the class, instead of giving them yourself, guides you in assessing understanding, increases students' confidence, and helps students think of themselves as sources of knowledge. Be prepared for new directions and ideas!

Assessment

We as teachers want to prepare students to reason, problem solve, make connections, and communicate about mathematics, yet we must also prepare them for standardized tests consisting mostly of computation, with one or two word problems. We are often held accountable for those test results.

We also assess students and ourselves daily in order to create tasks, guide students' thinking, pace the lessons, and evaluate the day's procedures. We give tests, assign written work, observe small groups, interview students one on one, watch them work, ask questions, and evaluate class discussion.

Some concerns have arisen that students taught from a manipulative base do not test well. Our students have been very successful on standardized tests. We teach from a manipulative base and use the basal for worksheets, assignments, and tests. Often, we do not assign anything until students have worked with the manipulatives for several days and have connected writing with the concrete activities. It is a mistake to go to the abstract, written-only problems too soon.

If you have taught all three steps, students will have an appropriate knowledge of the abstract symbols and how they connect to the concrete. They also will have more tools for problem solving.

When students work with manipulatives, daily assessment of their progress is made easier. You can quickly see whose blocks are not positioned correctly and who is slow at starting. Students can see what others are doing and by comparison evaluate their own activities and understanding.

Because you can see students' mistakes, they can be caught early, and you can guide students' exploration or to use questions to suggest a different tack. Thus, the chance is less that a student will do every homework problem wrong. In going over written work, ask what would be happening with the blocks. Often students will catch their own errors, since the written algorithm closely corresponds to the concrete.

Staff Development

Most elementary teachers have heard about the above-mentioned Standards and wish to improve their teaching but are unsure how to do so. Pre-service teachers also need to know the best methods of presentation.

Standard 4: Knowing Mathematical Pedagogy

The pre-service and continuing education of teachers of mathematics should develop teachers' knowledge of and ability to use and evaluate—

- instructional materials and resources, including technology;
- ways to represent mathematics concepts and procedures;
- instructional strategies and classroom organizational models;
- ways to promote discourse and foster a sense of mathematical community;
- means for assessing student understanding of mathematics.

(Reprinted with permission from *Professional Standards for Teaching Mathematics*, copyright 1991 by the National Council of Teachers of Mathematics.)

Teachers need to focus on creating learning environments that encourage students' questions and deliberations—environments in which the students and teacher are engaged with one another's thinking and function as members of a mathematical community. In such a community, the teacher-student and student-student interaction provides teachers with opportunities for diagnosis and guidance and for modeling mathematical thinking, while, at the same time, it provides students with opportunities to challenge and defend their constructions. (Reprinted with permission from *Professional Standards for Teaching Mathematics*.)

Teachers have to develop a structure to identify, assess, and use appropriate mathematical instructional materials. This structure should be developed from the teacher's knowledge of basic mathematical concepts, a recognition of what information is necessary for each specific skill, as well as an understanding of the connections between concrete, visual, graphical, and symbolic representations of those skills. It should include the knowledge of different ways to present

these representations for each mathematical skill and task. This book provides some ways to help teachers with their development of this internal structure; it is aimed at helping teachers learn about a variety of concrete materials and a range of ways to use them to explain different mathematical concepts. The book also focuses on how to make the connections between the concrete and more abstract representations understandable for the students.

Because this book is tied to the Standards, it makes an ideal basis for in-service or pre-service presentations. Teachers involved in hands-on doing of the lessons become more confident in using the materials and instructional techniques. By working through several skills within a strand and its related strands, they can see both the abstract and concrete connections between operations.

Practicing teachers are bound by the curriculum of their district and by the time constraints inherent in their work. Consequently, although they want to leave a workshop or class with ideas leading to improved instruction, they also want those ideas to translate easily into improved, usable lessons.

Group activities promote communication and even greater understanding. Having groups of teachers solve or propose problems, find more tie-ins to real-life math or extensions to other curricular areas, can help them develop practical ideas. They can write notes within each lesson, thereby making it more probable that what is learned in in-service training will affect what is taught to the students.

How to Use This Book

Don't Panic—Start Here

For many of us teachers the Standards are exciting yet overwhelming. How can we balance the desire to implement a new approach with the need to cover the growing curriculum, assess with prescribed tests, stay within a tight schedule, write meaningful comments on student papers, and all the rest? We need support, time, and the kind of knowledge that easily translates into actual lessons.

By no means does this book explain completely how to teach mathematics well. It focuses on the use of manipulatives as one tool for helping students construct meaningful understandings of mathematics. It offers a start—a way for teachers to become comfortable with new ways of presenting material.

Time is short. Manipulative and inquiry lessons take longer, both initially and because you need to include the connecting stage. You may fear you will never cover the curriculum or that students will not have the written skills to pass the required tests. Halfway through the year, you may start to get that familiar feeling of panic. We know it happens because we've been there.

An interesting thing happens, however, as the skills become more difficult. Because of the groundwork done earlier in the year, students often see new skills as a "free ride" (Bohan, Harry, "Mathematical Connections: Free Rides for Kids," *Arithmetic Teacher*, vol. 38, no. 3 [November, 1990], pp. 10-14.), something they can figure out because they already know how a particular operation works. Because they often see advanced lessons as requiring not new skills but logical extensions of what they have already learned, they begin to grasp concepts more quickly. Therefore, subsequent skill acquisition occurs at a much faster pace.

Using Lessons

Pick what looks interesting to you. Geometry and measurement are easy areas to begin with, using selected lessons. If, however, you begin to teach an operation such as subtraction using manipulatives, students will do better if you teach all subtraction that way. This helps the students draw the necessary connections. Manipulating place value blocks for 1 hour during the year won't be very effective in helping students understand subtraction problems.

You also need to keep to the sequence of skills within a strand. Keeping to the sequence gives students the steps of understanding they will need to construct a coherent whole. The Scope and Sequence section lists sub-skills for each lesson, and these are also identified within lessons by the symbol ■.

We also often extend skills as we are teaching them. If students have learned to add 2-digit numbers, they are delighted to find they can add numbers in the millions the same way, especially if they do it in the hallway on large sheets of paper taped to the walls. They are proud that they can do this feat.

Students need to see math both as something that works in the real world and as an abstractness. They need to know that 2 + 3 equals 5 not just with buttons, but also with fingers, etc. The symbols stand for the buttons and the ideas. We allow students to use physical materials for as long as they want. As connections are made, students come to see that it is easier and faster to work with just the symbols and that the symbols can then be used to solve problems it would be difficult to set up physically. The procedures that include activities at the connecting level are marked with the symbol □.

We have tied the written algorithms directly to the manipulation of the materials since math language only represents what happens in the real world. Consequently, look carefully at the illustrations showing the written algorithm in each lesson. Changes are suggested to assist students in making this connection. Division, especially, is a change, but students learn it more quickly and are more adept at error analysis since they can tie it to what was happening with the blocks.

The lessons are more directed than perhaps is desirable; the eventual goal is an inquiry-type lesson. Again, we offer a start. For those teachers accustomed to teaching from a manual, for new or pre-service teachers, the script is there. You may feel just as comfortable reading through it ahead of time and presenting it on your own. You know best what kinds of problems and scenarios appeal to your students. It may be that dividing sheep just doesn't engage them as much as anteaters dividing up an ant nest, or aliens dividing their toes to fit into shoes before they land.

As you use each lesson, we suggest that you mark it with the chapter and page numbers of the corresponding section of your textbook, and that you file the lessons by chapters. For a new basal, you can easily refile the lessons. Earlier lessons, good to use as antecedent skills, can be placed at the beginning of the appropriate chapter. Resource room teachers may prefer to keep the lessons organized by strands since they usually teach more than one grade level.

Parent Involvement

Parents are interested in helping their children succeed in school, but many have their own anxieties about assisting with written math homework. Try sending students home with materials, such as laminated place value mats, and the assignment to teach their parents how it is done at school. One student taught multiplication with peas and french fries! Whole families have become involved in finding hundred board patterns. Some parents say they have understood written multiplication and division for the first time.

The Practice and Extension section in each lesson offers activities, challenges, games, and tie-ins with real-life uses of math. These also are good ways to have students and parents work together. You might suggest some of the activities if you send newsletters home with your students. Another good resource is *Family Math* (Jean Kerr Stenmark, Virginia Thompson, and Ruth Cossey, the Regents, University of California, Berkeley, California, 1986).

Parents often are willing to donate materials such as frozen dinner plasticware, buttons, and items for treasure boxes. They also can be asked to help make place value mats of file folders or to cut bills or decimal bars for students use. Reproducibles have directions for these.

Other materials to have cut out or made are number lines to have on hand; pattern blocks, geoboards, fraction bars, and place value materials made from plastic needlepoint mesh; and coins. See the Manipulative Information section for directions on making these and more.

Reproducibles good to send home include
counter-trading boards:
   play games with materials found at home
multiplication/division table:
   patterns
   fact practice
   multiples and skip counting

pattern block sheets:
    fraction practice and games
    geometry—angles, polygons
    patterns

Multiplication Clue Rhymes:
    practice facts, students and parents can invent more

Multiplication Aids 1 and 2:
    finger math for multiplication

Number Find Samples 1 and 2:
    use also for addition and subtraction by covering every third line of numbers

bills (imitation paper money):
    make change
    games with dice for skill practice

decimal bars:
    color in decimal amounts and play matching or other games

geoboard paper:
    laminate and send home with markers for multiplication, fractions, and geometry

The benefits to this kind of homework are more than skill reinforcement. Students learn as they teach and are proud to show off their skills. Parents feel more comfortable helping with math and are pleased to be offered a low-stress way to become involved with their children's education.

Working with Manipulatives

General

Read the Manipulative Information section for ideas on specific materials; you will find that many are available in your school or classroom already.

Set up general rules for using manipulatives with the class at the beginning of the year. Each time a new material is introduced, discuss its safe use and where it will be kept in the classroom. Allow students time to play with any new manipulative. In their play, they will learn some of its properties.

Materials are manageable! Be aware that it is initially more time consuming to teach using manipulatives. It may seem to take twice as long to teach a lesson, and you may feel you will be unable to cover the year's objectives. But, you *can* cover the objectives, and you will be pleased with the final results.

Plan to use more than one manipulative to teach and practice each skill. Students are at different stages in constructing their understanding of mathematics. The use of a new tool will help them re-evaluate this understanding and will often provide some connections for those students whose grasp of skills is tenuous.

A final word about manipulatives and math anxiety. We don't allow students to say "I don't get it," but have them say, "I don't *quite* get it *yet*." This creates an expectation and trust in the students that they *will* understand the material. They know

- it will be presented in several ways, with several different manipulatives;
- it's all right if they don't understand well at first;
- they can use the manipulatives for as long as they feel a need to; and
- they have a teacher, each other, and their previous experience to draw on for help.

Their comfort and confidence levels increase, and the amount of math anxiety decreases.

Storage and Day-to-Day Use

Collections of materials are used more often if they are accessible. Use permanent storage containers for each type of manipulative, with both lid and container marked to indicate the contents. Try

    coffee cans
    envelopes in a shoe box
    ice-cream buckets with lids
    margarine tubs with lids
    frozen dinner plasticware
    cardboard pencil boxes
    plastic and cardboard sweater and shoe boxes

For day-to-day use, have enough microwave or other plasticware trays or tubs for each child. Materials can be counted out just once into the trays. The filled trays can be stacked for easy distribution and collection each day. Materials are then also available if students want to use them at other times.

When students have to share, keep materials for each group in reclosable freezer bags. Use a holepunch to punch a hole in the bags so that the bags will lie flat. Label with a permanent marker, or include an inventory list in each bag to help keep materials in place.

Using the Overhead Projector and Transparencies

Commercial manipulative sets for the overhead are available, although most manipulatives silhouette nicely. When color is important or the real materials are larger than you wish, use the reproducibles, either as-is or reduced in size, to make heavyweight transparencies. Draw others by hand on heavy acetate, color with a permanent marker, and cut out.

Buy colored transparency pens and a spray bottle. Write on transparencies or the glass itself, spray with water, and wipe off with paper towels. You can mark patterns in different colors, write numbers beside manipulatives, etc. Three-hole punch your transparencies, and keep them in a three-ring notebook with a punched sheet of plain paper behind each one. Use dividers to sort by categories to help you quickly find what you want.

Choose the reproducibles appropriate for your grade level. The following are useful as transparencies: counter-trading boards, geoboard paper, graph paper, hundred boards, number lines, moon stations, and place value mats.

Manipulative Information

What is it? What can I use in its place? How can I make it?

In this section are listed descriptions, alternatives, and directions for making the materials used in the lessons. See the grade level charts for lists of materials you will need. Plan to have enough for at least every two students. Some commercial sources are listed at the end of the section.

Not everyone can afford to buy commercial materials. Try garage sales, thrift stores, and asking for donations from parents and commercial businesses. Ask parents to help make materials. If you do make your own, use sturdy materials. It is relatively inexpensive to have a printer run off your master patterns on card stock, which comes in bright colors. For laminating, try using clear self-adhesive paper. If you chill it in the freezer before using, it is easier to work with. The Education Center, Inc., offers a non-heat laminating dispenser and film that work very well.

Attribute blocks

Sets vary in shape, color, size, and thickness: circles, rectangles, triangles, squares, and sometimes hexagons, each in four colors and a variety of sizes. Loops or circles are available to aid in sorting by attribute. To make your own attribute sets, see "Paper shapes."

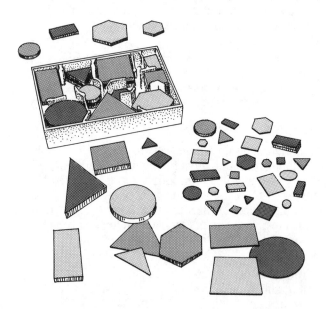

Chalkboards, individual

Available commercially. Use dark-colored poster board or railroad board cut to approximately 9" × 12". Use old cotton socks for erasing and store in coffee cans or shoe boxes, with a piece of chalk in each sock.

Containers

The best ones stack for easy storage. Many are available commercially.

bowls
egg cartons
frozen dinner, microwave plasticware
half-pint milk cartons from school lunches
margarine tubs

Counters

Commercial ones are available in all shapes, sizes, and colors. Some are one color on one side and another on the second. Transparent ones may also be used on the overhead.

If you get different colors, you can use them as counter-trading materials. You can spray-paint your own materials.

beads
beans
buttons
construction paper—small squares
craft sticks
paper clips
poker chips
washers

Counter-trading materials

A place value board with places marked with colors instead of values so that it can be adapted to various bases. Available commercially as chip-trading materials. Use with chips or counters (see above) to match the colors. See Reproducibles for boards.

Cubes, non interlocking

Commercially available in various sizes, in one color or many. Some 1 cm cubes have a mass of exactly 1 g, which is nice for measurement. See "Interlocking cubes and things" for cubes that snap together.

Cuisenaire® rods

Ten different-colored proportional lengths, representing 1 through 10. The one cube is a cubic centimeter. You could also use strips of colored graph paper.

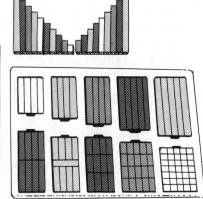

Decimals

We do not advise revaluing the place value materials for decimals. If a one is made the size of a hundred flat, many students will not understand the relationship of a tenth to one. Available commercially are decimal stamps and Decimal Squares, which are cards marked with a variety of decimals amounts.

Decimal bars

See Reproducibles for these bars, which are marked with decimal divisions and match paper money bills in size. Duplicate 25 of each per student in the same color as the U. S. paper money. You can also fill in various amounts with a marker, duplicate, and laminate.

Make a transparency, and color desired amounts in with pen. See Reproducibles for file-folder place value mats with decimal extensions.

Decimals—graph paper

Cut 1/2" graph paper into 10 × 10 squares and label: 1. Cut 1 × 10 strips and label: 1/10 = 0.1. Cut 1 × 1 squares and label: 1/100 = 0.01. A sheet and a half of paper will make 3 ones, 23 tenths, and over 20 hundredths; laminate first to make a permanent set. Use grains of rice for thousandths—about ten cover a hundredth square, thereby preserving the size relationships. Store in envelopes.

Dice

Available in several sizes and colors, blank or with numbers. Mark blank dice with a marker or with stick-on dots. Try the fuzzy ones intended to be hung in cars.

Foam rubber dice: Use a long, narrow strip of foam rubber as wide as it is thick—1" to 3". Cut it into cubes with a single-edge razor blade, and mark dots or numbers with a permanent marker. Sponge dice: Use dense sponges. Cut with a knife, and mark with a permanent marker.

Fractions

Many kinds are available: bars, circles, squares, ones that stack, cards, and tiles.

> Cuisenaire® rods
> felt fraction bars
> paper fraction bars (see below)
> paper plate fraction circles

Fraction bars—paper

Use 3" × 18" strips of construction paper: red, blue, orange, green, and yellow, one of each color per student. The red piece is left as the whole unit.

Have students fold the blue strip in half, crease the fold well, and cut on the line to make two halves. The orange strip makes fourths: first fold and cut into

halves, then fold and cut each half to make fourths. Continue in the same way, making the green strip into eighths and the yellow into sixteenths. Store in a business-size envelope, folding the red strip to fit. For a set extending to eighths or less, 3" × 12" strips can be used. Use as above for fractions wanted.

Geoboards

Available in 8" or 10" sizes, with a 5 × 5 pin arrangement. Rubber bands in different colors fit around the pins. Some can be used side by side for a larger number of pins, and some have pins in a circle on the back. See Reproducibles for geoboard paper, which can be substituted. If paper is laminated, students can use markers.

To make your own boards, which can be grouped together, use rubber cement to temporarily attach graph paper of appropriate size (see Reproducibles for 1" graph paper) to boards for marking nail arrangement. Pound in 25 finishing or round-top nails for each board at the marked points. Try to have all nails extending to the same height.

> 5" board: nails 1" apart, 1/2" margins
> 7 1/2" boards: nails 1 1/2" apart, 3/4" margins
> 10" board: nails 2" apart, 1" margins
> circles: mark center and every 30° or less around the circle

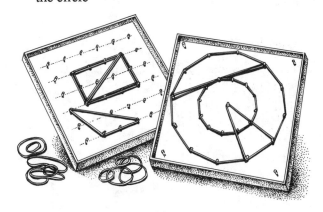

Geometric solids

Sets are available in wood, foam, or plastic, with varying pieces per set. Also available are plastic shapes that link together to construct both polyhedra and two-dimensional shapes. See the illustration on the following page.

> cones—ice-cream cones, thread cones (available at some fabric stores)
> cylinders—toilet paper rolls, oatmeal boxes
> triangular prisms—put three sharp creases in a toilet paper roll; some candies are triangular prisms
> rectangular prisms—cereal boxes, etc.
> sphere—marbles, balls, oranges, shapes made from clay, paper mâché, etc.

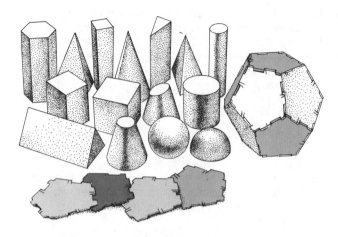

Interlocking cubes and things

Interlocking cubes snap together and are available in many colors and in sizes starting at 1 cm. Unifix® cubes join in a straight line; Multilinks™ connect on all six sides. The cubes can be made into rods or sticks.

Some sets include interlocking prisms, which are good for teaching fractions and spatial awareness. Other sets consist of squares and triangles that snap together or color-coded plastic rods that fit together with plastic connectors. These can be used to make polyhedrons and other solid geometry structures.

Measurement—materials to measure

Water is messy but interesting, because 1 L of water has a mass of 1 kg. Students enjoy discovering that fact. Provide towels or rags.

> beans
> O-shaped cereal
> pasta, especially the colored kind
> popcorn, popped and unpopped
> rice

Measurement—sets of containers

Have some containers that are of glass or clear plastic. You at least need clear measuring cups. Canning or jelly jars are alternatives. Use a permanent pen to make a line all the way around the containers to mark the desired capacities. You will need identical containers for demonstrating relationships among units.

Cup measures:

> ½-pint milk cartons with tops cut off
> 8-oz paper cups

Pint measures:

> pint half-and-half cartons with tops cut off
> pint jars

Quart measures:

> quart milk cartons
> plastic soda bottles with tops cut off and edges taped
> quart jars

Gallon measures:

> pails
> two ½-gallon cartons taped together
> gallon milk containers

Money—bills

Play money is available. See Reproducibles for our bills, $1 to $100,000. Run off back-to-back for two-sided bills. Use different colors for different denominations, starting with green for $1. Bills fit on file-folder place value mats (see Reproducibles) and work also with decimal bars (see Reproducibles).

Money—coins

Available as coins and stamps. Use coin stamps on tag board, then cut the board first into squares.

> counters—designate colors as amounts
> washers—spray-paint them

Number line—Secret Code

A long banner 6"–9" wide, divided into squares numbered 1–100, one number per square. Put high on the wall or cut into groups of ten squares and use as a large hundred board. It's a good idea to make this and put it up before the first day of school.

> bulletin board or chart paper cut and colored
> computer banners, colored with markers
> large number cards, colored with markers

Numbers are coded:

> multiples of 2: red heart, upper left corner
> multiples of 5: blue square lower right corner
> multiples of 10: green diagonal line
> odd numbers: brown
> even numbers: black

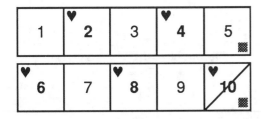

If you prefer, laminate and mark the squares with an overhead pen. Use for multiples, divisibility, number sentences, patterns, and so on. We mark complex number sequences and have students find the rule.

Paper shapes

Use construction paper or colored card stock. Cut triangles, circles, and squares in three or four sizes, each in three or four colors. Laminate first for permanence.

Pattern blocks

Very useful sets of six different-shaped blocks that relate to each other; e.g., six triangles cover a hexagon. See Reproducibles for full-size patterns and color descriptions. If you must substitute, reproduce on the heaviest paper possible, or print on colored card stock. A paper cutter works well. Hope for a parent with a jigsaw who will cut some from thin wood.

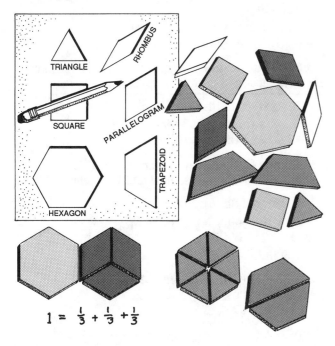

$$1 = \frac{1}{3} + \frac{1}{3} + \frac{1}{3}$$

Place value and base ten materials

Place value materials are extremely useful, and we suggest you have a set for the overhead as well. Commercial block sets are three-dimensional, based on a cubic centimeter one cube. Ten rods and hundred flats are marked to show the divisions into cubes. Hollow, cardboard thousand cubes that hold ten hundred flats each are less expensive than wood or plastic. Some sets link together for building larger amounts.

If you make your own place value sets from paper, laminating the paper before cutting it is a good idea. Counters can be used to represent 1000s. Allow 20–25 ones and tens, and 10–12 hundreds per student set.

> buttons or beans for 1s, craft sticks for 10s
> computer paper borders—for 1s, 10s
> counter-trading materials—see Counter-trading
> Cuisenaire® rods for 1s and 10s
> interlocking cubes—for 1s, 10s
> milk carton, ½ gallon—slice off the top, turn upside down for 1000s cube

Place value—graph paper

Follow cutting directions for "Decimals—graph paper." Label 10×10 square as 100; 1×10 bar as 10; and 1×1 square as 1. Store in envelopes.

Place value—plastic mesh

Individual sets to 100s can be made from plastic needlepoint mesh, seven squares per inch or larger, available from craft and needlework stores. It is less expensive to use only one color of mesh. If you prefer different colors, get 3 bright colors: one each for ones, tens, and hundreds. Use clear for thousands.

If you use only one color, determine the number of hundreds that can be cut from one sheet. This will vary according to the size of the sheets of mesh. Remember that you lose a row of holes each time you cut. Then figure the number of tens you can cut from each sheet after the hundreds are cut. Any extra mesh left after cutting the tens can be used for ones.

Next figure how many more tens you will need, and cut them from new sheets. Use any extra for ones.

To cut: A paper cutter works well for hundreds, tens, and long strips of ones. Cut the ones apart with scissors. For each thousand, stack 10 hundreds and fasten opposite corners with two paper-covered wire twisters for plastic bags. Store in reclosable plastic freezer bags.

Tangrams

A seven-piece puzzle set that fits together to make a large square. To make your own, start with a 5" × 5" square of construction paper. Fold from corner to corner into a triangle shape. Press the fold flat and cut or tear. You now have triangle A and triangle B.

Triangle A: fold and tear into two smaller triangles. Set aside. These are the large triangles.

Triangle B: fold the top point down to the midpoint of the base. Check that you have a triangle and a trapezoid. Press and tear. Set triangle aside. This is the medium triangle.

Trapezoid: fold in half, a vertical fold from midpoint of base to midpoint of top. You now have smaller trapezoids C and D.

Trapezoid C: fold in half at the midpoint of the base. You have a square and a small triangle. Press and tear.

Small trapezoid D: with longest point of the base to the left, fold right-hand edge of trapezoid up to lie along top edge. You now have a small triangle and a parallelogram. Press and tear.

Total: 1 square, 2 small triangles, 1 medium triangle, 2 large triangles, and 1 parallelogram.

Tiles

Available in wood or plastic in various colors. To make your own from paper, color if necessary, laminate, and cut with a paper cutter.

   1" × 1" ceramic tiles left over from tile stores
   1" × 1" construction paper, tag board, or card stock squares
   1" × 1" graph paper squares

Treasure boxes

Collections of many small objects that are in the same category but have differences can be assembled. Send notes to parents early in the fall, asking them to help collect such items. Fill cardboard pencil boxes with these small objects, one category per box. Some suggestions:

   buttons
   keys
   candy wrappers (at Halloween)
   gum wrappers
   shells
   beans and pasta—various kinds
   old jewelry
   business cards

Where can I find it?

Catalogs are numerous. Listed are some we have found particularly useful. Teacher stores are another source and often have their own catalogs, which may be quite complete.

Activity Resources Company, Inc. Many materials and books. Especially good for intermediate materials.

   P.O. Box 4875
   Hayward, CA 94540
   (415) 782-1300

Creative Publications. Many materials and resources. Separate catalog of primary-level material as well.

   5040 West 111th Street
   Oak Lawn, IL 60453-9941
   1-800-624-0822

Cuisenaire Company of America, Inc. Many resources and materials, some with free teacher guides.

   12 Church St., Box D
   New Rochelle, NY 10802
   (914) 235-0900
   1-800-237-3142

Dale Seymour Publications. Materials, many teacher resources, and posters.

   P.O. Box 10888
   Palo Alto, CA 94303-0879
   outside California: 1-800-USA-1100
   in California: 1-800-ABC-0766

Delta Education, Inc. Many manipulatives and teacher guides.

   P.O. Box 915
   Hudson, NH 03051-0915
   outside New Hampshire: 1-800-258-1302
   in New Hampshire: call collect 889-8899

Didax, Inc. Materials, games, and resources.

One Centennial Drive
Peabody, MA 01960
(508) 532-9060
1-800-458-0024

The Education Center, Inc. Non-heat laminating dispenser and film for do-it-yourself laminating. Construction materials, games.

1607 Battleground Ave.
P.O. Box 9753
Greensboro, NC 27429
1-800-334-0298

Educational Teaching Aids (ETA). Many different manipulatives.

620 Lakeview Parkway
Vernon Hills, IL 60061
(708) 816-5050
1-800-445-5985

Lakeshore Learning Materials. Infant through elementary. Manipulatives, some resources.

2695 Dominguez St.
P.O. Box 6261
Carson, CA 90749
(213) 537-8600
1-800-421-5354

National Council of Teachers of Mathematics. A wide range of offerings from the latest in research to the immediately useful. Books, videos, back issues of *Arithmetic Teacher, Mathematics Teacher,* and *Journal for Research in Mathematics Education,* article reprints, and NCTM yearbooks.

1906 Association Drive
Reston, VA 22091
(703) 620-9840

Summit Learning, Inc. Materials and resources.

P.O. Box 493
Ft. Collins, CO 80522
1-800-777-8817

Scope and Sequence

Number Skills

	4	5	6

1. Patterns in number sequence: addition or subtraction in the rule
    addition in the rule
    subtraction in the rule
    graphing sequences
	•	•	•

2. Patterns in number sequence: multiplication or division in the rule
    multiplication in the rule
    division in the rule
    graphing sequences
	•	•	•

3. Patterns in number sequence: multiple operations in the rule
    identify patterns and possible operations
    graphing sequences
	•	•	•

Notes: Exponents; see Multiplication Skill #10
    Prime and composite numbers; see Multiplication Skill #11
    Prime factorization; see Multiplication Skill #11			

Place Value

	4	5	6

1. Place value through 9,999
    regrouping and expanded notation
    compare numbers through 9,999
	•		

2. Place value through 999,999
    regrouping and expanded notation
    compare numbers through 999,999
	•	•	

3. Place value through 999,999,999		•	•
4. Round to the nearest 10 and $10	•	•	
5. Round to the nearest 100, 1,000, $100, and $1,000	•	•	•

Addition

	4	5	6

1. Add 3-digit numbers
    with regrouping, no zeros
    with regrouping, with zeros
    mixed digit addends
	•		

Note: Addition with money: see Decimals Skill #5			

Subtraction

	4	5	6
1. Subtraction facts: missing numbers	•		
2. Subtract 3-digit numbers: check with addition and subtract 1- or 2-digit subtrahends	•	•	•
Note: Subtraction with money: see Decimals Skill #5			

Multiplication

	4	5	6
1. Multiplication facts: products to 81	•		

2. Commutative property of multiplication
    multiplication chart
    fact families
    prove equalities
	•		

3. Relationship of multiplication to division
    recognize relationship
    missing factors
	•	•	•

4. Multiples of 10: multiply 10s by 1-digit numbers
    multiples of 10
    multiply 10 by 1-digit numbers
    multiply multiples of 10 by 1-digit numbers, no regrouping
    multiply multiples of 10 by 1-digit numbers, with regrouping
    traditional algorithm
	•		

5. Multiply with more than two factors	•	•	

6. Multiply 2-digit numbers by 1-digit numbers
    partial products
    traditional algorithm
	•		

7. Multiply 100s by 1-digit numbers
    partial products
    traditional algorithm
	•		

8. Multiply 3-digit numbers by 1-digit numbers
    partial products
    traditional algorithm
	•	•	•

9. Multiply by 10, multiples of 10, and 2-digit numbers
    multiply 1-digit numbers by 10 and multiples of 10, partial products
    multiply multiples of 10 by 10 and multiples of 10, partial products
    multiply 2-digit numbers by 10 and multiples of 10, partial products
    multiply 2-digit numbers by 2-digit numbers, traditional algorithm
    multiply 3-digit numbers by 2-digit numbers
	•	•	•

10. Exponents
    understand exponents
    graphing exponential numbers
		•	•

11. Prime numbers, composite numbers, and prime factorization
    prime numbers and composite numbers
    Sieve of Eratosthenes
    prime factorization
		•	•

Note: Multiply money; see Decimals Skill #10			

Division

	4	5	6

1. Understand division; division facts
    understand division using arrays
    divide with two kinds of objects, no regrouping
    divide with two kinds of objects, with regrouping
    divide with base ten materials
    develop facts, relate division to multiplication
	•		

2. Multiplication and division fact families: relate division to multiplication	•		

	4	5	6
3. Use multiplication to check division	•	•	

4. Missing dividends and divisors
    missing dividends
    missing divisors
	•	•	

5. Divide 2-digit numbers by 1-digit numbers
    no regrouping
    with regrouping, 2-digit quotients
    with regrouping, 1-digit quotients
    zeros in the quotient
	•	•	

6. Divisibility by 2, 5, 3, 6, 9, 4, and 8	•	•	•

7. Divide 3-digit or larger numbers by 1-digit numbers
    no regrouping
    with regrouping
    2-digit quotients
    zeros in the quotient
	•	•	•

8. Divide 2- and 3-digit numbers by 2-digit numbers
    divide by 10 and multiples of 10
    divide by 2-digit numbers; estimates and multiples
    estimates too low: adapt written format
	•	•	•

9. Find averages
    understand averages
    explore effect of number size on averages
	•	•	•

Note: Divide money; see Decimals Skill #12			

Fractions

	4	5	6

1. Understand and write fractions
    identify fractions
    different fractions of a whole
    fractions equal to 1 and 0
    find a fraction of a number
	•	•	

2. Compare fractions
    like denominators, same-size whole
    like denominators, different-size wholes
    unlike denominators
	•	•	•

3. Find equivalent fractions
    use equivalency chart
    use multiplication
	•	•	•

4. Order fractions
    like denominators
    unlike denominators
	•	•	•

5. Simplify fractions and find the greatest common factor
    simplify fractions
    greatest common factor
    use prime factorization to find the GCF
	•	•	•

6. Add and subtract fractions: like denominators	•	•	•

	4	5	6

7. Rename mixed numbers and improper fractions
    understand improper fractions and mixed numbers
    rename mixed numbers using addition
    rename mixed numbers using multiplication
    rename improper fractions using subtraction
    rename improper fractions using division
	•	•	•

8. Add and subtract mixed numbers: like denominator
    add mixed numbers, no regrouping
    add mixed numbers, with regrouping
    subtract mixed numbers, tenths only
    subtract mixed numbers, fractions other than tenths
	•	•	•

9. Find a common denominator: least common multiple and least common denominator
    understand common denominator
    find LCM and LCD
		•	•

10. Add and subtract fractions: unlike denominators		•	•
11. Round fractions to the nearest whole number	•	•	•

12. Add and subtract mixed numbers: unlike denominators
    add mixed numbers
    subtract mixed numbers, no regrouping
    subtract mixed numbers, with regrouping
		•	•

13. Multiply a fraction by a fraction and multiply a fraction and a whole number
    multiply a fraction by a fraction
    multiply a fraction of an amount by a fraction of an amount
    multiply a fraction and a whole number
		•	•

14. Divide a whole number by a fraction
    divide a whole number by a fraction
    understand invert and multiply by the reciprocal
		•	•

15. Divide a fraction by a fraction			•
Notes: Relate fractions to decimals; see Decimals Skill #1 Change fractions to decimals; see Decimals Skill #14			

Decimals

	4	5	6

1. Relate fractions to decimals: recognize and order tenths
    relate fraction tenths to decimal tenths and place value
    relate decimals and fractions equivalent to tenths
    order tenths
    order fractions and decimal tenths
	•	•	

2. Add and subtract tenths
    add tenths
    subtract tenths
	•	•	

3. Recognize and order hundredths
    understand hundredths
    order hundredths
	•	•	

4. Compare and order tenths and hundredths
    understand tenths and equivalent hundredths
    compare and order tenths and hundredths
	•	•	

	4	5	6

5. Add and subtract to hundredths
    add to hundredths
    subtract to hundredths
    add and subtract money
	•	•	

6. Understand thousandths and equivalent decimals to thousandths
    understand thousandths
    understand equivalent decimals to thousandths
		•	•

7. Compare and order decimals to thousandths		•	•
8. Add and subtract to thousandths		•	•

9. Round decimals to the nearest tenth, hundredth, and whole number
    round to the nearest tenth or hundredth
    round money to the nearest $0.10
    round decimals to the nearest whole number
    round money to the nearest $1.00
	•	•	•

10. Multiply decimals and whole numbers
    no regrouping
    with regrouping
    multiply whole numbers and money amounts
	•	•	•

11. Multiply decimals by decimals
    multiply tenths by tenths
    multiply hundredths by tenths
    multiply mixed decimals by decimals
    multiply mixed decimals by mixed decimals
		•	•

12. Divide decimals by whole numbers
    divide decimals by whole numbers
    divide money amounts by whole numbers
	•	•	•

13. Divide by decimals
    divide whole numbers by decimals
    divide decimals by decimals, whole number quotient
    divide by decimals, decimal or mixed decimal quotient
		•	•

14. Change fractions and mixed numbers to decimals
    change fractions to decimals by changing the denominator to a power of 10
    change fractions to decimals using division
		•	•

Note: Decimal skills as percents; see Ratio and Percent Skills #2 and #3			

Ratio and Percent

	4	5	6

1. Understand ratios and proportions
    understand ratio
    find equal ratios using multiplication
    find equal ratios using division
    understand properties of proportions
	•	•	•

2. Relate fractions, ratios, and decimals to percent
    understand percent; change fractions to percents using equivalent fractions
    change ratios to percents using cross products
    relate decimals to percent
    write tenths and thousandths as percents
    percents larger than 100%
    percents smaller than 1%
		•	•

	4	5	6

3. Calculate percents
  find a certain percent of a number
  find what percent one number is of another
  find a number when the percent of it is known
			•

Geometry

	4	5	6

1. Patterns in geometric shapes: two and three dimensions
  attribute patterns
  positional change patterns
  building-on patterns
  relate numbers to patterns
  three-dimension patterns
  relate numbers to three-dimensional patterns
	•	•	•

2. Understand and classify angles
  90°
  30°, 45°
  measure with protractors
  relationships of angles
	•	•	•

3. Understand and find perimeter
  understand perimeter
  relate perimeter and area
  find formula for the perimeter of rectangles
	•	•	

4. Classify triangles by sides and angles
  classify by sides
  classify by angles
	•	•	•

5. Find lines of symmetry
  understand symmetry
  multiple lines of symmetry
	•	•	

6. Find the sum of the angles: triangles and polygons
  in right triangles
  in any triangle
  in quadrilaterals
  in any polygon; find formula
	•	•	•

7. Understand area
  area with whole units
  area with half units
  area of rectangles; find formula
  area of squares
  area of shapes of more than one rectangle
	•	•	•

8. Find area: triangles and parallelograms
  area of right triangles; find formula
  find area of acute and obtuse triangles; find formula
  area of parallelograms; find formula
		•	•

9. Classify solid figures
  understand face, edge, and vertex
  classify solid figures
  three-dimensional spatial visualization
	•	•	•

10. Understand congruence, similarity, and scale	•	•	
Note: Volume: see Measurement Skill #10			

	4	5	6
1. Measure length by inches, feet, and yards; measure to fractions of inches 　inches 　feet 　yards 　measure to the nearest ½" and ¼" 　measure to the nearest ⅛" and 1/16"	•	•	•
2. Change one unit of length to another: inches, feet, and yards 　change larger to smaller units 　change smaller to larger units 　compute using mixed measurements	•	•	•
3. Measure length by centimeters, meters, and millimeters; use decimal notation 　centimeters 　meters 　millimeters; use decimal notation with centimeters and millimeters 　use decimal notation with meters and centimeters	•	•	•
4. Change one unit to another: centimeters, meters, and millimeters 　change one unit to another 　compute using mixed measurements	•	•	•
5. Understand capacity: cups, pints, quarts, and gallons 　cups, pints, quarts, and gallons 　change one unit to another 　compute using mixed capacities	•	•	•
6. Understand capacity: liters and milliliters 　liters 　milliliters 　change one unit to another 　compute using mixed capacities	•	•	•
7. Measure temperature and read thermometers 　measure temperature 　find changes in temperature above and below zero	•	•	•
8. Understand pounds and ounces 　pounds 　ounces 　change one unit to another 　compute using mixed weights	•	•	•
9. Understand kilograms and grams 　kilograms 　grams 　change one unit to another 　compute using mixed masses	•	•	•
10. Measure volume 　understand and measure volume 　measure volume 　find formula for the volume of a rectangular prism	•	•	•
Notes: Perimeter; see Geometry Skill #3 　　　Area; see Geometry Skills #7 and #8			

Reprinted with permission from *Curriculum and Evaluation Standards for School Mathematics*, copyright 1989 by the National Council of Teachers of Mathematics.

Note: We have correlated the lessons in this book to the 5–8 Standards. Standard 11: Probability is not included in this book.

Standard 1: Mathematics as Problem Solving

In grades 5–8, the mathematics curriculum should include numerous and varied experiences with problem solving as a method of inquiry and application so that students can—

- use problem–solving approaches to investigate and understand mathematical content;
- formulate problems from situations within and outside mathematics;
- develop and apply a variety of strategies to solve problems, with emphasis on multistep and non-routine problems;
- verify and interpret results with respect to the original problem situation;
- generalize solutions and strategies to new problem situations;
- acquire confidence in using mathematics meaningfully.

Standard 2: Mathematics as Communication

In grades 5–8, the study of mathematics should include opportunities to communicate so that students can—

- model situations using oral, written, concrete, pictorial, graphical, and algebraic methods;
- reflect on and clarify their own thinking about mathematical ideas and situations;
- develop common understandings of mathematical ideas, including the role of definitions;
- use the skills of reading, listening, and viewing to interpret and evaluate mathematical ideas;
- discuss mathematical ideas and make conjectures and convincing arguments;
- appreciate the value of mathematical notation and its role in the development of mathematical ideas.

Standard 3: Mathematics as Reasoning

In grades 5–8, reasoning shall permeate the mathematics curriculum so that students can—

- recognize and apply deductive and inductive reasoning;
- understand and apply reasoning processes, with special attention to spatial reasoning and reasoning with proportions and graphs;
- make and evaluate mathematical conjectures and arguments;
- validate their own thinking;
- appreciate the pervasive use and power of reasoning as a part of mathematics.

Standard 4: Mathematical Connections

In grades 5–8, the study of mathematics should include the investigation of mathematical connections so that students can—

- see mathematics as an integrated whole;
- explore problems and describe results using graphical, numerical, physical, algebraic, and verbal mathematical models or representations;
- use a mathematical idea to further their understanding of other mathematical ideas;
- apply mathematical thinking and modeling to solve problems that arise in other disciplines, such as art, music, psychology, science, and business;
- value the role of mathematics in our culture and society.

Standard 5: Number and Number Relationships

In grades 5–8, the mathematics curriculum should include the continued development of number and number relationships so that students can—

- understand, represent, and use numbers in a variety of equivalent forms (integer, fraction, decimal, percent, exponential, and scientific notation) in real-world and mathematical problem situations;
- develop number sense for whole numbers, fractions, decimals, integers, and rational numbers;
- understand and apply ratios, proportions, and percents in a wide variety of situations;
- investigate relationships among fractions, decimals, and percents;
- represent numerical relationships in one- and two-dimensional graphs.

Standard 6: Number Systems and Number Theory

In grades 5–8, the mathematics curriculum should include the study of number systems and number theory so that students can—

- understand and appreciate the need for numbers beyond the whole numbers;
- develop and use order relations for whole numbers, fractions, decimals, integers, and rational numbers;
- extend their understanding of whole number operations to fractions, decimals, integers, and rational numbers;

- understand how the basic arithmetic operations are related to one another;
- develop and apply number theory concepts (e.g., primes, factors, and multiples) in real-world and mathematical problem situations.

Standard 7: Computation and Estimation

In grades 5–8, the mathematics curriculum should develop the concepts underlying computation and estimation in various contexts so that students can—

- compute with whole numbers, fractions, decimals, integers, and rational numbers;
- develop, analyze, and explain procedures for computation and techniques for estimation;
- develop, analyze, and explain methods for solving proportions;
- select and use an appropriate method for computing from among mental arithmetic, paper-and-pencil, calculator, and computer methods;
- use computation, estimation, and proportions to solve problems;
- use estimation to check the reasonableness of results.

Standard 8: Patterns and Functions

In grades 5–8, the mathematics curriculum should include explorations of patterns and functions so that students can—

- describe, extend, analyze, and create a wide variety of patterns;
- describe and represent relationships with tables, graphs, and rules;
- analyze functional relationships to explain how a change in one quantity results in a change in another;
- use patterns and functions to represent and solve problems.

Standard 9: Algebra

In grades 5–8, the mathematics curriculum should include explorations of algebraic concepts and processes so that students can—

- understand the concepts of variable, expression, and equation;
- represent situations and number patterns with tables, graphs, verbal rules, and equations and explore the interrelationships of these representations;
- analyze tables and graphs to identify properties and relationships;
- develop confidence in solving linear equations using concrete, informal, and formal methods;
- investigate inequalities and nonlinear equations informally;

- apply algebraic methods to solve a variety of real-world and mathematical problems.

Standard 10: Statistics

In grades 5–8, the mathematics curriculum should include explorations of statistics in real-world situations so that students can—

- systematically collect, organize, and describe data;
- construct, read, and interpret tables, charts, and graphs;
- make inferences and convincing arguments that are based on data analysis;
- evaluate arguments that are based on data analysis;
- develop an appreciation for statistical methods as powerful means for decision making.

Standard 12: Geometry

In grades 5–8, the mathematics curriculum should include the study of the geometry of one, two, and three dimensions in a variety of situations so that students can—

- identify, describe, compare, and classify geometric figures;
- visualize and represent geometric figures with special attention to developing spatial sense;
- explore transformations of geometric figures;
- represent and solve problems using geometric models;
- understand and apply geometric properties and relationships;
- develop an appreciation of geometry as a means of describing the physical world.

Standard 13: Measurement

In grades 5–8, the mathematics curriculum should include extensive concrete experiences using measurement so that students can—

- extend their understanding of the process of measurement;
- estimate, make, and use measurements to describe and compare phenomena;
- select appropriate units and tools to measure to the degree of accuracy required in a particular situation;
- understand the structure and use of systems of measurement;
- extend their understanding of the concepts of perimeter, area, volume, angle measure, capacity, and weight and mass;
- develop the concepts of rates and other derived and indirect measurements;
- develop formulas and procedures for determining measures to solve problems.

Standards Correlation

	1	2	3	4	5	6	7	8	9	10	12	13
Number Skills 1	•	•	•	•	•		•	•	•	•		
Number Skills 2	•	•	•	•	•	•	•	•	•	•		
Number Skills 3	•	•	•	•	•	•	•	•	•	•		
Place Value 1		•	•	•	•		•	•		•		
Place Value 2		•	•		•	•	•	•				
Place Value 3		•	•	•	•	•	•	•				
Place Value 4		•	•	•	•		•	•				
Place Value 5	•	•	•	•	•	•	•					
Addition 1	•	•	•	•	•		•	•				
Subtraction 1	•	•	•	•	•	•	•	•	•			
Subtraction 2	•	•	•	•	•	•	•	•				
Multiplication 1	•	•	•	•	•	•	•	•				
Multiplication 2		•	•	•	•	•	•	•	•	•	•	
Multiplication 3	•	•	•	•	•	•	•	•	•	•	•	
Multiplication 4	•	•	•	•	•	•	•	•				
Multiplication 5	•	•	•	•	•		•		•		•	
Multiplication 6	•	•	•	•	•		•					
Multiplication 7	•	•	•	•	•	•	•					
Multiplication 8	•	•	•	•	•		•					
Multiplication 9		•	•	•	•		•	•				
Multiplication 10		•	•	•	•	•	•	•	•	•		
Multiplication 11		•	•	•	•	•	•	•		•		
Division 1	•	•	•	•	•	•	•	•		•		
Division 2		•	•	•	•	•	•	•	•	•		
Division 3		•	•	•	•	•	•		•	•		
Division 4	•	•	•	•	•	•	•	•	•		•	
Division 5	•	•	•	•	•	•	•	•				
Division 6	•	•	•	•		•	•	•		•		
Division 7		•	•	•	•	•	•	•		•		
Division 8		•	•	•	•	•	•	•				
Division 9		•	•	•	•		•	•		•		
Fractions 1		•	•	•	•	•	•		•		•	

	1	2	3	4	5	6	7	8	9	10	12	13
Fractions 2		•	•	•	•	•		•	•	•	•	
Fractions 3		•	•	•	•	•	•	•	•	•	•	
Fractions 4		•	•	•	•	•		•	•	•		
Fractions 5		•	•	•	•	•	•	•		•	•	
Fractions 6		•	•	•	•	•	•	•			•	
Fractions 7	•	•	•	•	•	•	•	•	•		•	
Fractions 8	•	•	•	•	•	•	•	•	•		•	
Fractions 9		•	•	•	•	•	•	•	•		•	
Fractions 10	•	•	•	•	•	•	•	•			•	
Fractions 11		•	•	•	•	•	•	•	•	•	•	
Fractions 12	•	•	•	•	•	•	•				•	
Fractions 13	•	•	•	•	•	•	•	•	•		•	
Fractions 14	•	•	•	•	•	•	•	•	•	•	•	
Fractions 15	•	•	•	•	•	•	•	•		•	•	
Decimals 1	•	•	•	•	•	•		•	•	•	•	
Decimals 2	•	•	•	•	•	•	•	•	•	•		•
Decimals 3	•	•	•	•	•	•		•	•			•
Decimals 4	•	•	•	•	•	•		•	•			•
Decimals 5	•	•	•	•	•	•	•	•				•
Decimals 6		•	•	•	•	•		•				•
Decimals 7		•	•	•	•	•		•	•			•
Decimals 8		•	•	•	•	•	•					•
Decimals 9	•	•	•	•	•	•	•	•				
Decimals 10	•	•	•	•	•	•	•	•				•
Decimals 11	•	•	•	•	•	•	•	•	•	•		•
Decimals 12	•	•	•	•	•	•	•					
Decimals 13	•	•	•	•	•	•	•	•	•	•		•
Decimals 14	•	•	•	•	•	•	•	•				
Ratio and Percent 1	•	•	•	•	•	•	•	•	•	•	•	•
Ratio and Percent 2	•	•	•	•	•	•	•	•		•		
Ratio and Percent 3	•	•	•	•	•	•	•	•	•	•		
Geometry 1	•	•	•	•	•	•	•	•	•	•	•	
Geometry 2		•	•	•			•	•	•	•	•	•
Geometry 3	•	•	•	•	•		•	•	•	•	•	•

	1	2	3	4	5	6	7	8	9	10	12	13
Geometry 4	•	•	•	•				•		•	•	•
Geometry 5	•	•	•					•		•		
Geometry 6	•	•	•				•	•			•	•
Geometry 7	•	•	•	•		•	•	•	•	•	•	•
Geometry 8	•	•	•	•		•	•	•	•	•	•	•
Geometry 9		•	•	•				•		•	•	
Geometry 10		•	•	•				•			•	•
Measurement 1		•	•	•	•	•	•			•	•	•
Measurement 2		•	•	•	•	•	•	•		•		•
Measurement 3		•	•	•	•		•			•	•	•
Measurement 4	•	•	•	•	•		•	•		•		•
Measurement 5		•	•	•	•	•	•	•	•	•		•
Measurement 6		•	•	•	•		•	•		•		•
Measurement 7	•	•	•	•	•	•	•	•	•	•		•
Measurement 8		•	•	•	•	•	•	•	•	•		•
Measurement 9		•	•	•	•	•	•	•	•	•		•
Measurement 10		•	•	•	•		•	•	•	•	•	•

Materials Needed at Each Grade Level

Many materials may be purchased through catalogs and at teacher stores. You will need at least enough for student pairs; catalogs will have guidelines for sets. We have also listed many alternatives in the Manipulative Information section. Many materials, such as cards, dice, and counters, also can be used for the Practice and Extension activities in a variety of strands.

R: a Reproducible for this

R/lam: a Reproducible for this; we suggest laminating it back to back with another Reproducible for permanence.

S: student-made materials, generally from Reproducibles

Grade 4

	Number Skills	Place Value	Addition	Subtraction	Multiplication	Division	Fractions	Decimals	Ratio and Percent	Geometry	Measurement
attribute blocks										•	
coins—1¢, 10¢								•			
containers—small, for general use											•
counters, various colors—20 or more/student		•	•	•	•	•	•	•	•		•
counter-trading materials to 100,000s— 1 set/student or pair		•	•		•	•					
cubes—1 cm (good to have larger sizes as well); 20+/student	•			•	•	•	•			•	•
Cuisenaire® Rods							•	•			•
decks of cards—1/pair; at least have 1 teacher deck		•			•						
dice—1 set/pair		•	•			•					
geoboards—1/student or pair					•	•	•			•	•
graph paper—½", 1 cm—R	•	•	•	•	•	•	•	•		•	•
index cards		•			•						
interlocking cubes						•	•			•	•
measurement sets for capacity, weight—1 or more											•
objects—small, collections of various kinds, some similar (e.g., buttons, beans, tiles); 20 or more/student				•		•			•		•
pattern blocks					•	•				•	
place value materials to 1000s—1 set/student or pair		•	•	•	•	•	•	•			•
protractors—1/student or pair										•	
scales—a variety of types including balance scales; 1 or more											•
Secret Code number line (see Manip. Info. section)	•				•	•					
solid geometry sets—1 or more										•	
tangrams—1 set/student or pair										•	
thermometer—1/pair or group											•
tiles—20 or more/student	•				•	•	•			•	

	Number Skills	Place Value	Addition	Subtraction	Multiplication	Division	Fractions	Decimals	Ratio and Percent	Geometry	Measurement
treasure boxes—(see Manip. Info. section) 1/group				•					•		
S—bills to $100,000 (see Manip. Info. section)		•		•	•	•	•	•			
S—decimal bars to 1/100; 25 of each/student								•			
S—decimal extensions for file-folder place value mats; 1/student								•			
S—file-folder place value mats to 100,000s; 1 file folder/student		•	•		•	•		•			
S—fraction bars; 1 set/student							•				
S—graph-paper decimals to hundredths (see Manip. Info. section)								•			
R/lam—counter-trading boards to 100,000s; 1/student or pair		•	•		•	•					
R/lam—equivalency charts; 1/student or pair							•	•			
R/lam—hundred boards; 1/student					•	•					
R/lam—moon stations; 1/student							•				
R/lam—place value mats to 1000s; 1/student or pair		•	•	•	•	•					

Grade 5

	Number Skills	Place Value	Addition	Subtraction	Multiplication	Division	Fractions	Decimals	Ratio and Percent	Geometry	Measurement
attribute blocks										•	
coins—1¢, 10¢								•			
containers—small, for general use											•
counters, various colors—20 or more/student		•			•	•	•	•	•		•
counter-trading materials to 100,000s—1 set/student or pair					•	•					
cubes—1 cm (good to have larger sizes as well); 20+/student	•				•	•	•		•	•	•
Cuisenaire® Rods								•			•
decks of cards—1/pair; at least have 1 teacher deck		•		•							
dice—1 set/pair						•					
geoboards—1/student or pair					•	•	•		•	•	
graph paper—1/4", 1/2", 1 cm—R	•	•		•	•	•	•	•	•	•	•
index cards		•			•						
interlocking cubes						•	•		•	•	
measurement sets for capacity, weight—1 or more											•
objects—small, collections of various kinds, some similar (e.g., buttons, beans, tiles); 20 or more/student								•	•		•
pattern blocks					•		•			•	

	Number Skills	Place Value	Addition	Subtraction	Multiplication	Division	Fractions	Decimals	Ratio and Percent	Geometry	Measurement
place value materials to 1000s—1 set/student or pair				•	•	•	•	•	•		•
protractors—1/student or pair										•	
scales—a variety of types including balance scales; 1 or more											•
Secret Code number line (see Manip. Info. section)	•					•					
solid geometry sets—1 or more										•	
tangrams—1 set/student or pair										•	
thermometer—1/pair or group											•
tiles—20 or more/student	•				•	•	•			•	
treasure boxes—(see Manip. Info. section) 1/group									•		
S—bills to $100,000 (see Manip. Info. section)		•		•	•	•	•	•			
S—decimal bars to $^1/_{1000}$; 25 of each/student								•	•		
S—decimal extensions for file-folder place value mats; 1/student								•			
S—file-folder place value mats to 100,000s; 1 file folder/student		•			•	•		•			
S—fraction bars; 1 set/student							•				
S—graph-paper decimals to thousandths (see Manip. Info. section)								•			
R/lam—counter-trading boards to 100,000s; 1/student or pair					•	•					
R/lam—equivalency charts; 1/student or pair							•		•		
R/lam—hundred boards; 1/student					•	•	•				
R/lam—moon stations; 1/student							•				
R/lam—place value mats to 1000s; 1/student or pair		•		•	•	•					

Grade 6

	Number Skills	Place Value	Addition	Subtraction	Multiplication	Division	Fractions	Decimals	Ratio and Percent	Geometry	Measurement
attribute blocks										•	
coins—1¢, 10¢								•			
containers—small, for general use											•
counters, various colors—20 or more/student		•			•	•	•	•	•		•
counter-trading materials to 100,000s—1 set/student or pair					•	•					
cubes—1 cm (good to have larger sizes as well); 20+/student	•				•	•	•			•	•
Cuisenaire® Rods							•				•
decks of cards—1/pair; at least have 1 teacher deck			•		•						

	Number Skills	Place Value	Addition	Subtraction	Multiplication	Division	Fractions	Decimals	Ratio and Percent	Geometry	Measurement
dice—1 set/pair						•					
geoboards—1/student or pair					•		•		•	•	
graph paper—¼", ½", 1 cm—R	•	•		•	•	•	•	•	•	•	•
index cards		•			•						
interlocking cubes							•	•		•	•
measurement sets for capacity, weight—1 or more											•
objects—small, collections of various kinds, some similar, (e.g. buttons, beans, tiles); 20 or more/student							•			•	•
pattern blocks							•			•	
place value materials to 1000s—1 set/student or pair		•		•	•	•	•	•	•		•
protractors—1/student or pair										•	
scales—a variety of types including balance scales; 1 or more											•
Secret Code number line (see Manip. Info. section)	•					•					
solid geometry sets— 1 or more										•	
tangrams—1 set/student or pair										•	
thermometers—1/student or pair											•
tiles—20 or more/student	•				•	•	•			•	
treasure boxes—(see Manip. Info. section) 1/group									•		
S—bills to $100,000 (see Manip. Info. section)				•	•	•	•	•			
S—decimal bars to ¹/₁₀₀₀; 25/student								•	•		
S—decimal extensions for file-folder place value mats; 1/student								•			
S—file-folder place value mats to 100,000s; 1 file folder/student		•			•	•		•			
S—fraction bars; 1 set/student							•				
S—graph-paper decimals to thousandths (see Manip. Info. section)								•	•		
R/lam—counter-trading boards to 100,000s; 1/student or pair					•	•					
R/lam—equivalency charts; 1/student or pair							•	•			
R/lam—hundred boards; 1/student					•	•	•				
R/lam—moon stations; 1/student								•			
R/lam—place value mats to 1000s; 1/student or pair				•	•	•					

Labels for File Folders, Dividers, or Book Sections

Each teacher has his or her preferred method of organizing materials. If you like organization, photocopy these labels onto heavier paper. If you do not like organization, skip this page. Here are some ways you might use these labels.

If you file materials for each textbook chapter in a separate file folder:

Use the "Chap.____" labels for file folders keyed to textbook chapters. Tear out the lessons you need, and file them in the appropriate folders.

If you use loose-leaf notebooks:

Tear out and file the whole book by strand using the strand labels with purchased notebook dividers.

Or, use the "Chap.____" labels and notebook dividers. Tear out the lessons you need, and file by textbook chapter.

Or file the whole book by strands, but have dividers for textbook chapters as well. File the lessons you actually use by chapter.

If you like to keep your books intact:

Use the strand labels and tape to the edge of the first lesson in each strand to facilitate finding the desired lessons.

Front Pages	Multiplication	Measurement	Chap. _____	Chap. _____
Number Skills	Division	Reproducibles	Chap. _____	Chap. _____
Place Value	Fractions	Ratio and Percent	Chap. _____	Chap. _____
Addition	Decimals	Chap. _____	Chap. _____	Chap. _____
Subtraction	Geometry	Chap. _____	Chap. _____	Chap. _____

Number Skills 1

Skill: To find patterns in number sequences: addition or subtraction in the rule

Secret Code number line (see Manipulative Information section)

graph paper: of any size

markers

Time: 2+ periods

Materials:

1 cm cubes or tiles

rulers: 1 per student

Anticipatory Set

Write the following number sequence on the board: 31–34–37–35–38–41–39. Ask what number comes next. (42) Students probably will not see that the pattern is +3 +3 –2 +3 +3 –2. Leave the sequence on the board for later solving. Do not tell students what the next number is.

Procedure 1

To find patterns: addition in the rule

Use *cubes or tiles, ruler, plain paper,* and the *Secret Code number line.*

Have students draw a horizontal line across their paper halfway down. This will be the base line. Instruct students to place one cube on the line. To the right of that, they place another cube. A second cube goes directly above it on the paper. Finally, they place three cubes. Do they see a pattern?

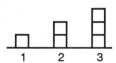

Students respond: The lines of cubes get bigger by one each time. They write the numbers 1, 2, 3 in a horizontal line, about 1/2 inch apart, on the bottom half of their paper.

Have students lay a ruler along the tops of the cubes. What do they notice? (the top cubes all touch the ruler along a diagonal)

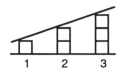

This is a regular pattern; the number of cubes increases by the same amount each time. How did we get from the 1 to the 3? (added 1 each time) We

can see they increase by one when we look at the cubes. What other way can we find the increase from one number to the next?

Students respond: Subtract the smaller from the larger.

What would be the next number? (4) We can find the difference between numbers by looking at the cubes or by subtracting. If you write how you got from one number to the next, it will help you see a pattern and you can predict the following number:

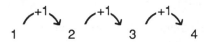

Students next place cubes for the sequence 2–3–5–6–8 on their papers. They also write this, as before.

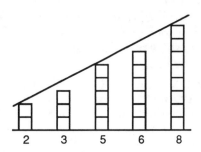

Have students lay their rulers along the tops of the cubes. What do they notice? (Not all the top cubes touch the ruler) The columns of cubes will touch the ruler if they form a regular series. Which columns do touch? (every other one) Every other time the same amount is being added. What would the next number of cubes be?

Students count cubes to see how much is added each time. They write +1 +2 +1 +2 above and between their numbers in the form shown above. They find the next number is 9.

What two ways could you find the pattern? (from the blocks and by subtracting)

Circle the following numbers on the Secret Code number line for students to solve: 0–1–3–6–10–15. (+1, +2, +3, +4, +5)

Procedure 2

To find patterns: subtraction in the rule

Use cubes or tiles, rulers, plain paper, and the Secret Code number line.

Repeat the procedure, using subtraction sequences. Use: 6–5–4–3; 7–6–4–3–1. Students should note that the direction of the ruler is reversed in subtraction. The numbers used to solve the sequence will be negative, as the numbers are decreasing.

Use the Secret Code number line as before. Circle: 35–34–31–30–27. Tell students the series is read on the number line from right to left this time, and challenge them to solve it. (–1, –3, –1, –3) Students should realize that they also could solve the series starting with 27 and adding numbers.

Procedure 3

To graph sequences

Use *graph paper, markers,* and *rulers.*

Have students draw a horizontal line across their paper six squares down from the top as a base line. Have them start at the base line and color a vertical column of squares for each number. Dictate the following series: 1–2–3–2–3–4–3–4.

Students color squares for the sequence and use their rulers to help show patterns. They write the series below the base line.

Have students put a dot at the midpoint of the top of each column. They use a ruler to draw a line connecting the dots. Ask: What does the graph tell us?

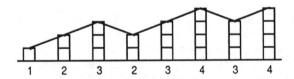

| 1 | 2 | 3 | 2 | 3 | 4 | 3 | 4 |

From the directions the line takes, students should see that they have both subtraction and addition. There is a regular series. The next number would be five.

Remind students that we can subtract to get the difference between numbers. Have students write +1 +1 between 1 and 2, and 2 and 3. What is the difference between the 3 and the next number, 2? (1) Will this be a +1 or a –1?

Students respond: Minus 1; the number is getting smaller. They finish writing the numbers.

Dictate sequences which include both addition and subtraction until students are competent in them.

Have them solve the problem from the Anticipatory Set. Then have them predict what the next three numbers would be.

Practice and Extension

Have students create sequences on the back of *graph paper.* Then turn the paper over and color in the sequence. Remind them that they must repeat the sequence for the pattern to become clear. Have them write a story problem to go with the sequence. Now they can exchange and try to solve each other's problems. Students may enjoy posting the more interesting designs made by the sequences.

Number Skills 2

Skill: To find patterns in number sequences: multiplication or division in the rule

Time: 1–2 periods

Materials:

cubes or tiles: about 20 per student

rulers: 1 per student

graph paper: of any size

markers

Anticipatory Set

Write the following sequence on the board: 1–2–6–12–36. Ask what number comes next. (72) Students probably will not see that the pattern is ×2 ×3 ×2 ×3. Leave sequence on the board for later solving.

Procedure 1

□■

To find patterns: multiplication in the rule

Use *cubes or tiles, rulers,* and *plain paper.*

Have students draw a horizontal line across their paper halfway down. This will be the baseline. Write 1–2–4–8 on the board. Instruct students to place one block on the line, then two blocks, then four blocks, then eight blocks. Be sure blocks make flat vertical lines on the paper.

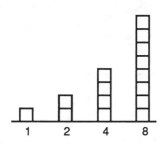

Students write the numbers in a horizontal line on the bottom half of their paper. Do they see a pattern?

Have students try to lay a ruler across the tops of the blocks:

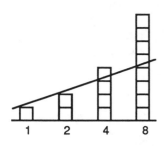

Students discover that this sequence is not formed by repeatedly adding the same numbers, for if it were the ruler would touch the tops of all the columns.

The numbers get large very quickly, which is a clue to remember. Ask: How can we get from the first number to the second? (add 1) How can we find how much to add?

Students respond: Subtract to find the difference between each number and the next.

On the board write +1 above and between the 1 and 2. Find the amounts to be added and mark them on your written sequence. Can you predict the next number?

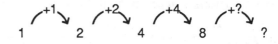

What have you discovered?

Students may notice that the same number is not added each time, and that each new number added is the same as the preceding number in the sequence.

Addition didn't help us here. The ruler showed us that. Is there another way to get from 1 to 2?

Students respond: Multiply by 2.

Write ×2 above the +1 in the sequence. Try to get from one number to the next by multiplication. What do you discover when you do that?

Students write ×2 above their addition numbers, in the form shown above. They discover a regular sequence.

What are the differences between sequences made by addition and those made by multiplication?

Students respond: The numbers get bigger more quickly with multiplication; the tops of the columns don't line up in a straight line as they do with addition.

Repeat this exercise with several other multiplication sequences.

Procedure 2

To find patterns: division in the rule

Use *cubes or tiles, rulers,* and *plain paper.*

Write: 9–3–1 on the board.

Students place blocks, write the sequence, and check with rulers.

The ruler slants downward to the right. Ask: What kind of sequence have you had before that gave the ruler a similar slant? (subtraction) Why does the ruler slant this way?

Students respond: The numbers are getting smaller.

But, does the ruler show that this sequence is made by subtraction?

Students respond: No, the ruler does not touch the tops of all the columns.

What do you notice about the size of the numbers? (they get smaller very quickly) How else could you get from 9 to 3? (divide by 3)

Students write ÷3 above their numbers.

What do you notice about both multiplication and division sequences? (the numbers go up and down quickly, and the columns don't line up with the ruler)

Provide students with more sequences to practice with. Ask them to first make predictions of what operations will be found in the rule.

Procedure 3

To graph curves of multiplication and division sequences

Use *graph paper, markers,* and *rulers.*

Have students draw a horizontal line across their paper near the bottom as a baseline. Have them start at the baseline and color a vertical column of blocks for each number. Dictate the following sequence: 3–6–12–24.

Students color blocks for the sequence and use their rulers to help themselves see patterns. They write the sequence to the side. They should recognize it as a multiplication sequence and be able to write ×2 above the numbers. If not, instruct them to write *all* ways to get from each number to the next.

Have students draw a line connecting the midpoints of the top blocks of the columns. Point out to them that they can smooth out their line to make a curve. (see illustration)

What pattern do they see? Where would the line go for the next number?

Students can see that the line is not straight and would rise even more quickly as the sequence progresses.

Sequences made by addition and subtraction give straight lines and sequences made by multiplication and division give curves on a graph.

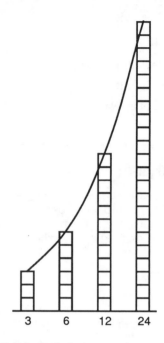

Write: 2–4–8–16–8–4–2.

Students color numbers and write the sequence to the side. They write ×2 ×2 ×2 ÷2 ÷2 ÷2 between the numbers and graph the tops of the columns.

If necessary, give students more sequences until they are competent.

Have them solve the problem from the Anticipatory Set. After solving, what would be the next number? What would they have to do to reverse the sequence? (÷3, ÷2)

Practice and Extension

Have students create sequences for others to solve on *graph paper.* Remind them that they must repeat the sequence for the pattern to become clear. Have students create a story problem to go with each sequence. They then exchange papers and see if they can solve each other's patterns.

Tell students they have worked hard at a job. Their boss says he will double their salary each month. Have students start with a salary of one dollar, chart several months' numbers, and make predictions about their future earnings.

Number Skills 3

Skill: To find patterns in number sequences: multiple operations in the rule

Time: 1–2 periods

Materials:

cubes or tiles

rulers

graph paper: of any size

markers

Anticipatory Set

Use *cubes or tiles, rulers,* and *plain paper.*

Have students draw a horizontal line across their paper halfway down. This will be the baseline. Write 1 2 3 on the board. Instruct students to place one block on the line, then two blocks, then three blocks. Be sure the blocks are in a flat vertical line on the paper. Students also write the sequence at the side of their paper.

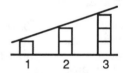

Have students lay ruler along the top edge of the blocks to see if the column tops all touch a straight line. Review that for addition and subtraction sequences the column tops line up and make a straight graph line.

Repeat with 1 2 4 8. Review that the numbers in multiplication and division sequences change size quickly and make curves rather than straight lines on a graph.

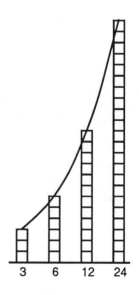

Procedure 1 □■

To identify patterns and possible operations

Use *cubes or tiles, rulers,* and *plain paper.*

Write 1 2 3 6 12 7 2 3 4 8 16 11 6 on the board. These numbers make two complete series or patterns formed by following the same rule. Instruct students to place blocks in a horizontal line. They should also write the sequence at the side of their paper.

Ask: Can you use your rulers to find patterns which will help you discover the rule and predict the next number?

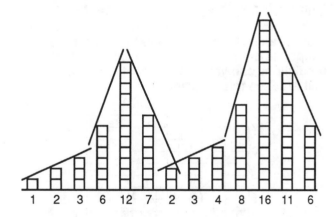

Students should discover that this is a complex series. Although there are several parts of it which line up with the ruler and could be formed by addition or subtraction, other parts rise and fall quite steeply.

Have students mark a dot at the midpoint of each top block then remove the blocks and connect the dots to graph the sequence. Ask what they notice.

Students respond: There are two patterns. One part of each pattern goes up very quickly and doesn't make a straight line. Those parts could be made by multiplication. The rest of the graph is in straight lines and could be made by addition and subtraction.

Tell the students: Between each of your written numbers, write all the ways to get from each number to the next. If you think a section is multiplication, write that way first. Find a rule that will work for both patterns.

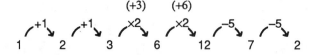

Students discover that although there are several ways to get from some numbers to the next, the pattern is:

$$+1 \quad +1 \quad \times 2 \quad \times 2 \quad -5 \quad -5$$

Repeat procedure with different patterns until students are comfortable with it.

Procedure 2

To graph sequences

Use *graph paper*, *rulers*, and *markers*.

Have students draw a horizontal baseline across their paper near the bottom. Have them start at the baseline and color a vertical column of blocks for each number in the following sequence, which you dictate:

1 2 4 8 4 2 3 6 12 6 3

Students color columns of blocks to represent the sequence and write the numbers to the side of their sheets of papers.

Have students use their rulers to connect the midpoints of the columns' top blocks. Ask: What predictions can you make about the operations that produce this sequence?

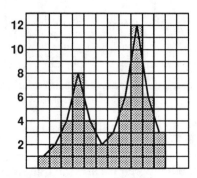

Students should be able to see that part of the graph probably shows multiplication and division. It forms a quickly rising and falling curve.

Say: This is a tricky series. Write all the ways to get from each number to the next. If you have made predictions about sections of the sequence, write that way first.

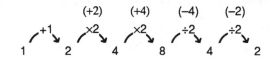

Students should see the pattern is:

$$+1 \quad \times 2 \quad \times 2 \quad \div 2 \quad \div 2$$

Students will find that there are several ways to get from some numbers to the next. They will have to find out which one is used when the pattern is repeated.

Repeat procedure if necessary. When students are comfortable with it, have them label two axes of a graph from 0 to 30. The horizontal axis will be the position of each number in the series. The vertical axis is the value of each number.

Write: 1 3 9 2 6 12 5. Have students write the sequence to the side and graph it.

Students graph series and look for repeating patterns.

Repeat above procedure to help students solve the sequence. The solution is:

$$\times 3 \quad \times 3 \quad -7$$

Practice and Extension

Have students create sequences for others to solve on *graph paper*. Remind them that they must repeat the sequence for the pattern to become clear. Have students create a story problem to go with each sequence, and make predictions from the graph.

Place Value 1

Skill: To understand place value through 9,999: regrouping, expanded notation, and comparing

Time: 2+ periods

Materials:

blank file folders, or tag board: 1 per student

rulers

scissors

1 die

counter-trading materials to 1000s

deck of cards: 1 for the teacher

See Reproducibles for: bills to 1000s—run off in different colors, directions for file-folder place value (pv) mats to 1000s; 1 per group, counter-trading boards to 1000s

Anticipatory Set (do this a day ahead)

Use *bills, pv mat directions, file folders, rulers,* and *scissors.*

Working in groups of four, students cut bills apart.

Hand out folders, directions, and rulers to each group. Each student will make one pv mat using the rulers to make each section equal. Have groups work with the sheet of directions to complete making file-folder pv mats to 1,000.

If folders are laminated, they will last the year and students can write directly on them with markers.

Procedure 1

To understand thousands: regrouping and expanded notation

Use *bills* and *pv mats.*

Give students some numbers to 999, and review reading of the expanded form, saying: __hundreds, __tens, __ones.

Have students place bills for the number 4,856 onto pv mats and read with you: four thousands, eight hundreds, five tens, and six ones.

Hold up a $1, and have them "add one."

Students place bills and read chorally: Four thousands, eight hundreds, five tens, and seven ones.

Continue adding $1 bills and reading until you have 10 $1 bills. Ask: What happens next?

Students respond: Regroup. They trade 10 $1s for a $10 and read chorally the expanded form for 4,860.

Hold up $10, and add tens until you reach 4,890. Add one more $10. Ask what happens next.

Students place bills and respond: Regroup for 100. They read the new amount.

Ask: What do you notice about the thousands?

Students respond: It's like the smaller numbers.

Now hold up combinations of bills, for example, one $100, five $10s, and four $1s.

Students place this amount on their pv mats below the 4,900, add, and regroup as needed.

Ask: What number do we have now?

Students respond: Five thousands, zero hundreds, five tens, and four ones.

Continue the procedure, giving amounts up to $9,999 that need more than one regrouping.

Procedure 2

To write numbers to 9,999

Use *die, bills,* and *pv mats.*

Divide the class in half, and play Money Madness to see which half finishes with the greatest amount.

Generate numbers for each side in turn by throwing the die. Make up stories to go with the numbers, such as inheriting $3,612. Have students place bills on their mats in the places dictated.

After placing a 4-digit number, students write the number on paper. Members of the group check each other. They add subsequent numbers, keeping a running total.

It is important for students to understand that the written form is just a description of what is actually happening. Students need much practice at this step.

After students become confident about the process, they can move to writing the problem first, and then checking with bills.

Procedure 3

To compare numbers to 9,999

Use *counter-trading boards* and *counter-trading materials.*

Have students place a colored counter over the labels on their mats if their mats are not color-coded.

Have students work in groups and place 1,111 on the mats. Ask: Are these ones all the same? (no)

How many ones to make one ten? (10) To make one hundred? (100) A thousand? (1,000)

Have students add one counter to a place of their choice. Who has the largest number?

Students place materials and discuss. They see that students who placed the counter in the thousands column have the largest number.

Write 2,111 on the board. Who has the next smaller number?

Students with 1,211 respond.

Discuss that the value of a number depends on its place. Repeat for 1,121 and 1,112.

Have students remove all but 1,111. This time have them add one additional block to *two* places of their choice.

What place should we look at first to find the largest number? (thousands) Why?

Repeat for other places.

Could we make a chart to be sure we have listed all the numbers in order? The biggest number will have what in thousands? (2) And in hundreds? (2) Repeat questions for rest of numbers so that the chart reads:

2,211
2,121
2,112
1,221
1,212
1,122

Repeat the procedure with other numbers to give students as much practice as is necessary.

Students write all possible numbers and then order them on paper after comparing them to their materials.

Later, have students write numbers in order and then check with materials. Students need much practice at the stage of both writing and using manipulatives.

Procedure 4 □

To practice comparing and writing numbers through 9,999

Use *pv mats, bills,* and the *deck of cards.*

Draw five cards; face cards are zeros. Have students decide where to put each digit on their pv mats. The object is to get the largest (or smallest) number.

Students must place each bill before the next card is drawn. They are allowed to ignore one number but must decide before the next number is drawn.

See who has the most thousands on their mat, then the most hundreds, and so on.

Students read each number in their group and write them in order.

Practice and Extension

Hand out *number lines,* and have students use *one color crayon or marker* to number to 1,000 by tens. Use *another color* to mark the hundreds. Using a *third color* and *another number line,* number by thousands to 10,000. Post the lines by thousands vertically. Place the lines by tens horizontally between thousands to give a visual representation of value.

Have students say address numbers. Have them become aware that certain numbers are *not* said as thousands, such as phone numbers, house numbers, sometimes years. Students compare their house numbers and the last four digits of their phone numbers. They work in groups and order the numbers from least to greatest.

Ask what would happen if we added *$1* more to the *bills* in Procedure 1; or one more *counter* to 9,999 *counters?* Let students experiment and discover the need to trade up to a larger number than they have a place for on their *mats.* Explain that this number is the ten thousands place number.

Use *dice* and generate four numbers. Have students write the largest or smallest number possible using those four digits. Have students explain why the number they wrote is the largest or smallest possible; make sure their explanations include the idea that the value of a number depends on its place. How many numbers can be made from the numbers shown on the dice? How did the students know if they had found them all? Did they look for patterns to help them? Does it make a difference if some of the dice-generated numbers are the same?

Place Value 2

Skill: To understand place value through 999,999

Time: $\frac{1}{2}$ period per procedure

Materials:

file-folder place value (pv) mats to 100,000s
scissors

counters: color-coded to 100,000s
6 index cards: 1 pv place name per card
10 index cards: 1 digit, 1 to 9 per card
graph paper: $\frac{1}{2}$" squares
large blank index cards: 1 per student
deck of cards
See Reproducibles for: directions for file-folder pv mats to 100,000s, bills to 100,000s—in different colors

Anticipatory Set

(*If making pv mats, do a day ahead.* Have each group make 1 pv mat; see directions.)

Use *pv mats, bills,* and *scissors.*

Have students cut apart bills and place various money amounts to $99,999 on their mats. Then have them read the numbers to each other.

Have students write down their phone numbers, discarding two digits to make a readable 5-digit number. Then have them read these to each other.

Procedure 1 ◼

To understand hundred thousands

Use *pv mats* and *bills.*

Write a number to 999,999 on the board. Draw a roof over the thousands' places.

Remind students that when a number is larger than 999, it lives in a house called *thousands.* The places are still called ones, tens, and hundreds, but now *thousands* is part of their name.

Cover all but the ones place. Ask: What number is this? Continue uncovering one digit at a time.

Students read each number, emphasizing the Thousands family name when they get to it.

Dictate numbers to 999,999.

Students pool their bills to put the amounts on their pv mats. They read the value of the numbers in the thousand house before saying the house name. *The comma is the clue to say the house name.*

Procedure 2 ◻◼

To regroup and use expanded notation

Use *pv mats, counters,* and *index cards with numbers and place value names.*

Dictate the number 888,888.
Students place counters on the mats for the number.

Read chorally: Eight hundred thousands, eight ten thousands, eight thousands, eight hundreds, eight tens, eight ones.

Write on the board: 800,00 + 80,000 + 8,000 + 80 + 8.

Draw a place value card and a number card. Example: a thousand card and a five card.

Students place that amount below the counters already on their mats and chorally read it. Example: five thousands, zero hundreds, zero tens, zero ones.

Students add and regroup as necessary.

Write the number on the board, using expanded notation.

Repeat the activity until students become adept at the skill. Then challenge them by drawing more than one pv card and number. Students should become comfortable with a variety of possible place changes.

When students are competent in the procedure, they write each new sum after making it with the counters. They write both standard and expanded forms.

Students need much practice at the stage of both using manipulatives and writing.

Procedure 3 ◻

To practice reading and writing numbers through 999,999

Use *graph paper* and *scissors.*

Have students write 0–9 in separate 1" × 1" graph paper squares across the top of their paper and cut out the squares.

Students draw a place-value chart on their remaining graph paper and arrange six of the digit squares on it to make a number. Working in pairs they read their numbers to their partners, both as standard numbers and using expanded form.

They rearrange the digit squares to make different numbers, reading and recording each new number. They exchange papers and read the partner's list of numbers, placing digit squares on pv charts to aid reading, if needed.

Procedure 4 ■

To compare numbers through 999,999

Use *pv mats* and *counters*.

Students place a color-coded counter over each place name on their mats. They write down their phone numbers, discard one digit, and represent the resulting 6-digit number with counters on their mats.

Ask: Who has the most tens? The fewest thousands? Continue until all places have been discussed.

Which is greater, one in the thousands place, or nine in the hundreds? Why?

Students respond: Each 1 in the thousands place is worth 10 hundreds. They read their numbers.

Next have students cover all but the ones place and compare 1-digit numbers. Continue uncovering and comparing until all places have been compared.

Repeat with other numbers until students are competent in the skill.

Procedure 5 □

To practice comparing numbers through 999,999

Use *large blank index cards*.

Students choose a 6-digit number and write it as large as possible on an index card. They hold the card in front of them at chest level, and the class sequences these numbers by lining up.

Extend practice by having students return to their seats and then having all even numbers order themselves on one side of the room and all odd numbers on the other.

Repeat with multiples of various numbers, if students know the rules for divisibility.

Display the completed whole-class sequence.

Now dictate several numbers for students to write and then to order. Have them check with the number display for accuracy.

Procedure 6 □

To practice comparing numbers through 999,999

Use *pv mats, bills,* and *deck of cards*.

Draw seven cards, one at a time; faces are zeros.

As each digit is drawn, students decide where to put it onto their pv mats, using the correct bills for that place. They try to get the largest/smallest number.

Bills must be placed before the next card is drawn. They are allowed to ignore one number but must decide before you draw the next number.

See who has the most hundred thousands on their mat, then the most ten thousands, and so on.

Students read each number in their group and write numbers in order.

Practice and Extension

Discuss with students when it would be useful to compare and order numbers to 1,000,000. For example, warehouse inventory numbers need to be sequenced for easy access.

Have students make a class chart ordering their phone numbers. Are the numbers close together or far apart when placed on a *number line?* Why?

Have student pairs see who can make the largest 6-digit number, the smallest 6-digit number. Why did they choose the digits they used?

Save *lists of 6-digit numbers* to exchange with other groups for reading. Have students organize and graph the numbers on *graph paper*.

Students use a *deck of cards* and play in pairs. They each draw seven cards and arrange them to be the highest possible number. Tens and face cards count as zero. The winner gets 1 point. After 5 points, the game changes to making the smallest number. The first one to 10 points wins the game. How do their strategies change? Where are the zeros placed in each round?

Use a *die, pv mats,* and *counters or bills*. Students work in pairs. Each chooses a number and places it on his or her mat. The die is tossed: An even number means the larger number wins; an odd number means the smaller one wins. Students play for a set amount of time.

Place Value 3

Skill: To understand place value through 999,999,999

Time: 2 periods

Materials:

file-folder place value (pv) mats to 100,000s

12" × 18" tag board: 1 per student

paper: in 3 colors, cut into 4½" × 2" rectangles; 10 of each per student

markers

blank 4" × 6" index cards: 1 per student

deck of cards

See Reproducibles for: directions for file-folder pv mats, bills to 100,000s—in different colors

Anticipatory Set

Use *file-folder pv mats, tag board, paper rectangles,* and *markers.*

Have students place tag board along the left-hand side of their pv mats to make an added part that shows millions. Label as done with thousands. Remind students that the comma tells you to say the family name. Have students label their paper rectangles: $1,000,000, $10,000,000, and $100,000,000, one color per denomination.

Have students write down their phone numbers and also two other numbers, one with nine digits and one with eight digits. Save them for Procedure 1.

Procedure 1　　　　　　□■

To read and write numbers through 999,999,999

Use *pv mats, paper bills and numbers from the Anticipatory Set,* and *bills.*

Draw a place value chart to millions on the board. Give students a 3-digit number to place on their mats; write the number on the chart.

Students place and read the number.

Have students add three more numbers to the left of the first number, resulting in a number in the hundred thousands. Write this on the chart.

Say: We now have a family name in our number. What is it? (thousands) How is the thousands family number like our first number?

Students respond: They both have ones, tens, and hundreds places.

Ask: What do you think about our next family, the millions family?

Students respond: It also has ones, tens, and hundreds places.

Add three more numbers as before.

Students place and read the resulting number, emphasizing the family names.

Point to various digits, and have students name their place.

Repeat the procedure with new numbers. Students should place and read the resulting number each time you add a digit.

Have students repeat the procedure until all are able to give correct oral responses.

Now have students work in groups of three or four to place bills on their mats to represent their numbers from the Anticipatory Set. Can a designated reader from another group correctly read the number shown?

Go around the class, reading the numbers shown. Continue until all numbers have been read.

Students then write a list of the numbers used in their group. They check each other, making sure that the family names of millions and thousands are used in the appropriate places. They also check to see that the commas have been placed correctly.

Dictate numbers, and have students place and then write them. Students need much practice at the stage of both manipulating the bills and writing the numbers.

When students are competent in the skill, they can write first and then check with the bills.

Procedure 2　　　　　　□■

To compare numbers through 999,999,999

Use *list of numbers from Procedure 1* and *index cards.*

Each student chooses one number from the group list and correctly writes it as large as possible on an index card. That is to be his or her name in this procedure.

Holding the card in front, students introduce themselves to each other, using the correct verbal form of the number.

Have students order themselves in a line around the room from least to greatest.

Repeat the procedure, but have students order themselves the opposite way.

Were they next to the same number? What did that tell them about the process of ordering numbers?

Students continue the exercise until they are comfortable with the use of larger numbers.

Have students place cards on the chalk rail for a number line. Write random numbers for them to order. They should check with the number line.

Procedure 3 ☐

To practice using numbers through 999,999,999

Use *pv mats, bills, paper bills from the Anticipatory Set,* and *deck of cards.*

Draw nine cards, one at a time; face cards and tens will represent zeros. As each card is drawn, have students decide where to place that number. The goal is to have the largest or smallest number.

Students each decide where to place a digit and then place bills and rectangles on their mats representing the numbers.

After all nine cards are drawn and the bills placed, discuss who has the most hundred millions, ten millions, and so on. Who had the largest number? The smallest?

Students then take turns, in groups, reading their numbers to each other.

Practice and Extension

Students use their *numbers* to make addition problems. Can they reach the billions when adding the large numbers?

Have students predict how they would say, or read, a 10-digit number, an 11-digit number, a 12-digit number. Can they see the similarities to millions? That is, do they use the ones, tens, and hundreds places and the family name?

Students make the numerals 0 to 9 on *squares of paper.* They work in pairs and draw numbers to see who can make the largest 7-digit, 8-digit, and 9-digit numbers.

Can they use their *pv mats* and *bills* to make up a game in which the first student to reach 1,000,000,000 wins?

Place Value 4

Skill: To round numbers to the nearest 10 and $10

Time: 2+ periods

Materials:

clear tape

scissors

crayons or markers in two colors

file-folder or other place value (pv) mats to 100s or 1000s

pv materials to 100s

counters (any color): 1 per student

See Reproducibles for: number lines to 100—1 per student, Rounding Rhyme—1 copy per student, directions for file-folder pv mats to 1000s, or use pv mats to 100s, bills to 100s—in different colors

Anticipatory Set

Use *number lines, clear tape, scissors,* and *crayons or markers.*

Have students cut apart and tape strips into one long line, and label each longer mark by tens. They use a different color to label all numbers ending in five.

Discuss that we don't always need to know exact numbers. Sometimes we can estimate.

Procedure 1

To round numbers from 1 to 99

Use *number lines from Anticipatory Set, copies of the Rounding Rhyme,* and *blank sheets of paper.*

Have students count on the number line, tapping each tick mark and emphasizing the multiples of ten. Explain that rounding is a way of estimating, or making a good guess. Ask: What on the number line looks the most round?

Students identify zero.

Tell students that a round number must end with a zero or more than one zero.

Have them look at the number line and put their finger on the mark for 14. Put another finger on the nearest number that ends in zero. What is it? (10)

Emphasize that sometimes it's more and sometimes it's less than the number we started with.

Students repeat procedure as you give: 7, 23, 18, 46, 12.

Have students write 16, 23, 18, 46, 62, and 35 on their paper.

Since we are rounding to the nearest 10, they should underline each digit in the tens place as a reminder.

Pass out the Rounding Rhyme and read with the class, using a rap rhythm:

Mark the place,
Look to the right.
Four or less are out of sight!

Five and up
Will buy one more,
Before they, too, are out the door.

In those empty
Right-hand spaces,
Zeros keep the proper places.

Have students check the underlined number in 16. Is the space to the right five or up? (yes)

What does the rhyme say to do? (buy one more)

Have students write 2 over the 1 in the number 16. Because rounded numbers end in zero, what should we put in place of the 6?

Students respond: A zero. They write a zero over the 6.

Have students check their answer on the number line. Is 20 the closest 10 to 16?

Continue the procedure with 23. What does the rhyme say to do to the number 3?

Students respond: It's out of sight. They write a zero over the 3 and leave the 2 alone. They check the answer on their number lines.

Repeat with 18, 46, 62, and 35.

Point out that the rhyme tells us that we can buy one more with 5. Even though it's not closer to either the higher or the lower ten, it's halfway, so we can keep on going up.

Continue rounding practice with many numbers, especially ones ending in 5.

Students say the rhyme, write the numbers, cross out and replace, and then check on the number line.

Discuss when rounding is useful.

Procedure 2

To round money amounts above and below $99

Use *pv mats, number lines from Anticipatory Set, bills, counters,* and *Rounding Rhyme.*

Dictate $53 to the students and have them place the bills on their mats. They may use a counter under the number in the 10s place to mark the place to which they're rounding.

Tell students: We're rounding to the nearest ten, or $10. Remember that sometimes we'll end up with more money, sometimes less.

On your number lines, we rounded higher at the halfway mark. How many dollars is halfway to $10?

Students respond: $5.

If we have $5 or more, we can regroup or "buy" a $10 bill. What will we do with less than $5?

Students discuss that rounded numbers end in zero. They will have to get rid of amounts under $5.

We have $53. Is $3 enough to buy $10? (no) What do we do? (get rid of it)

Students remove the $3. They check with both the number line and Rounding Rhyme to reinforce the concept.

Repeat with other 2-digit amounts, including $99.

Students place the bills, write the number, round the bills, then round the number.

Discuss with students how being able to round dollar amounts might help when grocery shopping. Where else would the skill be useful?

Students discuss other situations. They also compare this skill to other estimating skills they have learned.

Dictate a 3-digit number which the students place on their mats. Point out that they are still rounding to the nearest 10, not 100.

Students practice rounding with money, writing the numbers as well. They check with the number line and Rounding Rhyme.

As students' grasp of the concept improves, give numbers with 9 in the tens place and numbers above 5 in the ones place. Such numbers will force regrouping and change the hundreds number.

When students are competent, have them round numbers on paper first, then check each one with bills and the number line. They can also use the Rounding Rhyme to check their results.

Procedure 3 □

To practice rounding to the nearest 10

Use *pv mats, pv materials, number lines from Anticipatory Set*, and *Rounding Rhyme*.

Follow Procedure 2, using place value materials.

Students should both manipulate the materials and write their numbers. They should use the number line and the Rounding Rhyme as aids.

Remind the students that "buying one more" really means "trading up" on the pv mats. How can they prove this?

When they are comfortable with rounding, ask more abstract questions. What is the highest

number that rounds to 90? (94) The lowest one? (85) The highest that rounds to 230? (234) What does 999 round to? (1,000)

Practice and Extension

Estimate sums of two 2-digit numbers by rounding both numbers and adding them.

Have students round the number of students in each classroom and add the rounded numbers to arrive at an approximate school size. Have them compare this number to the answer they get when they add the actual numbers. When might they choose one procedure over another?

Have pairs of students use *cards* in turn to generate large numbers. They round the numbers, keeping a running total. After so many turns, the winner is the student with the higher total.

Place Value 5

Skill: To round numbers to the nearest 100, 1000, $100, and $1,000

Time: 1 period per procedure

Materials:

place value (pv) materials to 100s

file-folder or other pv mats to 1000s

graph paper: ¹/₂" or larger squares

20 large cards: labeled 0, 500, 1,000, etc., to 9,500

counters: 4 different colors; 1 of each color per student

See Reproducibles for: directions for file-folder pv mats, if needed; or other pv mats to 1000s, Rounding Rhyme, number lines to 1000—1 per student, bills to 1000s—in different colors

Anticipatory Set

Use *pv materials, pv mats,* and *copies of the Rounding Rhyme.*

Write 10 different 3-digit numbers on the board. Have students choose one of the numbers and represent it with counters on their place value chart. Review rules for rounding to nearest 10 and have them round their numbers to the nearest 10. Read all rounded numbers. What do the students anticipate will be the rule for rounding to the nearest 100?

Pass out the *Rounding Rhyme* and review with the class using a rap rhythm.

Mark the place,
Look to the right.
Four or less are out of sight!

Five and up
Will buy one more,
Before they, too, are out the door.

In those empty
Right-hand spaces,
Zeros keep the proper places.

Procedure 1 ☐■

To round 3-digit numbers

Use *number lines, copies of the Rounding Rhyme,* and *paper.*

Have students mark the number lines from 0 to 1,000 by hundreds. Then have them count, tapping each tick mark and emphasizing the multiples of 100.

Review that rounding is a way of estimating, or making a good guess.

Have them look at the number line and put their finger on the mark where 134 would be. Ask: What is the nearest hundred? Emphasize that sometimes it's more and sometimes it's less than the number we started with.

Students respond: The nearest 100 is 100. They check with fingers on the number line.

Have students write: 476, 223, 598, 746, and 351 on their paper.

Say: Since we are rounding to the nearest 100, you should underline the digit in the hundreds place as a reminder. What does the rhyme say to do for 476?

Students respond: We can buy one more.

Have students write 5 over the 4 in the number 476. Tell students that when rounding to the hundreds place, we ignore the ones place. The only number to the right that we look at is the one in the tens place. Because rounded numbers end in zero, what should we do to the 7 and 6?

Students respond: The right-hand spaces are zeros. They write zeros over the other two numbers, and then they write the rounded number.

Have students check their answers on the number line. Is 500 the closest 100 to 476? Ask what the rhyme tells us to do with 223.

Students respond: The 2 and 3 are out of sight. They write a zero over the 2 and 3, leaving the 2 hundred number unchanged. They check the answer on their number lines.

Repeat with the other numbers. Point out that for 351, we follow the rhyme, even though 50 is not closer to either hundred on their number line.

When students become adept at rounding numbers above 100, introduce numbers below 100. Have students round numbers over 51, under 49, then 50. Discuss which is closer to 50, 0 or 100. Remind them, that halfway buys the next number when rounding.

Practice with many 3-digit numbers. Discuss when rounding to nearest 100 is useful.

Procedure 2 ☐■

To round numbers to nearest 1,000

Use *graph paper, copies of the Rounding Rhyme, counters (1 color),* and *cards with numbers.*

Have 10 students come to the front of the room. Give each student a card to hold up, and a new name: 0, 1,000, 2,000, 3,000, and so on.

Ten more students take a counter and a card and place themselves as 500, 1,500, 2,500, and so on.

Ask: What we have made? (a human number line)

The remaining students rename themselves one at a time and take an appropriate place in the line.

Which thousand is closest to each of these students? How about the students with counters? Discuss.

Students place cards on the chalk tray for a number line. They discuss and predict a rule for rounding to the nearest 1,000.

Next have students use graph paper to make a pv chart and write 4,732 on it.

Ask: If I were number 4732, to whom would I be closest? (5,000) If I am a rounded number, what do I need to end in? (zeros)

Students underline the four in the thousands place and write a five over the four and zeros over the other numbers.

Students write other 4-digit numbers. They check first on the number line and then with the Rounding Rhyme before rounding the numbers.

Discuss using rounding to get an estimated answer. Why is this useful? (to see whether their answers to problems are reasonable)

Give students a 5-digit number to place on their mats. They are still rounding to the nearest 1,000. What will happen to the 10,000s place? (nothing, unless ten hundreds need to be regrouped as a thousand)

Have them round 49,900. Ask what other numbers would force regrouping.

When they are comfortable rounding, ask more abstract questions. What is the highest number that rounds to 9,000? (9,499) The lowest one? (8,500) The highest that rounds to 12,000? (12,499) What does 99,999 round to? (100,000)

Procedure 3 □ ■

To round to the nearest $100 and $1,000

Use *pv mats, bills, number lines, copies of the Rounding Rhyme,* and *counters.*

Dictate $563 to the students and have them place bills and round the amount to the nearest 100. They may use a counter under the number in the hundreds place to mark that place. Have students check their answers on the number line.

Repeat with other 3-digit numbers, including 999.

Students place the bills, write the number, round the bills, then write the rounded number.

Introduce a 4-digit number for the students to place on their mats. Point out that they are still rounding

to the nearest 100. **Ask: How could you use the number line to check? Does the rounding change the number in the thousands place? (not usually)**

Students practice rounding with money, writing the numbers, and checking with the number line.

Students will need a lot of practice with the skill when the rounded number is in the middle of the original number. Include some 5-digit numbers to round to the nearest 1,000.

When students are competent in the skill, they round numbers on paper first and then check with bills or the number line.

Repeat the procedure using money with cents by having students place a counter on the mat between the hundreds and tens places, or by using decimal extensions to the pv mat. See Reproducibles for directions for making extensions.

Have students practice rounding amounts to the nearest dollar and 10 dollars. If using decimal extensions, also round dollar and cent amounts to the nearest $100 and $1,000.

Practice and Extension

Have students estimate sums or differences of two 3- or 4-digit numbers: Round both numbers and add or subtract. Have students do problems both with and without rounding. When is this estimating skill useful?

Have students bring in *advertisements*. Who can be the first to round all the amounts and arrive at a total?

Have students think up shopping trips on which they need to estimate money amounts to the nearest dollar, such as grocery shopping, birthday parties, and so on. Students exchange problems for peers to solve.

Students can play First to Reach $1,000,000. They use *pv mats, bills ($1,000 to $100,000),* and *4 dice.* Students start with $1,000 and throw all four dice. They arrange them to make the largest possible number and then round that number to the nearest 1,000. They place that many bills on their mats. The first one who needs to trade for $1,000,000 is the winner.

Addition 1

Skill: To add 3-digit numbers and mixed-digit numbers

Time: 1+ periods

Materials:

graph paper: ½" squares; 1 sheet per student

scissors

file-folder or other place value (pv) mats to 1000s

pv materials to 1000s, use counters as 1000s

dice: 1 per group

crayons or markers

counter-trading materials to 1000s

See Reproducibles for: directions for file-folder pv mats to 1000s, pv mats to 1000s, counter-trading boards to 1000s, or use color-coded pv mats to 1000s

Anticipatory Set

Use *graph paper* and *scissors*.

Have the class make recording strips by cutting graph paper into strips, four squares wide. Label the top squares: "1000s," "100s," "10s," and "1s." Review the place names, and introduce a thousand cube.

Review 2-digit addition problems.

Procedure 1

To add with regrouping; no zeros

Use *pv mats, pv materials,* and *recording strips from Anticipatory Set.*

Draw a pv chart on the board or overhead. Introduce this story: Liam kept a diary but only remembered to write in it on 129 days the first year. The second year, he wrote in it on 213 days. On how many days did he write in the diary?

Students place materials and chorally read the numbers. Then they draw a line below the materials and push all below the line. See the illustration. They start with the ones and regroup as needed. They read the sum chorally.

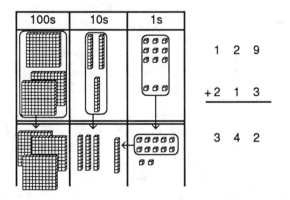

Now have student groups generate their own addition problems, creating story situations that have 3-digit numbers in them. They should be recording, as well as working out the problems with materials.

Groups present problems and answers to the class.

Procedure 2

To add with regrouping; including zeros

Use *pv mats, pv materials, dice,* and *recording strips from Anticipatory Set.*

Use a die to generate a 3-digit number: ones, tens, then hundreds. Have students place materials and record on their recording strip as you write the number.

Tell students: The second number is tricky. You may use only numbers that are 4, 5, or 6.

Have each group throw a die to obtain the second addend. What should happen for those who didn't get an allowed number? (Use a zero.)

Emphasize this is a place holder, and make sure all zeros are recorded. Students *cannot use a zero in the hundreds place* but must continue to throw dice until they have an allowed number.

Students throw dice, place materials, record numbers, add materials, and record total.

Continue the procedure until students are competent in the skill.

Procedure 3

To practice writing addition problems

Use *counter-trading materials, counter-trading boards, crayons or markers, dice,* and *recording strips from Anticipatory Set.*

Students need to understand that the written form is just a description of what is actually happening with their materials. They need much practice at this step.

Students color-code their recording strips.

Copy Illustration 2a, found on the following page, onto the board. Use this to demonstrate the form for students as you work through the procedure.

Students use dice to generate numbers, put two groups of counters on the mat, and record as before. They push down all the counters representing ones, and then the tens and hundreds, recording the total number in *each* column (Illustration 2a).

Say: Start with the ones counters, and regroup if necessary. Cross out the original number of ones on your recording sheet. Write the new number of ones below, and show any necessary regrouping in the tens column. Circle the regrouped number (Illustration 2b).

Recording Sheet

1000s	100s	10s	1s
	1	6	4
	+ 2	5	7
	3	11	11

2a

Recording Sheet

1000s	100s	10s	1s
	1	(+1) 6	4
	+ 2	5	7
	3	11	1̸1̸
			1

2b

Demonstrate Illustration 3a and say: Add all tens and record them like this. Continue to illustrate as in 3b and have students regroup tens as shown.

Recording Sheet

1000s	100s	10s	1s
	1	(+1) 6	4
	+ 2	5	7
	3	1̸1̸	1̸1̸
		12	
			1

3a

Recording Sheet

1000s	100s	10s	1s
	(+1) 1	(+1) 6	4
	+ 2	5	7
	3	1̸1̸	1̸1̸
		1̸2̸	
	4	2	1

3b

Continue step-by-step with students through the problem.

Students generate, work, and record some addition problems using this recording method. They record each separate step after doing it with the blocks.

When students are comfortable with the process, have them do problems on paper first and then check with the counters.

When they can do this easily, introduce the shortcut method of recording regrouping in which intermediate totals are not recorded. Remind them to continue circling the regrouped number.

Students check with blocks and write the complete recording procedure until they are comfortable with the shortcut method.

Procedure 4

To add mixed digit numbers

Use *counter-trading boards, crayons or markers, colored counters,* and *graph paper.*

Students use graph paper to make recording charts, and label them with colors or color names instead of numbers.

Present a story problem for students to place, record, and solve. Example: Lucy's Lamp Shop sold 374 table lamps and 26 floor lamps last month. How many total lamps were sold?

Before solving, have students look for patterns adding to 10. Remind them of rounding for estimating, and have them estimate an answer.

After placing materials, recording, and estimating, students solve problems for an exact total.

Have students now take turns giving uneven-digit problems for the whole class to estimate and then solve.

Students move to doing problems without manipulatives when they are comfortable with the process.

Practice and Extension

Use the *same materials as in Procedure 3*. Have students write down their first number, generate the second, and try to add them mentally. They write down their answer and check with the counters.

Have students use their *textbooks*, round the numbers, and add to get an estimate before doing the final addition. Have them check the two results to see whether their final sum is reasonable.

Extend the process to include 4- and 5-digit numbers. Set out problem situations for students to solve. Example: First Elementary School has 1,842 students. Second Elementary School has 964 students. How many elementary students are in the district? (Use look for tens and estimating before solving problems.)

Have students bring in *pictures of catalog items* costing amounts over and under $100. Students play in pairs using *pv mats* and *bills*. Students turn over two items and add amounts both with bills and on paper, ignoring any decimal amounts. The winner is the student who spent the most/least after three turns.

Have students extend practice to adding 3-digit numbers, using more than two addends. Use *pv mats*, place, record, and total. (356 + 178 +101) They may use *any of the manipulatives* to check.

Subtraction 1

Skill: To use subtraction facts: missing numbers

Time: 2 periods

Materials:

counters: 2 colors; 18 each per student pair

treasure box or other objects: 36 per group

markers

clear tape

scissors

2 cm × 18 cm graph paper strips: 1 per student

1 cm cubes: 18 per student

See Reproducibles for: number lines to 25—1 per student, graph paper with 1 cm squares

Anticipatory Set

Use *counters* and *paper.*

Have each pair of students tear a sheet of paper into thirds and place these in a line on their desks. One student then takes counters and displays an addition fact; the other student reverses the order and displays the related subtraction fact with other counters. Discuss the different addition and subtraction facts they have displayed. Review all the subtraction fact families that the students have learned previously, and explain that now they are going to look at them a different way.

Procedure 1

To develop recognition of the missing number

Use *paper pieces from the Anticipatory Set* and *objects or counters.*

Have each group of four take three pieces of paper and set two close together as the *problem;* the other goes to the right and is designated as the *answer.*

Have students place 16 objects on the *answer* paper and then take 7 more objects and place them on one of the *problem* papers.

How many do they need to place on the other problem paper so that they will have 16 total?

Students place objects and respond: 9.

Relate this to the fact 9 + 7 = 16. Remind them of fact families, and place the following equation on the board: ? + 7 = 16.

Ask: What number should be in the place of the question mark? How can you find the answer? What math process will you use?

Students respond: 9. We subtracted to find the answer.

Have students now place 18 of the objects on the *answer* paper. Say: Take some of the other objects and to place them on a *problem* paper. What problem question have you created?

After discussing the problems, place them on the board, with question marks in the places stated.

Students discuss the numbers that should be in place of the question marks.

Discuss responses, and complete the equations.

Procedure 2

To count up to find a missing number

Use *number lines, markers, tape, scissors,* and *counters.*

Have students tape together the number lines and use markers to number from 1 to 25.

Use story problems such as: I want to plant a dozen rosebushes. I can plant 5 in the front yard. The rest will go in the backyard. On the board write 5 + ? = 12.

Students place a counter on the number 5. They use the second color counter and place counters on 6, 7, 8, 9, 10, 11, and 12.

Ask: How many of the second color counters did you use? (7) How many rosebushes will I plant in the backyard?

Students should be able to respond: 7.

Let a student write the subtraction solution, 12 − 5 = 7, on the board.

Continue with other story problems. Write the equations on the board, and have students place counters and count up to arrive at an answer.

Then write the addition fact that proves the subtraction fact is correct; you now should have the two related facts on the board.

Procedure 3

To develop the concept of subtracting to find the missing number; to write equations

Use *cm graph paper strips, cm cubes,* and *paper.*

Discuss the relationship between addition and subtraction.

Have students number the cm strips, one number per square, from 1 to 20.

Have students place a cube on the number 12. This is another way to discover how many rosebushes should be planted in the backyard, if we are going to plant 5 in the front and have 12 total rosebushes.

Students place cubes and count back 5 numbers, using 12 as the first number, arriving at a subtraction answer.

Ask: Where did you place your last cube? (on the 8) How many numbers don't have cubes? (7)

Emphasize fact families, and tell students that the equation they just solved looks like this: write 5 + ? = 12 on the board.

Ask: What number do you think you would land on if you started at 12 and counted back 7 numbers?

Students respond: 6. Five numbers would not have counters. They count to see whether they are correct.

Write the equation 12 – 7 = 5 on the board.

Now place the equation 12 – ? = 7 on the board. How should this kind of question be answered?

Students respond: Subtract 7 from 12. They write the problem on paper and tell you the completed equation should read 12 – 5 = 7.

Discuss that they took a known total and subtracted a known amount to "find" the unknown number in these equations.

Write more equations with question marks on the board. Have students copy them on paper, and then have them lay cubes onto their cm strips. Example: ? + 7 = 13. Have students suggest a story scenario to go with each equation.

Students look at the strip and, starting at the number 13, cover 7 squares—orally counting backward—13, 12, 11, 10, 9, 8, 7 are covered.

Ask: What is the next number?

Students write the equation, cover numbers, and respond: 6.

That is the number that goes in the equation on the board. Six numbers are *without* cubes. Now write 6 + 7 = 13, and have students copy this under the equation with the question mark.

Continue the process with the other equations on the board until students have written all the combinations that total 18.

Be sure to include some equations that are subtraction, solved by subtraction, like 15 – ? = 8.

Now introduce the form students will see in many textbooks of [ ] + 7 = 13. (Use an empty box instead of brackets if your textbook uses a box in place of missing numbers.)

Discuss that the brackets (or box) could be replaced with a question mark. Students need to

comprehend the reading of these types of equations to ensure that they are able to understand what question is being asked.

Students discuss that even though the equation is addition, the problem actually is solved with subtraction. They should see that the correct answer then could be proven by using the addition sentence originally given.

Continue the procedure with problems that have answers of 19 and 20.

Expand the concept to include such equations as [ ] + 12 = 25 and 28 – [ ] = 16. Students should see that in order to answer the question, they need to subtract what is known to arrive at the unknown.

Students make up problems with larger numbers and solve as a class.

Allow students to use manipulatives as long as they feel a need to do so.

Practice and Extension

Challenge students to create story problems, such as: I have 18 marbles, and 12 of them are blue. How many are not blue? Students start at the number 12 and use *counters* to represent marbles. They count up to 18 from 12 and see that they used 6 counters; so 6 of the marbles were not blue.

Have students work together to make up problems and exchange with another pair of students to solve.

Use *worksheets* from the textbook that students have solved in earlier processes. Punch out or cover one number, and have them discover what that number was.

Have students use the *addition/subtraction table* in their textbook to find the missing number in equations. This is good practice for those students who are not as fast as is desired when using subtraction facts.

Subtraction 2

Skill: To subtract 3-digit numbers: to check with addition and to subtract 1- or 2-digit subtrahends

graph paper: ¹/₂" or larger squares; 1 sheet per student
deck of cards

See Reproducibles for: pv mats to 100s, bills to 100s—in different colors

Time: 3 periods

Materials:

1" × 1" squares with 1–9 on them: 1 set per group

place value (pv) materials to 100s

Anticipatory Set

Use *number squares.*

Give student groups this problem: Take the numbers one through nine, and use them all in any order to correctly form a 3-digit subtraction problem and answer. Each number may only be used once.

At the end of 5 minutes, see whether anyone has found an answer. If so, let them demonstrate. If not, put the problem shown on the board. There are other solutions.

$$\begin{array}{r} 954 \\ -683 \\ \hline 271 \end{array}$$

Does anyone have an idea how to prove the answer is correct? Encourage discussion. This skill is something the students have done previously in simpler terms.

Procedure 1 ☐■

To develop the concept of checking with addition

Use *pv mats, pv materials,* and *graph paper.*

Students make individual place value recording strips to hundreds on graph paper, one square per place.

Have students work in groups and place materials to represent 167 on their mats. They place those for 276 below, as in Illustration 1a.

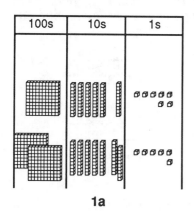

100s	10s	1s

	H	T	O
	1	6	7
	2	7	6

1a   **1b**

Students write these two numbers on their graph paper, leaving a top set of squares blank. (Illustration 1b)

Have students add the numbers by pushing all blocks in each column to the *top* of their mat, regrouping to reach a total of 443 (Illustration 2a).

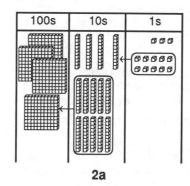

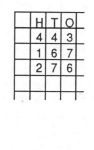

100s	10s	1s

	H	T	O
	4	4	3
	1	6	7
	2	7	6

2a   **2b**

Students write this total *above* the first two numbers they wrote on their graph paper chart. (Illustration 2b)

Ask: If 443 is the total, what would you have left if you took away 167 in materials?

Students show with materials.

How could we show this on paper?

Students respond: Place a minus sign in front of 167.

What kind of problem did we start with? (addition: 167 + 276)

What kind did we just do? (subtraction: 443 – 167) How are these two problems related?

Students discuss and write a minus sign beside and a line under the first two numbers, as shown.

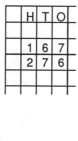

	H	T	O
	4	4	3
–	1	6	7
	2	7	6

Repeat with another problem, and then have students take the materials they subtracted and prove their answer is correct.

Students discuss their regrouping, subtraction, answers, and possible ways to prove it is correct.

If they do not come up with addition as a way of checking, suggest they recall what they just did with the manipulatives. It will have more meaning if they arrive at the conclusion for themselves.

Continue the procedure until the students are comfortable with the idea of subtracting and adding as related and reversible activities.

Procedure 2

To practice 3-digit subtraction; to check with addition

Use *pv mats, bills,* and *paper.*

Repeat Procedure 1, using the mats and bills.

Relate the minuends to the amount of money students started with, the subtrahends to items purchased, and the difference to the amount they have left.

Then have them return items and receive their money back. This amount, added to what they had left, should equal what they started with.

Students make up stories to go with the process.

Students use bills and write each step as they do it. When confident with the skill, they solve the problems on paper first and then check with the bills.

Make sure they understand that the written form is just the way of writing on paper what they can show and prove with manipulatives.

Procedure 3

To regroup with zeros

Use *pv mats* and *pv materials.*

Discuss regrouping and previous 3-digit subtraction problems with students.

Have students place 550 on their mats. Ask them to take away 135 blocks.

Students regroup a 10, pull down materials to be subtracted, and discuss what they did.

Ask: What would happen if we wanted to take away 167?

Students discuss the additional regrouping needed.

Now have students clear their mats and place 400.

Will they need to regroup to subtract 136? (yes) Stress that we can only regroup one place at a time.

Students refer to the problem before and to previous experience with subtraction problems to regroup the materials to show 3 hundreds, 9 tens, and 10 ones.

Can they prove that the materials still total 400?

Students add and find the total value is still 400.

Ask: If you now take away 136, how many will you have left?

Students subtract and respond: 264.

Continue the procedure until the students are competent with the regrouping process. Be sure to use numbers with zero in only the tens place, as well as those with two zeros.

Procedure 4

To practice checking subtraction with addition

Use *pv mats, bills, graph paper,* and *paper.*

Tell students they have $500 to spend, which they should place on their mats. Choose items that will interest them, costing $296; $94; $10, and so on.

Because the placement of the zeros is varied, students will have to think about what they are doing, not just repeat the previous procedure.

Have students make a recording strip:

Students pull down amounts to be subtracted, writing each step as they do it with blocks. After doing the subtraction, they prove and record the addition check.

After students are competent in the skill, they can begin working and checking the problems first on paper and then proving them with the manipulatives.

Expand the checking part of the instructions so that the students are able to do it all on only one extra line. *Students need to show regroupings in the subtraction and circle the carried number in the checking part:*

Students need much practice with this checking skill.

Procedure 5 ◻■

To subtract 1- or 2-digit subtrahends

Use *pv mats, bills, deck of cards,* and *graph paper.*

Have students take the graph paper and label ones, tens, and hundreds in squares at the top of the paper.

Have students place $436 on their mats and write it on the graph paper under the correct place value headings.

Students place bills and write the number.

Ask: What would happen if you wanted to take away a 2-digit number? How would you subtract a 1-digit number?

Students discuss that they will not be subtracting from the hundreds, and in the second case they would not subtract from the tens either.

Draw a card. That is the number the students will subtract. (Jacks are 11, queens are 22, and kings are 33.) Sometimes draw one card, sometimes two. The answer will be the minuend for the next subtraction problem.

Students write numbers, read chorally, and then do the problem. As they do each step with bills, they write the corresponding step on their graph paper, keeping their place value columns lined up correctly.

It is important for students to understand that the written form is just a description of what is actually happening. Students need much practice at this step.

You can make this more meaningful by having students make up a story problem to go with the exercise: amounts spent on a shopping trip, change received, and so on.

After doing several problems, have students discuss a problem like 305 – 53, with 0 in the tens place.

Students discuss and practice regrouping over zero.

Now draw three cards for the minuend and two for the subtrahend. Tens and faces count as zeros.

Write some of the problems on the board in a horizontal format.

After students become confident about the process, they can move to doing the problem first on paper and then checking with bills.

Extend activities so that the students can see the same math procedure works for 4-, 5-, and larger-digit numbers. When using these larger minuends with a variety of subtrahends, check to see that students remember to keep place value in mind as they place numbers.

Students can use *newspapers* for data and ideas to write word problems using 3-digit numbers; encourage them to use both addition and subtraction questions when writing the problems. Students exchange problems, estimate answers, and try to solve each other's problems.

Have students use a *deck of cards* to generate problems. The first three turned over are one number, the second three are another number. Face cards and tens are zeros. They subtract the smaller number from the larger, using the *manipulative of their choice.* Challenge teams to make up games to share.

Use *dice* to generate problems. The first three throws give the minuend, the next two throws give the subtrahend. If they throw a 1, make it a 0 instead. See who has the most/least left after three turns.

Using *bills,* students race to spend all their money, and get to a zero amount. Choose a starting amount of 3 or more digits. Then use *dice* to generate a 2- or 3-digit number to subtract. As they get closer to zero, they use fewer dice. Students make up story problems, such as: Now I am going to the store with $____ to buy a swim suit costing $___. My change will be $___. As an alternative if time is short, see who has the least (or most) money left after three to five turns.

Let a student try to teach a lesson on borrowing. Other students should pretend not to know how to regroup and should follow the "teacher" directions exactly.

Have students bring in *mail-order catalogs* of expensive items. Who can start with $999 in *bills,* buy a variety of items, and come closest to spending all their money?

Expand money concepts to include subtracting *dimes* and *pennies* as well as dollars. Does the basic concept change? (no)

Have students work on other solutions for the problem given in the Anticipatory Set. How many different solutions can they find?

Practice and Extension

Challenge students to write story problems using 3-digit numbers; their partners work the problems and check their work with addition. Next partners reword problem so that, using the same three numbers, it becomes an addition question and answer.

Multiplication 1

Skill: To learn multiplication facts: products to 81

Time: 2–3 periods

Materials:

pattern blocks: 4–6 of same shape per group

place value (pv) materials to 10s

cubes or tiles: any size; about 100 per group

graph paper: ½" or larger squares; 3 sheets per student

Secret Code number line (see Manipulative Information section)

markers: 4 colors per student

See Reproducibles for: pv mats to 100s—1 per student, and 1 per group, number lines to 25—1 per student, number lines to 100—1 per student

Note: If students learn their facts using place value materials, it will be easier for them to learn 2-digit multiplication.

Anticipatory Set

Use *pattern blocks.*

Working in groups, students find how many total sides are on their shapes. How did they find the answer? Did they multiply, add, or count?

Hold up three hexagons. How many sides in all? How did they arrive at the answer?

Have students combine their shapes into two figures. How many sides does each new figure have? If students have two identical shapes, how can they find the total number of sides? Review the concept of multiplication.

Procedure 1 ☐■

To develop facts using place value

Use *pv materials* and *pv mats.*

Working in groups, students place five rows of six cubes in the ones place and write numbers on the individual pv mats.

Count the materials to get a total of 30.

Group Mat		Individual Mat	
10s	1s	10s	1s
	66666 6		6
	66666 6		6
	66666 6		6
	66666 6		6
	66666 6		6
			30

Ask: Do we need to regroup? Why? How many digits can be written in one place? (the most is 9) Be sure students understand the place value system.

Students regroup and show 30 on group mats with rods and cubes. They show regrouping and rewrite numbers.

Group Mat		Individual Mat	
10s	1s	10s	1s
	66666 6		6
	66666 6		6
	66666 6		6
	66666 6		6
	66666 6		6
			30
		3	0

Show students how to write this as multiplication.

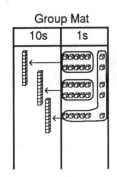

Group Mat		Individual Mat	
10s	1s	10s	1s
	66666 6		6
	66666 6		6
	66666 6		6
	66666 6		6
	66666 6		6 ×5
			30
		3	0

Explain that the circle around the × 5 indicates that these are just the directions for how many groups of six they take.

Continue the procedure, following these steps with students covering most of the facts.

Students demonstrate the numbers with materials, writing serial addition on small mats, regrouping as needed, and writing regrouping on paper. They then write the multiplication fact shown.

Procedure 2 ☐■

To develop multiplication sentence form using arrays

Use *cubes or tiles, graph paper,* and *markers.*

Working in large groups, students build several rectangles with their cubes and then discuss how many cubes they used to build each rectangle.

Emphasize that rows are the across lines, like rows of seats in an auditorium, and columns are down lines, like columns of a building.

Students discuss the number of rows in each rectangle and how many cubes in each row or column.

Say: These two numbers can make up part of a multiplication sentence: row × column; r × c. Have students write down the numbers for one structure and then count the total number of cubes used.

This is the third number in the multiplication sentence, row × column = total. Make a chart on the board or overhead showing the formula, r × c = t.

Have students write a multiplication problem and find the answer by doing serial addition or multiplication.

Students write down the numbers and count the total number of cubes for each of their rectangles. They record these as multiplication facts.

Now have students work individually to draw squares or rectangles on graph paper.

Tell students that the number in each row is the same as the number of columns in the rectangles drawn. Have students discuss how many rows and columns are enclosed by the shapes they have drawn.

Students write down the numbers for one rectangle and then count the total number of squares enclosed.

Instruct students to write down the multiplication sentence that each of their figures shows, as was done in the earlier activity.

Students write down the numbers and count the total number of squares for each of their rectangles. They continue to make figures and write multiplication facts. They color and label their arrays for a class chart.

Procedure 3

To discover patterns of multiples

Use *number lines to 25 and 100, colored markers,* and *Secret Code number line.*

Students fill in number lines to 25 and use different colored markers to show a series of jumps of twos, threes, fours, and fives:

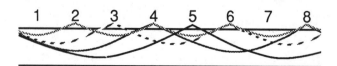

Ask: Do you see any patterns?

Did you notice where jumps landed on the same number? Could you make any predictions about a longer line?

What multiplication facts have you just shown on the number line? What similarities do you see to the Secret Code number line?

Students repeat with number lines to 100 using sixes, sevens, eights, and nines. Can they think of picture clues to add to the class Secret Code number line?

Practice and Extension

Use *Number Finds* (see Reproducibles), and have students follow directions, circling adjacent numbers. Students also name their monsters and write a descriptive paragraph about them. Later they can make their own number finds for others to solve.

Students play Concentration with *index cards.* The fact is on one card and the answer is on another.

Have students make their own *flash cards of facts* (self-correcting answers on the back) to use in pairs or to make up games for other students to play.

Have students list ways that knowing multiplication facts can be useful to them when they go shopping.

Read *Multiplication Clue Rhymes,* and go over procedures for *Garden Glove Multiplication* and *Finger Nines* (see Reproducibles). Send the sheets home.

Students create story problems that use multiplication, show it with *counters,* and act it out. Example: A birthday party has 7 children invited. Each is to have 4 balloons. How many balloons are needed?

Multiplication 2

Skill: To understand the commutative property of multiplication

Time: 1 period

Materials:

graph paper: ¹/₂" squares; several sheets per student

scissors

cubes: any size; 10 per student

rulers

narrow strips of tag board: 2 per student

light-colored markers: 1 per student

geoboards and rubber bands: 1 per student pair

See Reproducibles for: multiplication/division tables—1 per student, geoboard paper—1 sheet per student

Anticipatory Set

Use *graph paper, scissors,* and *cubes.*

Have each student cut a 5" × 5" square. Have students start in the upper left hand corner with 1 and number across to 10 and down the left side to 10, one number per square.

Using the leftover graph paper, have students cut out several smaller squares and rectangles and place these pieces on their 5" × 5" square lined up with the top left corner.

Review rows and columns. What multiplication facts using rows and columns do their rectangles show?

Have them use different corners of their rectangles for placing. Does this change the fact? The answer?

Have each student build a wall with some of the cubes. Choose some walls to describe to the class. How tall, and so on, are they? What would happen to the walls if the earth shifted and the walls fell down? Would the same amount of total materials still be there?

Procedure 1

To make multiplication charts

Use *graph paper (1 sheet per student), rulers, multiplication/division tables, tag board strips,* and *markers.*

Distribute the graph paper and tables. Explain that the students will be charting all of the answers to multiplication facts.

Have students use rulers to outline a square 12 spaces across and 12 spaces down. They should darken the first horizontal line down from the top and the first vertical line from the left-hand side as in the illustration.

Say: A times sign goes in the upper left-hand square and the numbers 0 to 10 go in the remaining squares across the top and down the left side.

Students finish labeling the chart and then fill in the products for rows 0 to 3 while you distribute tag board strips.

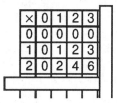

Tell students to find the product of 2 × 3 and then 3 × 2. What do they notice? (Answer is the same.)

Challenge students to explain how the strips could be used to find products.

Allow students to experiment with the strips; let a student who finds how to place them and read the answer, explain to the class.

Students complete their charts, highlighting every other row and column (even numbers) with markers to aid in finding products.

Ask students to find patterns on their multiplication/division tables.

Students find and draw loops around patterns. They discuss the class's findings.

Have students practice finding facts using the table and tag board strips.

Cover matrices with clear self-adhesive paper or laminate them. This treatment will keep them useful for the entire year.

Alternate Procedure 1

To generate multiplication tables

Use *graph paper (1 sheet per student), rulers, cubes, markers,* and *tag board strips.*

Have students use rulers to outline a square 12 spaces across and 12 spaces down on their graph paper. They should darken the first horizontal line down from the top and the first vertical line from the left-hand side as in the illustration.

Review that the numbers on the left are rows, and numbers on the top are columns. Have students put an × in the corner and label the top and side as shown in the illustration above.

Say: We wish to fill in the total number of cubes in each square. Start with an array of one row, one column.

Students build that array, count the squares, and write 1 in the first blank chart box. They continue to fill in numbers across, building the array first, counting the objects, and writing the number.

As the numbers get larger, students work in groups so that they have enough manipulatives.

Question students about possible uses of a matrix, and point out patterns as suggested earlier.

Students may take turns explaining different sets of multiplication facts.

Procedure 2 □■

To understand the commutative property of multiplication using fact families

Use *cubes, geoboards and rubber bands,* and *geoboard paper.*

Have students work in pairs and build a row of five cubes. On top of this row they should build another row of five cubes, making a structure five cubes wide and two cubes high. Ask: How many cubes did you use? (10) This shows two groups of five.

Now have students place the structure vertically so that they have two columns of five rows. How many cubes? (10) This shows five groups of two. We call this the commutative property of multiplication.

Students discuss that the commutative property is similar to fact families that they have worked with before.

On the board write $5 \times 2 = 10$ and $2 \times 5 = 10$.

Repeat the procedure with 4×5, 3×5, and 6×2. Higher grade levels may work with more complicated problems following the same pattern.

Students write the multiplication sentence shown by each set of problems.

Have students now work in pairs with geoboards and geoboard paper. One encloses a rectangle 3 by 4. How many squares are enclosed? (12) The other student encloses a square that is 4 by 3.

Ask: How many squares are enclosed? (12) Are these equal in size? (yes) What are the equations shown by these figures?

Students respond: $3 \times 4 = 12$ and $4 \times 3 = 12$. They continue to work with the geoboard, checking commutative properties of several sets of facts, copying the designs onto the geoboard paper, and writing the times facts shown.

Procedure 3 □

To prove equalities

Use *graph paper* and *scissors.*

Have students work in pairs. Have one partner cut out any size rectangle and label it with the fact it represents. Example: $7 \times 6 = 42$. Have the other partner cut out the commutative shape and label it.

Students cut and label the rectangles.

Have students lay rectangles on top of each other and count squares to prove they are equal. Encourage students to show higher multiplication facts.

Students continue to create buildings by cutting rectangular shapes; and the peer partners construct a same-size building using the commutative fact.

Make a class chart of all buildings, showing the two commutative facts together.

Practice and Extension

Use *flash cards* and play Concentration, finding the two commutative facts in order to win the round.

Give students several sets of facts to answer with their *multiplication/division tables.* As students find the answer to one fact, they are to write down the corresponding commutative fact and then check their table for accuracy.

Can students think of a way to prove whether the commutative property of multiplication would still be true for higher numbers, such as 12×36? Would using *graph paper* help?

Suggest that students keep their *multiplication charts* out when doing multiplication problems so that lack of memorization of the facts will not prevent them from learning a new concept.

Have students add other patterns to show multiples to the classroom *Secret Code number line.* This line can be adapted to use for any set of multiples or prime numbers.

Multiplication 3

Skill: To understand the relationship of multiplication to division; missing factors in equations

Time: 2 periods

Materials:

1" tiles, or alternatives: about 24 per student pair
geoboards and colored rubber bands: 1 per student pair

counters: 20 per student
thin tag board strips: 1 per student
graph paper: any size; 1 sheet per student
See Reproducibles for: multiplication/division tables—1 per student

Anticipatory Set

Use *tiles* and *blank sheets of paper.*

Review that rows are across and columns are down. Compare them to rows of seats and columns of buildings. Review that the number of rows times the number in the row equals the product.

Students experiment with materials and find a way to show both multiplication and division facts. They compare what they discovered. How are facts alike?

Have students record their numbers with the appropriate signs on the paper. How would they find the answer for a fact they haven't learned?

Procedure 1

□■

To discover relationships

Use *tiles* and *multiplication/division tables.*

Explain that the tiles are pigs in a pigpen. A farmer has divided them into four lines but needs to keep them from running into the cornfield next door.

Demonstrate on the board that a partial fence around a group looks similar to a division symbol.

Model for the students as they do an example. Ask: How many rows are shown? (4) How many columns? (3) What multiplication fact is shown? (4 groups of 3: 4 × 3 = 12)

How would knowing the multiplication fact help with division? Encourage discussion and remind students of fact families in addition and subtraction.

Ask: What division fact is shown? (12 divided into 4 groups: 12 ÷ 4 = 3)

What if we turned the group of tiles sideways?

Students respond: It would show 3 groups of 4: 3 × 4 = 12; or 12 divided into 3 groups: 12 ÷ 3 = 4.

Students continue discovery exercises.

Review with students how to use tables to find answers to multiplication facts. Can they find division answers on the same table?

Students use tiles to set up models of multiplication arrays; they make up stories that require division to solve, write the equations, and check their answers with the multiplication/division tables.

Procedure 2

□

To write and use relationships

Use *geoboards and rubber bands, counters, multiplication/division tables,* and *tag board strips.*

Have students put bands around four groups of three, sides touching to make a 4 × 3 rectangle. Then have them put another color band around the whole group.

Write the multiplication fact that this shows. (4 × 3 = 12) Ask: What division fact could this show? (12 ÷ 4 = 3) How are these alike?

Students continue to explore the facts using their geoboards and writing the facts on paper. It is important for students to understand that the written form is just a description of what is happening.

Have students now use groups of counters to work with higher facts.

Student groups show 3 groups of 7 and write the fact with its answer. Then they take 21 other counters and "share" them among 7 groups.

Continue with more examples, making up stories to go with the "sharing." Be sure students see the relationship with the multiplication fact.

Students work in pairs to make up problems and solutions to share with the rest of the class. They check their facts with their tables, using tag board strips to read along columns or rows.

Procedure 3

To develop the concept of missing factors

Use *counters*.

Put the following illustration on the board, and discuss the relationship of multiplication and division: The number of groups or rows times the number in a group is the total.

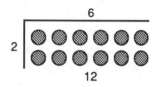

Write 2 × 6 = ? on the board.

Each student makes one row of 6 counters. Underneath that they make another row of 6 counters. Students count and reach the answer of 12.

Now write 2 × ? = 12. Have students make two rows of one counter each on their desks.

Students pick up enough more counters to total 12 and divide these between the two rows. They report 6 are in each row.

Now write ? × 6 = 12. Ask: How you could find the answer with the counters?

Students respond: Take 12 counters, and separate the 12 counters into groups of 6.

Ask: How many groups? (2)

Repeat with other missing factors until students are adept at the skill and begin to realize they can use division to solve these kind of problems.

Students make up word problems to go with missing factor problems. Example: Six students are playing 12 games. How many games can each play?

Continue the procedure until students are aware of all the places for missing numbers in multiplication problems and are comfortable with the process of using division to find what the missing number is.

Procedure 4

To practice finding missing factors

Use *graph paper, multiplication/division tables*, and *tag board strips*.

Have students draw a rectangle that encloses 12 squares. The top and bottom sides are to be 4 squares long. Write ? × 4 = 12.

Students draw around the space. They tell you the other sides are three squares tall.

Continue with such problems as 3 × ? = 15, ? × 7 = 21, describing walls to be constructed from blocks.

Students work with graph paper or the matrices and find the missing factors. They use the tag board strips to read along columns or rows. As soon as they feel ready, they try solving equations without drawing rectangles.

Tell students that using letters in place of the question mark is the way math equations are written in algebra. Have them create some problems they could pose in algebraic language.

Practice and Extension

Have students use *problems from the textbook* and make up situations to solve that require knowing the related procedure. For example, if the problem is to find how many apples are 8 baskets of 7 apples, they find that answer on the *multiplication/division tables* and reword the problem: I have 56 apples and 8 baskets. How many apples are in each basket?

Have students think of *counters* as cars in a parking lot, or cans to be put into different recycling containers, and so on. Students make up multiplication or division story problems. Their partner shows the fact with counters, writes it, and adds to the story, using the opposite operation.

Have students make up story problems that require finding a missing factor. Students write the problem and solve it on the back of the paper. They exchange with a partner who first estimates a reasonable answer and then tries to solve the problem.

Have students bring in *newspaper advertisements*. Give each student a specific amount of money to spend. If an item is a certain price, how many of each can be bought? Students should write the equations before solving the problems. Encourage them to write the equations in algebraic language.

Multiplication 4

Skill: To understand multiples of ten and how to multiply tens by 1-digit numbers

Time: 3 periods

Materials:

light-colored markers in 2 colors: 1 of each per student

place value (pv) materials to 1000s, use counters as 1000s

file-folder or other pv mats to 1000s

2" × 3" × number cards as shown in Illustration 1a: 1 set ×2 to ×9 per student

See Reproducibles for: hundred boards—1 per student, number lines to 1000, pv mats to 1000s, or directions for file-folder mats, graph paper with 1 cm squares

Anticipatory Set

Use *hundred boards, number lines,* and *markers.*

Have students highlight (or mark) all tens on hundred boards and number lines. Do they see a pattern? Ask: How many are three tens, four tens, and so on.

Count off the students by tens. How does counting by tens help us with our number system? Students should relate to our base ten place value system.

Procedure 1

To recognize and use multiples of 10

Use *pv materials, pv mats, graph paper, markers,* and *completed hundred boards and number lines from Anticipatory Set.*

Have groups place one ten rod in the tens place and say "one ten, zero ones." Continue adding tens until they have 10 rods in the tens place.

Review regrouping. Continue having students add tens and read chorally until reaching 200.

Dictate some higher multiples of 10 for students to place. Have them read each new number and the resulting total. Continue to 990.

Ask: What would happen if we added 10 more? What earlier activity does this remind you of? Discuss.

Students take graph paper and color in 10 squares.

How many are colored? (10) Color in 10 more squares. How many are colored now? (20) How many are two groups of 10? (20)

Continue until students see the pattern. Discuss patterns and how multiples of 10 are written.

How can knowing multiples of 10 help us in math?

Students discuss rounding numbers to the nearest 10 as a way of estimating answers and of being sure the answer for a problem is reasonable.

Instruct students to look at the marked hundred board and number line. Have them count off 3

tens. What is the total? (30) Continue with 6 tens, 11 tens, 23 tens, and so on.

Students make up problem situations for the class to estimate answers and then solve.

Procedure 2

To multiply 10 by 1-digit numbers

Use *pv mats, materials,* and *× number cards.*

Note: *Do not teach multiplying the digits and annexing the zero.*

Since multiplication problems are solved right to left, the following procedure tends to eliminate some later math confusion for certain students.

In this procedure students work with materials only, while you write on the board, showing partial products.

Have students put a ten rod on their mat. Ask: How many tens? (1) How many ones? (0)

Write 10 on a place value chart on the board.

Tell students they need five tens in all on their mats. Place a ×5 on the board below the 10 as in Illustration 1b on the next page.

What value does each rod represent? (10) How many tens? (5) How many ones? (0) How many in all? (50)

Did they add or count to get the answer? Discuss.

Say: We can also multiply to arrive at an answer.

Have students take 4 of the 10 rods off their mats. Under the remaining rod they should place the ×5 card as in Illustration 1a on the following page.

The "times five" is just the directions.

What you have on your mats now represents the problem 5 × 10.

You already know how to multiply 1-digit numbers by other 1-digit numbers. When we multiply 2-digit numbers, we first multiply the ones as we did before and then we multiply the tens.

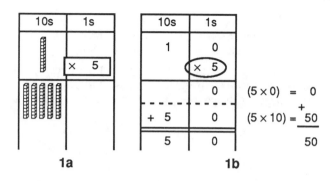

1a   1b

$(5 \times 0) = 0$
$(5 \times 10) = 50$
$= 50$

What are five groups of no ones?

Students respond: Nothing.

So we have no one cubes in our answer. How can I show this on the board?

Students respond: Put a zero in the ones place.

Place a 0 in the ones column, and to the side of the problem write $5 \times 0 = 0$ as shown in Illustration 1b.

How many tens did the directions say we needed? (5)

Now you need to place those five ten rods onto your mats.

Emphasize groups of 10. **How many groups of 10 are below the directions on the mat? (5)**

So we have five ten rods in our answer. What number have you made with your rods?

Students respond: 50.

Write 50 in the board example as shown. Beside that write the partial product: $5 \times 10 = 50$.

First we multiplied the zero ones by five, and then we multiplied the one ten by five. We get a final total by adding the two answers together.

Finish the board example as in Illustration 1b.

Continue with other examples, emphasizing "groups" of tens and the place value. Students should use only materials. You show on the board a written mathematical description of what is happening.

Procedure 3   ◻◼

To multiply multiples of 10 by 1-digit numbers; no regrouping

Use *pv mats, pv materials, × number cards,* and *paper.*

In this procedure students work with materials and write on a pv chart. You write the problem on a board chart with partial products on the side as shown in Illustration 2b.

Have students fold paper in half and label ones and tens. Next have them place a group of two tens on their pv mats.

Say: This is the number of juice boxes in a package. You want to know the number of boxes in three packages. First put directions on your mats.

Under the two ten rods students place the ×3 card. (Illustration 2a)

Instruct students to write 20 on their paper charts, and under that a circled ×3 as the directions. (Illustration 2b)

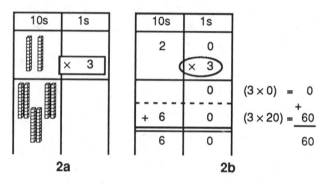

2a   2b

$(3 \times 0) = 0$
$(3 \times 20) = 60$
$= 60$

What does the ×3 mean?

Students respond: It's "just the directions" for how many groups we want of our starting number.

As students respond to questions, show the process on the board with partial products, as in illustration 2b.

How many cubes are in the ones place? (none) How many is three groups of none? (none) Where on our charts would we show that?

Students respond: Put a zero in the ones place because we are multiplying ones.

Now what do the directions tell us about the tens?

Students respond: We need three groups of two tens. They place three groups of two tens on their mats below the directions.

What is the total of three groups of two tens?

Students count and respond: 60.

Where in the answer would we show this?

Students respond: Put a six in the tens place, because we are multiplying tens, and a zero in the ones place.

Review: **First we multiplied the zero ones by three, and then we multiplied the two tens by three.**

How do we get the total number of juice boxes? (add) Complete the example on the board.

Practice the procedure, keeping the products under 100. Have students work with the materials and record their work on the paper charts.

Procedure 4   ◻◼

To multiply multiples of 10 by 1-digit numbers; with regrouping

Use *pv mats, pv materials, × number cards,* and *paper.*

This time have students divide their paper into three columns and label 100s, 10s, and 1s.

Using the same procedure as before, challenge students to show 3 groups of 50 on both mats and paper, circling the ×3 and using their ×3 card.

Students do as instructed and make up a word problem to go with their block problem.

Ask: After you multiply, how many ones in all? (0) How many tens? (15) Do you have a problem?

Students respond: Too many tens are in the tens place. We have to regroup.

Students regroup with materials and on charts as shown:

100s	10s	1s			
	5	0			
		× 3			
		0	(3 × 0)	=	0
1	1̸5			+	
1	5		(3 × 50)	=	150
1	5	0			150

What do we have once we regroup? (one hundred and five tens) Is this like any other regrouping we have done?

Students should relate this to the previous skills of regrouping in simpler multiplication and addition.

Students complete the problem by adding partial products.

Continue the procedure with problems up to 90 × 9. Ask students whether they can see a pattern. Discuss.

Procedure 5   □ ■

To develop the traditional algorithm

Use *prepared pv paper to 100s* and *counters*, if needed.

Stress to the students that since the ones answer in these problems is always zero, they can eliminate that line of partial products.

Introduce the form:

100s	10s	1s			
	5	0			
		× 3			
1	5	0	(3 × 0)	=	0
				+	
			(3 × 50)	=	150
					150

Still emphasize that they are multiplying ones first and then tens. They can take the shortcut in this type of problem because when we have tens, we have zero digits in the ones place.

Allow students to use counters to help solve the problems.

When students begin working independently, have them use graph paper—one number to a square, or have them turn lined paper sideways. Either aid will help them remember to keep their numbers in the right columns and to place the zeros where needed.

Practice and Extension

Have students look at their marked *hundred board* and count off numbers of tens. Ask for examples of when the mental skill of knowing tens would be useful. Discuss estimating costs, etc., with students.

Students make up problems that use groups of 10 and exchange them with other students. They see whether they can use their knowledge of multiples of 10 to arrive at the answer mentally. They check accuracy with the *hundred board.*

Go around the room, and orally count the number of fingers in the room, with each student taking a turn: "one student—10 fingers, two students—20 fingers . . . ." Continue with toes, giving each student the chance to participate twice in the counting activity.

Now you can teach the following shortcut:

1. Drop zero down into ones place.
2. Multiply the number in the tens place by the number of groups.

Hand out *catalog advertisements* and *bills.* Have students round prices to the nearest $10. Example: Shoes are $37. Round to $40, and then buy 3 pairs. About how much did they spend? How many different ways can they spend $100?

Have students use *bills* and play a shopping game in which every item they buy will cost $10. They throw a *die* to see how many items they can buy. After three turns, the student with the most items bought correctly is the winner.

Have students predict how they would multiply hundreds by 1-digit numbers. Can they also predict how they would multiply thousands by 1-digit numbers?

Multiplication 5

Skill: To multiply with more than two factors

geoboards, or geoboard paper

graph paper: any size

See Reproducibles for: geoboard paper, place value (pv) mats to 100s—1 per group

Time: 2 periods

Materials:

counters: two colors; 6 of each color per student

pattern blocks: several of each kind per group

Anticipatory Set

Use *counters*.

Have students make a rectangle of two groups of three counters. Repeat for another rectangle.

How many in the first rectangle? (6) How many in the second rectangle? (6) How many in all? (12) Both arrays show that $2 \times 3 = 6$, and together they show that two of these arrays equal 12, or $2 \times 2 \times 3 = 12$.

If two students combine their arrays, they have four arrays that equal 24, or $4 \times 2 \times 3 = 24$. This is what we will learn today.

Procedure 1

To discover the process of multiplying by more than two factors

Use *pattern blocks*.

Have students set out two triangles. Ask: How many sides are on each? (3) How many sides are displayed altogether? (6) What multiplication sentence do the students think this shows?

Students respond: $2 \times 3 = 6$.

Now have students set out two more triangles. How many sides on each? (3) How many sides on this new set? (6) How many sides on both sets together? (12) How do the students think this multiplication sentence should be stated?

If students respond that two groups of six equal 12, relate back to the first sentence of $2 \times 3 = 6$. Since we have two sets of these numbers, we are showing the complete multiplication sentence is $2 \times 2 \times 3 = 12$.

Now continue with various numbers of different shapes. Have students practice with some multiplication sentences that start with the number one as a factor.

Students display blocks, state the multiplication sentence shown, and check with each other for accuracy.

Procedure 2

To practice multiplying by more than two factors

Use *geoboards, or geoboard paper and graph paper*.

Have students enclose one group of two squares. Ask: How many squares in all? (2) What multiplication fact is shown? ($1 \times 2 = 2$)

Have students enclose a second group of two squares, not touching the first. Now how many squares in all? (4) What multiplication sentence is shown by the entire geoboard? ($2 \times 1 \times 2 = 4$)

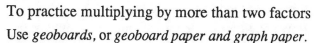

Have them enclose a third group of two squares. Now what multiplication sentence is shown? ($3 \times 1 \times 2 = 6$) If students do not see how it changed, encourage discussion so that they can see that they now have three sets of one times two.

Continue with other number examples that can be completed on the geoboard.

Students work with the lower numbers on the geoboards or geoboard paper until they are comfortable with the process.

Hand out graph paper. Now introduce some larger numbers. Ask students to make a square of two times three. How many squares are enclosed? (6)

Tell them to make three more just like the first. How many total squares have they enclosed? ($4 \times 2 \times 3 = 24$) Use story problems about acres of land or squares of chocolate.

Students complete drawings, compare answers, and check each other for accuracy. At this point students are not writing but are only giving oral answers using the manipulatives. After students are confident with this process, they can move to the next stage.

Procedure 3

To write the process of multiplying by more than two factors

Use *pv mats, counters,* and *paper.*

Have students work in groups for the beginning of this exercise, with each student recording after the group uses the manipulatives.

Have students place counters representing two rows of three on the pv mat. Ask: What multiplication sentence is shown by this array? ($2 \times 3 = 6$)

Now have them place a second group of two rows of three. How many in all? (12) What is the complete multiplication sentence shown? ($2 \times 2 \times 3 = 12$) Write the complete multiplication sentence on the board.

Students place counters and write the equation on their paper.

Make sure students understand that the written form they are learning is just a description of what is actually happening with their counters and pv mats.

Now have them place a third group of counters. How many in all? (18) What multiplication sentence is shown now? ($3 \times 2 \times 3 = 18$) If all do not agree, discuss why this is so, and continue the practice.

Students continue placing counters, deciding what the multiplication sentence is, and writing the complete equation on their papers.

Students continue using counters to demonstrate and find products of $2 \times 3 \times 3$, $3 \times 4 \times 3$, $5 \times 2 \times 3$, etc.

After students become confident with the process, they can move to writing the problem first and then checking each step with their counters.

After students understand the concept, move on to using larger numbers. Have students create story problems that have more than two factors.

Start students with this example. Students pretend they order supplies for the school and need to find total numbers of toilet paper rolls. The problem could be stated: 6 rolls in each package, 4 packages in each box, 4 boxes in each carton. How many rolls of toilet paper are in each carton? They can use counters to represent the rolls and draw squares to represent the packages.

Practice and Extension

Allow students to use *calculators* to solve more difficult situations, in which the final answer is found by multiplying with more than two factors.

Give the class one 2-digit number and two 1-digit numbers, and have students make up story problems using those numbers. For example: Ms. Orr's fourth-grade class of 27 students is selling light bulbs. Each student will try to sell 6 packages, and each package contains 4 light bulbs. How many light bulbs does the entire class hope to sell?

After writing the problem on paper, the students solve the problems on the back of the paper and then exchange with a partner. The partner first estimates a reasonable answer, remembering the last lesson of multiplying tens, and then solves the problem. Both students compare answers. Encourage students to diagram their problems, as well.

Another example could be painting the walls of the schools. They can find the area of a wall, multiply by the number of gallons that will cover that area, and they by the number of walls to be painted.

Have some students interview the school custodian to ask how he or she determines the toilet paper order for the school.

Multiplication 6

Skill: To multiply 2-digit numbers by 1-digit numbers

Time: 4 periods

Materials:

file-folder or other place value (pv) mats to 100s or 1000s

pv materials to 100s

× number cards: as shown in Illustration 1; 1 set ×2 to ×9 per student

counters in 3 colors: 25 of each color per group

See Reproducibles for: pv mats to 100s—1 per student, directions for file-folder pv mats, if needed

Anticipatory Set

Use *pv mats* and *pv materials*.

Have students work in pairs and place three tens and two ones on their mats. Now tell them to place an identical group below the first one. They now have two groups of materials both representing 32 on their mats. How many do they have in all? (64) What process did they use to get that number? (Some will say add, others multiply.)

Now have them add another group of materials representing the number 32 on the mats. How many groups of 32 do they have now? (3) Now it will be better to multiply. Students could still find the total by adding, but when the numbers are higher, multiplication is easier.

Procedure 1 ■

To introduce partial products: assumes students can multiply ten by 1-digit numbers

Use *pv mats, pv materials,* and *× number cards.*

In this procedure students work with materials only, and you write on the board showing partial products.

Have students work in pairs and place materials representing 11 on their mats (Illustration 1). Now have the students place the ×2 card under the 11 on their mats. Explain that these are the directions for the problem.

Students place the card and draw a line to separate the problem from the answer.

Ask: What does the two tell us?

Students respond: To make two groups of 11. Students place two groups of materials representing 11 below the line on their mats:

How much would two groups of 11 be?

Students push materials together and respond: 22.

Say: You added the two 11s together.

Could we have first multiplied the ones by the two, then multiplied the tens by the two, and added the answers? (yes) Let's see whether this is so.

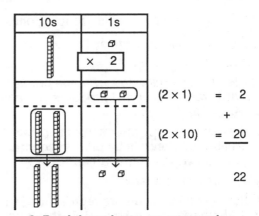

1. Serial addition.

Have students remove the answer materials from their mats. What are two groups of one one? (2)

Students place two one cubes below the directions.

What are two groups of one ten? (20, or 2 tens)

Students place two ten rods as shown in Illustration 2. They push all materials to the bottom for a total.

	10s	1s			

$(2 \times 1) = 2$

$+$

$(2 \times 10) = \underline{20}$

22

2. Partial products, no regrouping.

On the board, total the partial products as shown.

Continue with other groups of materials on the pv mats and other × number cards. Do not use numbers that require regrouping at this point.

Emphasize multiplying the ones and then the tens, adding them together, and reading the resulting total.

Students place groups of materials, multiply as directed by the cards, and find the products.

Now you can introduce some simple regrouping problems such as 2 × 16 for the students to place, regroup, and arrive at an answer. Students are not writing on paper at this stage. Write problems and partial products on the board while students work with the materials.

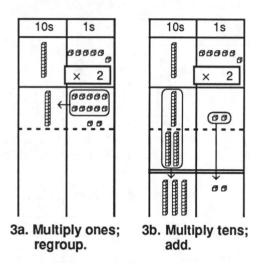

3a. Multiply ones; regroup.   **3b. Multiply tens; add.**

After students are comfortable with making separate groups of materials and arriving at the answers, use some simple problems to see whether they can predict the answer before placing materials. Continue with this procedure until all seem familiar with the process.

Procedure 2

To develop partial products; regrouping ones

Use *counters,* × *number cards,* and *paper.*

In this procedure students work with counters and write on a pv chart. You write the problems on a board chart with partial products at the side as shown in Illustration 7.

Have students make pv charts from two sheets of paper as shown. They will be placing counters on one chart and writing on the other.

Draw a chart on the board.

Have students place counters representing the number 15 on their mats. Under this they should place the ×5 card.

Put the problem on the board chart, and have students copy it onto their second chart, circling the ×5.

Ask: How many is 5 × 5 ones?

Students respond: 25 ones. They place 25 one counters below the line on one chart. They write 25 in the ones column on the other as shown:

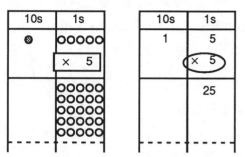

4. Multiply ones by five.

Write (5 × 5) = 25 on the board.

Do we have too many ones? (yes)

Students regroup.

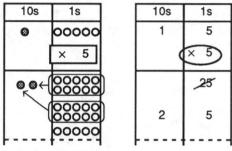

5. Regroup ones.

We no longer have 25 ones. Any written problem is just a description of what we are actually doing. How should we show this?

Students respond: Cross out the 25. Write a five in the ones column and a two in the tens column.

We've multiplied everything in the *ones* column by five. Now we need to multiply everything in the *tens* column by five.

Ask: How many is 5 times 1 ten?

Students place counters and respond: 5 tens.

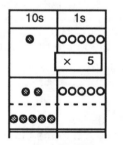

6. Multiply tens by five.

Let's write down what you did with the counters. How many ones? (0) How many tens? (5)

Write (5 × 10) = 50 on the board below the (5 × 5) = 25.

Students write 50 below the 25.

We followed all the directions. How do we find out how many in all? (add)

Students push down all counters that are below the directions. They add the partial products in the ones and tens columns. They find the final answer is 75.

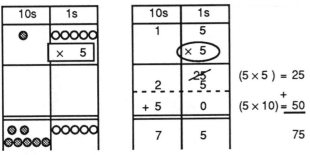

10s	1s		10s	1s	
⊛	○○○○○		1	5	
	× 5			(× 5)	
			2	2̶5̶ / 5	(5 × 5) = 25
			+ 5	0	(5 × 10) = 50
⊛⊛ ⊛⊛⊛	○○○○○		7	5	75

7. Add partial products.

Total the partial products on the board. Do both the materials and the numbers show 75? (yes)

Repeat with other numbers. Have students work with the counters, writing down each step as in the illustrations.

Students need much practice at this stage. They should continue writing the partial products to the side of their problem as they are shown in Illustration 7.

After students become confident about the process, they can move to writing the problem first and then checking each step with the counters.

Procedure 3 ◻◼

To develop a traditional algorithm

Use *counters* and *paper*.

Have students make pv charts and write 15 on one. On the other have them place counters. Under both tell them to put a circled ×5. You write on the board. Students first use counters *and then* write steps as instructed.

Ask: What do we multiply first? (ones)

Students multiply ones:

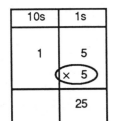 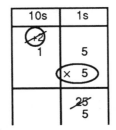

10s	1s		10s	1s
1	5		⊕+2̶ / 1	5
	(× 5)			(× 5)
	25			2̶5̶ / 5

8a. Multiply ones. **8b. Regroup ones.**

We have 25 in the ones column. Can we have that many ones? (no, we need to regroup)

Draw a line through the 25, and place a 5 below it.

Where does the two belong? (tens column)

Yes, but we still have a one in the tens column to multiply, so we have to put this two on hold for a while.

Place a circled +2 above the one in the tens column as shown in Illustration 8b.

We've taken care of the ones column. Now what does the one on our chart represent? (1 ten) How many is 5 × 10? (50)

When we worked before, we put the tens product on a separate line. But, when we multiply tens, do we ever have any ones? (no)

So we can put the number for the tens answer in line with the ones number. We don't really need to use a separate line for it:

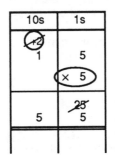 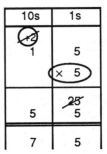

10s	1s		10s	1s
⊕+2̶ / 1	5		⊕+2̶ / 1	5
	(× 5)			(× 5)
5	2̶5̶ / 5		5	2̶5̶ / 5
			7	5

9a. Multiply tens. **9b. Find total.**

How do we find our total? (add)

We had two tens on hold from regrouping the ones. In order to get a final answer, we need to remember to add those two tens to the five tens we got from multiplying tens.

Draw a double line, and add to find the final answer.

Students finish the problem. (See Illustration 9b.) They make sure to cross out the circled +2 after adding it, proving that they remembered to take care of the regrouped number.

Review the process for this problem to check for understanding. Have students check their results.

Students check their results with the counters.

Repeat the entire process with many other problems, including some that result in regrouping tens.

It is important for students to understand that the written form is just a description of what is actually happening. Students need much practice at this step.

Students continue to use counters, writing each step as they do it. When they are comfortable with the process, they will see that they can write any regrouping in one step rather than the two steps shown in Illustration 8b.

Call their attention to the similarity to regrouping in addition.

After students become competent in the skill, they can move to writing the problem first and then checking each step with their counters. Remind them to circle the regrouped number and to cross it out after they have taken care of it.

Practice and Extension

Have students use *counters* and *pv mats* to make up games to play in which they have to multiply 2-digit numbers by a 1-digit number in order to "move" or win.

Take *checkerboards* and put problems on the spaces. Play as in regular Checkers except the students have to answer the problems correctly in order to move.

Have students write original problems, solve them on a separate sheet, and then give the problem to a partner to solve. Example: A piano has 88 keys. If 7 pianos are on the stage, how many piano keys are on the stage? Will the answer be more than 400? How do you know? (Students explain their process of estimating.)

Multiplication 7

Skill: To multiply hundreds by 1-digit numbers

Time: 1 period

Materials:

file-folder or other place value (pv) mats to 1000s

2" × 3" × number cards as shown in Illustration 1a:
1 set ×2 to ×9 per student

counters color-coded to 100s

See Reproducibles for: number lines to 1000—1 per student, graph paper with 1 cm squares—4 sheets per student, pv mats to 1000s, directions for file-folder pv mats

Anticipatory Set

Use *number lines, graph paper,* and *plain paper.*

Count by tens to 100. Count by hundreds to 1,000. Review how to write the number 1,100.

Students number by hundreds from 100 to 1,000 on the number line. Discuss patterns. Then they cut graph paper into 10 × 10 squares to represent hundred flats.

Students draw three vertical lines on their paper to make four columns, and label them 1000s, 100s, 10s, and 1s.

Procedure 1

To multiply hundreds by 1-digit numbers; partial products

Use *pv mats, × number cards,* and *prepared graph paper hundred flats from Anticipatory Set.*

Note: *Do not teach multiplying the digits and annexing the zeros.*

Since multiplication problems are solved right to left, the following procedure tends to eliminate some math confusions.

Have students place a hundred flat on their mats. Ask: How many 100s? (1) How many 10s? (none) How many 1s? (none)

Write 100 on the board in a place value chart.

Tell students you want five 100s in all.

Students place four more 100s on their mats.

What value does each flat represent? (100) *Emphasize that we are working with groups of 100.*

How many 100s? (5) How many 10s? (none) How many 1s? (none)

What is the total of the manipulatives? (500) Did they add or count to get the answer?

We know how to multiply 5 × 10; we can also multiply to find the answer to 5 × 100. Do you think the problems will be similar?

Students discuss.

On the chart on the board write a circled ×5 under the 100. Remind students that the directions are circled to help them remember what to do.

Instruct students to take four of the hundred flats off their mats. Under the remaining hundred flat on their mat they should place the ×5 card, as in Illustration 1a. This represents the problem 5 × 100 = ?.

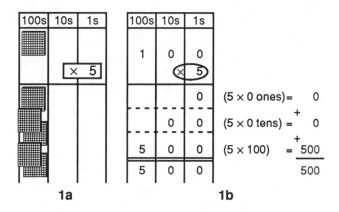

1a   1b

You know how to multiply 1-digit numbers by other 1-digit numbers. How many is 5 × 0? (none)

How can I show that on the board?

Students respond: With a zero in the ones column.

You already know how to multiply tens by 1-digit numbers. How many tens are on your mats? (none)

We place that answer on the second line in the tens column. The second zero "holds" the ones column.

Place these numbers on the board with the partial products to the side, as shown in Illustration 1b.

How many hundred flats are on your mat? (1) What did the directions say we needed to do?

Students respond: We need five groups of 100. They place five hundred flats on their mats under the line.

What number do your flats show? (500)

Write 500 in the board example as shown.

***Review the process:* First we multiplied the zero ones by five and got zero. Next we multiplied the zero tens by five and got zero.**

Last we multiplied the 100 by five and got 500. We get a total by adding those three answers.

Repeat the procedure, emphasizing groups of hundreds and the place value.

Have students place a hundred flat on their mats. This is the number of pepperoni slices on the giant party-size pizza from Marcella's Magnificent Pizza.

Have them place three more hundreds. Now they show the number of pepperoni slices on four of the pizzas. Have them write the number 400 on their pv papers.

Students place materials on their mats and write 400 on their papers. Students want to buy four more pizzas. This will be a second group just like the first.

Students place the ×2 card under the four hundred flats on their mats.

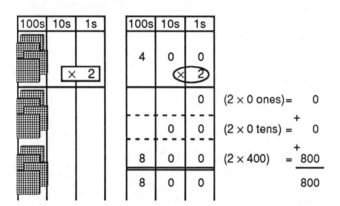

100s	10s	1s	
4	0	0	
		(×)(2)	
		0	(2 × 0 ones) = 0
			+
	0	0	(2 × 0 tens) = 0
			+
8	0	0	(2 × 400) = 800
8	0	0	800

Write the number 400 and a circled ×2 on the board as shown. Why did I draw a circle around the ×2?

Students respond: Those are the directions. They place a circled ×2 under the 400 on their pv paper.

Ask the same kind of questions as before. Finish the problem on the board while students do the same on mats and papers.

Does your answer on paper show the same number as your flats on the place value mat? (yes)

Repeat the procedure.

When students are confident with the procedure, continue with problems up to 9 × 900, with regrouping. Ask students whether they see a pattern. Discuss responses.

After students are competent using the manipulatives and writing the problem, they can begin writing the problem first and then checking with the materials.

Procedure 2 ☐■

To develop a traditional algorithm

Use *prepared paper* and *counters*, if needed.

Stress to the students that since the ones and tens answers in these problems are always zero, they can "double up" those lines in the problem.

Introduce the form:

100s	10s	1s
4	0	0
		× 2
8	0	0

Still emphasize that they are multiplying ones first, then tens, and then hundreds. They can take the shortcut in this type of problem because when we have hundreds, we have zero digits in the ones and tens places.

Students use counters to help solve the problems until they are no longer necessary.

When students begin working independently, have them use graph paper—one number to a square, or turn lined paper sideways. Either aid will help them remember to place numbers in the correct columns and to place zeros where needed.

Practice and Extension

Now you can teach the shortcut:

1. Drop a zero into the ones place.
2. Drop a zero into the tens place.
3. Multiply the digits.

Have students make up word problems using groups of hundreds and exchange for peers to solve.

Have students use *catalogs*. They round prices to the nearest $100 and purchase several of the same items. About how much did they spend? How many ways can they purchase multiples of items totaling $1,000?

Can students predict how to multiply ten thousands by 1-digit numbers? Can they predict how to multiply millions by 1-digit numbers? What can they generalize about multiplying any number that has zeros in all places except the largest?

Multiplication 8

Skill: To multiply 3-digit numbers by 1-digit numbers

Time: 3 periods

Materials:

file-folder or other place value (pv) mats to 1000s

pv materials to 1000s; use counters as 1000s

2" × 3" × number cards as shown in illustration 1a: 1 set ×2 to ×9 per student

counter-trading materials to 1000s

markers in 3 colors

See Reproducibles for: pv mats to 1000s—1 per pair, directions for file-folder pv mats to 1000s, counter-trading boards, bills to 1000s—in different colors

Anticipatory Set

Use *pv mats* and *pv materials*.

Have student pairs place materials for the number 132 on their mats and then place an identical group below the first one. They now have two 132s on their mats.

Ask: How many do you have in all? (264) What process did you use to get that number? (most say add)

Now have them add another 132 to the mats. How many groups do you have now? (3) You could still find the total by adding, but when the numbers are higher multiplication is easier.

We know how to multiply 2-digit by 1-digit numbers. How we could expand that to this problem? Discuss.

Procedure 1 □■

To use partial products

Use *pv mats, pv materials,* and *× number cards.*

In this procedure students work with materials while you write the problem on the board.

Have student pairs place materials for the number 111 on their mats with the ×2 card underneath.

Ask: What does the ×2 tell us? (to make two groups of 111)

Students draw a line and place two groups of 111 on their mats. (Illustration 1a)

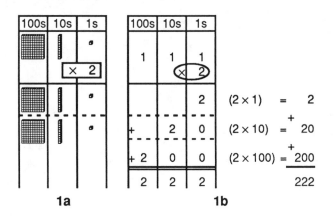

1a   **1b**

How much would two groups of 111 be?

Students push materials together and respond: 222.

Tell students they have added, but they could have multiplied. Have them clear materials from below the line. Tell them to do the problem again, using multiplication, while you write each step on the board as in Illustration 1b.

How many one cubes do you have? (1) How many do the directions say we need? (2) Write 2 × 1 = 2.

Students place two one cubes below the line.

How many ten rods are on your mats? (1) How many are two groups of 10? (20) Write 2 × 10 = 20.

Students place two ten rods.

How many hundreds are on your mats? (1) How many are two groups of 100? (200) Write 2 × 100 = 200.

Students place two hundred flats.

I wrote just what you did on your mats. Remember how we multiplied 2-digit numbers before, and tell me how to finish the problem.

Students respond: Add the three amounts together. They add materials together and tell you to write 222.

Repeat with other numbers. When students seem familiar with the process, have them write each step with you as they do it with materials.

It is important to include the stage of connecting the concrete materials to the writing of the process.

Procedure 2 □■

To develop a traditional algorithm

Use *counter-trading boards, counter-trading materials, markers, × number cards,* and *paper.*

Have students draw vertical lines to separate paper into three columns and label them "Ones," "Tens," and "Hundreds." Have them color-code these charts and place counters for 234 on their counter-trading boards.

Say: There are 234 people at a conference, and each needs four note pads. How many note pads must be provided? How would we show this as a multiplication problem?

Students place a ×4 card under the 234 on their boards and write 234 with a circled ×4 on their chart. They will use materials and then write each step with you as they do it.

Make sure students understand that this is an abbreviation of the process they learned in Procedure 1 and that it is still just describing what is actually happening as they do it.

Say: Make four groups of four. Where does that answer go? (ones column) (You write the 16 as shown, as students follow your example.) Do we need to do something with them? (regroup)

Students regroup counters and cross out the 16.

How many ones are left? (6) (You write a six in the ones column. Students continue to write as well.)

We haven't multiplied the three in the tens column yet. We need to put the one from regrouping on hold for a while. Put a one with a small plus sign at the top of the tens column. We circle it to remind us to add it in later.

How many are four groups of 30? (120)

Where would the zero go? (ones column) Since adding zero won't change the total of ones, we don't need to show the zero. We don't need to write this product on a separate line anymore.

We place the 12 in the tens column. Do we need to do anything else?

Students respond: Add the +1 to the 12. That makes 13 tens. They do this with materials and in writing.

Now what should we do? (regroup)

Students regroup on their boards, cross out the 13, make it a 3, and place a +1 in the hundreds column.

We still have another number to multiply. What is four groups of 200? (800) As before, the zeros won't change the column totals of tens or ones, so we don't have to use a separate line. Where would the eight go?

Students respond: In the hundreds column.

What happens to the regrouped +1 in the hundreds column? (add to the eight) Show this on the board, and point out that their written problems show just what they did with the materials.

Repeat the procedure with other numbers. Students need much guided practice on these steps.

Procedure 3 ☐

To practice multiplication

Use *bills, pv mats,* and *paper.*

Have student groups generate their own problems. They should place the bills and then multiply on the mats as in Procedure 2.

Students do problems with bills and write each step on a group sheet of paper. They share their problems with the rest of the class, along with their solutions.

Have each student now create a problem. Post these for other students to prove with the bills.

Practice and Extension

Students can play Money Madness. Use *bills to 1000s* and *pv mats.* Divide the class into teams, and have each start with $1,000. Use *number cards* or *dice* to generate numbers in turn for a 3-digit number and a multiplier.

Use story problems like the sale of stock, pairs of shoes bought, and so on. Teams predict answers before multiplying, then compare their actual answer with their prediction.

When all team members have the correct answer, flip a *two-sided coin* or *counter* to see whether the answer is to be added or subtracted from a running total for the week.

Extend activities to four or more digits by 1-digit multiplication, a free-ride skill, as they already know the process. Do part of a large number problem each day for a week. Have students predict the final answer. At the end, see how close the estimate was.

Skill: To multiply by ten, multiples of ten, and 2-digit numbers

Time: 1 period per procedure

Materials:

light-colored markers: 2 colors; 1 set per student

place value (pv) materials to 1000s; use counters for 1000s

18 blank index cards: 1 set per student

counter-trading materials

See Reproducibles for: hundred boards—1 per student, directions for file-folder pv mats, pv mats to 1000s, bills to 100s—in different colors

Anticipatory Set

Use *index cards, markers,* and *hundred boards.*

Students write an × and one number per card: ×1 to ×9 and ×10 to ×90. These are shown in Procedure 4 and used in *all* procedures.

Next students color each multiple of 10 on the hundred board. How do we multiply 10 by a 1-digit number?

Students color multiples of 3 to 36 with another color. Where did they color the same number? (30) Discuss the fact family $3 \times 10 = 30$ and $10 \times 3 = 30$.

Explain that we are beginning to learn 2-digit multiplication and that the first one we work with is 10 times a simple number.

Procedure 1

□■

To multiply 1-digit numbers by 10 and by multiples of 10; to understand partial products

Use *pv materials to 10s, pv mats, × number cards ×10–×90, and paper.*

Have students place a group of four one cubes on their group pv mats.

On the board write 10×4 vertically, circling the 10.

Ask: What is the 4? (the number we start with) What is the ×10?

Students respond: The directions.

Have students place nine more groups of four one cubes on their mats. (Illustration 1a)

Students finish with 40 one cubes on their mats. They say they have 10 groups and this shows $10 \times 4 = 40$.

Students should see the need to regroup. (Illustration 1b) After regrouping, they tell you they have 4 groups of 10 and this shows $4 \times 10 = 40$.

Reinforce with students that fact families will help them solve 10 times a simple number.

Draw a pv chart around the board problem, and write the total.

Continue with other 1-digit by 10 problems. Ask: Do you see a pattern to multiplying by 10?

Students should see that the answer never has any ones. They should recognize the similarities to multiplying 10 by a 1-digit number.

Repeat only until students understand the process. Move on to the next activity, multiplying by multiples of 10.

Say: A rancher has 20 corrals with 8 broncos in each. Ask: How could we find out how many wild horses he or she has in all?

Students use materials and work in small groups. Discuss how they arrived at an answer.

What if the rancher had 10 corrals with 8 broncos in each. How many wild horses would there be?

Students respond: 80 because $10 \times 8 = 80$.

Have students draw the following headings on paper as you demonstrate on the board.

Be sure students understand that this form is a way of describing by writing what is actually happening.

# of corrals		horses in each	total
10	×	8	80
20	×	8	?

If the rancher has 20 corrals, he or she has 10 + 10 corrals.

We know $10 \times 8 = 80$ and we could add another $10 \times 8 = 80$. How many is 80 + 80? (160) Place that on your chart.

10s	1s

1a

1b

What if there were 30 corrals? That would be $(10 \times 8) + (10 \times 8) + (10 \times 8)$, or $80 + 80 + 80$. What is the total?

Students respond: 240. They chart 30×8 and 240.

Do you see any patterns? You may want to suggest students look at $1 \times 8 = 8$; $2 \times 8 = 16$; $3 \times 8 = 24$.

Continue to fill in the chart and discuss responses until students can understand the pattern.

Say: Whenever you multiply by 10 or multiples of 10, you end up regrouping. This means you have moved the numbers over a place on a place value chart.

When we multiply by 10s, will there ever be any ones? (no) Why not?

Demonstrate on the board, showing the products to the side as in the following chart.

Make sure students understand and can see the patterns and relationships developed.

Assign student groups different multiples to work with and have them add their results to the chart.

	×100	×10	×1	
			8	(1 × 8)
		8	0	(10 × 8)
	8	0	0	(100 × 8)
	×200	×20	×2	
		1	6	(2 × 8)
	1	6	0	(20 × 8)
1	6	0	0	(200 × 8)
	×300	×30	×3	
		2	4	(3 × 8)
	2	4	0	(30 × 8)
2	4	0	0	(300 × 8)

Procedure 2

To multiply multiples of 10 by 10 and by multiples of 10; to show partial products

Use *pv materials to 10s, pv mats*, and *× number cards ×10–×90*.

Students do not write the problem until the concept is understood. Demonstrate the written form on the board.

Place 10×20 on the board. Ask: How would you place the rods and cubes on your mats?

Students respond: Place a group of two ten rods on the mat, with a ×10 card below.

Students use manipulatives as you write each step on the board with partial products as shown in the next column.

Move step by step through the problem, emphasizing each separate partial product.

100s	10s	1s	
	2	0	
	×1	0	
		0	(0 × 0) = 0
	0	0	(0 × 20) = +00
	0	0	(10 × 0) = +00
+2	0	0	(10 × 20) = +200
2	0	0	200

After 10×20, ask: Do we need to regroup? (yes) How many times? (2) Will there be any ones in the answer? Any tens?

Students trade twenty tens for two hundred flats. They tell you they have no ones and no tens in the answer.

Review: In the ones column we had no ones times no ones, which equals zero, or nothing. We also know that no ones times two tens is nothing.

Ten times no ones is no tens. Ten times two tens is 20 tens. We had to regroup, and we have found that 10 times 20 equals how many?

Students add the columns and respond: 200. They continue to complete problems similar to this one.

Do students see the same or similar patterns as in the earlier charting exercise? In what ways?

When students are competent with this part, you can move on to multiplying by multiples of 10.

Students are now writing problems as they work with manipulatives.

Procedure 3

To multiply 2-digit numbers by 10 and by multiples of 10; to move to only two partial products

Use *pv mats, bills, × number cards ×10–×90*, and *paper*.

Student pairs use bills and then write problems while you demonstrate on the board. They now know that no ones are in these kinds of partial products and can learn to use only two products.

Write the problem 10×36 on the board, circling the 10. Have students place bills on their mats and answer questions as in Procedure 2.

100s	10s	1s	
	3	6	
	×1	0	
	6	0	(10 × 6) = 60
+3	0	0	(10 × 30) = +300
3	6	0	360

We know multiplying 1-digit numbers by tens; and multiples of ten by tens. So, what is 10×6? (60) Show where to write that.

Students copy $10 \times 6 = 60$ on their papers.

Ask: What is 10×30? (300)

Students copy as you complete the problem.

Have students write down the multiplication sentence proved with their bills. ($10 \times \$36 = \$360$)

Students continue to build numbers, multiply by 10, write the partial products on paper, and then write down the multiplication sentence proven.

Ask: Do you see any pattern to your answers? Discuss. Move on to multiplying by multiples of 10.

Say: The buyer for a large department store pays $24 for each pair of men's shoes he orders. He needs 20 pairs. How much will this cost?

Students place bills until they have 20 groups of $24 on their mats.

Place the following problem on the board. Show students how this describes what they have just done with bills.

100s	10s	1s		
	$2	4		
	×2	0		
	8	0	$(20 \times 4) =$	80
+4	0	0	$(20 \times 20) =$	+400
$4	8	0		480

Ask the same type of questions as before. Continue showing the partial products on the board, and have students show them on their papers.

After students have practiced with the bills and are competent in the skill, they move to the stage of first doing each step on paper and then checking with bills.

They must understand that the written form is just a description of what they have been doing.

Continue until students have mastered this concept. This mastery takes many repetitions.

When students begin working on paper, have them turn lined paper sideways so that they do not "lose" some of the needed zeros. *Remember to do this in all the rest of the activities.*

Challenge students to build on the skill of multiples of 10 and predict how to multiply by hundreds or thousands. See the Practice and Extension for other ideas.

Now you can teach students to write down the pattern of placing the zero in the ones column and then multiplying by the tens digit in the multiplier.

Procedure 4

To multiply 2-digit numbers by 2-digit numbers; to develop a traditional algorithm

Use *pv mats, pv materials or counters, all × number cards, bills,* and *paper.*

Say: I've invited 30 people for a spaghetti dinner. My recipe says that I'll need 12 of the 13-ounce jars of sauce. I could buy larger jars and save money, but how will I know how many to buy? What do I need to know?

Students discuss that you will need to know the total number of ounces needed.

I could add 23 twelve times. Do we know a short-cut for adding the same number over and over? (multiplication) Write 12×13 on the board.

You may not realize it, but you already know how to solve this problem. We'll split up the jars. Some of you will find the total of the first ten and some will find the total for the last two.

Half the class solves the problem 2×23. The other half solves the problem 10×23. One student from each group explains the steps the group completed to find the answer and why.

You found 230 ounces in ten jars and 26 ounces in two jars. How do I find how many ounces in all? (add the totals together and get 256 ounces)

Repeat with other problems. Include multiplication by numbers above 20. When students fully understand the process say: You've been doing a lot of writing to solve these problems. Let's find a way to combine the separate steps into one problem.

Students draw vertical lines to divide a paper into thirds or fourths. They label the columns "Ones," "Tens," and "Hundreds."

Write 12×13 vertically on the board, drawing a circle around the 12.

Ask: What is the 13? (the number we started with) What is the ×12? (the directions)

Students place the number 13 on their mats with the ×10 card below. On top of that card they place the ×2 card as shown.

We know how to do 2 groups of 13, and that is our first step. How many are in 2 groups of 3 ones.

Students place cubes and record $2 \times 3 = 6$.

What's next? (multiply 2×10)

How many are in 2 groups of 1 ten? (20)

We have multiplied 13 by 2. What do the materials show? (26)

You can already do the next step. Take away the ×2 card. What kind of problem is this?

Students respond: 10 times a 2-digit number.

How many are in 10 groups of 3? (30)

How many are in 10 groups of one 10?

Students respond: 10 tens, or 100.

How many do you have in 10 groups of 13? (130)

We can look at this as two problems, each of which we know how to complete:

```
   13          13          26
   x2    +    x10    =   +130
   26          130        156
```

Ask: What is the next step? (add)

Students push materials together and read the total: 156.

Do both the numbers and the materials show the same total? (yes)

First we multiplied by the number in the ones column. Then we multiplied by the number in the tens column and added to find the total.

Repeat the procedure with 11×11.

Students practice on mats and paper, first using their manipulatives and then recording each step on paper.

Continue the procedure with other lower 2-digit numbers until students grasp the concept, and then move to numbers that require regrouping.

Regrouping procedure:

Have students place 13 groups of 26 on their paper mats and write 13×26 as shown:

100s	10s	1s	
	2	6	
	×1	3	
	7	8	$(3 \times 26) = 78$
+2	6	0	$(10 \times 26) = +260$
3	3	8	338

First multiply the ones. How many are 3 groups of 6 ones? (18 ones) Do we need to regroup? (yes)

When we write problems, what do we do with a regrouped number to hold it for future use?

Students respond: Place 8 in the ones column and a circled +1 above the tens column. They record this.

Ask: How many is 3×2 tens? (60) Do we need to write the 0 in the ones column?

Students respond: No, we can write 6 in the tens place.

Complete the multiplying of 3×26, *crossing out the circled regrouped number after adding it to the tens answer as shown.*

How do we multiply by tens?

Students respond: When we multiply by 10, the number in the ones place is zero and the other numbers go in the tens column and hundreds column.

Multiply by 10, ask questions, and have students respond.

Students write numbers and tell you that the final step is to add the columns. They finish the problem.

Continue the procedure until all students have grasped the concept. Make sure the students understand that the written form is just a description of what they were able to prove with the different manipulatives.

Have students create problems. Example: A day has 24 hours. How many hours are in two weeks?

Shortcut traditional algorithm:

Do not do this activity until students have demonstrated competency in completing the problems in the preceding procedures.

Write the following problem on the board, and have students copy it. Do not include answers.

100s	10s	1s	
	2	8	
	×3	4	
1	1	2	
+8	4	0	
9	5	2	

Ask: How many are 4 groups of 8 ones? (32 ones) Place the 2 in the ones column, and place a circled +3 above the tens number.

Students complete the problem step by step with you.

How many are 4 groups of 2 tens? (8 tens) Add the +3, and you have how many tens? (11 tens, 110) Cross out the regrouped number, and place a 1 in the tens column and a 1 in the hundreds column.

Next we multiply by the tens number. How many are 30 groups of 8 ones? (240) Place a 0 in the ones column, a 4 in the tens column. Place a circled +2 above the crossed-out +3 as shown.

Students can see why it is very important to remember to cross out a regrouped number after it has been added in.

How many are 30 groups of 20? (600) Since the last two digits of that number are zeros, we can place it on the same line as a shortcut. We still have a +2 on hold, however. What shall we do with it?

Students respond: Add it to the 6.

Say: That makes the number in the hundreds column 8.

Ask: How do we get a total? (add)

Students add and arrive at the final answer. (952)

Continue verbal, as well as physical, practice of this procedure since students often forget steps when they start using this shorter form of writing.

If students have trouble, they can use manipulatives and partial products to check their work.

Procedure 5

To multiply 3-digit numbers by 2-digit numbers; to develop a traditional algorithm

Use *pv mats, bills, all × number cards,* and *paper.*

Since students have already learned multiplying by 1-digit and 2-digit numbers, they can write those products as the partial products.

Write the following problem on the board, and complete the steps as students respond to questions.

1000s	100s	10s	1s	
		⟨1⟩		
	$2	1	7	
		×1	2	
	4	3	4	(2 × 217)
+2	1	7	0	(10 × 217)
$2	6	0	4	

Have student pairs place $217 on their mats and place × number cards as before.

What do you have to do first? (multiply 2 × 7 = 14)

Students place bills, trade, and see that they have one ten and four ones. They write the regrouped number in a circle with a + sign to remind them to add.

Ask step-by-step questions, emphasizing groups of ones, tens, and hundreds.

When you are ready to multiply the hundreds number by the tens number, ask: What would the rule be? Where would the answer go?

Students discuss the need to place the number in the thousands place: 1 ten × 1 one = 1 ten; 1 ten × 1 ten = 1 hundred; 1 ten × 1 hundred = 1 thousand; each time you multiply by 10, you add a zero.

Have students complete the problem. Continue the procedure until they understand the process.

Multiply some 3-digit numbers that have a zero in only the tens place. What problems are created?

Students need a great deal of practice at the connecting stage of working with manipulatives and writing down each step as they work in order to become truly competent in this skill.

Practice and Extension

Challenge students to make up problems that use multiples of 10 as part of the problem.

Make a class chart that shows multiples of 10 through the thousands.

Divide the class in half. Each half works 12 months each year. Generate 2-digit salary amounts for each month using *cards*. How much does each half of the class make the first year? Over a week's time, repeat the procedure for subsequent years, and keep a running total. What about taxes, bonuses, and so on? Which side earned the most money?

Have students work in pairs, and let them make up games using numbers at random to multiply as 2-digit problems. One student should solve the problem with the *mats and blocks,* and the other should solve the problem with *paper* and *pencil* in the accepted pattern.

Ask students to find how many months they have lived or how many months ago a famous person died.

Have students work in pairs, and let them make up games using numbers at random to multiply as 3-digit problems.

Have students use *catalogs* and choose several items that cost over $100. Roll two *dice,* and use the numbers as a 2-digit multiplier. They buy that many of each item. How much money do they need? If they buy 24 of each item chosen, how close can they come to $5,000 without going over? The closest one wins. They can do these exercises on *paper* only or with the *bills.*

Have students build on multiplying by two digits to multiplying by three digits. Include some with multipliers that have a zero in the tens place. What can they discover and prove about that line of partial products?

Have students estimate the number of days since an important event, like the Civil War, a world war, or a winning local team at the World Series or Super Bowl.

Multiplication 10

Skill: To understand exponents

Time: 1+ periods

Materials:

tiles, cubes, or counters

place value (pv) materials to 10s

graph paper: with ½" squares

markers

clear tape

Anticipatory Set

Use *tiles, cubes,* or *counters*.

Have students use tiles to make *squares* of different sizes. Can they see a pattern? (2 groups of 2, 3 groups of 3, etc.) How can we write two groups of two? (2×2) What about three groups of three? (3×3) Discuss that the factors are the same for a square number.

Procedure 1 □■

To understand exponents

Use *pv materials to 10s, tiles, or cubes,* and *paper*.

Say: In square numbers, we used each factor twice. We can write this with a math shortcut. First write the number you started with, like 3. This is called the base number.

We used the base number as a factor, and we show how many times we used it with a small number called an exponent.

Write 3^2 on the board.

We call this 3 squared, or 3 to the power of 2. $3^2 = 3 \times 3 = 9$. How would we write the square number made with 2? $(2^2 = 2 \times 2 = 4)$

Repeat for all the square numbers students made. Emphasize base, exponent, to the second power.

Ask: When might we have a number multiplied once by itself in real life? (area of a square) Let's see whether other exponents may be used besides 2.

Build $2 \times 2 \times 2$ with your materials.

Students build 2 groups of 2×2 squares. If they do not think of building a cube, suggest they put their blocks into the smallest space possible.

You built 2 twice, then you built *another whole group just like the 2×2* as you multiplied by the third 2.

What was our base number? (2) How many times did we use 2 as a factor? (3 times) What number will I use as the exponent? (3) $2^3 = 2 \times 2 \times 2 = 8$.

We call this 2 cubed because it makes a cube. We can also call it 2 to the third power.

Ask: What will 3^3 equal?

Students build 3^3. They write $3^3 = 3 \times 3 \times 3 = 27$. They discuss how quickly exponential numbers get larger.

Students discover that any number with an exponent of 1 is itself.

Students construct 10, 100, 1,000. They write $10 = 10^1$, $100 = 10^2$, $1{,}000 = 10^3$, $10{,}000 = 10^4$. They discuss any patterns found.

We are missing an exponent shortcut for the ones column. What might it be according to the pattern?

If students say 1^1, remind them that ours is a base ten system, and the base number must be 10.

Explain that any number with an exponent of 0 is 1, so $10^0 = 1$. (If students wish to extend the pattern further, decimal places are to the right of the ones. $10^{-1} = 1/10^1 = 1/10$, and $10^{-2} = 1/10^2 = 1/100$.)

Provide practice with materials and writing the numbers until students are competent in the skill.

Procedure 2 □■

To graph exponential numbers

Use *graph paper, markers,* and *tape*.

Have students start in the lower left corner with zero and number upward along the left side of the graph paper. Have them use markers to make a bar graph of the answers to 2^2, 2^3, 2^4, 2^5, and 2^6.

Each number should be one square wide. Students can tape several sheets of paper together as the numbers get larger.

Ask: What do you notice about exponential numbers?

Students respond: The numbers get big very quickly.

Have students put a dot at the midpoint of the top of each charted number. If they connect the dots, they will find a curve, since these are multiplication patterns.

Practice and Extension

Have students use *graph paper, tape,* and *markers* to chart other exponential numbers.

Have students set up a chart on lined paper, headed "Exponent = ___." On the next line they head columns: "Number," "Total," "Difference Between Totals," "Difference Between Differences." An Exponent = 2 chart will have *two* columns headed "Difference." An exponent of 3 will have *three* columns headed "Difference," and so on.

As an example, for the Exponent = 2 chart:

1. Students write down the first column: 1^2, 2^2, 3^2, 4^2, etc., to 10^2. They skip a line between each number.

2. The totals are 1, 4, 9, 16, 25, 36, 49, 64, 81, 100.

3. On the lines between the totals, in the first Difference column, they would write 3 (the difference between 1 and 4), 5 (the difference between 4 and 9), 7, 9, and so on.

4. On the lines between those first Difference numbers, in the second Difference column, they would write 2, 2, 2, 2, 2, 2, 2, 2. When the exponent is 3, the last Difference column reads all 3s.

Exponent = 2

Number	Total	Difference Between Totals	Difference Between Differences
1^2	1		
		3	
2^2	4		2
		5	
3^2	9		2
		7	
4^2	16		2
		9	
↓	↓	↓	↓
		19	
10^2	100		2

Multiplication 11

Skill: To understand prime numbers, composite numbers, and prime factorization

Time: 1+ periods

Materials:

cubes, tiles, or counters

light-colored markers: 1 per student

See Reproducibles for: hundred boards—1 per student

Anticipatory Set

Use *cubes* or *tiles*.

Have students make as many different rectangular arrays as possible with 12 cubes or tiles, writing down each one as they complete it. Discuss factors of a number, and have students circle the factors for 12. Each factor may only be circled one time.

Procedure 1

To find factors; to understand prime and composite numbers

Use *cubes, tiles,* or *counters*.

Draw a chart on the board, headed "Number," "Factors," "Prime," "Composite." Write the numbers from zero to nine in a vertical line in the Number column.

As you give each number, have students make all the rectangular arrays possible and list the multiplication fact for each array. Then have them circle all the *different* factors for that number. If a factor is circled once for a number, it should not be circled again.

Students start with two tiles and find the facts are 2×1 and 1×2. They find the factors are 1 and 2.

Number	Factors	Prime	Composite
0			
1			
2	1, 2	×	
3	1, 3	×	
4	1, 2, 4		×
5	1, 5	×	
6	1, 2, 3, 6		×
7	1, 7	×	
8	1, 2, 4, 8		×
9	1, 3, 9		×

On the chart, list 1 and 2 as factors and then, *without saying why*, put an × in the Prime column.

Students take three tiles or cubes. They find the factors are 1 and 3.

On the chart, list 1 and 3 as factors and, *without saying why*, put an × in the Prime column.

Students take four tiles or blocks. They find the factors are 1, 2, and 4.

On the chart, list 1, 2, and 4 as factors and, *without saying why*, put an × in the Composite column.

Continue the procedure through the number nine. Ask students whether they can see what makes a number prime or composite.

Lead them to discover that prime numbers have exactly two factors, the number itself and one. Composite numbers have more than two factors.

Students explore the number zero. It has no factors. Draw a line through both Prime and Composite columns.

Repeat for the number one. It has only one factor, so it too is neither prime nor composite.

Explain that with smaller numbers it is easier to find all the factors since you know all the multiplication facts.

Ask: Can you think of an organized way we could make sure we had all the arrays for a larger number, like 34?

Students suggest building a 1×34 array, then a 2×17 array, and so on.

Ask whether they are using division. Since 34 divides into 2 parts without any remainders, we know 2 will be a factor of 34. What will the multiplication fact be? (2×17)

Students make all possible arrays for 34 and find the factors are 1, 2, 17, and 34. Thirty-four is not prime.

Repeat with numbers of 35, 36, and 37.

Ask: What if you can't find a smaller number except one that will divide evenly into your number?

Students respond: That means our number is prime, so 37 is prime.

Procedure 2 □■

To find prime numbers using the Sieve of Eratosthenes

Use *hundred boards* and *markers*.

Think about the number 122. Ask: Is it a prime number? If we can find a factor besides 1 and 122, we don't have to go any farther in testing it.

Is 122 even or odd? (even) So 2 is a factor. Since 122 is divisible by 2, 122 isn't prime.

What about 123? Is it even or odd? (odd) So 2 is not a factor. Why wouldn't I have to see whether 123 was divisible by any other even numbers?

Students should respond: They would have 2 as a factor, and we already know 2 isn't a factor.

You only have to try dividing by prime numbers, since all composite numbers have a prime number as a factor. If you knew all the prime numbers, you could more easily decide whether a number such as 397 was prime or composite.

A Greek mathematician named Eratosthenes (200 B.C.) developed a way to find prime numbers. The method is called the Sieve of Eratosthenes.

Using your hundred board, circle the number two because it is a prime number. Now cross off all the multiples of 2.

Ask: Why are all the numbers you crossed off composite numbers? (they all have 2 as a factor)

Go back to the beginning: three is the next number that is not crossed off. Circle it because it is prime and then cross off all larger multiples of three. What is the next number that is not crossed off? (5) Is five prime? (yes) Circle it, and repeat the procedure.

Students repeat the procedure until no more numbers can be crossed off. The numbers left are prime numbers. They discover the prime numbers under 100 are: 2, 3, 5, 7, 11, 13, 17, 19, 23, 29, 31, 37, 41, 43, 47, 53, 59, 61, 67, 71, 73, 79, 83, 89, and 97.

Have students highlight all the primes with markers. Then have them explore all possible patterns.

Procedure 3 □■

To understand prime factorization

Note: For using prime factorization to find the GCF or GCD, see Fractions 5. For using prime factorization to find the LCM or LCD, see Fractions 9.

Use *cubes, tiles, or counters,* and *paper.*

If students have trouble using a factor tree for prime factorization, have them use materials as they work.

Students list the number to be factored at the top of the page. Then they find an array that can be made from that number of cubes or tiles. They list the two factors below their original number, the smaller factor to the left. They circle any prime factors.

For factors that are not prime, they make an array of the *factor.* Once they have found the factors of *that* number, they write these down, using the same procedure as before. They continue until all prime factors have been found and circled.

Example: Prime factorization of 16:

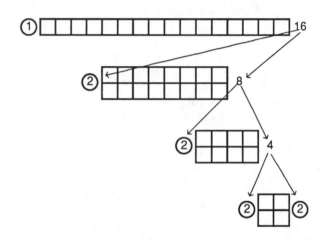

The circled numbers are the prime factors of 16. The prime factorization of 16: $1 \times 2 \times 2 \times 2 \times 2$, or 1×2^4.

Practice and Extension

Have students explore:

Christian Goldbach (1690–1764) stated: Every even number greater than 2 is the sum of two primes. This is known as Goldbach's Conjecture. Example: $4 = 2 + 2$, $6 = 3 + 3$, $8 = 3 + 5$, and so on.

The primes two and three are consecutive integers. Is there another pair of consecutive integers both of which are prime? Why or why not?

Twin primes are prime numbers that differ by only 2, such as 11 and 13. How many other twin primes can students find?

Division 1

Skill: To learn division facts

Time: 4 or 5 periods

Materials:

counters of 2 colors: buttons, cubes, tiles, or 1" × 1" paper squares

graph paper: ¹/₂" squares

markers: to match colors of counters

geoboards and rubber bands

interlocking cubes

Cuisenaire® rods

place value (pv) materials to 10s

dice: 1 per student pair

See Reproducibles for: pv mats to 100s, division paper, bills to 10s—in different colors

Note: Eventually, you want students to be able to divide using a base ten format. Students need to understand how to divide several kinds of groups (tens and ones, for example), how to trade from one kind of group to the other (trade a ten for ten ones), and how to record their actions in a base ten format.

By teaching each of the following procedures, you increase the chances of students' thinking of "facts" in a base ten format. Division of any 2- or 3-digit number by a 1-digit number then becomes a logical extension of what has gone before.

Anticipatory Set

Use *counters*.

Have students lay out 15 counters as shown below. Explain that the lines across are called *rows,* like a row of seats in an auditorium. The lines up and down are called *columns,* like columns holding up a building. Do students have other memory aids? Have them build arrays of specified rows and columns.

Procedure 1

To understand and use the $\overline{)}$ symbol

Use *counters* and *paper*.

Have students write 15 below their counters.

Say: These are a farmer's 15 pigs. He has them in three lines. However, he doesn't want them to get away, so he puts a fence around them. Draw a fence as shown.

The farmer walks around to the front of the lines. (Show on the board where the three will go.) How many lines does the farmer see? (3) Write the three in the correct place. The pigs have been divided into three lines, or groups.

The farmer needs to know how many pigs are in each line, so he walks around to see. Indicate on the board where the five will go.

How many pigs in each line? (5) Write the five in place. Five pigs are in each line.

This fence is used as one of our division symbols. It shows 15 pigs divided into three groups with 5 in a group. You could also think of the problem as 15 pigs divided into five columns with 3 in each column.

Have we done anything with rectangles or arrays before?

Students respond: This is like multiplication.

Repeat with other numbers. Write the array and written division problem on the board as before. Any remainders can be written as leftovers or written as remainders

When students are comfortable with arrays, they work in pairs. One student works with the counters while the other writes the problem. As each step is done with the counters, the result is put onto paper. They write the related multiplication fact and make up stories to go along with their manipulations.

Procedure 2

To practice the concept and writing of division, using arrays

Use *graph paper and markers* or *geoboards and rubber bands*.

Have students use graph paper or geoboards and outline an array of their starting number. Example: If the starting number is 18 and it is to be divided by three, students will make a rectangle three squares high. See the illustration on the following page.

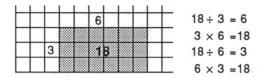

$$18 \div 3 = 6$$
$$3 \times 6 = 18$$
$$18 \div 6 = 3$$
$$6 \times 3 = 18$$

Students write the resulting number of columns above the rectangle and then write the division and multiplication facts discovered.

Procedure 3 ◻▪

To divide with two kinds of objects; no regrouping

Use *two colors of counters*, *plain paper*, and *markers*.

Say: Sam had jelly beans left over from his lunch, which he decided to give to two friends. Take eight red counters for eight red jelly beans.

Sam also had four yellow jelly beans. Put them to the right of the red jelly beans, and draw a line between them because there are two different kinds of jelly beans. Draw a division fence above them. (Illustration 3a)

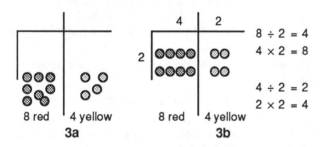

$$8 \div 2 = 4$$
$$4 \times 2 = 8$$

$$4 \div 2 = 2$$
$$2 \times 2 = 4$$

Ask: How many friends do we have? (2) Let's put the two here to show how many groups we will have. (Illustration 3b) Divide the red beans into two lines.

How many red beans are in each group? (4) I'll show the divided beans and put the four up here to show how many red beans each friend got. (Illustration 3b)

Say: Divide the yellow beans to see how many each friend will get.

We still have two friends. How many will each friend get? (2) I'll put the two up above the yellow jelly beans.

Does anyone see a division fact I can list?

Students respond: $8 \div 2 = 4$, $4 \div 2 = 2$.

I'll list these on the board to the side.

Could we check our results with math? Who sees something they've seen before?

Students respond: It's like multiplication. $4 \times 2 = 8$ red jelly beans and $2 \times 2 = 4$ yellow jelly beans.

Write these facts next to the division facts.

Say: Take all the jelly beans for the first friend and put them in a pile to the side. Do the same for the second friend. How many jelly beans in all for each friend?

Students respond: They get 4 red beans and 2 yellow beans—6 in all.

Repeat the procedure with other stories and numbers. Extra beans can be written to the side with a +.

When students are comfortable with the skill, they work in pairs. One works with the counters, and the other records results. The recorder draws a picture of the counters using markers and places the results on the chart.

Students need much practice at this stage of both manipulating materials and recording results. As they become confident in the skill, have them try to predict the result before using the materials.

Procedure 4 ◻▪

To divide with two kinds of objects; with regrouping

Use *interlocking cubes* and *plain paper*.

Say: Today we will be handing out gum to friends. The gum comes in packs of five. Take some of your interlocking cubes and make them into packs of five.

Students do this.

Let's start with three packs and two pieces. Put them on your paper, and draw a line between them.

Now draw a division fence above because we are going to divide among two friends. (Illustration 4a)

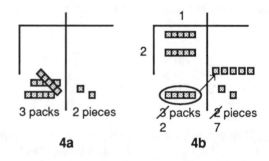

Ask: How many friends? (2) I'll write that to the left. Divide your three packs among two friends.

Students do this. They comment that one is left over.

How many packs does each friend get? (1)

On the board draw the divided packs. (Illustration 4b)

Say: Each group has one in it, so I'll write the one in the pack column. What does this show?

Students respond: How many packs each friend gets.

What can we do about the extra pack?

Students respond: Break it into single pieces. They do this.

We only have two packs now. I'll cross out the three and put a two.

Make sure all your pieces are on the "pieces" side of your paper. How many single pieces do you have now? (7)

Divide your seven pieces for your two friends. If any are left over now, just put them to the side and we'll save them for later.

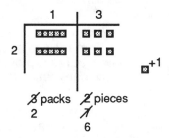

Students divide the pieces and put one piece to the side.

How many pieces does each friend get?

Students respond: Each friend gets three pieces. One is left over.

Where will I show this?

Students respond: Above, where the pieces are.

Finish the problem on the board. List any division and multiplication facts students see.

Repeat the procedure with other combinations.

As students become adept at dividing and trading, change the value of the packs. Have six pieces in a pack, or four pencils in a bundle, or three anteaters for each anthill.

Ask questions: How many packs and pieces did we start with? How many packs and pieces did each friend get? Any left over? What division and multiplication facts did you find?

Procedure 5

To practice division with two kinds of objects; with regrouping

Use *Cuisenaire® rods* and *paper.*

Repeat Procedure 4 with different materials and different values. This time have students record the division after completing each step with the manipulatives.

Procedure 6

To divide with base ten materials

Use *pv materials, pv mats, division paper,* and *dice.*

Repeat Procedure 3 with ten rods and one cubes. Start with numbers that do not require trading, such as 24 ÷ 2. On the board write the problem as shown in the illustrations below.

Have students place materials for 24.

10s	1s		10s	1s
			2	4

Say: We are giving out erasers, which are packaged in tens. We'll give them evenly to two friends.

Write the two on the board, and have students divide their rods and cubes into two groups.

10s	1s		10s	1s	
			1	2	Tens
					$2 \div 2 = 1$
					$1 \times 2 = 2$
			2	4	Ones
					$4 \div 2 = 2$
					$2 \times 2 = 4$

Ask: How many groups of tens did you make? (2) How many eraser packages in each group? (1) Where can I record that?

Students respond: Above, in the tens column.

Yes, if you divide tens, you get a certain number of tens and your answer is in tens.

What division fact did you show? (2 pkgs. ÷ 2 = 1) Write this on the board.

How can we check that our division is right?

Students respond: With multiplication. $1 \times 2 = 2$.

How many groups of ones, or single erasers, did you make? (2) How many erasers are in each group? (2) Where can I record that?

Students respond: Above, in the ones column.

Yes, if you divide ones, you get a certain number of ones and your answer is in ones.

What division fact did you show? (4 ÷ 2 = 2) Write this on the board.

How can we check that our division is right?

Students respond: With multiplication. $2 \times 2 = 4$.

Divide 2-digit numbers with and without trades, recording the results on the board after each trade. Ask the same questions for each problem.

In recording regrouping, make sure students cross out original numbers and write in new amounts for *both* tens and ones, as in illustrations 4a and 4b.

Practice also with 1-digit numbers. Make sure students understand where to place the answer.

When students are comfortable with making divisions and trades, they begin writing. Working in pairs, one uses the materials, and one records each step. They keep a list of division and multiplication facts they discover. Dice can be used to generate problems: The first two numbers are the dividend; the third is the divisor.

Work through several problems with students before having them work on their own. Students need much practice at the connecting stage of both writing and using concrete materials.

Procedure 7

To practice and record division

Use *pv mats, dice, division paper,* and *bills.*

Repeat Procedure 6 with different materials. Use dice to generate the problems. Have students make up story situations to solve with division. They should use the words *divisor, dividend,* and *quotient* in describing their problems.

Procedure 8

To develop knowledge of facts; to relate division to multiplication using a multiplication chart

Use *pv materials, pv mats,* and *graph paper.*

Have students outline a square on their graph paper 12 spaces across and 12 spaces down. They should write an × in the upper left-hand corner and the numbers 0 to 10 in the remaining spaces across the top and down the left-hand side.

	0	1	2	3
0				
1				
2			2	4
3				

Have students start with two one cubes and divide them by two. Ask: How many in each group? (1) What is the division fact? (2 ÷ 2 = 1) What is the related multiplication fact? (1 × 2 = 2)

Can you find a place on this chart where you could put the number you started with? Pretend

the upper left-hand corner of the blank squares is your division fence.

Students place two in the appropriate place.

Now have students divide four by two. Repeat the procedure, having students repeat both division and multiplication fact. Place four in the appropriate place.

Continue through the multiples of two. Do students see a pattern?

Some may recognize multiples of two.

Have students recite the multiples of two as they check their materials. How many times did they say a multiple? Does this relate to the answer to their division problem?

Suggest that as they divide by two, they are taking groups of two from their total each time to put in lines. The answer at the top of their division problem tells how many times they removed a group of two.

Continue through the matrix, writing both division and multiplication facts. Pay particular attention to dividing zero and dividing a number by itself.

Practice and Extension

Have students use any of the materials listed to make up division problems. They can act them out with friends.

Have students work individually, and give each student 15 $1 *bills.* The mall is having Dollar Days. Each item they find at the mall costs $3, so they will be dividing their money into groups of $3. They are to keep a record on paper of each purchase and the amount left. Students complete the exercise, continuing to subtract until they have no money left. How many items were they able to buy? (5)

Have students pool their money and work in pairs. They are to take the $30 and divide it into equal groups by spending an equal amount of money at each store. How much do they spend at each store, and how many stores do they visit before all their money is gone? (answers will vary)

Students can make *division flash cards* to use in Concentration (facts on one card and answer on another).

Division 2

Skill: To learn multiplication and division fact families: to relate division to multiplication

Time: 2 periods

Materials:

1" tiles: ceramic, plastic, or 1" × 1" paper squares

1 cm cubes

light-colored markers

scissors

geoboards and colored rubber bands

interlocking cubes

counters

narrow strips of tag board: 2 per student

See Reproducibles for: graph paper with 1 cm squares—1 sheet per student, multiplication/division tables—1 per group

Anticipatory Set

Use *tiles* and *blank sheets of paper.*

Review with students that rows are the across lines and columns are the down lines. Compare them to rows of seats and columns of buildings. Have students make and discuss several arrays. Does every number make an array? (Yes, it at least has 1 × itself.)

What if we turn the group of tiles so that the rectangle is sideways? (Illustration 2b)

Students respond: It would show 3 groups of 4: $4 \times 3 = 12$; or 12 divided into 3 groups: $12 \div 3 = 4$.

Write these on the board, and bracket them as a fact family. Relate this to addition/subtraction fact families.

Have students suggest other groupings and show their groups with the tiles. Write the fact families on the board until the students understand the procedure. They then can see how many families they can discover and record.

Procedure 1

To use arrays to discover fact families

Use *tiles* and *paper.*

Have students make a 3 × 4 array as shown above.

Explain that the tiles are pigs in a pigpen. The farmer has divided them into four lines but needs to keep them from running into the cornfield nearby.

Demonstrate on the board that a partial fence around a group looks similar to a division symbol:

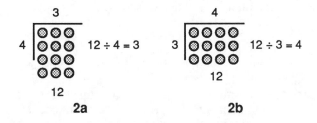

2a   **2b**

Model for the students as they do an example (Illustration 2a). Ask: How many rows are shown? (4) How many columns? (3) What multiplication fact is shown? (3 in each group × 4 groups: $3 \times 4 = 12$)

What division fact? (12 divided into 4 groups: $12 \div 4 = 3$) Write these on the board.

Procedure 2

To draw and write fact families

Use *graph paper with 1 cm squares, 1 cm cubes, markers,* and *scissors.*

Have students work in groups to explore arrays of fact families. Have students start by labeling their paper: "Fact Families for Six." Take six cubes and make a row. Ask: What fact family can I show with this rectangle?

Students respond: $1 \times 6 = 6$, $6 \times 1 = 6$, $6 \div 1 = 6$, $6 \div 6 = 1$. They form the rectangle with cubes, color the graph paper to match, and write the fact family below:

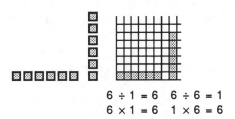

$$6 \div 1 = 6 \quad 6 \div 6 = 1$$
$$6 \times 1 = 6 \quad 1 \times 6 = 6$$

Students explore fact families in this manner, making as many rectangles as possible with each number. Groups can cut out and post their discoveries.

How were they sure they got all the combinations? What do they notice about the shapes of the rectangles? What patterns do they see? Can they tell you how multiplication and division are related?

Procedure 3

To practice and write fact families

Use *geoboards and rubber bands.*

Have students put a band around a 3 × 4 rectangle. Then have them use another color band to make four separate rectangles as shown:

$12 \div 4 = 3$
$3 \times 4 = 12$

What multiplication fact is shown? (3 × 4 = 12) What division fact could this show? (12 ÷ 4 = 3)

How are these alike? Have students reposition the bands for a 4 × 3 rectangle and write the rest of the fact family. (4 × 3 = 12 and 12 ÷ 3 = 4)

Continue with more examples.

As students do each step with the geoboards, it is important for them to understand that the written form is just a description of what is happening.

Students continue to explore both the multiplication and the division facts they can discover. When they are comfortable, have them predict the fact family for each new dividend before using the geoboard.

Procedure 4

To practice and write fact families

Use *interlocking cubes.*

Write 12 ÷ ? = ? on the board.

Have students build a stick of 12 cubes. Ask: How many ways can you separate the stick into equal groups?

After students have done this, ask how many are in each group. How many groups do you have? What multiplication and division facts did you discover?

Write the facts discovered on the board, and continue until you have covered all desired facts.

Procedure 5

To use the multiplication/division table to find facts

Use *multiplication/division tables, light-colored markers, counters,* and *strips of tag board.*

Have students color in the six and position the strips:

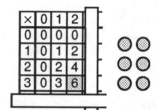

Say: The six you colored tells how many counters to start with. We'll use the far left column as our first directions. The number is three, so divide the six counters into three groups. How many in each group? (2) Do you see that answer anywhere?

Students respond: In the top row above the starting 6.

Ask: What division fact did we show? (6 ÷ 3 = 2) What multiplication fact did we show? (2 × 3 = 6)

Write these on the board.

Say: Now try the *top* directions. They say to divide your six counters into two groups. How many in each group? (3) Do you see that answer anywhere?

Students respond: In the side column, next to the 6 we started with.

What is the division fact? (6 ÷ 2 = 3) And the multiplication fact? (3 × 2 = 6)

Write the complete fact family on the board. Repeat until students understand the procedure.

Students then work in groups to color squares, use the strips, divide the counters, and write the facts.

Do they see any patterns? Will they have to do all the higher numbers to know whether the chart works for them?

Practice and Extension

Have students use *counters* to show three groups of seven and then write the multiplication fact with its answer. Then have students take 21 other counters and "share" them among 7 sections of an *egg carton.* Have students write the division fact this shows and find the other facts that are related. Have them continue with more examples, making up stories to go with the "sharing." Students can work in pairs to make up problems and solutions to share with the rest of the class. They can exchange problems to solve.

Division 3

Skill: To use multiplication to check division

Time: 2+ periods

Materials:

geoboards and rubber bands: 1 set per group

interlocking cubes or counters: 24 per student pair

12-month calendars (not leap year): 1 per group if possible, if not—1 large teacher calendar

markers: 4 colors per group

file-folder or other place value (pv) mats to 100s or 1000s

pv materials to whatever place you wish

See Reproducibles for: directions for file-folder pv mats, pv mats to 100s—1 per student, division paper—2 sheets per student

Anticipatory Set

Use *geoboards and rubber bands.*

Have student groups enclose a 2×3 rectangle. What multiplication and division facts are shown by this figure?

Repeat, having students make shapes and record multiplication and division facts found. Share results with the class, discussing fact families.

Procedure 1 ■

To develop the concept by checking division facts

Use *interlocking cubes or counters* and *paper.*

Have students work in pairs and draw a partial fence on their paper. Tell them to place 24 counters to show 24 cows in a field.

Say: A farmer has three barns and wants to divide these cows evenly so that each barn has the same number of cows. What kind of a math problem will this be? (division) Write 3)24 on the board.

Say: Put a three outside the fence. This number gives the directions. Put your 24 cows into three rows.

Ask: How many cows are in each row or barn? (8) Place the answer above the fence, as in a division problem.

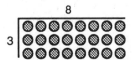

Say: The farmer wants to make sure all cows are taken care of. To check, he sees eight cows in each of three barns.

Ask: What kind of problem is this? (multiplication) Write $8 \times 3 = 24$ on the board. Ask: Do you notice anything about our two problems?

Students may see the numbers are the same but used differently; the starting and ending numbers are the same.

Relate this to fact families. Repeat the procedure until students understand that multiplication and division are related and can be used to check each other.

Procedure 2 ■

To check division of 2-digit numbers by 1-digit numbers

Use *calendars, markers,* and *paper.*

Give each student group a calendar. *If using only one teacher calendar, adapt this to be a whole-class activity.* Ask: How many days are in a year?

Some students will know the correct number: 365.

How many months are those days divided into? (12)

Do all the months have the same number of days? (no) How many days does February have? (28)

How many days are in a week? (7) How can I find how many *weeks* are in February?

Students respond: Divide 28 days by 7.

Write 7)28 on the board. How could I check?

Students respond: Count on a calendar and add up the weeks. Multiply number of days by number of weeks.

How would I write this check the quickest way in math language? ($4 \times 7 = 28$) Write this on the board.

So if a month had 28 days, it would have four weeks. Now look at March.

Students see that March has 31 days.

How do we find the number of weeks in March?

Students respond: Divide the 31 days by 7. Students use the calendar and see that the answer is not even.

Write 7)31 on the board.

Have students place a red dot on the first seven numbers, a blue dot on the second seven numbers, a green dot on the third seven numbers, and a black dot on the fourth seven numbers.

Say: We divided the 31 days by 7 and show 4 weeks. How can we check using math language?

Students respond: Multiply 4×7.

Write $4 \times 7 = 28$ on the board.

I've checked and find that March has 28 days. Is that right?

Students respond: No, it has 31; some days have no dots on them. We need to add the extra days that didn't divide into weeks.

Repeat with other months. Show the remainder when doing the division problem on the board.

After developing the concept, you can expand to as many digits as you desire. Emphasize to students that the process and procedures remain the same.

Procedure 3 □

To divide and write a multiplication check

Use *pv mats*, *pv materials*, and *division paper*.

Have students place two ten rods and six one cubes on their mats and write 26 on their division paper.

Say: I want to divide this into two groups.

Write 2)26 on the board.

Students write the problem on their division paper. They divide the two ten rods into two lines and then divide the one cubes. After each step with their materials, they write on paper what they did.

Ask: What is 2)26? (13) I want to be able to check that to make sure all the blocks are accounted for. What do your blocks show now? (2 groups of 13)

Write $2 \times 13 =$ on the board.

Did you use all the blocks (yes) So $2 \times 13 = 26$? (yes) Put your blocks together to check that you have what you started with.

Students do this and then write the multiplication check in the proper column on their paper.

I started with 26, divided it into two groups, and then multiplied back to check. What if I make a mistake?

Students respond: The numbers won't match.

Draw a smile line from the number you started with to the product you ended with:

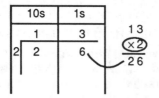

Say: If I see you haven't really *looked* at the match, I will draw a line back. This turns your smile into a banana, which is something you don't want to see!

Repeat the procedure with other problems until students understand the concept.

Now introduce checking with remainders. Have students put two ten rods and seven one cubes on their mats. Write 2)27 on the board.

Students write the problem, divide blocks, and write a check. They notice the materials didn't divide evenly, so it doesn't check.

The reason we check is to make sure all the materials are accounted for. Not all the blocks could be put into the two groups. What could we do with the remainder blocks to get our starting number? (Add them back in.)

Demonstrate how to add the remainder by writing it in under the multiplication problem and adding.

Provide practice with both materials and written work until students understand the concept.

Have students do problems that have regrouping, as well as remainders, such as 3)47.

Practice and Extension

Have students make up word problems to solve with *bills* and to check with multiplication.

Have students use *cards* or *dice* and work in pairs. The first two or three numbers turned over are the dividend for both, the following two are separate divisors. Students do problems and check. The winner is the student with the larger quotient or remainder.

Give students remainders, and have them build problems to fit. What problems can't be built with a given remainder? (ones with a smaller divisor)

Division 4

Skill: To find missing dividends and divisors

Time: 2 periods

Materials:

Use several of the following (about 20 per student):
tiles

1" × 1" construction paper squares
1 cm cubes
counters
See Reproducibles for: bills—1s only

Anticipatory Set

Use *one of the manipulatives in the Materials list.*

Write $3\overline{)15}$ with 5 above. Review with students that this shows 15 divided into three groups with five in a group. Have students construct arrays that show this. Have them draw the division fence around their array and write the division sentence.

Repeat for 12 ÷ 2 and 16 ÷ 4.

Procedure 1

To find missing dividends

Use *one of the manipulatives in the Materials list.*

Write on the board: ? ÷ 2 = 6. Say: We don't know how many we started with, but what does the two mean?

Students respond: Something is divided into 2 groups, or we have groups of 2.

Ask: What does the six mean?

Students respond: The 6 means we have 6 in a group, or 6 groups of 2.

Have students build an array that shows two groups with six in a group.

Students do so and discover they have used 12 tiles:

⬡⬡⬡⬡⬡⬡   12 ÷ 2 = 6
⬡⬡⬡⬡⬡⬡

What if I had written the problem as $2\overline{)??}$ with 6 above? Would this have been easier to solve? (yes) Why?

Students respond: It looks more like what we are doing with tiles.

What does this suggest to you?

Students respond: Rewrite the problem.

Give students several more missing dividend problems. Each time, have them identify the meaning of each number, build the array, and write the complete division sentence as in the illustration above.

Ask them to be able to explain how they went about solving the problems.

Students solve problems.

What ways did you find to solve these problems? For example: ? ÷ 2 = 6.

Students respond: Some laid out groups of 6, some did groups of 2, some noticed they could multiply to find the answer.

Some of you laid out groups and added them. Do you know a shortcut way of adding same-sized groups? (multiplication)

Yes, you are multiplying the number of groups by the number in each group. Do we ever use multiplication in doing a regular division problem?

Students respond: Yes, when we multiply back to find out how many of our total we've been able to put into groups so far.

You could also solve this by thinking of multiples. How would that work?

Students respond: If you used multiples of 6, you find the second multiple of 6, since you have 2 groups.

Often a problem can be solved in many ways. Now try ? ÷ 3 = 13. Use either tiles or paper and pencil, and rewrite the problem first if you wish. That's a lot of tiles. Do you know a faster way?

Students arrive at an answer. They discuss multiplying to find the missing dividend.

Have students construct problems for others to solve. They should make up story problems to go along. For example: I started with a mystery amount of money. I spent it on 2 tapes, each costing $6. How much money did I start with?

Continue the procedure until students demonstrate an understanding of how to find missing dividends.

Procedure 2

To find missing divisors

Use *another of the manipulatives from the Materials list.*

Write on the board 12 ÷ ? = 6. What does the 12 mean?

Students respond: How much we start with.

Ask: What does the question mark stand for?

Students respond: How many groups 12 is divided into, or the size group we'll take out.

What does the six mean?

Students respond: 6 are in each group, or we have 6 groups.

Say: Use 12 tiles to build an array that has 6 in a group. Find how many groups you have.

Students do this. They have two groups.

What if I had written ?)$\overline{12}$? Would this have been easier to solve? (yes) Why?

Students respond: It looks more like what we are doing with tiles on the paper. We could rewrite the problem.

Give students several more missing divisor problems. Each time, have them identify the meaning of each number, build the array, and write the complete division sentence, as in the Procedure 1 illustration.

Ask them to be able to explain how they went about solving the problems.

Students solve the problems.

What ways did you find to solve these problems? For example: 12 ÷ ? = 6.

Students respond: Some laid out groups of 6 until they had used up 12 tiles. Some recognized it as a division problem, dividing 12 by 6. Some recognized that they could think of multiples of 6 until they reached 12, a multiplication problem.

Have students build a 6 × 2 array. This shows 12 ÷ 2 = 6. Have them turn their array around. What does this show?

What is the total in each case? (12) In one we have groups of six, and in one we have groups of two.

Discuss the relationship of multiplication and division and that a problem often may be solved in many ways.

Give students more difficult problems, and have them use either tiles or paper and pencil. They should rewrite the problem first.

Add estimation questions at this time, such as: What number would be too big? Too small? What two numbers will the answer come between?

Students now construct problems for others to solve. They make up story problems to go along. For example: I started with 18 buttons. I need to sew 6 on each shirt. How many shirts can I put buttons on?

Continue the procedure until students are able to explain the process of how to find missing divisors.

Practice and Extension

Have students take handfuls of *tiles* and construct problems. Have students discuss how to handle remainders.

Have students write division problems and work in pairs to play Missing Numbers. They throw a *die* or use a *two-colored counter:* An even number or a certain color means they cover the *divisor* with a *counter.* An odd number or the other color means they cover the *dividend.* They switch problems and solve them, keeping a total of the missing numbers found. The lowest score at the end of five rounds wins.

Division 5

Skill: To divide 2-digit numbers by 1-digit numbers

Time: 1 week

Materials:

counters: 27 per group

file-folder or other place value (pv) mats to 100s or 1000s

pv materials to 10s

dice: 1 per student pair

See Reproducibles for: directions for file-folder pv mats, pv mats to 100s—1 per group, division paper—4 sheets per student, bills to 10s—run off in different colors

Note: If students are not used to dividing with base ten materials on a place value mat, do Division 2, Procedures 3 and 4. This will reinforce basic division concepts and provide a concrete base for the written division algorithm.

The written format in Procedures 3 to 5 is a change from the standard form. No "bring down" is used because nothing is brought down when dividing objects. DMSB—divide, multiply, subtract, and bring down, becomes DMSR—divide, multiply, subtract, and regroup. Send a note home to parents, explaining that this way of writing the problems more accurately reflects division. Otherwise, you will soon find out who is getting help at home.

Anticipatory Set

Use *counters* and *paper*.

Say to student groups: Imagine that 3 students have up to 27 marbles (counters) between them. Write as many problems and solutions as you can using those facts.

After 5 to 10 minutes, discuss results.

Procedure 1 □■

To establish the concept of dividing 2-digit by 1-digit numbers

Use *pv mats, pv materials to 10s,* and *dice.*

Say: Today we'll be dividing yo-yos, which come ten to a package. Your ten rods will be one package. One cubes will be separate yo-yos. You have 24 yo-yos. Show that with blocks on your mats.

On the board write the problem as in Illustration 1b.

1a **1b**

We'll give the yo-yos evenly to two friends.

Write the two and the division fence on the board as in Illustration 2b. Say: Divide yours into two groups.

Students divide rods and cubes as in Illustration 2a.

2a **2b**

Tens
$2 \div 2 = 1$
$1 \times 2 = 2$

Ones
$4 \div 2 = 2$
$2 \times 2 = 4$

Ask: How many groups of tens did you make? (2) How many whole packages are in each group? (1) Where can I record that?

Students respond: Above, in the tens column.

Yes, if you divide tens, your answer is in tens.

Draw in the divided rods and the 1 on the board.

What division fact did you show? ($2 \div 2 = 1$) Write this on the board.

How can we check that our division is right? (with multiplication: $1 \times 2 = 2$)

How many groups of ones, or single yo-yos, did you make? (2) How many yo-yos are in each group? (2) Where can I record that?

Students respond: Above, in the ones column.

Yes, if you divide ones, your answer is in ones. Write the one cubes and the 2 on the board.

What division fact did you show? ($4 \div 2 = 2$)

Write this on the board.

Ask: How can we check? (with multiplication: $2 \times 2 = 4$)

How many yo-yos in all does each friend get?

Students respond: One ten and two ones equals 12 yo-yos.

How could I check the whole problem? (with multiplication)

Write and solve 2 × 12 on the board.

Repeat with other 2-digit numbers *with and without regrouping,* recording only the results on the board after each step.

When students are comfortable with making divisions and trades, have them write results. In pairs, one should do problems with blocks, and one should record each step as in Illustration 2b. Work through several problems with students before having them work on their own.

Students need much practice at this stage of both writing and using concrete materials. They should check all results with multiplication. See Division 5 for checking division with multiplication.

Use dice to generate problems: The first two numbers are the dividend, and the third is the divisor. Discuss what to do with remainders.

Repeat the procedure with different materials.

Procedure 2

To develop a written algorithm; no regrouping

Use *pv materials* and *pv mats.*

Write 36 ÷ 3 on the board in a place value format.

Tell students that 36 bats go evenly into 3 caves. This time when we divide, we will record *all* steps.

Students place three ten rods and six one cubes at the bottom of their mats.

We'll make a chart that will help us when we don't have blocks. Every time we take out enough to put one more bat into *each* cave, how many have we taken out? (3)

The second time, how many total bats are now taken care of? (6) Another time? (9) We're talking about multiples of three. Make a chart:

Number of Groups Out	Bats Divided
1	3
2	6
3	9

We'll start by dividing the ten rods into three groups. Look at the chart of multiples, and predict how many groups of three ten rods we'll be able to take care of.

Students predict 1 group of 3. They divide their rods.

Ask: How many ten rods are in each cave? (1) How many bats so far in each? (10) Where will I write that?

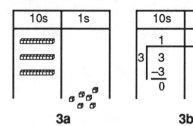

3a **3b**

Students respond: Above, in the tens column.

Yes, if you divide tens, you end up with tens. One is in each cave. 3 ÷ 3 = 1. How could I check that? (with multiplication) Yes, I multiply back 1 × 3 = 3 to check that I divided right and to see how many bats I've taken care of.

How do I see on paper whether any tens are left? (subtract those taken out) I'll write it this way (Illustration 3b)—no groups of 10 bats are left.

I wrote exactly what you did to find no more ten rods. Written numbers just show what would be happening if we used blocks all the time.

Now what bats do you have to divide?

Students respond: 6 in the ones column.

Do you see anything on your multiples chart that would help you predict the answer?

Students respond: 2 groups of 3 bats take care of all 6 bats. They divide the one cubes. (Illustration 4a)

4a **4b**

Where do I write this? (Above the ones. If we divide ones we get ones.)

How do I check that no bats are left? (multiply) I multiply 2 bats in each cave times 3 caves and find I've taken care of 6 more bats. (Illustration 4b)

How do I see whether any are left? (subtract)

Look at the bat piles. How many total bats do you show in each cave? (12) What have we written at the top of our problem? (12)

Let's check the whole problem. How many caves? (3) How many bats in each cave? (12)

Write 3 × 12 on the board, and have students solve it with you.

Say: Check that the answer equals the number you started with.

Repeat with other problems. Emphasize that you are writing just what they do with the blocks.

Students work in pairs. One works with the blocks, and a partner records each step as in Illustration 4b. They make multiples charts and try to predict the answer to each problem before using the blocks.

Students need much practice at this stage of both using the blocks and writing the process. With practice, they should be able to do the problem first on paper and then check with blocks.

Procedure 3

To divide 2-digit by 1-digit numbers with regrouping; 2-digit quotients

Use *pv mats*, *division paper*, and *pv materials or bills*.

When we divide 2-digit numbers, sometimes we have to regroup. We're going to figure out how to write this down so that our written problem shows exactly what we do when we divide.

We'll start with 47 socks that we want to put into 3 boxes. They come in packages of 10, and we have 7 extra.

Write 47 ÷ 3 on the board.

Students place blocks for 47 on their mats.

Ask: How should we start? (make a multiples chart)

Number of Groups Out	Socks Divided
1	3
2	6
3	9
4	12

You want to divide four packages of socks. Would anything on your multiples chart help you predict the answer? (1 × 3 = 3)

But we have *four* packages of 10 socks.

Students explain the one package left is not enough to divide evenly. They divide and find one package for each box, with one left over. (Illustration 5b)

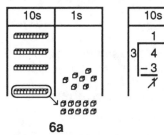

5a　　　　**5b**

How do I write this? (put a 1 in the tens column) How do I check how many socks are in boxes?

Students respond: Multiply 1 package times 3 boxes.

How can I tell how many are left over? (subtract) I show one left over. That's exactly what you have with your blocks.

What can you do about the leftover package?

Students respond: Trade it for 10 single socks. They do this and find they have 17 ones. (Illustration 6a)

I need to show the regrouping in my problem. How many tens do you have left? (none) I'll cross out the one leftover ten.

Do I still have seven ones? (no) I'll cross that out and write what we have now, 17. (Illustration 6b)

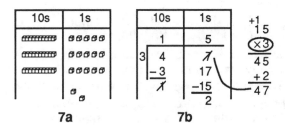

6a　　　　**6b**

Now divide 17 into three groups. Check the multiples chart, and make a prediction.

Students respond: 5 × 3 = 15, some will be left over.

Why can't I use 6 × 3?

Students respond: That would take 18, and you don't have 18 socks. They divide the blocks and discover there are 5 socks in each box, with 2 left over.

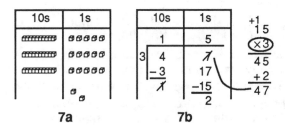

7a　　　　**7b**

Where will I write the five single socks in each box? (in the ones column) How do I check? (multiply) Finish the problem on the board. (Illustration 7b)

What is left to do? (check the whole problem) Multiply with students: 15 socks in 3 boxes is 45 socks. Is that what we started with?

Students respond: No, 2 were left over. Add those to the socks we did put in boxes.

Repeat with other problems. If the tens digit is only one or two more than the divisor, students will not have to exchange more than two ten rods.

When students are comfortable with the skill, have them begin writing each step on division paper as you write on the board.

When they can write each step accurately, student pairs make multiples charts and try to predict the answer to each step. One student works with the blocks, while the other records each step.

Students need much practice at this stage of both using the blocks and writing the process.

Procedure 4

To divide 2-digit by 1-digit numbers with regrouping; 1-digit quotients

Use *pv mats*, *division paper*, and *pv materials or bills*.

Write 27 ÷ 3 on the board. Have students place materials and develop a chart of multiples. Now tell students to start by dividing the tens.

Students respond: We don't have enough tens to put into three groups.

Say: You show no tens as having been divided. I could put a zero in the tens column, but we don't write numbers starting with zero. What's the next step? (regroup the tens for 20 ones)

Follow the previous procedure to finish the problem. Remind students that when we divide ones, we get ones and need to put the answer in the *ones* column:

10s	1s	10s	1s
			9
3)2̸	1̸	3)2̸	1̸
	27		27
			−27
			0

What if I put the nine in the *tens* column. What would the nine be worth? (90)

That would mean I divided 27 into 3 groups and got 90 in each group. That would be wonderful if I were dividing money, but it's just not possible.

Do several more problems of this type with students. After each step with the blocks, have them write on their division paper as you work on the board.

When students feel comfortable with the skill, they do each step first on paper and then check with the materials.

Procedure 5

To divide with zeros in the quotient

Use *pv mats*, *division paper*, and *pv materials or bills*.

Place 30 ÷ 3 on the board, and have students place blocks. Have students make a chart of multiples and divide their ten rods. Record this on the board.

Say: We have zero ones. What's zero divided into three groups? (zero) If I leave the ones column blank and say my answer is 1, what's the problem?

Students respond: We have 1 ten, not just 1.

We need zero as a placeholder. How many blocks total do you show in each group? (10) I have to show the same thing in my answer.

10s	1s
1	0
3)3	0
−3	−0
0	0

Repeat with other problems. Students write on division paper after each step, as you work on the board. When they feel comfortable with the process, have them do each step first on paper and then check with the manipulatives.

Practice and Extension

Use any of the following materials: *two-colored counters, different-colored counters, chip-trading materials, interlocking cubes, bundled craft sticks,* or *bills.* Use *cards* or *dice* to generate numbers for division problems. Students can work in teams, one using the manipulative and one writing on paper.

Play Money Madness. Divide the class into two teams. Have them use *$90 in bills* and *pv mats.* Use *cards* or *dice* to generate divisors. In turn, teams are given a divisor and must divide their money and then write the problem on paper. Remainders are discarded. The team whose money lasts longer is the winner.

Explore problem solving with remainders. Example: Mae needed 13 feet of string, which came 6 feet to a package. How many packages did she need? By having students use manipulatives or draw pictures, it becomes clear that Mae will need to buy an extra package.

Write two identical division problems such as $2)\overline{\,}^{\,4}$ on the board. You will play against the class. Use *cards* or *spinners* to get numbers to fill in. Remainders are allowed.

Other types of problems are $)\overline{25}$.

Ask such questions as, If I divide by six, how many numbers will end up with a remainder of one?

Division 6

Skill: To understand divisibility by 2, 5, 3, 6, 4, and 8

Time: 1–2 periods per number

Materials:

Secret Code number line (directions in Manipulative Information section)

light-colored markers: 3 per student

objects: cubes, or counters

See Reproducibles for: hundred boards—1 per student where called for, bills to 100s—in different colors

Anticipatory Set

Use *Secret Code number line.*

Several days before each lesson, you may want to mark the number line with all or some of the multiples involved and ask the students to figure out what the coded numbers have in common.

Write on the board the number of students in the class. Can the class can be divided evenly in half or into groups of two? As students number off, even numbered students stand. Write the odd numbers on the left of the board and the even numbers on the right.

Point out that the numbers on the right, the multiples of two, meant we had completed another pair, or that we divided the last two students evenly into teams. Do they see any patterns to the numbers? When might it be helpful to know whether a number can be divided evenly?

Procedure 1　□■

To understand divisibility by 2 and by 5

Use *hundred boards* and *markers (2 colors).*

We're going to discover how to tell, without counting off, whether a number can be divided evenly into groups of two or five.

Have students use one color marker to color in the *top half* of all the multiples of 2, from 1 to 50. Relate this to counting off by twos.

Ask: Can you predict will happen on the rest of the board? (yes) Can you complete the board without counting? Why?

Students discuss patterns and then complete the board.

What do you notice about the numbers you colored? Remember, we're looking for a rule that will tell us whether a number can be divided evenly by two.

Have students discuss. They should notice odd and even numbers. If they do not see that colored numbers end in zero, two, four, six, and eight, ask whether numbers ending in three are divisible by two. Numbers ending in five?

Tell students to take their other marker and color in the *bottom half* of all the multiples of 5, from 1 to 50.

1	2	3	4	5	6	7	8	9	10
11	12	13	14	15	16	17	18	19	20
21	22	23	24	25	26	27	28	29	30
31	32	33	34	35	36	37	38	39	40
41	42	43	44	45	46	47	48	49	50
51	52	53	54	55	56	57	58	59	60
61	62	63	64	65	66	67	68	69	70
71	72	73	74	75	76	77	78	79	80
81	82	83	84	85	86	87	88	89	90
91	92	93	94	95	96	97	98	99	100

Ask: Were there any patterns? What will happen on the rest of the board? Is it possible to complete the board without counting?

Students discuss and complete the board.

Now we're looking for a rule that will tell us whether a number can be divided evenly by five. What do you notice about your new numbers?

Students discuss that they end in zero or five. If they do not see this, ask whether any numbers ending in three are divisible by five.

What can we see about the overlapping numbers? Lead students to discuss the following ideas:

What can be said about numbers ending in zero? In any even number? In five?

What would happen if we used a thousand board?

What have we learned about multiples that we could make into two division rules?

Students discuss, write two class rules, and check their theories by practicing 3-digit numbers.

To start, suggest 110. Is it divisible by 2? By 5?

Students predict, and check by counting by twos and fives.

Procedure 2

To practice identifying divisibility by 2 and by 5

Use *objects (differing amounts to each student).*

Have each student write down his or her number of objects. Ask: Will that amount be divisible by two? Why or why not?

Students discuss and then prove their answers by trying to divide their objects into two groups.

Have each student record how many objects he or she had in each group and how many *more* are needed to be able to divide by two.

Students should realize that if the number was not divisible by two, then they needed only one more object to make it possible. They discuss why this is so.

Now ask each student to predict whether his or her objects can be divided evenly into five groups.

Students discuss and then prove their answers by trying to divide their objects into five equal groups.

Ask: Which amounts were divisible by five? Why? (They ended in 0 or 5.) Did some amounts divide evenly into both two and five groups? Which were those? (Those ending in 0.)

Students whose objects were not divisible by five record how many *more* objects they would need in order to divide into five equal groups. (from 1 to 4) They discuss why they wouldn't need five more.

Put a chart on the board with headings such as the following across the top:

Even + Even	Even + Odd	Odd + Odd	Both ÷ by 2	Both ÷ by 5
22 + 24 = 48 (even)			22 + 24 = 48 (even)	

Pairs join their objects and chart their results. They discuss results and reasons:

```
even + even  =  even
even + odd   =  odd
odd + odd    =  even
both ÷ by 2  =  even, ÷ by 2
both ÷ by 5  =  even or odd, ÷ by 5
```

If they join their amount with another group, can they predict divisibility of the new total?

Procedure 3

To understand divisibility by 3

Use *hundred boards (1 per student), markers (1 color per student),* and *bills to 100s.*

Tell students to use only one color marker to color in all the multiples of 3 to the number 60 on their hundred boards, circling any patterns they find.

1	2	3̶	4	5	6̶	7	8	9̶	10
11	12̶	13	14	15̶	16	17	18̶	19	20
21̶	22	23	24̶	25	26	27̶	28	29	30̶
31	32	33̶	34	35	36̶	37	38	39̶	40
41	42̶	43	44	45̶	46	47	48̶	49	50
51̶	52	53	54̶	55	56	57̶	58	59	60̶
61	62	63	64	65	66	67	68	69	70
71	72	73	74	75	76	77	78	79	80
81	82	83	84	85	86	87	88	89	90
91	92	93	94	95	96	97	98	99	100

Ask: Can you mark the rest of the numbers that divide evenly by three without counting? (yes) If there were more numbers, what would you expect to have happen? (pattern would continue)

Students discuss patterns and then finish coloring in the multiples of three on the hundred board.

Say: Take some of your money. Make the total a multiple of three. Now divide your money into three equal piles.

Students discover that any multiple of three is divisible by three.

Imagine you want to share money with two friends so that you all have the same amount. We need a way to tell which numbers divide evenly by three. How are all of these numbers alike?

Students discuss. They probably will not be able to discover the rule.

Write numbers that are divisible by three on the left of the board, and those that are not on the right. Add the digits for each.

Ask: Now can you find a pattern?

If students can't discover the rule, give them a hint to check which digit totals are colored on their hundred boards. It may take a while before they discover they should add all the individual digits of a number. If the resulting number is divisible by three, so is the original number.

Students write a rule about dividing by three, working in groups or pairs for this part of the exercise.

After writing the rules, each group of students tests their theory by choosing random numbers, predicting whether or not they are divisible by three, and then dividing by three to check.

Have the class discuss and decide on one way to word the rule about dividing by three.

Procedure 4

To practice identifying divisibility by 3

Use *objects (differing amounts to each student).*

Adapt Procedure 2 to explore and predict divisibility by three. Students record exact amounts.

Procedure 5

To understand divisibility by 6

Use *hundred boards, markers (3 colors per student),* and *bills to 100s.*

Have students use one color to color in the top third of squares that are multiples of 2, to the number 60 on their hundred boards.

Review divisibility by 2: numbers that end in 0, 2, 4, 6, or 8.

Repeat with another color to color in the middle third of numbers to 60 divisible by 3.

Review divisibility by 3: numbers whose digits add to a number that is divisible by 3.

Use the third color to color the bottom third of all numbers to 60 that are multiples of 6. We are looking for a rule to tell which numbers are divisible by 6.

1	2	3	4	5	6	7	8	9	10
11	12	13	14	15	16	17	18	19	20
21	22	23	24	25	26	27	28	29	30
31	32	33	34	35	36	37	38	39	40
41	42	43	44	45	46	47	48	49	50
51	52	53	54	55	56	57	58	59	60
61	62	63	64	65	66	67	68	69	70
71	72	73	74	75	76	77	78	79	80
81	82	83	84	85	86	87	88	89	90
91	92	93	94	95	96	97	98	99	100

Students do the activity, discuss patterns, and finish coloring in the multiples.

They should discover the rule: Numbers divisible by six are divisible by both two and three. They discuss the need to make two divisibility checks.

Give students 3-digit numbers to test. Ask students to predict divisibility and then to use bills to actually divide the amount into six piles.

Procedure 6

To practice identifying divisibility by 6

Use *objects (differing amounts to each student).*

Adapt Procedure 2 to explore and predict divisibility by six. Students record exact amounts.

Procedure 7

To understand divisibility by 9

Use *hundred boards, markers (1 color per student),* and *bills to 100s.*

Adapt Procedure 3 for divisibility by 9. A number is divisible by 9 if the sum of its digits is divisible by 9. For example, 243: 2 + 4 + 3 = 9, 9 ÷ 9 = 1. The number 243 is divisible by 9.

Adapt Procedure 2 for practice and exploration of the skill.

Procedure 8

To understand divisibility by 4

Use *hundred boards, markers (1 color per student),* and *bills.*

Tell students to use only one color marker to color in all the multiples of 4 to the number 60 on their hundred boards, circling any patterns they find.

We are looking for a rule that will tell us which numbers are divisible by four.

1	2	3	4	5	6	7	8	9	10
11	12	13	14	15	16	17	18	19	20
21	22	23	24	25	26	27	28	29	30
31	32	33	34	35	36	37	38	39	40
41	42	43	44	45	46	47	48	49	50
51	52	53	54	55	56	57	58	59	60
61	62	63	64	65	66	67	68	69	70
71	72	73	74	75	76	77	78	79	80
81	82	83	84	85	86	87	88	89	90
91	92	93	94	95	96	97	98	99	100

Ask: What patterns did you find?

Can you mark the rest of the numbers that divide evenly by four without counting? (yes)

Students discuss patterns and then finish coloring in the multiples of four on the hundred board.

Imagine you want to share money with three friends so that you *all* have the same amount. We need a way to tell which numbers divide evenly by four. How are all of these numbers alike?

Students probably will not be able to discover the rule.

Write numbers that are divisible by four on the left of the board, and those that are not on the right.

Write a 1 in front of each number to change it to a number in the hundreds. Draw one circle around *all but the hundreds digit* in each number. Now can you find a pattern?

Divisible by 4   Not Divisible by 4
1(36)
                            1(37)
                            1(38)
                            1(39)
1(40)

If students can't discover the rule, have them divide the circled numbers by four.

Students should discover that if the number formed by the tens and ones digit is divisible by four, the entire number is divisible by four. *They do not need to check the hundreds or thousands digit because 100 and 1,000 always divide by four.*

Give students 3-digit numbers to test. Ask students to predict divisibility and then to use bills to actually divide the amount into four piles. Explore how we know when leap years will occur.

Procedure 9   □ ■

To understand divisibility by 8

Use *bills to 100s.*

We will be looking for a rule to tell which numbers are divisible by eight. Assign students consecutive amounts to test, starting with $124.

Say: Divide your amount, if possible, into *four* piles. Record your result. Then see whether you can divide it into eight piles. Record your result. Add both results to a class chart.

Divisible by 4	Divisible by 8	Not Divisible by 4 or 8
124		
		125
		126
		127
128	128	
		129
		130
		131
132		

Discuss patterns in the chart.

If students do not see the rule, *circle the entire number* in the Divisible by 8 column. The rule: A number is divisible by 8 if the number formed by the hundreds, tens, and ones digits is divisible by 8. They do not need to check the digits above the hundreds because those will always divide by 8.

Give students 3- and 4-digit numbers to test. Ask students to predict divisibility and then to use bills to actually divide the amount into eight piles.

Practice and Extension

Students keep tallies recording how many numbers on their hundred board that they could divide by two. Show them that the common way of marking tallies is a way of counting multiples of five. (卌). Why might people in the past have chosen to use fives to count?

Have students work in pairs and use *dice* or *cards* to generate separate 3- or 4-digit numbers. They get 2 points if their number is divisible by 2, 3 points if it divisible by 3, and so on. Results are checked with a *calculator.*

Have students make up story problems in which they would be dividing by three. They can use *dice* to generate numbers, predict divisibility, and then divide with *bills, objects,* or *calculators.* They get points for numbers that work.

Skill: To divide 3-digit or larger numbers by 1-digit numbers

counter-trading materials to 100s

See Reproducibles for: directions for file-folder pv mats if needed, pv mats to 100s, division paper, bills to 100s or larger—in different colors, counter-trading boards to 1000s

Time: 4–5 periods

Materials:

place value (pv) materials to 100s; use counters for 100s if needed

file-folder or other pv mats to 1000s

Note: Make sure students can divide 2-digit by 1-digit numbers easily. If they cannot, teach them the procedures in Division 5 first. Students will catch on quickly to dividing 3-digit or larger numbers and will become competent in the skill in a shorter time.

The written format is a change from the standard form. No "bring down" is used because nothing is brought down when dividing objects. DMSB—divide, multiply, subtract, and bring down, becomes DMSR—divide, multiply, subtract, and regroup. Your students will think of some way to remember this! Send a note home to parents, explaining that this way of writing the problems more accurately reflects division. If you don't, you will soon find out who is getting help at home.

Anticipatory Set

Use *pv materials*.

Have students make 3-digit numbers with blocks and then divide them into three groups. Discuss similarities to previous division. Did anyone have to regroup? Can students make a problem that requires only one trade? Repeat until students can make trades easily.

Procedure 1

To divide 3-digit by 1-digit numbers with no regrouping; to develop a written algorithm

Use *pv materials* and *pv mats*.

Write 366 ÷ 3 on the board in a place value format. This could be 366 tapes shipped to 3 stores, the same amount to each store.

Say: This time when you divide, I'm going to record on the board all the steps you do.

Each time we take out enough to send one more tape to *each* store, how many do we take out? (3) The second time, how many are now sent? (6) Once more? (9) We have multiples of three, since we're dividing by three.

Make a chart on the board:

Number of Groups Out	Tapes Already Divided
1	3
2	6
3	9

Students place 366 at the bottom of their mats.

What do we divide first? (hundreds) Use the multiples chart, and predict how many groups of three hundred flats we'll be able to take care of.

Students predict one group of three. They divide:

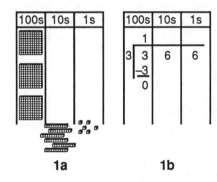

1a   **1b**

Ask: How many hundreds in each group? (1) How many tapes for each store? (100) Where do I write that?

Students respond: Above, in the hundreds column.

Yes, if you divide hundreds, your answer is in hundreds. One hundred in each store: 3 ÷ 3 = 1. How could I check that? (with multiplication) I multiply a group of 100 tapes times 3 stores to check that I divided right.

With real tapes you can *look,* but how do I see on paper whether any hundreds are left? (subtract those taken care of) I subtract and find no groups of hundreds tapes left to divide. (Illustration 1b)

I wrote *exactly what you did* to divide the hundreds. Written math language just shows what would be really happening if we used blocks all the time.

Now what tapes do you have to divide?

Students respond: 6 in the tens column.

You want to divide 6 groups of 10 tapes. Can you use the multiples chart to predict the answer?

Students respond: 3 groups of 2 would take care of all 6 tens. They divide the ten rods. (Illustration 2a)

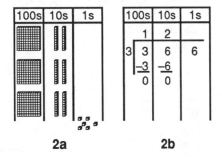

2a   2b

Ask: How many groups of 10 tapes go to each store? (2) Where should I write this? (above the tens)

How do I check that I divided right? (multiply) Two groups of 10 tapes in each store times 3 stores; I've taken care of 60 more tapes. How do I see whether any are left? (subtract) (Illustration 2b)

Repeat the procedure to divide the ones:

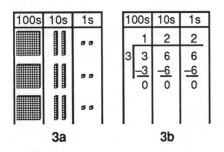

3a   3b

What do the blocks show for each store? (122) What does the written problem show? (122)

Let's check the *whole* problem. How many stores? (3) How many tapes in each store? (122)

Write 3×122 on the board, and have students solve it, checking that the answer agrees with the number of starting tapes.

Give students other problems to do with their blocks. For each one, make a chart of multiples and work through the recording on the board. Emphasize that you are writing just what they do with the blocks.

When students are confidently able to tell you what to record, go on to Procedure 2.

Procedure 2 ☐■

To write 3-digit divided by 1-digit problems; no regrouping

Use *pv mats, division paper,* and *pv materials or bills*.

Have students work in teams of two. One works with blocks, while the other records each step as in Procedure 1. Have students together make the multiples charts. Work through problems with students until all are recording correctly.

As students gain confidence, they try to predict the answer to each problem before finding it with the blocks. Students need much practice at this stage of both using the blocks and writing the process.

Procedure 3 ☐■

To divide 3-digit by 1-digit numbers with regrouping

Use *pv mats, division paper,* and *pv materials or bills*.

Say: When you divide, sometimes you have to regroup. We'll write the regrouping so that our written problem shows exactly what we do with the blocks.

Write 463 ÷ 3 on the board: We have 463 buttons that need to go into 3 boxes. They come in packages of 100. Inside each package are bags of 10. We have 4 packages, 6 bags, and 3 extra buttons.

Students place blocks and chart the multiples.

Before you divide your packages of 100 buttons, predict how many will be in each box. Will the chart help?

Students respond: $1 \times 3 = 3$.

But we have *4* packages of 100 buttons.

Students respond: Yes, but you only have one package left. It's not enough to divide evenly. They divide and find one package for each box; one left over:

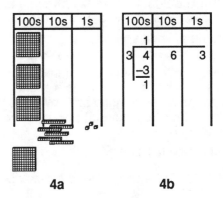

4a   4b

How do I write this? (a one in the hundreds column)

How will I check how many buttons I've put into boxes?

Students respond: Multiply 1 package of 100×3 boxes.

How can I tell how many are left over? (subtract) I show one left over, which is what you have with your blocks. (Illustration 4b)

What can you do about the leftover package?

Students respond: Trade it for 10 bags of 10 buttons.

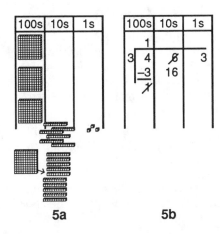

5a   **5b**

Say: I need to show the regrouping. How many hundreds do you have left? (none) *I'll cross out the 1 leftover hundred.* Do I still have 6 tens? (no) *I'll cross out 6 tens and write what we have now, 16.* (Illustration 5b)

Now divide 16 into 3 groups. Check the chart.

Students respond: $5 \times 3 = 15$. One will be left over.

Why can't I use 6×3?

Students respond: That would take 18, and you don't have 18 packages. They divide the blocks and discover 5 bags are in each box, with 1 left over:

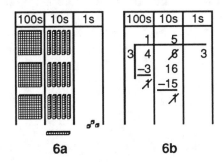

6a   **6b**

Where do I write the 5 bags of 10 buttons per box? (the tens column) How do I check? (multiply, then subtract)

Complete this step on the board. (Illustration 6b)

Repeat procedure to divide ones as shown in Illustration 7a and 7b.

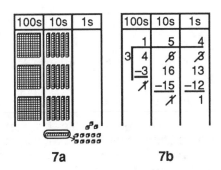

7a   **7b**

What is left to do? (check the problem) Write 3×154, and multiply with students: 154 buttons in 3 boxes is 462 buttons. Is that what we started with?

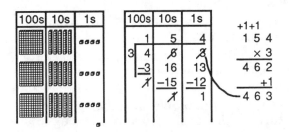

Students respond: No, 1 was left over. Add it to the buttons we did put in boxes.

Work through other problems with students. Pick numbers without a lot of blocks to trade.

When students are comfortable with the skill they write each step on division paper as you write on the board.

When they can write each step accurately with you, have them work in teams of two, charting the multiples and taking turns writing.

As students gain confidence, they do problems on paper before finding it with the blocks. They will need practice at the stage of both using the blocks and writing the process.

Procedure 4

To practice and write division of 3-digit by 1-digit numbers with regrouping

Use *division paper, pv mats or counter-trading boards,* and *bills or counter-trading materials.*

Have students practice with different materials, making up stories to go with their problems.

Some students will be able to divide using their facts, rather than making a multiples chart. Encourage the others to estimate the quotient and then check with the multiples chart.

Procedure 5　□■

To divide 3-digit by 1-digit numbers; 2-digit quotients

Use *pv mats*, *division paper*, and *pv materials or bills*.

Write 163 ÷ 3. Have students place blocks or bills and develop a chart of multiples. Start by dividing the hundreds.

Students respond: We do not have enough hundreds to put into three groups.

Say: You show no hundreds as having been divided. I could put a zero in the hundreds column, but we don't write numbers starting with zero.

Ask: What's the next step? (Regroup the hundreds for 10 tens.)

Follow Procedure 4 to finish the problem. Remind students that when we divide tens, we get tens and need to put the answer in the tens column.

Do several more problems of this type with students. After each step with the blocks, have them write on their division paper as you work on the board. When they feel comfortable with this skill, have them do each step first on paper and then check with the blocks.

Procedure 6　□■

To divide 3-digit by 1-digit numbers; zeros in the quotient

Use *pv mats*, *division paper*, and *pv materials or bills*.

Write 312 ÷ 3 on the board. Have students place blocks, chart multiples, and divide their hundreds. Record this on the board.

Now let's look at the tens.

Students respond: We don't have enough tens.

Ask: Now what? (regroup) What do I write in the tens column? (0) Why? (as a placeholder)

Students regroup and finish the problem:

	100s	10s	1s
	1	0	4
3	3	$\cancel{1}$	$\cancel{2}$
	−3		12
	0		−12
			1

What if I hadn't written anything in the tens column?

Students respond: The answer would be 14.

How many blocks total do you show in each group? (104) I have to show the same thing in my answer.

Do several more problems of this type with students. Have students write on division paper after each step with blocks. When they are comfortable with the skill, have them write first and then check the blocks.

Practice and Extension

Use any of the following materials: *different-colored counters, counter-trading materials, interlocking cubes, bundled craft sticks* or *bills*. Use *cards* or *dice* to generate numbers for division problems. Students can work in teams, one using the materials and one writing on the paper.

Play Money Madness. Divide the class into two teams. Have them use *$900 in bills* and *pv mats*. Use *cards* or *dice* to generate divisors. In turn, teams are given a divisor and a scenario, for example, to buy palm trees. They divide the bills and write the problem on paper. Remainders are discarded. The team whose money lasts longer is the winner.

On the board or *large sheets of paper taped together*, make a number one or two digits larger than the number of students in your classroom. Example: Many fruit flies are in your orchard. If they get trapped evenly, how many are in each of your six traps?

Each student gets a chance to do one part of the problem. Allow the problem to remain on the board, or taped on the wall, through several class periods so that you can help each student if needed and so that all can reinforce by giving oral feedback. Students are very impressed with being able to solve this extremely large division problem and discover it is as easy as a smaller number to solve; it just takes a little more time.

Division 8

Skill: To divide 2- and 3-digit numbers by ten, multiples of ten, and 2-digit numbers

Time: 4+ periods

Materials:

light-colored markers: 1 per student

file-folder or other place value (pv) mats to 1000s

pv materials to 100s

counter-trading materials to 100s

dice

See Reproducibles for: hundred boards—1 per student, directions for file-folder pv mats if needed, pv mats to 100s, division paper, bills to 100s or larger—in different colors, counter-trading boards to 1000s

Note: Make sure students can divide 2-digit by 1-digit numbers easily. If they cannot, teach them the procedures in Division 7 first. Then you will find students catch on quickly to dividing by 2-digit numbers. This actually will shorten the time it takes for students to become competent in the skill.

The written format is a change from the standard form. No "bring down" is used because nothing is brought down when dividing objects. DMSB—divide, multiply, subtract, and bring down, becomes DMSR—divide, multiply, subtract, and regroup. Your students will think of some way to remember this! Send a note home to parents, explaining that this way of writing the problems more accurately reflects division. If you don't, you will soon find out who is getting help at home.

Anticipatory Set

Use *hundred boards* and *markers*.

Have students take their hundred boards and color in three rows. Have them count how many are in each row and count how many rows. The number at the end of the row gives them the total number. Do they remember using hundred boards when they were learning to multiply? This time they want to discover how many tens are in each whole number. For example how many tens are in 30? In 36?

Continue coloring in rows and discussing the division problem shown. Repeat with multiples of 10.

Next call out random numbers, and have students tell the number of tens, twenties, or thirties in the number, until students can do this easily, using the hundred boards.

Procedure 1   ☐■

To divide 2- and 3-digit numbers by 10 and multiples of 10

Use *pv materials, pv mats, division paper,* and *hundred boards from the Anticipatory Set.*

Write 24 ÷ 10 on the board. Have students work in groups. We are selling cookies, and we have 10 customers. How many cookies will each customer get?

Make a multiples chart:

# Groups Out	Cookies Already Sold
1	10
2	20
3	30

Students place blocks for 24 at the bottom of their mats.

Say: You have 2 packages of 10 cookies each. Divide these equally among your 10 customers.

Students respond: We don't have enough to divide without regrouping. They regroup the 2 ten rods for 20 one cubes:

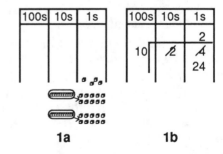

1a   **1b**

Ask: Do you have any more tens? (no) I'll cross out the tens.

Do you still have 4 ones? (no, we have 24) I'll cross it out and write 24 to show exactly what you did with the blocks. (Illustration 1b)

Now we need to divide 24 into 10 groups. Check the multiples chart, and predict the answer. Check your hundred board, as well.

Students see 2×10 would be 20. They divide the 24 ones into 10 groups and find 2 cookies for each customer, with 4 left over.

100s	10s	1s
		🍪🍪🍪🍪🍪🍪🍪🍪

100s	10s	1s
		2
10	~~12~~	~~24~~
		24
		−20
		4

2a   2b

You divided 24 into 10 groups and found 2 in each group. Where do I put my answer?

Students respond: Above the ones column because you are dividing ones.

How do I check to see for sure how many I've sold?

Students respond: Multiply 2×10.

How do I see whether any are left over?

Students respond: Subtract what you sold from what you started with; subtract 20 from 24.

Finish the problem on the board as in illustration 2b. Check with multiplication, reminding students they must add in the remaining four cookies that could not be sold. Leave the problem on the board.

Give students other 2-digit problems to divide by 10.

Students use materials and write each step on their division paper as you write on the board.

Discuss that the process is exactly the same as previous divisions. Students need much practice at this step of both using the materials and writing each step.

Students look for a pattern to dividing by 10 and should come to see that their answer is one place over from the number they started with. Relate this to the base ten system and changing places.

Write 221 ÷ 20 on the board. Say: 221 mosquitoes are going into 20 traps. How many mosquitoes are in each trap?

Make a multiples chart for 20, and have students talk through the problem *as if they were using materials*. Use the multiples chart and hundred boards to estimate.

Students write each step as you write on the board:

100s	10s	1s
	1	1
20 ~~2~~	~~2~~	~~1~~
	22	21
	−20	−20
	2	1

Do more problems until students can write the problems easily and estimate answers without the multiples chart.

Procedure 2   ☐

To practice and write division by 10 and multiples of 10

Use *dice, counter-trading materials and counter-trading mats*, or *bills and pv mats*.

Have students use dice to generate the 3-digit problems, as well as the multiples of 10. One can use materials, one records on paper, and a third student checks both.

Procedure 3   ☐ ◼

To divide by 2-digit numbers; to use estimates and multiples

Use *pv materials, pv mats, division paper,* and *hundred boards from the Anticipatory Set.*

Write 147 ÷ 12 on the board.

Say: You are owners of a bakery and have been baking muffins. You need to package them in boxes of a dozen, 12 to a box.

Ask: How many boxes will you be able to fill?

Students place 147 at the bottom of their mats.

Say: This time our multiples chart will be a little different. You can already divide easily by 10, or 20, or 30. We'll round 12 to 10 and put this estimate on our multiples chart as well:

# Groups Out	Muffins Out	Estimate
1	12	10
2	24	20
3	36	30

Students do first regrouping and show 14 ten rods and 7 one cubes on their mats.

Check the multiples chart. Predict the first answer.

Students see $1 \times 12 = 12$.

Ask: What would the estimate have been?

Students respond: We could take out a group of 10. They continue working through the problem.

100s	10s	1s
	1	2
12 ~~1~~	~~4~~	~~7~~
	14	27
	−12	−24
	2	3

Students use materials and write each step on their division paper as you do the problem on the board. They use the multiples chart and estimates to predict their answer.

Finish the problem and check.

Repeat the procedure with other numbers, using 11 or 12 as divisors. Most students should be able to move fairly quickly to doing the problem without the materials, since they have had much practice.

Encourage them to round the divisor and to use an estimate before dividing.

When students are competent in the skill, write 840 ÷ 37 on the board. The estimate will be different here:

# Groups Out	Number Out	Estimate of Number Out
1	37	40
2	74	80
3	111	120
4	148	160

Discuss why the estimates get farther from the actual number and that we round up at five or higher.

Encourage students to estimate without looking at the chart if possible. They do the problem and check.

If students have problems at this stage, have them do simpler problems, using the materials.

Procedure 4

To adapt the written format when estimates are low

Use *division paper* and *pv mats and materials, if needed.*

Write on the board:

1000s	100s	10s	1s
	1	2	
12⟋ 1̸	1̸5̸ 15 −12 8̸	3̸8̸ 38 −24 14	9

Ask: What is wrong here?

Students respond: You have too many left in the tens column. You can get another group of 12 out.

Ask: If I were doing this with the blocks, what would I do?

Students respond: Put another block in each of the 12 piles. If they are unsure of this, encourage them to use the pv materials.

I can do this in writing, as well. I'll show the second division above the first instead of erasing. What do I have to remember?

1000s	100s	10s	1s	
		1		
	1	2	2R5	= 132 R5
12⟋ 1̸	1̸5̸ 15 −12 8̸	3̸8̸ 38 −24 14 −12 2̸	2̸9̸ 29 −24 5	

Students respond: 1 + 2 = 3 tens in each group out.

I'll need to rewrite the answer to show what actually happened. Work through several problems with students until they are comfortable with this technique.

Practice and Extension

Have students roll *dice* to generate numbers. They roll four or five times and place the numbers on paper as a 2- or 3-digit number divided by a 2-digit number.

They then exchange their problem with a partner, and each works both problems. (This way they can help each other.) The problems should be checked by multiplying. When both students have worked the problem and checked it correctly, they are winners!

Have students bring in numbers from the *newspapers* and then divide by the number of students in the class. Example: We have 4,500 cattle. Each of the 25 members of the class would get how many cows? (180)

Relate dividing by 10 to metric measurement.

Division 9

Skill: To find averages

Time: 1+ periods

Materials:

tiles, counters, or interlocking cubes: 4 colors
dice

markers: to match counter colors; 1 per student
graph paper: of any size
See Reproducibles for: bills to 100s—in different colors

Anticipatory Set

Use *tiles, counters, or interlocking cubes.*

Give students a number of counters, and have them divide the counters evenly into three piles. Put aside any left over. Discuss that each group has the same number of counters; they are spread evenly. How did students know how to do this? Have students make other arrays, pointing out all are divided evenly.

Procedure 1 □ ■

To establish the concept of *average*

Use *tiles, counters, or interlocking cubes* and *paper.*

Draw the following chart (without the counters) on the board, and have students write it on paper.

Try 1 ⊗ ⊗ ⊗ ⊗	Try 1 ⊗ ⊗ ⊗ ⊗
Try 2 ⊗ ⊗	Try 2 ⊗ ⊗ ⊗ ⊗
Try 3 ⊗ ⊗ ⊗ ⊗ ⊗ ⊗	Try 3 ⊗ ⊗ ⊗ ⊗

Say: Carlos is practicing his free throws for basketball. On his first try, he gets four in a row before missing. Put four counters in a line beside Try 1. If using interlocking cubes, have students make a stick of four.

Students do this.

On his second try, he only gets two in a row before missing. Put two counters beside Try 2. On his third try, he gets six in a row before missing. Put six counters beside Try 3.

Students lay out counters as instructed.

Today we are going to find averages. We'll start by finding the average number of free throws Carlos made before missing. Your job is to discover what the word *average* means and how to go about finding it.

Rearrange your counters so that they show Carlos making the same number of baskets each try.

Students do this. They show four baskets at each try.

The average number of baskets Carlos made in three tries was four.

Repeat with other numbers and other stories, such as points scored in a dart game, scores on a test, and so on.

Ask: What do you think the word *average* means?

Students respond: Average is what you get if all of the numbers are spread evenly, or if people had scored the same amount each try.

Now we're going to look for a way to *find* averages of numbers or scores.

Take 15 counters. This is the total number of runs scored in three innings. Arrange them evenly over the three innings.

Students do this and discover they have five counters, or runs, in each line, or inning.

Each inning has the same number of runs. What is the average number of runs in an inning?

Students respond: 5.

What you just did, taking the total number of runs and dividing them among innings, is all there is to finding averages.

Suppose I said the total number of runs was 21. Can you tell me the average number of runs in 3 innings without using your counters?

Students respond: 7. They check with counters.

When students are comfortable with the concept, provide practice from the classroom: average number of T-shirts in each row, average number of people wearing blue in each row, or list test scores and have students figure the average score.

Students use counters as long as they feel the need.

Procedure 2 □

To practice finding averages

Use *bills ($1s)* and *dice.*

Have each pair of students use $40. Divide the class into two teams. Teams will keep track of the average bill amount per month, starting with January, to see who can spend the least amount of money.

Keep the amounts small so that the concept is clearer. You might want to explore *real* utility bills later.

Use dice to generate amounts for each team. The first throw is the gas bill. For example, $9. The second throw is the phone bill, which might be $5. The third bill is the water bill, which is $8.

Ask: How much is the average utility bill?

Students of the first team distribute bills into three piles and respond: $7 for January. If there are left-overs, students decide what to do with them.

	Team 1	Team 2
gas bill	$9	
phone bill	$5	
water bill	$8	
total	$22	

$$\begin{array}{r} \$7 \\ 3)\overline{\$22} \\ -21 \\ \hline 1 \end{array}$$

January

Repeat for the second team. Each time, have students discuss that they totaled the amounts and divided by the number of bills. When students are comfortable with the skill, have them do the averaging on paper, as well.

Students find and list January's average. They find the next 5 months, then the 6-month average.

Procedure 3

To find averages; to explore the effect of number size on averages

Use *tiles, counters, or interlocking cubes (4 colors), markers,* and *graph paper.*

Have students work in groups of four. Give each student a different color tile or counter. Have them lay out a number equal to the number of letters in their first name.

Students lay out counters, write down numbers, and reproduce on a group graph in the same colors:

Ann ● ● ●
Samantha ○ ○ ○ ○ ○ ○ ○ ○
Darien ◐ ◐ ◐ ◐ ◐ ◐
Tran ⊗ ⊗ ⊗ ⊗

Say: Now we want the average number of letters per name for the group. Have students move counters until they have the same number in each name row.

Students do this and make a chart of the end result.

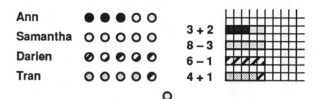

Ann ● ● ● ○ ○   3 + 2
Samantha ○ ○ ○ ○ ○   8 − 3
Darien ◐ ◐ ◐ ◐ ◐   6 − 1
Tran ⊗ ⊗ ⊗ ⊗ ⊗   4 + 1
○

Ask: How many counters did you have to rearrange? Compare by groups, and discuss charts and average number of letters per group.

Did any groups end with the same average number of letters? Do their charts look the same or different? Why?

What happens if one name is quite a bit longer than the other names? Does an average show a true picture of the group?

Discuss how one outlying amount might give a distorted picture of the whole group. This is even clearer if the experiment is repeated including both first and last names.

Procedure 4

To further explore the effect of number size on averages

Use *bills to 100s, markers,* and *graph paper.*

Repeat Procedure 3, using money. Relate this process to allowance or income. What happens if the person with the most triples his or her starting amount?

Practice and Extension

Use *geoboards and rubber bands,* and have students make a number of polygons or rectangles. Have them then adjust their figures to find the average area.

Students use *bills* and *dice.* They pretend that they are going shopping. The roll of the dice tells them how much they spend at each "store." After going to a set number of stores, the student must find the average amount of money he or she spent at each store. This may include the process of adding decimal points and zeros to the amounts in order to obtain the cents part of the answer.

Have students work such problems as: The average price of a bag of popcorn at four different stores is 89¢. What are possible prices found at each store?

Have the class use a survey to gather all-school data. They then find and graph the various averages possible.

Fractions 1

Skill: To understand and write fractions

Time: $1/2$–1 period per procedure

Materials:

construction paper cut into 3" × 18" strips—red, blue, orange, green, yellow: 1 of each color per student

scissors

business-size envelopes for storing completed fraction sets: 1 per student

counters in 4 colors: several of each per student

small paper bags: 1 per group

objects: cubes, beans, counters, etc.; 12 per student

pattern blocks

See Reproducibles for: bills to 100s—in different colors

Anticipatory Set

Use *construction paper strips, scissors,* and *envelopes.*

Make paper fraction bars for whatever fractions you wish; the red piece is left as the whole unit. Have students fold the blue strip in half and cut on the fold to make two halves.

The orange strip makes fourths: first fold and cut into halves; then fold and cut each half to make fourths. Continue in the same way, making the green strip into eighths and the yellow into sixteenths.

Discuss relationships as students fold. Have them label each piece and store them in a business-size envelope, folding the red strip to fit.

Save for Procedure 3 and for many future lessons.

Procedure 1

To identify fractions

Have six students stand at the front of the room. Write the headings "Boys" and "Girls" on the board.

Ask: How many are girls? (2) Two out of the group of six are girls. Write $^2/_6$ under Girls. We say this as two sixths.

Repeat for boys: $^4/_6$.

Write $^2/_6$ + $^4/_6$ = $^6/_6$ =1 as you explain: two of the six are girls, and four of the six are boys. Together they make all six of the group of six, one whole group.

Repeat with other groups until the class can dictate what you write.

Now use the class as a whole. Choose categories that will not overlap, such as hair color, eye color, ice-cream flavor preferences.

Ask: If you were ordering ice cream for a store, how would knowledge be useful?

Chart each set of results, and have the class dictate the appropriate fractions.

Procedure 2

To identify and write fractions

Use *counters* and *bags.*

Write headings on the board for each of the counter colors. Put a handful of mixed counters into a bag.

Have a student tally each counter under the appropriate heading as you draw them out of the bag:

Blue	Red	Yellow	Green	All
3	3	4	2	12

Three of the 12 are blue. What fraction is blue? ($^3/_{12}$) Write this under Blue. Repeat for the other colors.

Write plus signs between colors: 3 of the 12 are blue, + 3 of the 12 are red, and so on.

We've counted all 12 of 12 and have one whole bagful: $^3/_{12}$ + $^3/_{12}$ + $^4/_{12}$ + $^2/_{12}$ = $^{12}/_{12}$ = 1

Repeat until students understand the process. *Make sure you include some times when not all colors are represented.*

Students repeat the process in their groups. They each place a secret number of counters in the bag. One student tallies as they take turns drawing out the counters and putting them in color groups. Students agree on the total and appropriate fractions and equation to be written down.

Procedure 3

To write different fractions of a whole

Use *construction paper fraction bars from Anticipatory Set.*

Have students lay their red whole at the top of their desk. Have them find the color that has only two pieces and make a bar below the red one.

Students make a blue bar.

Continue until all bars are laid out. Ask: What do you notice about your bars?

1																

| $\frac{1}{2}$ |||||||| $\frac{1}{2}$ ||||||||

| $\frac{1}{4}$ |||| $\frac{1}{4}$ |||| $\frac{1}{4}$ |||| $\frac{1}{4}$ ||||

| $\frac{1}{8}$ | $\frac{1}{8}$ | $\frac{1}{8}$ | $\frac{1}{8}$ | $\frac{1}{8}$ | $\frac{1}{8}$ | $\frac{1}{8}$ | $\frac{1}{8}$ |

$\frac{1}{16}$	$\frac{1}{16}$	$\frac{1}{16}$	$\frac{1}{16}$	$\frac{1}{16}$	$\frac{1}{16}$	$\frac{1}{16}$	$\frac{1}{16}$	$\frac{1}{16}$	$\frac{1}{16}$	$\frac{1}{16}$	$\frac{1}{16}$	$\frac{1}{16}$	$\frac{1}{16}$	$\frac{1}{16}$	$\frac{1}{16}$

Students respond: All the same-color bars together make the same size as the red one. All the same-color pieces are the same size.

Look at the halves. The denominator shows how many equal parts in the whole. How do we write one of these two parts? ($\frac{1}{2}$) How about two of these two parts? ($\frac{2}{2}$) The numerator shows how many of the equal parts we have.

Have students pick up one, two, three, then four fourths. Write $\frac{1}{4}$, $\frac{2}{4}$, $\frac{3}{4}$, $\frac{4}{4}$. How many fractions can be made with fourths? (4)

Students should make a list of fractions, beginning with $\frac{1}{1}$ on the first line, and $\frac{1}{2}$, $\frac{2}{2}$ on the second. They continue to explore possible fractions from each color bar, looking for possible patterns.

Ask: What patterns do you see?

Answers might include: All bars are equal to a whole, the numerators increase until they equal the denominator, the number of fractions possible equals the number of parts. Students may notice that some fractions are equivalent to others.

What fraction of the whole bar is three green pieces? ($\frac{3}{8}$) Five yellow pieces? ($\frac{5}{16}$)

Continue practicing in this way. Have students write their answers when they feel comfortable identifying the fractional parts.

Procedure 4

To identify different fractions of a group of objects

Use *objects*.

Have each student make a group of 12 objects. This will be the whole group. Have them make 2 groups of 6.

Ask: How many parts do we have now? (2) Write $/2$ on the board. Are they equal in size? (yes)

Pull one of the groups toward you. What fraction name can we call this part? ($\frac{1}{2}$) Add the ^{1} to the $/2$ on the board.

Put the objects together into 1 group again. Now divide them into 3 equal groups.

Students divide the objects into 3 groups with 4 in each group. They identify each as a third or $\frac{1}{3}$ of 12. Next they name the possible fractions ($\frac{2}{3}$, $\frac{3}{3}$) as they pull the groups toward them.

Ask: What other fractions are possible with 12 objects? Are some not possible? Why?

Students explore the possibilities and write them down. They should realize that only factors of 12 can be fractional parts of 12.

Repeat with other numbers of objects. Make a large chart for the class results.

Procedure 5

To write fractions of a whole, using fractions equal to 1, 0

Use *pattern blocks* and *paper*.

Say: A yellow hexagon is one whole. Cover one yellow hexagon with red trapezoids. How many does it take? (2)

Students trace around a hexagon on their papers, divide it into two trapezoids and write $\frac{1}{2}$ on each part.

Hold up two trapezoids. Ask: How many of the two equal parts do I have? (2) If we have both equal parts, we can write the two halves as $\frac{2}{2}$.

What do you notice about having both of the trapezoids?

Students answer: They are the same as one hexagon.

We can write $\frac{2}{2}$ = 1 to show that both of two equal parts is the same as the whole.

Say: Now take the hexagon and cover it with green triangles.

Students cover the hexagon with six triangles and draw this on their paper.

How many equal parts do the triangles make? (6) We can call each part a sixth and write one part of six as $\frac{1}{6}$.

Students write $\frac{1}{6}$ on each triangle.

Hold up two triangles. How many of the six equal parts do I have? (2) How could I write this as a fraction? ($\frac{2}{6}$) Continue asking about increasing numbers of triangles until reaching $\frac{6}{6}$ = 1.

Now hold up *nothing*. How many sixths do I have? (none) How could I write this? ($\frac{0}{6}$)

Students trace the outline of a hexagon. They can mark it with a large × to show no parts and then label it ⁰/₆.

Repeat with other colors until students are comfortable with all possibilities. Have them use same-color blocks to make a chart to show all fractions possible with the blocks. Start each new color with the hexagon outline to represent zero parts of the fraction being explored:

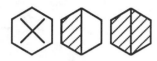

Students continue with their chart and designs to show a variety of fractional parts.

Have students look for patterns. They should see that more parts mean more fractions, all of the parts together equal one whole, and zero parts equal zero no matter what the denominator.

Procedure 6

To find a fraction of a number

Use *objects* and *bills*.

Have students make a row of 12 objects and find ¹/₄ of them:

Ask: If one of the fourths is three objects, how many objects are two of the fourths?

Students find ²/₄ of 12 is 6.

Have students find ³/₄, ¹/₃, ²/₃, ³/₃, and so on, of the row of 12. Emphasize first dividing the 12 into the equal parts called for.

Repeat the procedure with rows of various sizes.

Have each student take $100, which will be shopping money.

Say: New socks will cost ¹/₁₀ of your money. How much will that be? What do I need to do first?

Students respond: Divide the money into 10 groups by exchanging the $100 for 10 $10s. They make the exchange and find ¹/₁₀ of $100 = $10.

You have $90 left. New tapes will cost ²/₉ of that. How much is that?

Students divide their money into 9 groups, add 2 groups together, and find ²/₉ of $90 is $20.

Students work in pairs, using all their bills to create, solve, and write down problems.

Practice and Extension

Have students use *graph paper* and *markers*. Groups decide on categories. They outline a row as long as the number in the class and color in appropriate amounts, for example, ³/₂₅ live in brick buildings, ⁴/₂₅ live in wood buildings, and so on. They label the fractions.

Label *blank dice* with fraction amounts. Students use *fraction bars*. They throw a die and put out that amount. They add additional amounts each turn. If they can trade, for example, ¹/₄ for ²/₈, they do so to get the least number of pieces. The winner is the first to make a whole exactly.

Have students use *markers* or *crayons* and draw six identical pictures of trees, clowns, etc. They draw fruit on the trees or buttons on the clown suits, and then chart fractions: ²/₆ have 2 buttons, ⁴/₆ have 3 buttons; ³/₆ of the trees have red fruit, ¹/₆ of the trees have blue fruit, ²/₆ have green fruit.

Ask students to use a *multiplication chart* to figure out what fractional parts are possible for any number.

Have students bring in *advertisements* for items they are interested in purchasing. Allow them a certain amount of *money*, and have them identify the fractional amount of their money it would take to buy items.

Example: You have $50, and you may spend half of it. If you buy books for $15, how much will you have left? Student use *bills* to solve the problem, writing down each step on *paper*.

Use fractional amounts in daily directions, for example, ¹/₅ of each row, ³/₄ of the boys, ¹/₄ of 12 crayons, and so on.

Fractions 2

Skill: To compare fractions

Time: 3 periods

Materials:

interlocking cubes: 2 colors

graph paper: ½" or larger squares

markers

geoboards and rubber bands

scissors

objects: buttons, beans, counters; 20 per student

See Reproducibles for: geoboard paper, equivalency charts

Anticipatory Set

Use *interlocking cubes* or *graph paper and markers.*

Have students use interlocking cubes or graph paper to show various fraction amounts; e.g., $\frac{3}{4}$, $\frac{5}{12}$. Have them make up fraction word problems to go with the models. For example: Four foxes went hunting, and 3 went home. What fraction of the foxes went home?

Procedure 1 ☐■

To compare fractions with like denominators; same-size whole

Use *interlocking cubes, graph paper,* and *markers.*

Have each group make a stick of six cubes all the same color. Then have each student use graph paper to outline a horizontal row one square high and six squares wide, as in the illustration. Explain that this is the size of our whole stick.

Ask students to make another stick with five cubes of the original color and one of a different color. What fractional part of our whole is the *different-colored* cube?

Students respond: $\frac{1}{6}$. They color this on their graph paper.

Have students make sticks of two colors to show all possible the fractional parts of the whole.

Ask: What do you notice? Are there any patterns to these fractions? Have students write the fractions.

Students show and write $\frac{0}{6}$, $\frac{1}{6}$, $\frac{2}{6}$, $\frac{3}{6}$, $\frac{4}{6}$, $\frac{5}{6}$, and $\frac{6}{6}$.

They may notice the colors make a steplike pattern when lined up and that the numerators increase by one.

What fraction is more of the bar, $\frac{1}{6}$ or $\frac{5}{6}$?

Students respond: $\frac{5}{6}$.

We can say that $\frac{5}{6}$ is bigger than $\frac{1}{6}$ because it is more of our whole. We can show this: $\frac{5}{6} > \frac{1}{6}$.

Ask: Can you find another pair of fractions with our sixths in which one fraction is larger than another?

How could we make an organized chart that shows which fractions are larger than others?

Students decide as groups how to chart all possible combinations of larger and smaller fractions.

Help students see that organizing their chart makes it easier to read. Example: Start with $\frac{1}{6} > \frac{0}{6}$, and then move on to the $\frac{2}{6}$ relationships.

$$\frac{1}{6} > \frac{0}{6}$$

$$\frac{2}{6} > \frac{1}{6} > \frac{0}{6}$$

$$\frac{3}{6} > \frac{2}{6} > \frac{1}{6} > \frac{0}{6}$$

$$\frac{4}{6} > \frac{3}{6} > \frac{2}{6} > \frac{1}{6} > \frac{0}{6}$$

$$\frac{5}{6} > \frac{4}{6} > \frac{3}{6} > \frac{2}{6} > \frac{1}{6} > \frac{0}{6}$$

$$\frac{6}{6} > \frac{5}{6} > \frac{4}{6} > \frac{3}{6} > \frac{2}{6} > \frac{1}{6} > \frac{0}{6}$$

What rule can you find about comparing fraction sizes?

Students respond: Fractions with the same denominators can be compared by comparing their numerators.

Repeat the procedure, using different numbers of cubes in the whole. Have each group choose a different-size whole, make all possible fractions, and chart all possible combinations of larger and smaller fractions. Make a class chart from the group charts. Do they see any patterns?

Procedure 2 ◻◼

To compare fractions with like denominators; different-size wholes

Use *geoboards, rubber bands, geoboard paper, markers,* and *scissors.*

Have students make a rectangle two squares wide and two squares long and then divide it into halves with a rubber band around each half. Ask: How many squares is the whole we started with? (4) How many squares is each half? (2)

Students next make a rectangle two squares by four squares and divide it into halves.

Ask: How many squares is our whole now? (8) How many squares is each half? (4) Which is bigger?

Students respond: The half of the larger rectangle.

Say: You compared fractions using interlocking cubes and discovered you could put them in order by their numerators. Can I write 1/2 >1/2 for our geoboard halves? Why isn't this right?

Students respond: The numerators are equal, so one shouldn't be larger than another.

Can I add any information to make 1/2 > 1/2 possible and to show what's happening with the rectangles?

Students discuss. They should realize that they need to consider the size of the whole. This is shown on the geoboards: $\frac{1}{2}$ of 8 > $\frac{1}{2}$ of 4.

Have students repeat, dividing the rectangles into fourths.

Emphasize that students need to know the size of the whole, as well as the size of the fraction, before they can compare them. Can they think of any real-life situations in which this might be important?

Students find different ways to show $\frac{1}{2}$, $\frac{1}{3}$, $\frac{1}{4}$, etc. They color and label all combinations on geoboard paper, cut them out, and make a class chart.

Procedure 3 ◻◼

To compare fractions with unlike denominators

Use *objects* and *equivalency charts.*

Remind students that in order to compare fractions they need to know the size of the fraction and the size of the whole.

Ask: Which fraction is bigger, $\frac{3}{5}$ or $\frac{2}{4}$? What is our problem?

Students respond: The size of the whole is not the same. The denominators are not the same.

Give students 40 buttons or beans. Have students put them into two groups of 20 each. Ask: How do we show $\frac{3}{5}$ of the first 20 beans?

Students divide the beans into fifths and separate three of the fifths.

Now show $\frac{2}{4}$ of the second group of 20 beans.

Students divide the beans into four groups and separate two of the fourths.

How many beans are in $\frac{3}{5}$ of 20? (12) How many are in $\frac{2}{4}$ of 20? (10)

Which is the bigger fraction, $\frac{3}{5}$ or $\frac{2}{4}$? ($\frac{3}{5}$) What did we have to do to compare two fractions with different denominators?

Students respond: Make them fractions of the same-size whole.

Repeat with other fractions and other-size wholes, such as $\frac{5}{6}$ of 12 aliens had green hair, and $\frac{3}{4}$ had purple. Which was the more common color? Use also $\frac{3}{8}$ and $\frac{2}{4}$ (of 8 or 16).

Hand out equivalency charts. Point out that the size of the whole is the same for all fractions on the chart.

Have students start at the left and find the space taken up by various fraction amounts. They may use a pencil or ruler lined up top to bottom to find equivalent fractions.

Students use the chart to compare. They write the fractions using < or > to show relationships.

Practice and Extension

Have students use *fraction bars* or *circles cut into fractions* to compare fractions. Students can check on an *equivalence chart.*

Write fractions on *wooden cubes* to make fraction dice. Have students each throw die. The largest fraction is worth 1 point.

Have students make up fraction questions about the class; e.g., what fraction is larger, the fraction of students with brown hair or the fraction of students with blond hair?

Fractions 3

Skill: To find equivalent fractions

Time: 3 periods

Materials:

fraction bars (directions in Manipulative Information section) or Cuisenaire® rods

pattern blocks

objects: buttons, beans, counters; 48 per student pair

flat toothpicks: 15 per student pair

graph paper: ½" squares

thin, dark markers

See Reproducibles for: equivalency charts

Anticipatory Set

Have students make paper fraction bars, or use Procedure 1 as an Anticipatory Set.

Procedure 1

To learn the concept of *equivalence*

Use *fraction bars or Cuisenaire® rods* and *pattern blocks*.

Have students lay their whole fraction bar at the top of their desk. Below that have them lay the halves, etc. Review that the denominator is the number of equal groups in the whole and that the numerator is the number of those groups we have.

Have students pick up a ½ bar and see whether it is the same size as some other fractions.

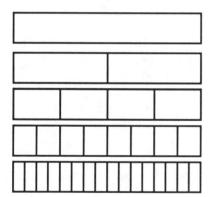

Students discover ½ = ²/₄ = ⁴/₈ = ⁸/₁₆. They write these relationships.

Explain that these are equal-sized, or equivalent, fractions. Have student discover and write all possible equivalencies.

Have the class use pattern blocks to discover other equivalencies. One yellow hexagon equals two red trapezoids, three blue parallelograms, or six green triangles:

Procedure 2

To generate and read an equivalency chart

Use *objects, toothpicks, graph paper, markers,* and *equivalency charts.*

Have student pairs make four rows with 12 beans evenly spaced in each row. Rows should be 3 to 4 inches apart. Each row is a whole of 12.

Have them separate the second row into two parts with a toothpick.

Ask: What do we call each part? (½)

Students use toothpicks to divide the third row into fourths and the fourth row into twelfths.

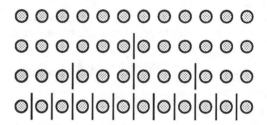

Have them notice whether any of the toothpicks line up. What do the lined-up toothpicks let us see? Have we used anything else that is similar?

Students respond: The toothpicks let us see where the equivalent fractions are. The fraction bars look like the beans and toothpicks.

Have students write all equivalencies discovered. Repeat with the rows divided into thirds and sixths.

Tell the class to leave their beans in place. Have students use graph paper to make an equivalency chart.

Students draw a row 1 square tall and 12 squares wide as their whole and directly below that outline five more identical rows.

Students leave the top row as their whole, divide the second row into halves, the third row into thirds, the fourth into fourths, the fifth into sixths, and the last into twelfths. They use markers to mark divisions.

Relate this graph to the groups of 12 beans and the equivalent fractions they found. Have students

make a list of equivalent fractions to the side of each graph paper bar. For example:

$1 = {}^2/_2 = {}^3/_3 = {}^4/_4 = {}^6/_6 = {}^{12}/_{12}$

${}^1/_2 = {}^2/_4 = {}^3/_6 = {}^6/_{12}$.

Students complete the chart and look for patterns.

Lead students to notice the multiplication relationship of equivalent fractions: Equivalent fractions are multiples of the original fraction; also, if the original denominator is three times the numerator, as in $^1/_3$, all fractions equivalent to $^1/_3$ will have this same relationship.

Hand out the equivalency charts. Show students how to read the fraction amounts on the chart, relating it to the graph paper chart they made and to the fraction bars.

Students use a ruler or pencil to see which fractions line up and thus are equivalent. They duplicate the chart with fraction bars if they wish.

matrix. Repeat for $^2/_3$. Two adjacent horizontal rows on the multiplication chart will list equivalent fractions.

Lead students to recognize that the numerator and denominator can be multiplied by the same number to find equivalent fractions.

Cut the matrices into horizontal rows. Line up different rows to find more equivalent fractions.

Have students rewrite *recipes;* they have lost all measuring cups except the $^1/_3$ or $^1/_8$ cup size, and must adapt.

Procedure 3 □■

To use multiplication to find equivalent fractions

Use *student-made chart of equivalent fractions from Procedure 2* or *equivalency charts*.

If students have not made a chart of equivalent fractions, have them use their charts to do so.

Ask whether students see any patterns. They need to find a rule that will work for equivalent fractions in general. Hint: Start with each original fraction, like $^1/_2$. How did we get to $^2/_4$? From $^1/_2$, how did we get to $^3/_6$?

Students notice that if you multiply both numerator and denominator by the same number, you have an equivalent fraction.

Ask: Why does this work? Have students compare $^1/_2$ and $^2/_4$ on their charts. Are there more fourths? (yes) Say: They are smaller, so there are more of them.

Repeat for other fractions. Emphasize the need to multiply the *original* fraction when generating a list of equivalent fractions.

Students find fractions equivalent to $^2/_4$ and $^4/_5$ on their charts. They use multiplication and compare results.

Have students generate charts of equivalent fractions using multiplication. Each fraction should be checked with the equivalency chart.

Practice and Extension

Have students list horizontally all fractions equivalent to $^1/_2$. Have them compare this list to a *multiplication*

Fractions 4

Skill: To order fractions

Time: 3 periods

Materials:

geoboards and rubber bands

*interlocking cubes in 2 colors or graph paper with ¹/₂"
squares and markers*

*fraction bars (directions in Manipulative Information
section) or Cuisenaire® rods*

objects: buttons, beans, counters; 36 per student pair

See Reproducibles for: equivalency charts

Anticipatory Set

Use *geoboards and rubber bands*.

Have students enclose a five-pin by five-pin square
on their geoboards. How many squares have they
enclosed? (16) Have students enclose a single square
inside the larger one. What fraction is it of the
whole? (¹/₁₆) Write this on the board.

Then have students enclose two squares, identify ²/₁₆,
and see which fraction is bigger. Continue increasing
area to develop the idea that like fractions can be
compared using their numerators.

Procedure 1 ☐■

To order fractions with like denominators

Use *interlocking cubes,* or *graph paper and markers*.

**Work in groups for cubes, individually for graph
paper.**

**Have groups make a stick of six cubes all the
same color. (Students using graph paper should
outline a horizontal row one square high and six
squares wide.) Explain this is the size of our
whole stick.**

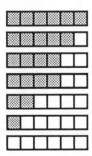

**Tell students to make another stick with five
cubes of the original color and one of a different
color. Ask: What fractional part of our whole is
the different-colored cube? (¹/₆)**

Students make sticks to show all possible fractional
parts of the whole. They write the fractions next to
the sticks.

Ask: What do you notice? Are there any patterns?

Students notice the colors make a step pattern when
lined up and that the numerators increase by one.

What fraction is more of the stick, ¹/₆ or ⁵/₆?

Students respond: ⁵/₆ is bigger because it is more of
our whole.

**Write ⁵/₆ > ¹/₆ on the board. Ask: Can you find
another pair of fractions with the sixths in which
one fraction is larger than another?**

Students decide as groups how to chart all possible
combinations of larger and smaller fraction pairs.

**Help students see that organizing their chart
makes it easier to read. Example: Start with ¹/₆ > ⁰/₆,
and then move on to the ²/₆ relationships. Ask:
What rule can you find about comparing fraction
sizes?**

Students respond: Like fractions can be compared by
comparing their numerators.

**Repeat the procedure, using different numbers of
cubes in the whole. The class could make a class
chart showing a variety of denominators. Students
should make up word problems for their fractions.**

Procedure 2 ☐■

To order fractions with unlike denominators

Use *fraction bars* or *Cuisenaire® rods*.

**Have students lay their whole bar across the top
of their desk; then put the two halves together,
below the whole; and then the fourths below the
halves.**

**Ask: Which bar is longer, ¹/₂ or ¹/₄? (¹/₂) The ¹/₂ is a
bigger part of the whole and is a bigger fraction.**

**Write ¹/₂ > ¹/₄ on the board. Have students find all
the fractions that are smaller than ¹/₂ and write the
relationships.**

Students then find all the fractions that are smaller
than ³/₄ and list their relationship to ³/₄.

**Give students three fractions and see whether
they can put them in order, first using the bars
and then on paper. Make a class chart of all the
relationships possible with the fraction bars.**

Procedure 3

To order fractions with unlike denominators; to relate the size of the denominator to fraction size

Use *objects* and *equivalency charts*.

Have student pairs make a row of 12 objects and divide the row into thirds. Ask: How many groups is that? (3)

Have them make a second row of 12 objects and divide it into fourths. How many groups is that? (4)

Students make a third row divided into sixths and respond that there are six groups.

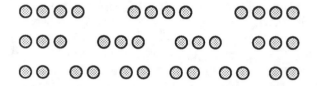

In each case, we started with how many objects? (12) This is the size of our whole. Compare sizes. Which is smaller, the group that is ¹/₄ of the 12, or the group that is ¹/₆ of 12? Why?

Students respond: The group that is a sixth because fewer objects are in it.

Which is smaller, a group that is ¹/₄ of the whole 12, or a group that is ¹/₃ of the 12? Why?

Students respond: The fourth because fewer objects are in it.

Have students write ¹/₆ < ¹/₄. Point out that the six and the four represent how many groups the whole 12 is divided into and that the ones tell how many of these groups we have.

Students compare ¹/₃ and ¹/₄. They write ¹/₆ < ¹/₄ < ¹/₃.

Do you see a pattern?

Students respond: As the denominators get smaller, the size of each group gets larger.

Have the class predict where ¹/₂ will come. (larger)

Change your row of sixths into halves of the 12. How many groups? (2) How many of these will we look at? (1) Does the size of the group fit our prediction? (yes)

If I divided my 12 objects into twelfths, would each twelfth be a large or a small group? Why?

Students respond: A small group. The groups are so many that only one object could be in each group.

Reinforce that as the fraction name—the denominator—gets larger, the size of each group gets smaller.

Repeat this procedure with groups of eight objects, emphasizing the number of groups the whole is divided into and comparing the size of each group.

Have students now compare ²/₈, ²/₄, and ²/₂ of the eight to see whether the relationships hold.

Students pretend their eight objects are silver dollars. They work in pairs to see who would have more money if one student held ³/₈ of their dollars and the other held ²/₄.

Review that they need to divide the whole into the number of groups that the denominator instructs and then to take the number of groups that the numerator instructs.

Hand out equivalency charts. Point out that the size of the whole is the same for all fractions on the chart.

Students start at the left and find the space taken up by various fraction amounts of the whole. They can use a pencil or ruler lined up top to bottom to help compare various fractions.

Have students compare various fractions to ¹/₂. Ask them to predict whether the fraction will be larger or smaller than ¹/₂. Then have students mentally compare two separate fractions. Explain that relating the fractions to ¹/₂ makes it easier to compare them to each other.

Practice and Extension

Have students make *index cards* of fractions on the *equivalency chart*. Each student draws several cards from his or her deck to put in order. Have students make up rules to play a game or to race ordering fractions.

Fractions 5

Skill: To simplify fractions and to find the greatest common factor

objects: cubes, tiles, or counters

See Reproducibles for: moon stations, equivalency charts

Time: 3+ periods

Materials:

pattern blocks

fraction bars (directions in Manipulative Information Section) or Cuisenaire® rods

Anticipatory Set

Use *pattern blocks* and *moon stations.*

Have students place two yellow hexagons on their moon station outlines. Call this shape a moon station, and have students pretend they have a pattern block that shape. This will equal one whole unit.

Have students build examples of all the ways to cover a moon station with blocks of one color: 2 yellow hexagons, 4 red trapezoids, 6 blue parallelograms, or 12 green triangles. Students should write the equivalent fractions:

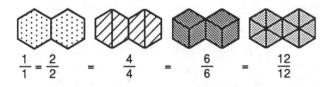

$$\frac{1}{1} = \frac{2}{2} = \frac{4}{4} = \frac{6}{6} = \frac{12}{12}$$

Procedure 1

To simplify fractions, using manipulatives only

Use *pattern blocks, pattern block equivalent fractions from Anticipatory Set,* and *moon stations.*

Ask: Do each of these fractions represent the same amount? (yes) *If* **we had a pattern block made in the shape of a moon station, which is the simplest fraction we could write to show this amount? ($^1/_1$) Using the smallest numbers possible makes the fraction in its simplest form.**

Let's find the simplest form for $^6/_{12}$. Which pattern blocks are twelfths? (green triangles) Cover a moon station with six of them. Now cover the same space with the fewest possible pieces. Use only one fraction size—one color, to do this.

Students find one yellow hexagon covers the same space. They start a chart: "Fraction" "Simplest Form."

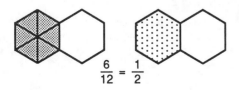

$$\frac{6}{12} = \frac{1}{2}$$

Students repeat with other fractions that simplify. Examples: $^4/_6$, $^8/_{12}$. They chart results.

Now introduce a fraction that is already in its simplest form. Have students start with $^{11}/_{12}$ and cover the same amount with another color block.

Students discover that they cannot use one color to cover the same amount as $^{11}/_{12}$.

Say: If you cannot find a way to show the same amount using fewer same-color pieces, you have discovered that $^{11}/_{12}$ is in its simplest form.

Students continue the procedure until they have charted all possible fraction/simplest form combinations. They look for any patterns. They may discover that the numerator and denominator can be divided by the same number to simplify a fraction.

Procedure 2

To simplify fractions using manipulatives only

Use *fraction bars* or *Cuisenaire® rods.*

Repeat Procedure 1, using fraction bars or rods. The largest bar represents one whole unit. Fractions possible are halves, fourths, eighths, and sixteenths. As students become more adept at the skill, have them predict the answer before using the bars. Have them chart results and look for any patterns.

Procedure 3

To simplify fractions using division; to understand the greatest common factor

Use *fraction bars or Cuisenaire® rods* and *equivalency charts.*

Have students show $^8/_{12}$ and find the equivalent fraction with the lowest, simplest numbers. ($^2/_3$) Write $^8/_{12} = ^2/_3$ on the board. Repeat for $^4/_8 = ^1/_2$ and $^2/_8 = ^1/_4$, adding to the list on the board. What patterns do students see?

If students do not notice that both numerator and denominator are divided by the same number, ask how (for $^4/_8 = ^1/_2$) to get from 4 to 1, and from 8 to 2.

Ask: Can we divide the numerator and denominator by the same number to get a simpler fraction?

Students use fraction bars to test this theory by finding the simplest form for $^2/_4$, $^6/_8$, and so on.

Say: We have discovered that we can get a smaller equivalent fraction by dividing the numerator and denominator by the same number. We have to find a number that is a *factor of both*. Write:

$$\frac{12 \div 2}{12 \div 2} = \frac{6}{6} \qquad \frac{6 \div 2}{6 \div 2} = \frac{3}{3} \qquad \frac{3 \div 3}{3 \div 3} = \frac{1}{1}$$

Ask: Do you know an easier way to simplify $^{12}/_{12}$?

Students respond: We could have divided the numerator and denominator both by 12.

Yes, if you divide by the largest possible factor in the first place, you save a lot of steps. The largest factor that both numerator and denominator have in common is called the *greatest common factor*.

Students use their equivalency charts to find simplest equivalent fractions for fractions. They identify the greatest common factor used to simplify the original fractions.

Continue until the concept is understood.

Procedure 4 □■

To use prime factorization to find the GCF (Multiplication 11 explains prime factorization.)

Use *objects* and *2 sheets of paper per student*.

In reducing fractions to simplest terms, we need to find a number that will divide both numerator and denominator evenly. We're looking for a factor that both share, or have in common. Since we want the smallest possible numerator and denominator, we need to divide by the largest possible number—the *greatest* (largest) *common factor* or *divisor*. We'll find the greatest common factor for $^{16}/_{30}$.

Students place two pieces of paper side by side and then make a 1×16 array with cubes on the left and a 1×30 array on the right. They factor the 16 first.

Students build a 2×8 array, writing results next to each step. The 2 is prime, so they circle the 2.

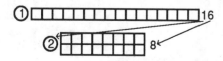

The 8 is not prime. Take 8 of the blocks and build a 2×4 array. Write down both 2 and 4, circling the 2, since it is prime:

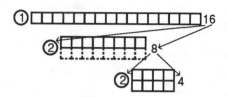

Next factor the 4 into a 2×2 array. Circle both 2s:

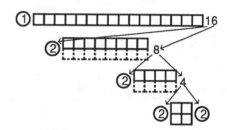

Repeat for 30.

Ask: What factors do both 16 and 30 have in common? (one 2) So 2 is the largest factor or divisor you can use, the greatest common factor.

Repeat for $^{12}/_{24}$.

What is the prime factorization of 12? ($1 \times 2 \times 2 \times 3$)

The prime factorization of 24? ($1 \times 2 \times 2 \times 2 \times 3$)

We are looking for the largest or greatest possible number to divide by. How many twos are common? (2) What else is a common factor? (3)

Since both share $2 \times 2 \times 3$, we can divide both by 12. Twelve is the GCF.

Ask: What would have happened if we had divided both 12 and 24 by 2, the first prime factor we found for both?

Students respond: We would have had to keep going. The fraction wouldn't be in the simplest form.

Repeat until students show understanding.

As students do each step with the blocks, they write the corresponding step on their paper. When confident they try on paper first, then check with blocks.

Students need to understand that the written form is just a description of what is actually happening.

Practice and Extension

Ask students how divisibility rules could help them simplify fractions.

Divide the class in half. Use a *deck of cards* to generate numerators and denominators of fractions to simplify. Award 1 point for each one simplified correctly.

Fractions 6

Skill: To add and subtract fractions: like denominators

Time: 3 periods

Materials:

fraction bars (directions in Manipulative Information section) or Cuisenaire® rods

pattern blocks

See Reproducibles for: moon stations

Anticipatory Set

Ask how many students are in the class. Have one student stand. Ask what fraction of the class he or she is. Review: The denominator is the number of equal parts in the whole; the numerator is the number of parts we're interested in.

Ask a second student also to stand. What fraction of the class is he or she alone? What fraction of the class are all the standing students? Continue adding students and emphasizing the adding of single-student fractions.

Procedure 1

To add fractions

Use *fraction bars or Cuisenaire® rods* and *paper*.

Have students lay their eighths in a row below their whole bar. Instruct them to separate $^1/_8$ and then add another $^1/_8$ to it. Ask: How many eighths do we have now? ($^2/_8$)

Write $^1/_8 + ^1/_8 = ^2/_8$ on the board.

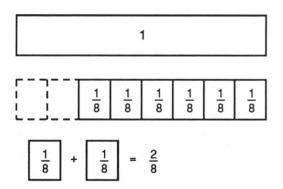

Have students add another $^1/_8$. How many eighths have we added now? ($^3/_8$)

Write $^2/_8 + ^1/_8 = ^3/_8$. Repeat for one more eighth.

Repeat the process with fourths and sixteenths, writing the process on the board as the students work.

Students separate the amount you call for, add the bars, and find the total.

Ask: Do you see any pattern to what you have written?

Students should see that you have added numerators.

Give students other fractions to add.

Write $^1/_4 + ^1/_4 = ^2/_8$ on the board, and challenge students to prove why this is wrong.

Students add $^1/_4$ and $^1/_4$ and match this against $^2/_8$. They see that two fourths are greater in size than two eighths.

Discuss adding the numerators but not denominators. The denominators refer to the number of equal parts of the whole; these don't change. Have students practice with bars only until they are comfortable with the process.

Now you can move to the stage where students write, as well as use manipulatives. As students do each step with the bars, they write the corresponding step on their paper.

It is important for students to understand that the written form is just a description of what is actually happening. Students need much practice at this step.

After students become confident about the process, they can move to writing the problem first and then checking each step with their blocks.

Procedure 2

To subtract fractions

Use *fraction bars* or *Cuisenaire® rods*.

Have students start with a bar of $^8/_8$. Direct them to pull down $^3/_8$. Ask: How many eighths do you have left? ($^5/_8$) Write $^8/_8 - ^3/_8 = ^5/_8$ on the board.

Next students pull down $^2/_8$ from their group of $^3/_8$. Ask: How many eighths are left? ($^1/_8$)

Write $^3/_8 - ^2/_8 = ^1/_8$ on the board. Repeat several times. Do you see a pattern?

Students respond: Only the numerators change.

Emphasize that the size of their bars didn't change—they are still eighths. Only the number of eighths we had left changed.

Give fractions for students to subtract, using other bars. Write the process on the board as they work.

Students create and solve fraction word problems using their bars. When they are competent in the skill, they also write down the process as they work with the bars.

Procedure 3

To add and subtract fractions

Use *pattern blocks* and *moon stations*.

Give each student pattern blocks and moon stations. Have them review how many of each color block it takes to cover a moon station. (2 yellow hexagons, 4 red trapezoids, 6 blue parallelograms, or 12 green triangles)

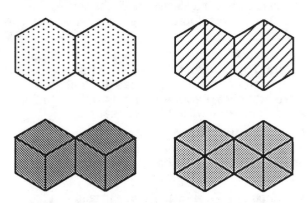

Repeat Procedure 1, using the pattern blocks. For example, have students place one red trapezoid on a moon station.

Ask: What fraction is covered? (¹/₄) Have them add another ¹/₄. How many fourths in all now? (²/₄)

For subtraction, have them cover ³/₄ of a moon station and then take away ¹/₄.

Continue giving fractions to add or subtract on the moon stations. Use halves, fourths, sixths, and twelfths.

Students write equations. When they are comfortable with the skills, they write equations first and then check with the blocks.

Practice and Extension

Give students fractions to add and subtract. Have students divide *moon stations* into fractional parts

and color in the required number on the *moon stations*. For subtraction they can use a light color to color in the first fraction and then a darker color to line through the fraction amount to be subtracted. They should write the problem under the moon station.

Use *place value blocks* with a ten rod as one whole, or *money* with $10 as one whole to work with tenths.

Have students change *recipe* ingredient amounts to all one denominator.

Have students write about a turtle who can't make up its mind. It walks forward ¹/₄ foot, forward another ¹/₄, backward ¹/₄ and then forward ³/₄. How far does it go in all? Have students do the intermediate equations as well.

Discuss temperature in tenths of degrees. What is normal body temperature? How much higher is a fever?

Fractions 7

Skill: To rename mixed numbers and improper fractions

Time: 4 periods

Materials:

pattern blocks

See Reproducibles for: moon stations, Marvin the Mammoth

Anticipatory Set

Use *pattern blocks* and *moon stations*.

Have students cover moon stations with fractional parts as you dictate: $^1/_4$, $^4/_3$, $^5/_6$, then $^2/_2$, $^4/_4$, and so on. Use fourths (trapezoids), halves, sixths, and twelfths.

Procedure 1

To understand improper fractions and mixed numbers

Use *pattern blocks* and *moon stations*.

Have students cover as many moon stations as possible with 5 fourths. Ask: If we call it $^5/_4$, have we named any whole numbers? (no) But do we have more than a whole moon station? (yes)

Five fourths is an improper fraction. It's more than a whole, but called by only its fraction name.

Ask: How many *whole* moon stations? (1) What else did you cover? ($^1/_4$ of a moon station)

You also made $1^1/_4$. An amount like this is a mixed number. It mixes wholes with extra fraction parts.

On the board show students how to write $1^1/_4$.

When we work with mixed numbers, we make all parts with the same fraction pieces. For $1^1/_4$, the whole must be made of 4 fourths. What about $2^2/_6$?

Students respond: It must be made of all sixths. They make other examples and write both numbers, using only one color block each time.

Repeat with 3 halves, 6 fourths, 9 sixths, and then have students make mixed numbers with a whole greater than one: 5 halves, 13 sixths.

Procedure 2

To change mixed numbers to improper fractions using addition

Use *pattern blocks, moon stations*, and *Marvin*.

Marvin the Mammoth, the mixed number muncher, eats only food in mixed number amounts. Have students cover one moon station taco with halves.

Ask: If we're working with halves, what *fraction* can we call a whole taco? ($^2/_2$) Write $1 = ^2/_2$.

Make $1^1/_2$ tacos with halves. What fraction is the *whole* taco? ($^2/_2$) How much of a second taco do we have? ($^1/_2$). We can call this $^2/_2 + ^1/_2$.

Can you name an equation *all in halves* that tells all the moon stations and parts? ($^2/_2 + ^1/_2 = ^3/_2$) What do we call $^3/_2$? (an improper fraction)

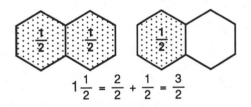

$$1\frac{1}{2} = \frac{2}{2} + \frac{1}{2} = \frac{3}{2}$$

Give more mixed number amounts for students to place until students are comfortable with breaking mixed numbers into fractional parts. Example: Write $2^1/_4$ on the board; have students break it into parts while you write:

$$2^1/_4 = ^4/_4 + ^4/_4 + ^1/_4$$
$$2^1/_4 = ^9/_4$$

Marvin continues to eat: $2^5/_{12}$ bushels of apples, and so on. Students both place blocks and write the equations. When students are competent in the skill they write first and then check with blocks.

Procedure 3

To change mixed numbers to improper fractions using multiplication

Use *pattern blocks, moon stations*, and *Marvin*.

Have students place $2^1/_4$, which could be pounds of fortune cookies. We eventually want to be able to know how many fourths in all without the blocks.

Students write: $2\frac{1}{4} = \frac{4}{4} + \frac{4}{4} + \frac{1}{4} = \frac{9}{4}$.

We have two groups of 4 fourths. What shortcut do we use to add same-size groups? (multiplication)

Two groups of 4 is how many in all? (8) Any more fourths? (1) What are $\frac{8}{4}$ and $\frac{1}{4}$? ($\frac{9}{4}$)

Repeat with other mixed numbers, for example, $2\frac{3}{6}$.

Ask: What fraction size do we have? (sixths) How many parts in each whole? (6) How many wholes? (2) How many sixths are in all the wholes? (12) Write: 2×6 sixths $= \frac{12}{6}$. How many are left over to add on? (3) Write: $\frac{12}{6} + \frac{3}{6} = \frac{15}{6}$.

Can students tell what to multiply and add by looking at the numbers? What does each number mean? Have them use arrows:

$$2\ \frac{1}{4}\ =\ \frac{9}{4}$$

Students should use or picture the blocks while they write. They make up Marvin problems for each other.

Procedure 4 □■

To change improper fractions to mixed numbers using subtraction

Use *pattern blocks, moon stations,* and *Marvin.*

Use 5 fourths to make moon stations. Each moon station is a whole chocolate pie for Marvin. He only eats food in mixed number amounts.

Ask: How many fourths in one whole pie? (4) How many in the other? (1). If we talk about the $\frac{4}{4}$ as 1 whole pie, and the other $\frac{1}{4}$ as $\frac{1}{4}$ of a pie, we have a mixed number: $1\frac{1}{4}$ pies.

How many fourths did you start with? (5) How many pies did you make? ($1\frac{1}{4}$) Write:

$$\frac{5}{4}\ =\ \frac{4}{4} + \frac{1}{4}$$
$$=\ 1 + \frac{1}{4}$$
$$=\ 1\frac{1}{4}$$

If we start with $\frac{8}{6}$, what size fraction are we working with? (sixths) How many whole ones can we make with $\frac{8}{6}$? (1) How many sixths left over? (2)

What mixed number would that be? ($1\frac{2}{6}$) Can you prove this by covering moon stations?

Students check with blocks and write each step.

Each time we subtract another group of 6 sixths, we make another whole.

Continue to give numbers in a story format. Also give improper numbers that result in two wholes, for example, $\frac{9}{4}$.

Procedure 5 □■

To change improper fractions to mixed numbers using division

Use *pattern blocks, moon stations,* and *Marvin.*

Write $\frac{9}{4}$ on the board. Have students cover moon stations with 9 fourths. Ask: If we couldn't use blocks, how could we discover how many moon stations we could cover?

Students respond: Subtract groups of 4 fourths.

What is a shortcut for subtracting equal groups? (division)

Ask: If you divide that 9 into groups of 4 to make whole ones, how many groups of $\frac{4}{4}$ do you have? (2) How many left over? (1) Check with your blocks.

Say: To change from an improper fraction to a mixed number, you divide the blocks, the numerator, into groups. The denominator tells you what size groups you need. Leftovers are the fraction part in the mixed number. Write:

$$\frac{9}{4}\ =\ 9 \div 4$$
$$=\ 2\frac{1}{4}$$

Repeat with Marvin's $\frac{9}{6}$ pots of peas, and so on.

Students do each step with the blocks, writing the step on paper. They need much practice using both blocks and paper and pencil before moving to using paper first and then checking with blocks.

Practice and Extension

Follow any or all of Procedures 1–3, 5–6 using *fraction bars* or *Cuisenaire® rods.* Students work in pairs or small groups to have enough bars for mixed numbers. They should use more than one manipulative to extend their understanding of the concept.

Use *place value blocks.* Use a ten rod as one whole. Pairs of students play Improper Challenge. One student names an improper fraction using tenths. The partner changes it to a mixed number while the first student checks with blocks. Score 1 point for a correct answer; 10 points is a game.

Use *1$ bills* and *counters* to play Improper Challenge or to follow Procedures 1–3, 5–6. Let $1 be one whole and a counter be 10¢ or $\frac{1}{10}$. This is more difficult because students are dealing with value rather than spatial relationships.

Fractions 8

Skill: To add and subtract mixed numbers: like denominators

Time: 4 periods

Materials:

place value (pv) blocks to 10s or Cuisenaire® rods: 1s and 10s

fraction bars (directions in Manipulative Information section) or Cuisenaire® rods

pattern blocks

See Reproducibles for: Marvin the Mammoth, moon stations

Anticipatory Set

Use *Marvin the Mammoth*.

Have students write addition problems involving Marvin, who only eats food in mixed number amounts. Example: Marvin ate $1^2/_8$ lbs of cake and $1^5/_8$ lbs of apples. How much more did he weigh after eating?

Procedure 1 ▫◼

To add mixed numbers; no regrouping

Use *pv blocks or Cuisenaire® rods* and *Marvin*.

A ten rod equals one whole; each one cube is $^1/_{10}$. Have students lay out one rod with three cubes to the right of it. Ask: What number have we made? ($1^3/_{10}$)

Have students place $1^5/_{10}$ below the $1^3/_{10}$.

Add your blocks together. How many tenths in all? (8 tenths) How many wholes? (2) Write:

$$\begin{array}{r} 1^3/_{10} \\ + \ 1^5/_{10} \\ \hline 2^8/_{10} \end{array}$$

Students place and add several more combinations of mixed numbers as you write the problems on the board. Sums of fractional parts should be below.

Ask: Do you see a pattern for adding mixed numbers?

Students respond: Add the fractions, add the wholes.

Dictate stories about Marvin. Include some in which students must add a mixed number and a fraction, or a whole number and a mixed number.

When students are comfortable with the skill, have them write each step as they do it, following your example.

Students may first write sums and then check with blocks when they feel competent in the skill.

Procedure 2 ▫◼

To add mixed numbers; with regrouping

Use *pv blocks or Cuisenaire® rods* and *Marvin*.

Have students place $1^3/_{10}$ and $1^7/_{10}$.

Ask: How many tenths all together? (10) How many wholes? (3) Can we do anything else?

Students respond: Regroup the $^{10}/_{10}$ as 1. They now have 2 wholes.

Demonstrate the form:

$$\begin{array}{r} 1^3/_{10} \\ + \ 1^7/_{10} \\ \hline 2^{10}/_{10} = 2 + 1 = 3 \end{array}$$

Dictate other mixed numbers to be added. The numerators should total 10.

Students write each step as they do it. They should be able to state: add the fractions, add the wholes, regroup if necessary, find the final total.

Now introduce sums with improper fractions. Dictate $1^6/_{10} + 1^5/_{10}$. How many wholes? (2) How many tenths? (11) What is $^{11}/_{10}$? (an improper fraction) What must we do?

Students respond: Regroup. They change the $^{11}/_{10}$ into $1^1/_{10}$ and arrive at a total of $3^1/_{10}$.

Demonstrate the form:

$$\begin{array}{r} 1^6/_{10} \\ + \ 1^5/_{10} \\ \hline 2^{11}/_{10} = 2 + ^{11}/_{10} = 2 + 1 + ^1/_{10} = 3^1/_{10} \end{array}$$

Students do more Marvin problems, writing each step as they do it until they feel confident enough to write first and then check with blocks.

Procedure 3 ▫

To practice adding mixed numbers

Use *fraction bars or Cuisenaire® rods or pattern blocks* and *moon stations*.

Follow Procedures 1–2, using alternate materials. First review changing improper fractions to mixed numbers if necessary. Students need much practice working with the manipulatives and then both working with materials and writing down each step to internalize the concepts.

Procedure 4 ☐■

To subtract mixed numbers; tenths only

Use *pv blocks or Cuisenaire® rods* and *Marvin*.

Let a ten rod equal one whole. Each one cube will be $^1/_{10}$. Have students place $3^6/_{10}$ as shown. Write:

$$3^6/_{10}$$
$$- \ 1^3/_{10}$$

Instruct students to pull down $1^3/_{10}$. Ask: How many wholes are left? (2) How many tenths are left? ($^3/_{10}$)

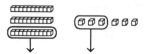

Dictate several more problems. Example: If Marvin had $3^5/_{10}$ pizzas and then ate 1 whole one and $^2/_{10}$ of one, how much would be left? *Do not dictate any problems yet that would require regrouping.*

Students write down each step as they do it with blocks. When they are comfortable with the skill, they work problems on paper first and then check with blocks.

Introduce regrouping **with the problem $4^3/_{10} - 2^5/_{10}$. Do we have a problem? (yes, not enough tenths) If we were subtracting with whole numbers, not fractions, what would we do? (regroup or rename)**

Can we do the same thing here? How many tenths does it take to make a whole? (10) We can get more tenths by renaming one of the wholes as 10 tenths. Write:

$$4^3/_{10} \ = \ 3^{13}/_{10}$$
$$- \ 2^5/_{10} \ = \ 2^5/_{10}$$

Students regroup to get $3^{13}/_{10}$. They then pull down $2^5/_{10}$ as you finish the problem on the board.

Dictate $3^2/_{10} - 1^4/_{10}$, $4^4/_{10} - 3^6/_{10}$, $4^4/_{10} - {^6/_{10}}$ as Marvin stories. Have students continue to work with blocks while writing as before.

Procedure 5 ☐■

To subtract mixed numbers; fractions other than tenths

Use *pattern blocks*.

Let a hexagon equal a whole. Have students place $2^3/_6$ as shown. Write $2^3/_6 - 1^1/_6$ on the board. Instruct students to pull down $1^1/_6$. Ask: How many are left? ($1^2/_6$)

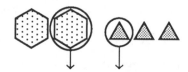

Students write each step as they do it.

Now introduce regrouping. **Write $3^2/_6 - 1^4/_6$ on the board. Ask: What is the problem? (not enough sixths)**

When we work with tenths, we group at 10. Ten tenths made a whole. When we work with sixths, what do we group at? (6; 6 sixths make a whole)

Students place $3^2/_6$, trade a yellow hexagon for 6 triangles to get $2^8/_6$, and solve the problem.

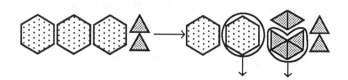

Dictate more problems involving regrouping. When ready, students do the problems first on paper and then check with the blocks.

Practice and Extension

Challenge students to choose another manipulative and to demonstrate subtraction of mixed numbers. They might choose *beans, fraction bars, bills, coins,* or *interlocking cubes*.

Have students write on *index cards* word problems that involve addition and subtraction of mixed numbers. They can trade problems to solve, or cards may be kept in a file.

Continue the saga of *Marvin the Mammoth, the Mixed Number Muncher*. Students may wish to compile a math book of problems and drawings for others to use with mixed numbers.

Fractions 9

Skill: To find a common denominator using LCM/LCD

Time: 2+ periods

Materials:

objects: buttons, beans, or counters; 40 per student

markers: two colors

pattern blocks

See Reproducibles for: equivalency charts, hundred boards

Anticipatory Set

Use *equivalency charts*.

Review comparing fractions with unlike denominators, using the equivalency chart. Then have students turn their equivalency charts face down.

Tell students they each have the same number of coins. Some students have $5/7$ of their coins in dimes, the rest in pennies. The other students have $2/3$ of their coins in dimes. Who has the most money? Why is this difficult to figure out without a chart?

Procedure 1   □■

To understand common denominator; manipulatives only

Use *objects*.

Remind students that in order to compare fractions, they need to know the size of the fraction and the size of the whole.

Ask: Which fraction is bigger, $3/5$ or $2/4$? What is the problem?

Students respond: The denominators are not the same. The pieces are not the same size; the whole may not be the same.

Give students 40 buttons or beans. Have them form two lines of 20 each. Twenty will be our whole. How do we show $3/5$ of the first 20 beans?

Students divide the beans into fifths and separate three of the fifths.

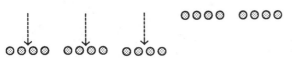

Now have students show $2/4$ of the second group of 20 beans.

How many beans are in $3/5$ of 20? (12) $12/20$ is *equivalent* to $3/5$. Write $3/5 = 12/20$.

How many are in $2/4$ of 20? (10) $10/20$ is *equivalent* to $2/4$. Write $2/4 = 10/20$.

We found $12/20$ is bigger than $10/20$, so which is bigger, $3/5$ or $2/4$? ($3/5$)

What is the size of our new whole? (20) What did we have to do to compare two fractions with different denominators?

Students respond: Make them fractions of the same-size whole.

Point out that we are substituting equivalent fractions with the same-size whole, the same-size denominator. We call this same-size denominator a *common denominator* because it is common to, or shared by, two fractions.

Can we choose just any denominator for a common denominator?

Students respond: No, It has to be one that will work for both fractions.

Repeat with other fractions and wholes, such as $3/8$ and $2/4$ (8), $3/7$ and $1/2$ (14). Use a story format or have students use the given numbers to make up situations for the class to solve.

Students write equivalencies as they discover them. They will need much practice at this level.

Procedure 2   □■

To understand least common multiple and least common denominator

Use *equivalency charts, hundred boards, markers,* and *objects (2 colors or types).*

Hand out equivalency charts. Ask: What are some fractions equivalent to $\frac{1}{2}$? ($\frac{2}{4}$, $\frac{3}{6}$, $\frac{4}{8}$, etc.) If we are working with $\frac{1}{2}$, the denominator of any equivalent fraction is going to be a multiple of what?

Students review that any fraction equivalent to halves will have a denominator that is a multiple of 2.

Repeat for $\frac{1}{3}$ and other fractions until students show understanding.

Hand out hundred boards. Say: We are going to compare $\frac{1}{2}$ and $\frac{1}{3}$ but need to find a denominator that will work for both. What multiples will you mark for $\frac{1}{2}$?

Students respond: 2. They mark all multiples of two with a dot of one color.

Now let's look at $\frac{1}{3}$. What do we know about the denominators of fractions equivalent to $\frac{1}{3}$? (They will be multiples of three.)

Students dot the multiples of three with a second color marker.

What number could we use that would be a multiple of *both* two and three? (6, 12, 18, etc.)

We'll use the smallest, or least, number that is a common multiple of both two and three. We call this number the *least common multiple* and abbreviate it LCM. What is the LCM of two and three? (6)

We need a common denominator for the fractions $\frac{1}{2}$ and $\frac{1}{3}$. We need to look for a multiple which will work for, *is common to,* both fractions we are comparing.

To keep things simple, we look for the smallest one possible and call it the *least common denominator.* This is abbreviated LCD.

Ask: What is the LCD for $\frac{1}{2}$ and $\frac{1}{3}$? (6) How is the LCD different from the least common multiple, the LCM?

Students respond: The number is the same. The LCM is the smallest multiple two numbers share. When we use the LCM as the same-size denominator for fractions equivalent to the ones we're working with, we call the LCM the LCD.

Students now use hundred boards and two colors or types of objects to mark multiples and to find the LCM for three and five, three and seven.

Repeat until students show competence in the skill.

Emphasize that the size of the fractions has to be the same to compare, add, or subtract them.

When students are comfortable with the hundred boards, have them list multiples of two numbers and choose the LCM on paper first and then check with the hundred boards.

Procedure 3

To visualize common denominators

Use *pattern blocks.*

If needed for understanding, use pattern blocks $\frac{1}{2}$ (red trapezoid) and $\frac{1}{3}$ (blue parallelogram). Say: We need to find a color/shape of pattern block that will cover each exactly. We are looking for a fraction size each can share, the same denominator.

Help students visualize covering both with another block color/shape: the green triangles representing sixths.

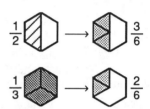

Have students physically cover original blocks and write findings. Relate this idea to equivalent fractions.

Repeat with manipulatives until students grasp the concept.

Practice and Extension

Challenge students to show LCDs using *fraction bars* or *equivalency charts.*

Have student bring in *grocery store advertisements* that show unlike fractions. Have them list all the situations they can think of as examples of when they might need to compare unlike fractions. Have them decide which item is the better buy.

Have student pairs use two *dice.* In turn, they throw the dice twice. For each throw, they create a fraction using either number as the numerator and find the LCD for the two fractions. They keep a running total of their LCDs. The winner is the student with the lower total after five turns. What strategies were they able to devise for choosing the fraction to make from their second throw?

Fractions 10

Skill: To add and subtract fractions: unlike denominators

Time: 2–3 periods

Materials:

pattern blocks

fraction bars (directions in Manipulative Information section) or Cuisenaire® rods

See Reproducibles for: moon stations

Anticipatory Set

Use *pattern blocks* and *moon stations*.

One moon station outline is one whole. Have each student use only one color block to make two fractions with the blocks, and make up an addition word problem to fit. They explain all parts of the fractions to a partner, and how they solved the problem.

Now have each moon station represent one measuring cup. If I have $3/4$ of a cup of sugar and $1/2$ of a cup of flour, can I get them both into the cup at the same time? Can they use one color block to solve this?

Procedure 1

To add fractions with unlike denominators

Use *pattern blocks* and *moon stations*.

Problem answers should be less than 1 until students have grasped the concept.

Have students place blocks on a moon station to make the fractions $1/2$ (1 yellow hexagon) and $1/4$ (1 red trapezoid). Ask: Can we add them together?

 $\frac{1}{2} + \frac{1}{4}$

If students answer $3/4$, say they have covered $3/4$ of a moon station, but how many actual fourths do they show? (still only 1)

Say: You show $1/2$ and $1/4$. In order to show only one fraction, you must have only one color block. Can you find an equivalent fraction for $1/2$? ($2/4$)

Change the yellow hexagon for two trapezoids.

Now what fraction is shown for the total? ($3/4$) Write on the board:

$$\begin{array}{r} 1/2 = 2/4 \\ + \ 1/4 = 1/4 \\ \hline 3/4 \end{array}$$

Next have students place blocks to solve $3/4 + 2/12$. Ask: Did you have to trade block colors? (yes) Why? What did you trade for? (all green twelfths) Now you have a problem you can do.

Write the problem on the board as before.

Review finding equivalent fractions or common denominators if necessary.

Repeat the process with $1/6 + 1/2$, and $5/12 + 1/6$.

Now move to problems with answers of 1 and larger, **and have students write each step with you.**

Have students solve $1/2 + 3/4$. Ask: What is different about this problem? (We have more than 1 whole.)

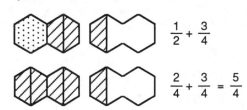

$\frac{1}{2} + \frac{3}{4}$

$\frac{2}{4} + \frac{3}{4} = \frac{5}{4}$

Since our final answer should never be an improper fraction, what do we need to do? (change to a mixed number; $5/4 = 1\frac{1}{4}$)

Repeat the process until students are comfortable with the skill. Then have them try to do the problem on paper first before checking with the blocks.

Procedure 2

To practice adding fractions with unlike denominators

Use *fraction bars or Cuisenaire® rods* and *paper*.

Follow Procedure 1. Have students first place one whole bar for comparison. They lay the fraction parts end to end to add them and then find bars of all one color that make up the same length as shown on the next page.

1		

$\frac{1}{2}$		$\frac{1}{4}$

$\frac{1}{2} + \frac{1}{4}$

$\frac{1}{4}$	$\frac{1}{4}$	$\frac{1}{4}$

$\frac{3}{4}$

Students place bars and write the steps. Then they try solving the problem on paper before checking with the bars. Give the fractions in story problem form.

Have students solve the problem from the Anticipatory Set without using manipulatives.

Procedure 3

To subtract fractions with unlike denominators

Use *pattern blocks, moon stations,* and *paper.*

Have students use only one color block to set up two fractions. Example: $^8/_{12}$, $^3/_{12}$. They make up a subtraction word problem to fit and then solve it.

Have students place blocks for $^1/_2$ on one moon station, and $^1/_4$ on another to show how much needs to be subtracted. Ask them to take $^1/_4$ away from the $^1/_2$, using the second moon station as a model. How can they do this?

Students see that they can change the $^1/_2$ (yellow hexagon) into $^2/_4$ (two red trapezoids) and then remove a fourth (trapezoid).

Ask: When have we had to change block colors, denominators, before? (to add fractions with different denominators)

Review common denominators.

Dictate $^{12}/_{12} - ^5/_6$.

Students cover one moon station with 12 twelfths and place 5 sixths on a second to see how much has to be removed.

Can you subtract enough twelfths to cover the $^5/_6$?

Students cover the $^5/_6$ with $^{10}/_{12}$.

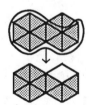

What did you change the sixths to? (twelfths)

Say: Instead of subtracting sixths, you found the common denominator and subtracted twelfths. I need to show this when I write it:

$$\begin{array}{r} ^{12}/_{12} = ^{12}/_{12} \\ - \quad ^5/_6 = ^{10}/_{12} \\ \hline ^2/_{12} \end{array}$$

Have students solve: $^3/_4 - ^7/_{12}$, $^1/_2 - ^3/_{12}$. Give the problems in story form.

Students place both fractions. They cover the subtrahend fraction with blocks taken from the minuend.

Ask: How is this different from subtracting fractions with the same denominator?

Students respond: Once you find a common denominator, it isn't different.

Have students practice with more problems, especially those given in a story format, until they are comfortable with the process. Write the process on the board.

Now move to the stage at which students write each corresponding step on paper, as well as use manipulatives.

Students need to understand that the written form is just a description of what is actually happening.

After students are confident in the skill, they can move to writing the problem first and then checking each step with their blocks.

Procedure 4

To practice subtracting fractions with unlike denominators

Use *fraction bars or Cuisenaire® rods* and *paper.*

Follow Procedure 3. Have students place bars and write down the steps. Then they try solving the problem on paper before checking with the bars.

After working through both procedures, allow students to choose a preferred manipulative to check their problems.

Practice and Extension

Have students use *recipes* with fractional amounts to make up and solve word problems.

Have them work in pairs to make up subtraction problems using unlike fractions. Example: $^5/_6$ of the class likes only vanilla ice cream. $^1/_{12}$ of the class likes only strawberry. How much of the class is left?

Challenge students to write a story about 12 months of their life. They must refer to fractional parts of the year *without* using 12 as a denominator. Caution them not to exceed 1 year. Example: For the first $^2/_{24}$ of a year, Alyson stuck to her New Year's resolution and did not use the magic crystal. However . . .

Fractions 11

Skill: To round fractions to the nearest whole number

Time: 1+ periods

Materials:

place value (pv) blocks or Cuisenaire® rods: 1s and 10s

pattern blocks

fraction bars (directions in Manipulative Information section) or Cuisenaire® rods

See Reproducibles for: Rounding Rhyme, moon stations

Anticipatory Set

Use *pv blocks* and *Rounding Rhymes*.

Have students place 1 ten rod on their desks, with 8 one cubes to the right. They should also write the number 18.

Review Rounding Rhyme, using a strong rhythm:

Mark the place,
Look to the right
Four or less are out of sight!

Five and up
Will buy one more
Before they, too, are out the door.

In those empty
Right-hand spaces,
Zeros keep the proper places.

Have students round 18 to the nearest 10. Have them also round 23, 8, and then 5. When they rounded 5, they rounded up to 1 ten rod.

What fraction of the ten rod is 5 cubes? ($^1/_2$)
$^1/_2$ rounds up to 1. What fraction is 3 cubes? ($^3/_{10}$)
$^3/_{10}$ rounds down to 0. Do they see a pattern?

Procedure 1

To round fractions to the nearest whole number

Use *pattern blocks* and *moon stations*.

Let one moon station be one whole. Have students place $^{11}/_{12}$ on a station.

Ask: Is $^{11}/_{12}$ closer to covering 1 whole moon station space, or no space? (1) Write $^{11}/_{12} \rightarrow 1$ as shown in the illustration.

Have them place $^2/_{12}$. Is $^2/_{12}$ closer to 1 or none? (none) Write $^2/_{12} \rightarrow 0$.

Have them next place $^6/_{12}$.

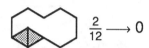

If the rule for rounding fractions is like the rule for whole numbers, is the $^6/_{12}$ closer to 1 or none? (1)

Think about a whole made of $^{12}/_{12}$. How many twelfths would make only *half* of the space? ($^6/_{12}$) You need six or more twelfths to round to a whole.

Say: Write all the twelfths from $^{12}/_{12}$ to $^0/_{12}$, with $^{12}/_{12}$ at the top of the list and $^0/_{12}$ on the bottom. Round each to 1 or 0.

Students write their chart. They make each amount with pattern blocks if they need to.

Think about a whole made of $^4/_4$. How many fourths would make only *half* of the space? ($^2/_4$) You need two or more fourths to round up.

Students chart and round all the fourths.

How many twentieths would you need to be able to round up? ($^{10}/_{20}$) Do they see a pattern?

Students should see that a numerator equal to half of the denominator will give them the point at which they round up. If they do not see this, continue with other fractions until the pattern becomes clear.

Students can be reminded that 5 of 10 one cubes is 5 and rounds up. $^5/_{10}$ is the same as $^1/_2$.

When students are comfortable with rounding fractions less than 1, have them place $1^5/_6$.

Is the *fraction* part closer to 1 or none? (1) We can call it 1 more whole moon station. Now how many moon stations do you have? (2)

Continue giving mixed numbers to round, ending with $1^1/_2$.

Students work with only blocks until they have grasped the concept. They then write the fractions as well, following the format shown above.

Procedure 2

☐

To round fractions using a number line

Use *fraction bars* or *Cuisenaire® rods.*

Follow Procedure 1, using fraction bars or Cuisenaire® rods. Students can lay out a whole bar and a ½ bar for comparison. Students should think of the left side of the whole as zero, and the right side as one.

Have students draw a line the same length as one whole on their paper.

Students mark 0 at the left end of the line, 1 at the right end, and ½ at a mark in the middle:

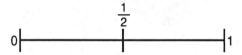

Have students use fraction bars to compare whether a fraction falls between 0 and ½ or between ½ and 1. Ask: Is it closer to 1 or none?

Students indicate each fraction's position on the fraction line as they round it. They give each other story problems to solve, such as running ⅛, ⅚, and ¹⁴/₂₀ of a mile. *About* how far is that? Would it be easier to round first or to add the fractions and then round?

Practice and Extension

Have student list weights or volume from *food containers that have fractions.* Have them compare adding all the amounts with and without rounding.

Have students use the financial section of the *newspaper* to pick stocks to follow. Do they do better or worse by rounding the fraction amounts they find?

Fractions 12

Skill: To add and subtract mixed numbers: unlike denominators

Time: 2–3 periods

Materials:

pattern blocks

fraction bars (directions in Manipulative Information section) or Cuisenaire® rods

See Reproducibles for: Marvin the Mammoth, moon stations

Anticipatory Set

Use *Marvin the Mammoth* and *pattern blocks*.

Marvin the Mixed Number Muncher is at it again. He ate 1⅙ jars of pickles in the morning and 2⁴⁄₆ jars in the afternoon. How much did he eat in all? Have students solve the problem, using the pattern blocks.

Procedure 1 ☐■

To add mixed numbers with unlike denominators

Use *pattern blocks, moon stations, Marvin the Mammoth,* and *paper.*

Two yellow hexagons equal one whole moon station.

Review adding mixed numbers with like denominators by having students add 1³⁄₆ + 1²⁄₆ and 1⁴⁄₁₂ + ³⁄₁₂.

Students place blocks, writing each step as they do it.

Review adding fractions with unlike denominators by having students add ³⁄₆ + ²⁄₁₂ and ¼ + ³⁄₆.

Students place blocks and write each step as they solve the problems. They substitute equivalent fractions as necessary to find the least common denominator.

Say: Marvin now eats 1⅙ of a container of chow mein in the morning, and another 1¼ in the afternoon. How much has he eaten so far?

Have students place 1⅙ and 1¼. Can they figure out how to solve this? Do they know enough?

Students try to solve the problem with blocks.

Point out that they have enough knowledge because they already know how to add mixed numbers and they already know how to add unlike fractions.

Dictate: 1⁵⁄₆ + 1¼. How is this different?

Students change fractions to twelfths, add the fractions, and discover they have an improper fraction.

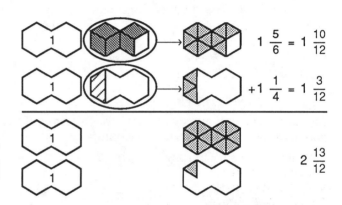

$$1\frac{5}{6} = 1\frac{10}{12}$$

$$+1\frac{1}{4} = 1\frac{3}{12}$$

$$2\frac{13}{12}$$

Remind students to reduce all fractions to simplest terms.

Students regroup ¹²⁄₁₂ as 1 and have 3¹⁄₁₂.

Continue to dictate mixed numbers in a story format for students to add.

Students solve problems with blocks. When they feel comfortable with the skill, they write each corresponding step as they do it. Next they try working on paper first, checking each step with the blocks. They look for the fewest blocks possible to reduce their answer to simplest terms.

Procedure 2 ☐

To practice adding mixed numbers with unlike denominators

Use *fraction bars* or *Cuisenaire® rods.*

Repeat Procedure 1, using fraction bars or Cuisenaire® rods. Emphasize that students already have the necessary skills for this process.

Procedure 3 ☐■

To subtract mixed numbers with unlike denominators; no regrouping

Use *pattern blocks, moon stations, Marvin,* and *paper.*

Let two yellow hexagons equal one whole. Review subtracting mixed numbers with like denominators. As an aid to visualizing subtraction, have students place separate blocks for the amount to be subtracted below the initial amount as a guide to how much must be removed.

Say: Marvin stored away $2^4/_6$ jars of pickles one morning but ate $1^2/_6$ jars of them in the afternoon. How much did he have left?

Students place the $2^4/_6$ above and $1^2/_6$ below. They remove the required amount from above and cover the $1^2/_6$ below, writing each step as they do it.

Review subtracting fractions with unlike denominators by having students subtract $^3/_6 - {}^2/_{12}$ and $^5/_6 - {}^2/_{12}$.

Students place the fractions with blocks. They substitute equivalent fractions as necessary to find the least common denominator and remove the required amount, continuing to write each step.

Have students write $1^5/_6 - 1^1/_4$. Can they figure out how to solve this? Do they know enough?

Students try to solve the problem with blocks.

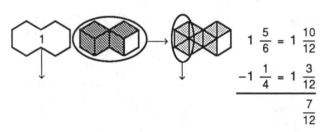

$$1\frac{5}{6} = 1\frac{10}{12}$$
$$-1\frac{1}{4} = 1\frac{3}{12}$$
$$\frac{7}{12}$$

Point out that the students have enough knowledge because they know how to subtract mixed numbers and how to subtract unlike fractions.

Students create and solve Marvin stories as you give them numbers to subtract.

Procedure 4

To subtract mixed numbers with unlike denominators; with regrouping

Use *pattern blocks, moon stations, Marvin,* and *paper.*

Dictate: $2^1/_4 - 1^5/_{12}$.

Students place $2^1/_4$ and use extra blocks below to place $1^5/_{12}$. They try to subtract.

Ask: How is this different from what we have been doing?

Students respond: We can't subtract unless we change the fractions to the same denominator. They change $^1/_4$ to $^3/_{12}$ and notice they still can't subtract.

When we work with base ten blocks and whole numbers, what do we do if we want to subtract 13 from 20? (rename 1 ten and 10 ones)

Can we do something similar here? (change a 1 to $^{12}/_{12}$) What number would we have? ($1^{15}/_{12}$)

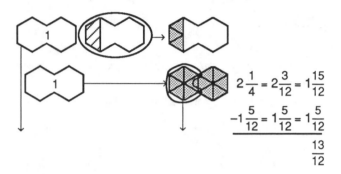

$$2\frac{1}{4} = 2\frac{3}{12} = 1\frac{15}{12}$$
$$-1\frac{5}{12} = 1\frac{5}{12} = 1\frac{5}{12}$$
$$\frac{13}{12}$$

How is this different from the subtracting we have been doing? (It is the same after the fractions have the same denominator.)

As students do each step with blocks, they write the corresponding step on their paper. They look for the fewest blocks possible to reduce their answer to simplest terms.

Continue to give stories about Marvin that have amounts to subtract. Include some in which a fraction is subtracted from a whole number.

When students are confident about the process, they write the problem first and then check each step with blocks.

Procedure 5

To practice subtracting mixed numbers

Use *fraction bars* or *Cuisenaire® rods.*

Repeat Procedure 3 or 4, using fraction bars or Cuisenaire® rods.

Practice and Extension

Have students mark *wooden cubes* or *foam dice* with fractions. They roll two *regular dice* and two *fraction dice* and then add or subtract the totals. The winner is the one with the highest (or lowest) total after five turns.

Have students use the *financial section of the newspaper* to write problems about the stock market that use mixed numbers and can be solved by adding or subtracting.

Fractions 13

Skill: To multiply a fraction by a fraction; to multiply a fraction and a whole number

fraction bars (directions in Manipulative Information section) or Cuisenaire® rods

objects: cubes, counters, or beans; 16 per student

geoboards and rubber bands

See Reproducibles for: equivalency charts

Time: 2–3 periods

Materials:

graph paper: any size; several sheets per student

markers: 2 light colors

Anticipatory Set

Use *graph paper.*

Write 4 × 3 on the board, and have students make a 4 × 3 rectangle. We have three rows *of* four. Repeat with 2 × 4, emphasizing two rows *of* four. Help them see they can use "of" for the multiplication sign.

Procedure 1

To multiply a fraction by a fraction using arrays

Use *graph paper* and *markers.*

Have students look at the 4 × 3 rectangle they made. This will be 1 pound. Marvin had $\frac{1}{3}$ lb of apples and ate $\frac{1}{4}$ of what he had. Shade one third:

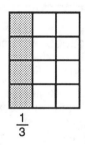

We want $\frac{1}{4}$ of $\frac{1}{3}$. Ask: How can we show this?

Students respond: Shade $\frac{1}{4}$. They do this:

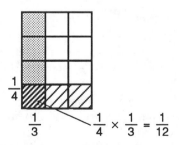

How many parts do we show that are the same size as the double-shaded square? (12) What is $\frac{1}{4}$ of $\frac{1}{3}$?

Students respond: One square, $\frac{1}{12}$ of the pound.

Write $\frac{1}{4} \times \frac{1}{3} = \frac{1}{12}$ on the board.

Repeat with other rectangles, continuing to add to the list of results on the board. Try a 10 × 10 rectangle, shading it to show $\frac{1}{5} \times \frac{1}{2} = \frac{1}{10}$, and a 4 × 4 rectangle for $\frac{2}{4} \times \frac{1}{4} = \frac{2}{16}$.

Students look for a pattern that will work for all cases. They write the problem and solution by each rectangle.

Discuss the findings: To multiply fractions, multiply their numerators and multiply their denominators.

Ask: Will this work for all fractions? What about $\frac{1}{3} \times \frac{6}{4}$? Start with a 3 × 4 rectangle, and divide it into fourths and thirds.

How many parts in all? (12) So we're working with twelfths. We have $\frac{6}{4}$ in our problem. Shade another 2 fourths to the side and shade $\frac{1}{3}$ of those fourths.

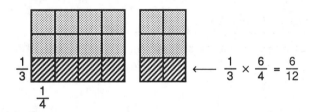

How many twelfths are shaded? (6) $\frac{1}{3} \times \frac{6}{4} = \frac{6}{12}$, the rule holds for improper fractions as well.

Students create and solve Marvin problems. They work with the graph paper as long as they need to.

Procedure 2

To multiply a fraction by a fraction using fraction bars

Use *fraction bars or Cuisenaire® rods* and *equivalency charts.*

Remind students that 3 × 4 means three rows *of* four. Ask: What do you think $\frac{1}{2}$ of $\frac{1}{4}$ could mean?

Have students find a bar worth $\frac{1}{4}$ and fold it in half to find $\frac{1}{2}$ of it. What bar is equal to this amount?

Students find that $\frac{1}{2}$ of $\frac{1}{4}$ equals $\frac{1}{8}$.

Write $\frac{1}{2} \times \frac{1}{4} = \frac{1}{8}$ on the board.

How many eighths would $\frac{2}{2} \times \frac{1}{4}$ be? (2) Write $\frac{2}{2} \times \frac{1}{4} = \frac{2}{8}$. Repeat with $\frac{1}{4} \times \frac{1}{4}$, and $\frac{3}{4} \times \frac{1}{4}$. Can students see a pattern to their answers?

Students should see they multiply the numerators and denominators when multiplying fractions.

Repeat until students are comfortable with the concept.

What about improper fractions? Write $1\frac{1}{2} = \frac{3}{2}$. Have students find $\frac{3}{2}$ of $\frac{1}{4} = \frac{3}{8}$ with their bars. This procedure works for all fractions.

Students use equivalency charts for further practice.

Procedure 3

To multiply fractions of amounts by fractions of amounts

Use *objects*.

Have students lay out 16 buttons and find $\frac{1}{4}$ of them.

Write $\frac{1}{2} \times \frac{1}{4}$ on the board. Ask: What word can we use when we see the multiplication sign? (*of*) Find $\frac{1}{2}$ of the group that is $\frac{1}{4}$ of the buttons.

Students separate their group of four into two groups with two buttons in each group.

We now have two buttons. What whole did we start with? (16) What fraction of the whole is $\frac{1}{2}$ of $\frac{1}{4}$? ($\frac{2}{16}$) Simplified, that is $\frac{1}{8}$. Write $\frac{1}{2} \times \frac{1}{4} = \frac{1}{8}$.

Repeat as in other procedures, trying $\frac{3}{2} \times \frac{1}{4}$ and $1\frac{1}{2} \times \frac{1}{4}$.

Procedure 4

To multiply fractions and whole numbers

Use *fraction bars* or *Cuisenaire® rods*.

Have students place a whole bar and a fourth bar. Write $3 \times \frac{1}{4}$ on the board. Say: We want three of the fourths. Can you show that?

Students place 3 fourths. The total is $\frac{3}{4}$.

Write $3 \times \frac{1}{4} = \frac{3}{4}$. Repeat with $4 \times \frac{2}{8}$ and $3 \times \frac{2}{6}$, and have students look for a rule.

Students respond: You multiply the whole number by the numerator of the fraction to get the product.

Ask: Can we relate this to what we know about multiplying fractions?

If students do not make the connection, ask if three can be written as a fraction.

Students respond: Three can be written $\frac{3}{1}$, so $3 \times \frac{1}{4}$ is the same as $\frac{3}{1} \times \frac{1}{4}$.

Multiplying whole numbers and fractions is just like multiplying fractions together. The answer is the product of the numerators over the product of the denominators.

Students create stories with numbers you give them. Make sure to include some improper fractions.

Procedure 5

To practice multiplying fractions and whole numbers

Use *geoboards and rubber bands*.

Let one square be our whole. Enclose a rectangle that has the value of 12, or $\frac{12}{1}$. Use another rubber band to show half *of* the first rectangle: $\frac{1}{2} \times \frac{12}{1}$. Ask: How many squares will you have?

Students respond: Six. They write $\frac{1}{2} \times \frac{12}{1} = 6$.

What are $\frac{2}{2}$ *of* 12, or $\frac{2}{2} \times \frac{12}{1}$? (12)

Write $\frac{2}{2} \times \frac{12}{1} = \frac{24}{2} = \frac{12}{1} = 12$. Point out that they are multiplying fractions by fractions; the answer is the product of the numerators over the product of the denominators.

Students suggest other problems of fractions of whole numbers they could solve on the geoboards. They write each step as they solve them. When they are competent in the skill, they write first and then check with the geoboards.

Practice and Extension

Bring in a *calorie chart,* and have students make up and solve problems about *Marvin's* diet. Have them figure the calorie amounts of their meals for several days.

Have students write and solve word problems for time and for distance: Marvin had $2\frac{1}{2}$ miles to walk to find his bushel of sandwiches, but he only walked $\frac{1}{4}$ of it before he tired. How far did he get? He had $3\frac{1}{4}$ hours of homework but could only work for $\frac{1}{8}$ of the time before he *had* to eat. How long did he work?

Fractions 14

Skill: To divide a whole number by a fraction

Time: 2 periods

Materials:

objects: buttons, beans, or counters; 12 per student

fraction bars (directions in Manipulative Information section) or Cuisenaire® rods

pattern blocks

Anticipatory Set

Use *objects*.

Write 12 ÷ 3 on the board. Remind students that this means 12 divided into groups of 3. Have students lay 12 buttons in a row. Point out that another way of stating each problem is to ask how many 3s are *contained in* the 12. How many *are* there? Did they make groups of 3s? Repeat for 12 ÷ 2.

Procedure 1

To develop the concept of dividing a whole number by a fraction

Use *fraction bars or Cuisenaire® rods* and *paper*.

Students work in groups and share fraction bars.

Keep the numerators at 1 until students are comfortable with the process.

Write 2 ÷ ¹/₄. This means 2 divided into groups of fourths. We can also ask how many fourths are *contained in* 2. If we were using buttons, we would have to break them into fourths to find out.

Say: Lay out two whole fraction bars, and find how many ¹/₄ bars are contained in two whole bars.

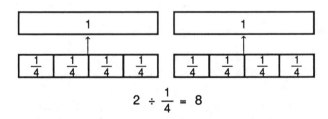

$$2 \div \frac{1}{4} = 8$$

Students discover that eight fourths are contained in two wholes. They start a chart: "Problem" "Answer." They write 2 ÷ ¹/₄ and 8.

Ask: How many fourths were in each whole? (4) How many in two wholes? (8)

Next write 3 ÷ ¹/₄. How many fourths are contained in three whole bars?

Students discover that 12 fourths are contained in 3 wholes. They chart 3 ÷ ¹/₄, 12.

Repeat with 2 ÷ ¹/₂ (4) and 3 ÷ ¹/₈ (24).

Ask whether students see a pattern in their chart.

Some students will see that they can arrive at the answer by *multiplying* the whole number by the denominator of the fraction. *(This is true because all numerators are kept at 1 at this stage.)*

Suppose we are dividing by fourths—dividing into groups of fourths. We would have to multiply the whole numbers by four to find out how many fourths in all.

If we divide specifically by ¹/₄, we only need one of the fourths in each group.

***Now move to numerators greater than 1.* Say: Now we'll get more complicated. We'll do 3 ÷ ²/₄. What does this mean?**

Students respond: How many groups of 2 fourths are contained in 3.

First find out how many fourths there are in all.

Students cover three whole bars with fourths.

How many fourths? (12) How else could we have found the answer?

Students respond: Multiply the 3 by 4 since there are 4 fourths in each whole.

Yes, we could multiply by the denominator to find 12 fourths in 3 wholes. We're dividing by ²/₄, though. Put those 12 fourths into groups with ²/₄s in each group. How many groups do we have?

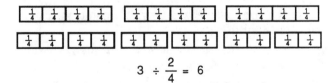

$$3 \div \frac{2}{4} = 6$$

Students put the 12 fourths into groups of 2 and discover there are 6 groups. They write 3 ÷ ²/₄, 6.

There were 12 fourths in all, and we divided them into groups of 2, ending up with 6 groups.

Have students practice with bars only until they are comfortable with the process.

With each problem emphasize *multiplying* by the denominator to find the total and then *dividing* by the numerator—the size of groups called for.

Students will need much practice at this stage to understand the concept.

Examples:

$$2 \div {}^4\!/_8 = 4 \text{ groups of } {}^4\!/_8\text{s}$$
$$3 \div {}^6\!/_8 = 4 \text{ groups of } {}^6\!/_8\text{s}$$
$$1 \div {}^3\!/_4 = 1 \text{ group and } {}^1\!/_3 \text{ of a group}$$

Go to Procedure 2.

Procedure 2

To understand invert and multiply by the reciprocal

Use *pattern blocks or fraction bars, student charts from Procedure 1,* and *paper.*

Say: We've found that to divide a whole number by a fraction, we multiply by the denominator to find total parts and then divide by the numerator to find the number of groups called for. When we write the process, we can use a shortcut.

Think of $6 \div 3$. We divide the 6 into 3 groups. What fraction is *each* of the three groups? ($^1\!/_3$) How else can we write $^1\!/_3$ of 6? ($^1\!/_3 \times 6$)

We have written our problem two ways: $6 \div 3$ and $6 \times ^1\!/_3$. What is the answer to $6 \div 3$? (2) What is the answer to $6 \times ^1\!/_3$? ($^6\!/_1 \times ^1\!/_3 = ^6\!/_3 = 2$)

When we divide by a number, we can do the problem in two ways. We can divide, or we can invert that number and multiply.

The proper term for a number that has had its numerator and denominator inverted is *reciprocal.* A number and its reciprocal will equal $^1\!/_1$ when they are multiplied together: $^3\!/_1 \times ^1\!/_3 = ^3\!/_3 = 1$.

Have students make 6 hexagons with 3 blue parallelograms each. Write $6 \div ^1\!/_3$ on the board.

Have students divide those six into thirds to find how many are contained in the six.

Students separate the hexagons into separate thirds and find 18 thirds.

Write $^6\!/_1 \div ^1\!/_3 = 18$. The question is how many thirds we have in 6, how many thirds we have times 6.

We've found that when we divide by a *whole number,* we can get the answer also by multiplying by its reciprocal.

Does this work for dividing by *fractions?* What is the reciprocal of $^1\!/_3$? ($^3\!/_1$) Instead of $6 \div ^1\!/_3 = 18$, we'll write $^6\!/_1 \times ^3\!/_1 = ^{18}\!/_1 = 18$.

We divided the 18 by 1, since one was in each group.

Now try $6 \div ^2\!/_3$.

Students cover the hexagons with thirds then put them into groups of two. $6 \div ^2\!/_3 = 9$.

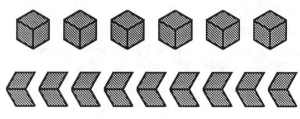

$$6 \div \frac{2}{3} = \frac{6}{1} \times \frac{3}{2} = \frac{18}{2} = 9$$

Write $^6\!/_1 \times ^3\!/_2$ on the board.

You multiplied by the 3 to find how many thirds and then divided by 2 when you put the thirds into groups. Is this the same as multiplying by the reciprocal of $^2\!/_3$?

Finish the problem to read: $^6\!/_1 \times ^3\!/_2 = ^{18}\!/_2 = 9.$

Students check their charts to see whether they could get the same results by multiplying by the reciprocals.

Repeat the procedure for $4 \div ^1\!/_2$, $3 \div ^2\!/_6$, and $4 \div ^3\!/_4$.

Students make hexagons, divide into the size groups called for, and solve the problem. They write the original problem, rewrite it as a multiplication problem, and then work with the blocks. After each step with the blocks they write the corresponding step on paper.

It is important for students to understand that the written form is just a description of what is actually happening.

After students become confident about the process, they move to writing the problem first and then checking each step with their blocks.

Practice and Extension

Students should make up and exchange story problems that divide whole numbers by fractions. Some examples may need to be given:

Clothes were collected for charity. In the collection were 16 sweaters. One fourth were cardigans and the rest pullovers. How many were cardigans? How many were pullovers?

Cut three sheet cakes into twentieths. How many people can you serve?

Skill: To divide a fraction by a
fraction

Time: 1+ periods

Materials:

*fraction bars (directions in Manipulative Information
section) or Cuisenaire® rods*

See Reproducibles for: equivalency charts—2 per
student

Anticipatory Set

Use *fraction bars* or *Cuisenaire® rods.*

Have students find $2 \div \frac{1}{4}$, *how many fourths are
contained in 2.* They lay out 2 wholes, and find how
many fourths it takes to cover them. (8) There are
8 fourths in 2. Repeat with $2 \div \frac{4}{8}$ (2) and $2 \div \frac{1}{2}$ (4).

Pose this problem: I have two cakes, and I divide
each into eighths. How many people can I serve? (16)
How do I write this as a math problem? Have students use the fraction bars to solve the problem.
$(2 \div \frac{1}{8} = 16)$

Explain that now there is only half of a cake left.
How many people can you serve—how many eighths
are left? The problem will be written as $\frac{1}{2} \div \frac{1}{8}$. How
can they solve it?

Procedure 1   ◻◼

To develop the concept of dividing a fraction by
a fraction

Use *fraction bars or Cuisenaire® rods* and *paper.*

**Continue the problem from the Anticipatory Set:
$\frac{1}{2} \div \frac{1}{8}$. Have students lay out their whole bar and
find the $\frac{1}{2}$. Say: We have to find out how many
eighths *are contained in* the $\frac{1}{2}$ bar.**

Students place eighths over the $\frac{1}{2}$ bar and find
4 eighths are in $\frac{1}{2}$.

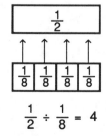

$$\frac{1}{2} \div \frac{1}{8} = 4$$

**Repeat the procedure with $\frac{8}{16} \div \frac{1}{4}$ (2) and $\frac{6}{8} \div \frac{2}{16}$
(6). Emphasize finding how many groups of a
certain size *are contained in* the original fraction.**

Students use the bars to find the answers. They chart
their results, looking for patterns.

**Continue the practice, giving problems with
mixed numbers as well: $1\frac{2}{4} \div \frac{2}{8}$ (6).**

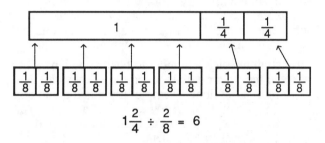

$$1\frac{2}{4} \div \frac{2}{8} = 6$$

**Write the mixed numbers as improper fractions
so that their chart entries will be consistent.**

Ask: Do you see any patterns in your charts?

Some students may see that they can invert and
multiply. Most should notice that they are coming out
with answers larger than one.

**Remind students that they know how to divide a
whole number like three by a fraction.**

**Ask: What do you have to do to the whole num-
ber before you invert the divisor and multiply?**

Students respond: Change it to that number over one,
like $\frac{3}{1}$.

**We've been using bars to divide fractions by
fractions. Is $\frac{3}{1}$ a fraction? (yes) Do you think we
could use this technique with a smaller fraction
like $\frac{2}{4}$?**

**Now move to the stage at which students write as
well as use the bars. Have students use bars and
write corresponding steps on paper as they work.**

Students rewrite their division problems as multiplication problems to see whether the answers are the
same.

**Dictate problems for students to solve. After they
become confident with the process, they can
move to working the problem first on paper and
then checking with their bars.**

Procedure 2

To practice dividing a fraction by a fraction

Use *equivalency charts.*

Repeat Procedure 1, using equivalency charts. After students find the first fraction, have them find how many of the second fraction are equivalent to, or *are contained in,* the first one.

Students work first with the chart and then with writing the problems as well. It is important that students understand that the written form is just a description of what is actually happening.

Practice and Extension

Students make up story problems for *Marvin the Mammoth.* Example: Marvin has $2\frac{1}{2}$ apple pies. He only wants to eat $\frac{1}{4}$ of what he has for dessert each meal. How many meals will his apple pie last?

Have students pick a number to be the quotient. They write all the fraction division problems they can that result in that quotient. Example: Eight is the quotient. Possible problems are $\frac{1}{2} \div \frac{1}{16}$, $\frac{4}{1} \div \frac{2}{4}$, and $\frac{4}{2} \div \frac{2}{8}$. Have students keep a chart of their equations and look for patterns to help them.

ACTIVITY MATH *FRACTIONS 15*

Decimals 1

Skill: To relate fractions to decimals: to recognize and order tenths

Time: 2+ periods

Materials:

graph paper: ½" squares

file-folder place value (pv) mats to 1000s

12" × 18" tag board for decimal extensions for pv mats

½" gummed dots: 1 per student

clear tape

rulers

pv blocks to 100s

scissors

counters: 1 per student

envelopes for storing graph paper decimals: 1 per student

See Reproducibles for: directions for file-folder pv mat decimal extensions, decimal bars for tenths—in the same color used for $1 bills, equivalency charts

Anticipatory Set

Use *graph paper.*

Have students outline a 1 × 10 square rectangle. Immediately below, they outline three identical rectangles. Label the top one "One." Divide the second rectangle in half and label "Halves." Divide and label the third as "Fifths." The bottom rectangle is "Tenths."

Have they seen a similar chart? (an equivalency chart) Have students discover all the fractions equivalent to tenths on the chart. Examples: ²/₅ = ⁴/₁₀; ½ = ⁵/₁₀.

Procedure 1 □■

To relate fraction tenths to decimal tenths and place value

Use *paper chart from Anticipatory Set, pv mats, tag board, directions for decimal extensions, gummed dots, tape, rulers, pv blocks,* and *decimal bars.*

Have students make decimal extensions, tape them to the right-hand side of their pv mats, and place a gummed dot for a decimal point. They should not label yet.

Next have students place one hundred flat, one ten rod, and one one cube on their pv mats. Write 111 on the board.

Ask: How many tens does it take to make 100? (10) What fraction of the hundred is each 10? (¹/₁₀)

Repeat for the relationship between 10 and 1.

If something is in the column to the right of the ones, how many of them it take to make a one? (10) What fraction of the one would it be? (¹/₁₀ of 1)

Have students replace the cube with a one bar and add a tenth bar in the column to the right.

Say: The whole bar is equal to a one. How many parts does the tenth bar have? (10) We are only interested in the shaded part. One part is shaded.

Ask: What fraction of one is it? (¹/₁₀) The shaded part is less than one whole. Find something similar on the graph paper chart.

Students find ¹/₁₀ on the chart.

How can we write ¹/₁₀ of one? (¹/₁₀)

Have students label "Tenths" on their decimal extensions. Fractions that are tenths are special in our number system because they can go on our place value chart.

We can also call them *decimal fractions* and write them in a special way.

You have placed a dot on your pv mat. Everything to the left is one whole or more. Everything to the right is less than one. This dot is a decimal point and goes in all numbers that have tenths in them.

Ask: How would I say the number we have on the mats? (one hundred eleven and one tenth) How would I write it? (111.1)

Have students place two more tenth bars on their mats and identify 111.3 both in words and numbers.

Students place whole numbers with decimal parts on their mats as you write them on the board. They chorally read each place and then write them, as well.

What must we do when we have 10 ones on the mat? (trade for a 10) What will we need to do when we have 10 tenths on the mat? (trade for 1 one)

Students place combinations of pv blocks on their mats, which will lead to trading. They chorally read each resulting number, as well as write it.

Procedure 2 □■

To relate decimals and fractions equivalent to tenths

Use *paper chart from Anticipatory Set, equivalency charts, scissors,* and *counters.*

Say: Miles are often measured in tenths. An odometer on your bicycle would be in miles and tenths of miles.

If I bicycled $\frac{1}{2}$ a mile, what would this be in tenths? ($\frac{5}{10}$) How many ways could you write this? ($\frac{5}{10}$, 0.5)

Students write: $\frac{1}{2} = \frac{5}{10} = 0.5$.

Continue until students are comfortable finding and writing decimal equivalents.

Ask: Can some fractions not be written as decimals? Why not?

Students respond: Not all fractions are equivalent to tenths. They use their equivalency charts to check this.

If I biked $2\frac{5}{10}$ miles, how would I see this on the odometer? (2.5) Repeat until students are competent in the skill.

Have students cut their graph paper chart into parts.

Students work in groups of three. One gives a number consisting of 1 and a decimal part, for example, 1.5 ounces of gold. The first student to assemble and write the number gets a point. They use counters for decimal points.

Procedure 3 □■

To order tenths

Use *graph paper, scissors, pv mats with extensions, envelopes,* and *paper.*

Have students cut out four 10 × 10 squares, label two of them "1," and cut the other two into 1 × 10 strips.

Ask: How many equal strips does it takes to equal the whole one? (10) Each strip is what fraction of the whole? ($\frac{1}{10}$) Review writing decimal tenths.

Have students place 1.2 on their mats and then 1.4 below.

Which is more, the 1.2 or 1.4? (1.4) When we have more tenths, the number is bigger. Write 1.4 > 1.2 on the board.

Have students add another seven tenths to the 1.2 to make 1.9 and then chorally read.

Ask: Which amount is more, the 1.4 or 1.9? (1.9) Why?

Students respond: It has more tenths.

Write 1.9 > 1.4 > 1.2 on the board.

Students continue to place numbers as you write them on the board. Use numbers both greater than and less one.

Have students place 1.9 and then add one more tenth strip. How many tenths do we have now? (10)

In our number system, whenever we get to 10 of anything, what do we need to do? (regroup)

Say: Decimals follow the same rule. What is equivalent to $\frac{10}{10}$ that we could trade for?

Students respond: 1 whole. They trade $\frac{10}{10}$ for 1 and chorally read: two ones and zero tenths.

Write 2.0 > 1.9 > 1.4 > 1.2 on the board. Ask: Do you see a pattern to which numbers are bigger?

Repeat, using amounts from 0.1 to 2.9.

Have students work in groups of three. Dictate three decimal amounts and have groups place and compare them. Then have them write the numbers in order of size.

When students are competent in the skill, have them order numbers on paper before checking with the strips.

Procedure 4 □

To order fractions and decimal tenths

Use *pv mats with extensions, pv blocks, decimal bars,* and *equivalency charts.*

Give story problems using decimals and fractions equivalent to decimals for students to place, solve, and write. Example: Half the class ate hot dogs, $\frac{1}{5}$ ate chicken, and $\frac{3}{10}$ ate tacos. Which food was most popular? Least popular?

Practice and Extension

Have students draw a map that includes several towns. They use a *graph paper 1 × 10 strip* to measure and mark the distances in miles and tenths of miles.

Have students predict and then record a week's mileage on their cars at home. Repeat for a second week and compare the accuracy of the estimates.

Duplicate sheets of *decimal bars for tenths,* and have students color in various amounts from 0.1 to 1.0. Students work in pairs to draw three bars, order them, and write the decimal amounts.

Have students make up word problems with distance and odometer readings. The emphasis should be on which trip covers the greatest or least distance.

Decimals 2

Skill: To add and subtract tenths

Time: 3 periods

Materials:

file-folder place value (pv) mats to 1000s with decimal extensions to tenths

pv blocks to 100s

decimal bars to tenths

coins: dimes, or counters; 20 per student

See Reproducibles for: directions for file-folder pv mats and decimal extensions, decimal bars to tenths—in the same color used for $1 bills, bills to 100s—in different colors

Anticipatory Set

Use *pv mats* and *pv blocks*.

Have students place one hundred, one ten, and one one on their mats. Ask: How many tens make 100? (10) Each ten is ¹/₁₀ of 100. Repeat for tens and ones. Have students place nine more ones on their mats. Have students add and subtract other amounts to review regrouping.

Procedure 1 □■

To add tenths

Use *pv mats, pv blocks,* and *decimal bars*.

Review with students the relationship between tenths and one whole. Tell students they will be responsible for measuring the progress of a team climbing Mt. Everest. The measurements will be done in meters and tenths of meters.

Have students clear their mats, since the climbing team is starting at ground level. The first day the team climbs 165.6 meters. Write this on the board.

Students place 165.6 on their mats and chorally read: 1 hundred, 6 tens, 5 ones, and 6 tenths of one.

The next day the team climbs 132.3 meters. Write the addition problem on the board, where a running total will be kept.

Students chorally read the amount and place 132.3 on their mats. They chorally read the total: 2 hundreds, 9 tens, 7 ones, and 9 tenths meters.

Add the total on the board. The third day the team climbs 123.0 meters. Write this on the board.

Students chorally read and place 123.0 on their mats. They regroup to get a total of 420.9 meters.

Do the problem on the board, calling attention to the regrouping. Ask: Do you see any pattern to adding with decimals?

Students may see that adding decimals is like adding whole numbers; you have lined up the decimal points. If they do not see this, erase the decimal point in the answer, and have students read the number.

The next day the climbing team went 101.8 meters. Have students place the amount but not total it.

Ask: How many tenths do you have in all? (17) In our number system we regroup when we have how many in any place? (10) Will this be true for decimals as well? (yes)

What are ten tenths equal to? (1) Trade ten tenths for one one and find the total distance climbed.

Students regroup and find the total of their blocks and bars is 522.7 meters.

Call attention to the regrouping in your addition on the board.

The team had a hard next day and only climbed 5 meters. Where should you write the five in the problem?

Students chorally read: 5 ones and 0 tenths. They discuss keeping the numbers lined up in the correct space. They place and total the blocks and bars.

Give more numbers from below, starting with 143.6. Keep a running total on the board.

Amount Added	Total	(Notes)
165.6	165.6	
132.3	297.9	
123.0	420.9	(regroup 1s, 10s)
101.8	522.7	(regroup tenths)
5	527.7	(no decimal part)
143.6	671.3	(regroup tenths, 1s)
100	771.3	(no decimal part)
39.9	811.2	(regroup all places)
80.7	891.9	

Proceed directly to Procedure 2.

Procedure 2 □■

To subtract tenths

Use *pv mats, pv blocks,* and *decimal bars*.

This is a continuation of Procedure 1. Otherwise, have students place 891.9 on their mats, the total meters climbed so far by the team on Mt. Everest.

Explain that a blizzard rages on Mt. Everest and the team has to retreat. Give students numbers of meters retreated each day: 103.2, 31.3, 123.1; *amounts do not include regrouping of decimals.*

Have students continue to chorally read the amount, emphasizing tenths of one.

Students remove blocks and bars as necessary as you do the problem on the board.

Next, introduce an amount to subtract that will include regrouping.

Ask: What do we do when we don't have enough tens on the mat for a subtraction problem? (trade 1 hundred for 10 tens)

What do we do if we don't have enough ones on the mat for a subtraction problem? (trade 1 ten for 10 ones)

What can we do if we don't have enough tenths to subtract? (trade 1 one for 10 tenths)

Students regroup on their mats.

Finish the problem, asking students whether the procedure looks familiar. (It is just like whole number subtraction.)

Dictate more decimal numbers to add and subtract.

Students do problems on their mats and write them on paper when they have understood the concept with blocks and bars.

Dictate several whole numbers to be subtracted from decimal amounts. Emphasize the correspondence of the numbers on the pv mat to the placement in the written problem.

Put the whole number in the decimal position, and challenge students to find your mistake on the board.

Procedure 3 □

To add and subtract using tenths

Use *bills, pv mats,* and *dimes or counters.*

Ask: How many dimes are in $1? (10) Each dime is what fraction of $1? ($^1/_{10}$) Tell students they are traveling in a country that has no pennies, only dimes, or tenths of dollars. One counter equals a dime or 0.1. They will need to keep track of their money.

Repeat the story-type format as in Procedures 1 and 2, with bills and counters. Start with an amount in the hundreds, and either buy items (subtraction) or earn money (addition).

Students take turns suggesting situations.

Continue to emphasize in the choral reading that the counters are $^1/_{10}$ of a dollar.

Now have students try problems first and then check their answers with manipulatives and pv mats.

Practice and Extension

Play Bicycle Race. Use four *dice, pv mats, pv blocks and decimal bars or bills and counters,* a *bag or can,* and *counters of different colors.* Divide the class into two parts, each part is to be a bicycle racing team. The distance is measured in kilometers.

The first die drawn from the can will be the hundreds amount, the second die will be the tens amount, the third the ones amount, and the fourth the decimal tenths amount. One color counter will represent addition and the other color subtraction.

Have each team start with the same amount. Draw a counter from the can. The first team will either add or subtract the subsequent number, depending on the color of the counter. Repeat for the second team.

Students place amounts and do the problem on paper. At the end of three rounds the team who has gone farther wins as long as all students on the team have the correct amounts on their mats and papers.

Decimals 3

Skill: To recognize and order hundredths

Time: 2–3 periods

Materials:

graph paper: ¹/₂" squares
scissors

envelopes: for storing graph paper decimals

file-folder place value (pv) mats to 1000 with decimal extensions to hundredths

See Reproducibles for: directions for file-folder pv mats and decimal extensions, decimal bars to hundredths—in the same color used for $1 bills, bills to 100s—in different colors

Anticipatory Set

Use *graph paper, scissors,* and *envelopes.*

Have students make graph paper decimals: Cut out four 10×10 squares. Label two of them "1." Cut the third into 1×10 strips, and label each "¹/₁₀ = 0.1." Cut 15 1×1 squares from the fourth. Review that it takes 10 tenths to make a whole. How many 1×1 squares does it take to make a whole one? (100) What would each square be called? (1 hundredth). Store the decimals in envelopes.

Have several students make 10 extra 10×10 squares and tape together to make a 10. Display a ten, a one, a tenth, and a hundredth so that students can see relative size.

Procedure 1 ☐ ■

To understand hundredths

Use *graph paper decimals from the Anticipatory Set* and *pv mats with extensions.*

Have students place 1 one square and 2 tenth strips on their desk. Ask: How much do we have? (1 one and 2 tenths) Write 1.2 on the board.

Students discuss that it takes 10 tenths to make one, 10 ones to make 10, and so on.

Have students place 5 hundredths on their desk. How do we write this as a fraction? (⁵/₁₀₀) We can write hundredths another way, as well. Have students put the hundredths to the right of the tenths. How do they think this is written in decimals? (1.25) Write 1.25 on the board.

Students chorally read: 1 one, 2 tenths of 1 whole, and 5 hundredths of 1 whole.

Have students place pv mats on their desks and put 1 one and 6 hundredths on the mats. Write 1.06 on the board.

Students chorally read the resulting number: 1 one, 0 tenths, and 6 hundredths. They label the hundredths place on their decimal extensions.

We don't have any tenths. What would the number be if I wrote 1.6 instead of 1.06 just because I didn't have any tenths? (The number would be 1 and 6 tenths.)

Students continue to place the numbers you dictate. Make sure to include numbers more than and less than one.

Students then start writing each number after they place and read it.

When students are adept at the skill, write numbers on the board for them to place. Students must first read the number and then place and write it.

Procedure 2 ☐

To practice reading and writing hundredths

Use *pv mats, bills,* and *decimal bars.*

Have students next place 1 hundred, 1 ten, 1 one, and 1 tenth on their pv mats with bills and decimal bars. Write 111.1 on the board.

Ask: How many tens does it take to make a hundred? (10) The hundred is divided into how many equal parts? (10) What fraction of the hundred is each 10? (¹/₁₀) Repeat for the relationship between 10 and 1, 1 and tenths, and tenths and hundredths.

Students label the hundredths column if not already labeled, and place one hundredth decimal bar.

The whole bar is equal to a one. How many parts does the bar have? (100) We are only interested in the shaded part.

One part is shaded. What fraction of one is it? (¹/₁₀₀) The shaded part is less than one whole. We can write it as ¹/₁₀₀, but we can also write it as a decimal fraction of 0.01.

How does this relate to the real world? When do we regularly use whole numbers and hundredths? (with money)

What is 0.1 in money? (dimes) What is 0.01 in money? (pennies) In money the decimal name is *cents.* We follow the rule that says the last decimal place is the family name; *cent* means hundred.

Give students numbers of bills and bars to place.

Students place and then read the amounts. When they are adept in the skill, they place amounts from written decimals. Then they write the amounts after placing and reading.

Make sure to include some with zero in the tenths place and some with zero in the hundredths place.

Procedure 3

To order hundredths

Use *graph paper decimals* and *pv mats with extensions.*

Have students place 1.06 on their mats, with 1 one and 2 hundredths below the 1.06.

Students chorally read: 1 one, 0 tenths, and 6 hundredths. They name the number as 1 and 6 hundredths. They repeat for the 1.02.

Ask: Which amount is more, 1.06 or 1.02? (1.06) When we have more hundredths, the number is bigger. Write 1.06 > 1.02.

Repeat with other numbers *without regrouping* until students are comfortable with the process.

Now work with regrouping to help students understand the difference between 1.09 and 1.10, and that 0.10 can be called either 1 tenth or 10 hundredths.

Have students place 1 one and 9 hundredths on their mats (1.09.) Add 1 more hundredth. How many hundredths do we have now? (10)

In our number system, whenever we get to 10 of anything, what do we need to do? (regroup) Decimals follow the same rule. What is equivalent to 10 hundredths that we could trade for? (a tenth)

Students trade 10 hundredths for 1 tenth and chorally read: 1 one, 1 tenth, and 0 hundredths.

Write 1.10 on the board. What else could we call this? (1.1)

Write the number 13, 542 on the board. Put a roof over the 13. Ask students to read the number, remembering the family name of thousands from earlier lessons.

Now add .10 after the number. The conventional way of naming this number is 13 thousand, 542, and 10 hundredths. The family name for decimals is always the name of the *last* place.

What if I did not have the zero? (It would end in tenths.)

Students continue to place and read as you dictate. They see that decimal numbers follow the same pattern as the whole numbers.

Write 0.5 on the board and have students place that amount. Have students read as both 5 tenths and 50 hundredths.

Continue dictating more tenth amounts until all students can place a written decimal amount and chorally read the resulting number both as tenths and as hundredths.

Students should now draw a pv chart on paper and write down each number. When they are competent in the skill, they write the numbers first and then check with the manipulatives.

Students work in groups of three. They take turns placing amounts on their mats as numbers are dictated. After comparing the numbers, they write the numbers in order of size.

When students are comfortable with the process, have them order numbers on paper before checking with the graph paper decimals.

Procedure 4

To practice ordering hundredths

Use *pv mats, bills,* and *decimal bars.*

Repeat Procedure 3 with the bills and decimal bars. Chorally read each number that you have students place, emphasizing the relationship of the hundredths as parts of one. Make sure students relate cents to hundredths and dimes to tenths.

Write money amounts on the board, and have students make up story problems with them.

Practice and Extension

Duplicate sheets of *decimal bars,* and have students color in various amounts from 0.01 to 1.0. They cut out the bars. Students can work in pairs to draw three bars, order them, and write the decimal amounts. The first one done gets 1 point.

For further activities see Measurement 3: Measure length by centimeters, meters, and millimeters; use decimal notation.

Decimals 4

Skill: To compare and order tenths and hundredths

Time: 2 periods

Materials:

graph paper decimals to hundredths, or ¹/₂" graph paper to make them (directions in Manipulative Information section and below)

scissors

clear tape

file-folder place value (pv) mats to 1000s with decimal extensions

See Reproducibles for: number lines to 1000, directions for file-folder pv mats and decimal extensions, decimal bars to hundredths—in the same color used for $1 bills, bills to 100s—in different colors

Anticipatory Set

Use *graph paper, scissors, tape,* and *number lines.*

If students have not yet made graph paper decimals to hundredths, they should do so: Have students cut out four 10×10 squares. Label two of them "1." Cut the third into 1×10 strips, and label each "¹/₁₀ = 0.1." Cut 15 1×1 squares from the fourth.

Review that it takes 10 tenths to make a whole. How many 1×1 squares does it take to make a whole one? (100) What would each square be called? (1 hundredth)

Have students cut out and assemble the number lines.

Procedure 1 □■

To understand tenths and equivalent hundredths; to compare and order tenths and hundredths

Use *pv mats with extensions, graph paper decimals and number lines from the Anticipatory Set,* and *paper.*

Write 0.01 on the board, and have students place 1 hundredth on their mats.

Students place and chorally read: 0 ones, 0 tenths, and 1 hundredth.

Students begin their number line at 0.01.

Now have students place another hundredth below the first.

Students chorally read and then write 0.02 on their number lines.

Repeat until reaching 0.09. Ask: Do you see a pattern?

Students respond: Decimals act like whole numbers.

Have students compare numbers on their number lines and mats: Which is bigger 0.02 or 0.05? Repeat until all are competent in the skill.

Have students add another hundredth. How many hundredths do you have? (10) Do you have a problem?

Students respond: You need to regroup. They regroup and have 0.10 on their mats and number lines.

On your mats you show 1 tenth, and on your number line you show 1 tenth and 0 hundredths. What will you call this amount?

Students respond: Some say 1 tenth, and some say 10 hundredths.

How many hundredths did it take to get that tenth? (10)

You have 10 hundredths. This is something special about decimals: The same amount can have several names.

Remember that a decimal's family name is the last place we're using on the pv mats. We're going to use the hundredths place.

Write 10,000 on the board. What is the *family* name of the part I've underlined? (thousands) What is the number? (10 thousand) We read the number we have in each section, then say its family name.

Have students put 1 hundredth below the tenth.

Students read each number: 10 hundredths, 1 hundredth. They compare positions and written numbers on the number line.

Ask: Why might you get mixed up?

Students respond: They both have a 1 and a decimal point.

How can you tell what to call the number?

Students respond: The family name is the last decimal place we're using; look at the place value position.

How many hundredths does it take to make a tenth? (10) Are 10 hundredths the same size as 1 tenth? (yes)

Sometimes a number will be written only in tenths. What could you do if you wanted to read it in hundredths?

Students respond: Use the hundredths place, and put a zero in it. They write the equivalency: 0.1 = 0.10.

Let's make another tricky comparison. Put 0.09 on your mats below the 0.10. Which number is bigger?

Students respond: 0.10

Yes, remember that 9 hundredths is not a tenth yet. Even though 9 is bigger than 1, a number's value comes from its position.

Students complete the number line to 0.50.

Repeat the procedure with other numbers until students are comfortable with the process. When reaching 0.20, compare it with 0.02 and 0.19.

Include equivalent tenths and hundredths. Also have students name numbers both as tenths and as hundredths. Have students write each number on the number line.

Students order a series of numbers on paper after placing them on their mats. When students are comfortable with the process, they order numbers on paper and then check with manipulatives.

Procedure 2

To compare and order numbers to tenths and hundredths

Use *pv mats, decimal bars, bills,* and *paper.*

Repeat Procedure 1 with bars and bills. Give numbers in a word problem format. Example: Compare distances in kilometers, volume in liters, money amounts, and so on. Include numbers in the hundreds, as well.

Make sure students compare numbers with only tenths to some numbers with hundredths, and some with no decimal part.

Students write problems on paper after placing and comparing amounts on their mats.

Practice and Extension

Use *index cards,* and have students make Decimal Decks. Write various amounts of decimals to tenths and hundredths, one per card. Students each turn over one card. The student with the larger card gets to keep both.

Students take 10 cards from a Decimal Deck and place in order from least to greatest. Another student checks.

Decimals 5

Skill: To add and subtract to hundredths

Time: 2 periods

Materials:

graph paper decimals to hundredths, or ¹/₂" graph paper and scissors to make them (directions in Manipulative Information section and Decimals 4)

file-folder place value (pv) mats to 1000s with decimal extensions

pv blocks: 10s and 100s

coins: pennies and dimes, or counters to represent them

See Reproducibles for: directions for file-folder pv mats and decimal extensions, decimal bars to hundredths—in the same color used for $1 bills, bills to 100s—in different colors

Anticipatory Set

Use *pv mats with extensions, pv blocks,* and *graph paper decimals.*

Have students place 1 hundred flat, 1 ten rod, 1 one, and 1 tenth from the graph paper decimals on their mats. How many tens make 1 hundred? (10) Each 10 is ¹/₁₀ of 1 hundred. Repeat for tens and ones, and ones and tenths. Have students add several numbers to review regrouping.

Procedure 1

To add to hundredths

Use *pv mats with extensions, pv blocks, graph paper decimals,* and *paper.*

When dictating decimal amounts make sure to say the amount in words rather than in numerals. Example: 0.2 is said as "two tenths."

Summary (for reference) Procedures 1 and 2:

Amount added	Total	Notes
1.01	1.01	
0.39	1.40	regroup 100ths
2.69	4.09	regroup 10ths
0.1	4.19	rewrite as 0.10
2	6.19	rewrite as 2.00
−1.06	5.13	
−1.06	4.07	regroup 100ths

Tell students that two teams of engineers are supervising separate sections of a highway overpass under construction. The engineers must follow the plans carefully to make sure the parts meet in the middle.

As engineers, students will measure the difference between the path the plans call for and what actually was built each day.

If the team has not built on the correct line, they will have to get back on the correct line when building the next day's section. Measurements are taken in feet to hundredths of feet.

Say: At the end of the first day, engineers find the team is 1.01 feet off.

Write 1.01 on the board, where you will be keeping a running total.

Students place the amount on their pv mats and chorally read: 1 foot, 0 tenths of a foot, and 1 hundredth of a foot. They name the number as one and one hundredth of a foot. They also write 1.01 on paper.

In spite of being careful, the second day's building is off 0.39 more of a foot.

Have students place the amount but not total it.

Ask: How many hundredths do you have now? (10)

In our number system we can't have more than nine in any place. Will this be true for hundredths as well? (yes)

What are 10 hundredths equal to? (1 tenth) Trade the 10 hundredths for 1 tenth, and find the total distance off.

Students read 0.39 of a foot. They write this below the 1.01 on their paper. After regrouping and adding their blocks and decimals, they do the addition on paper.

Again, the bulldozers must have slipped and the road is off another 2.69 feet. What is the total amount off the correct line now?

Students place, read, and write 2.69. After adding their blocks and decimals, they do the addition on paper. They arrive at 4.09 off.

The next day was better, only 0.1 of a foot off. Now what is the total amount off?

Students place, read, and write 0.1. After adding their blocks and decimals, they do the addition on paper. They arrive at 4.19 feet off.

Where did you write the 0.1 in your addition problem? (the tenths place) What is the rule for adding decimals?

Students respond: Line up the decimal points so that places are lined up correctly.

Remember that 1 tenth is the same as 10 hundredths, so you can write 0.10 instead of 0.1.

The next day the team has problems and is off by a full 2 feet.

What place does the two go? (ones place) How many tenths does two have? (0) How many hundredths? (0) How can we write two to help keep our places lined up? (2.00)

Students place, read, and write 2.00. After adding their blocks and decimals, they do the addition on paper. They arrive at 6.19 feet.

Go directly to Procedure 2.

Procedure 2

To subtract to hundredths

Use *pv mats with extensions, pv blocks, graph paper decimals,* and *paper.*

This is a continuation of Procedure 1. Students have 6.19 on their mats.

Say: As engineers, you decide to bring in another bulldozer operator. She is more successful and turns the road 1.06 feet closer to where it's supposed to be.

Students write –1.06 and remove 1.06 from their mats. They do the subtraction on paper as well. The overpass is now 5.13 feet from the correct line.

The new operator corrects another 1.06 feet.

Have students write and then place the amount.

Ask: Can we subtract 6 hundredths from 3 hundredths? (no) Where can we get more hundredths? (trade a tenth for 10 hundredths)

Have students regroup and subtract on their mats. Demonstrate on the board how to write the problem correctly. Have students do the subtraction on paper.

Continue to give amounts to be added or subtracted until students are comfortable with the skill. Encourage students to estimate the amount of correction required to arrive at zero deviation from the plan.

Procedure 3

To add and subtract with money

Use *pv mats with extensions, bills,* and *decimal bars or coins or counters.*

Relate tenths and hundredths to dimes and pennies. Repeat Procedure 1 with the bills and bars, but have students buy and sell items instead of build a road.

Include some amounts with only hundredths or tenths, and some with no decimal part.

Practice and Extension

Have students bring in *catalogs* of desired items. Allow each student $50. They are to "buy" items from a catalog and keep a running total. They try to come as close as possible to spending all their money without going over $50.

Use *Materials from Procedure 1, three dice, a bag or can,* and *two counters of different colors.* Divide the class into two engineering teams, and continue building the overpass from Procedure 1. The first die thrown will be the ones amount, the second die will be the tenths amount, and the third will be the hundredths. One color counter will represent addition and the other subtraction.

Have each team start with 10 feet of deviance. Draw a counter from the can. The first team will either add or subtract the subsequent number, depending on the color of the counter. Students place amounts and do the problem on paper. Repeat for the second team. At the end of three rounds the team who has come closest to zero wins, as long as all students on the team have the correct amounts on their mats and papers.

Decimals 6

Skill: To understand thousandths and equivalent decimals to thousandths

Time: 2 periods

Materials:

graph paper decimals to hundredths, or ¹/₂" graph paper and scissors to make them (directions in Manipulative Information section and below)

file-folder place value (pv) mats to 1000s with decimal extensions

scissors

rice: approximately 15 grains per student

markers: red, dark blue, and yellow

See Reproducibles for: directions for file-folder pv mats and decimal extensions, decimal bars to thousandths—in the same color used for $1 bills, bills to 100s—in different colors, decimal bar example sheets—several per student

Anticipatory Set

Use *graph paper decimals* or *graph paper and scissors*.

If students have not already done so, have them make graph paper decimals. They should cut out four 10 × 10 squares. Label two of them "1." Cut the third into 1 × 10 strips, and label each "¹/₁₀ = 0.1." Cut 15 1 × 1 squares from the fourth.

Review that it takes 10 tenths to make a whole. How many 1 × 1 squares does it take to make a whole one? (100) What is each square called? (1 hundredth) Label each 0.01.

Procedure 1

To understand thousandths

Use *graph paper decimals from the Anticipatory Set, scissors, rice, pv mats with extensions,* and *paper*.

Have students place 1 one square and 2 tenth strips on their mats. Ask: How much do we have? (1 one and 2 tenths)

Students write 1.2 on paper. They discuss that it takes 10 tenths to make 1, 10 ones to make 10, and so on.

Have students hold up 5 hundredths. How do we write this as a fraction? (⁵/₁₀₀) We can write hundredths another way, as well, since it has a multiple of 10 as a denominator.

Ask: How would ⁵/₁₀₀ be written as a decimal fraction? (.05)

Place the 0.05 on your mats. How much do you have in all?

Students chorally read: 1 one, 2 tenths of one whole, and 5 hundredths of one whole. They write: 1.25.

If we had a smaller place than hundredths, what do you think it would be called? (thousandths)

How many thousandths would it take to make 1 hundredth? (10)

Students label the thousandths place on their mats.

Have students take a hundredth square and draw 4 vertical lines and 1 horizontal line to divide the square into 10 equal parts.

Students try to cut pieces. They compare the size of the thousandths with the other decimals.

Hand out rice to students. The grains are about the same size as the paper thousandths, but are easier to work with.

Have students place 3 thousandths on their mats and chorally read the whole number: 1 one, 2 tenths of a whole, 5 hundredths of a whole, and 3 thousandths of a whole: 1.253.

When we read decimals, we take the family name from the last decimal place used, in this case thousandths.

How many thousandths would you have in *just the decimal part*? (253 thousandths)

How many in all? (1,253 thousandths)

Repeat with other numbers until students are adept at reading and placing decimals to thousandths.

Have students write each number after placing and reading it. Remind them that written math is just a description of what is actually happening.

Write 1.006 on the board.

Students place and chorally read the resulting number: 1 one, 0 tenths, 0 hundredths, and 6 thousandths.

We don't have any tenths or hundredths. What would the number be if I wrote 1.6 instead of 1.006 and left out zeros? (The number would be 1 and 6 tenths.)

Have students continue to place the numbers you dictate. Make sure to include numbers more than and less than one, and numbers with zeros.

Procedure 2

To understand thousandths

Use *pv mats*, *bills*, and *decimal bars*.

Have students place 1 hundred, 1 ten, 1 one, 1 tenth, and 1 hundredth on their pv mats. Write 111.11 on the board.

Discuss the relationship between tens, ones, tenths, hundredths, and thousandths.

Students place 1 thousandth decimal bar.

Say: The whole bar is equal to a one. How many parts does the bar have? (1,000) We are only interested in the one shaded part. What fraction of one is it? ($^1/_{1,000}$) We can write it as $^1/_{1,000}$, but we can also write it as a decimal fraction of 0.001.

When would we use numbers to thousandths in the real world?

Students discuss. They may suggest sports events, distances, or other measurements.

Repeat Procedure 1 with the bills and decimal bars. Chorally read each number before students place and write it. Emphasize the relationship of the thousandths as parts of one.

Procedure 3

To understand equivalent decimals to thousandths

Use *decimal bar example sheets* and *markers*.

Have students use the red marker to go over the divisions for tenths, on all three bars, and use the dark blue marker to go over the hundredth divisions on the hundredths and thousands bars.

Students next use the yellow marker to color in the first tenth of the tenth bar. They write 0.1 and read 1 tenth.

Say: Mark the same amount on the bar with hundredths. How many hundredths?

Students respond: 10 hundredths. They write 0.10.

What is the family name for decimals? (the last place used)

Do the amounts represent the same space? (yes) Is 0.1 the same as 0.10? (yes)

If you had 10 hundredth bars on your mats, what would you have to do? (regroup for 1 tenth) These are equivalent decimals because they mean the same amount.

Write 0.1 = 0.10 on the board.

Students chorally read: 1 tenth equals 1 tenth and 0 hundredths.

Have students color in the same amount on the thousandths bar. How many thousandths?

Students respond: 100 thousandths.

If you had 100 thousandths on your mats, what would you have to do?

Students respond: Regroup each 10 thousandths for 1 hundredth, and then 10 hundredths for a tenth.

Write 0.1 = 0.10 = 0.100 on the board. Have the class chorally read: 1 tenth equals 1 tenth and 0 hundredths equals 1 tenth, 0 hundredths, and 0 thousandths.

Have students color in one more tenth and repeat the process with 0.2 = 0.20 = 0.200. Have students look for a pattern.

Discuss when might you want to use thousandths or hundredths rather than just tenths.

Students next color in equivalent amounts on all three bars. They write each number on the back. They can trade bars with other students for practice reading and writing equivalent decimals.

Practice and Extension

Use *toothpicks, craft sticks,* and *rice:* 10 bundled sticks equal 10, 1 stick equals 1, 10 toothpicks glued together is a tenth, a single toothpick is a hundredth, and a grain of rice is a thousandth. Students work in pairs to place, read, and write numbers to thousandths.

Have students cut out *bars colored with equivalent decimals from Procedure 3.* They pool their bars in groups and play Concentration or Go Fish until they are adept.

For further activities see Measurement 3: Measure length by centimeters, meters, and millimeters; use decimal notation.

Skill: To compare and order decimals to thousandths

Time: 2 periods

Materials:

scissors

clear tape

markers: two colors per student

file-folder place value (pv) mats to 1000s with decimal extensions

See Reproducibles for: number lines to 1000, directions for file-folder pv mats and decimal extensions, decimal bars to thousandths—in the same color used for $1 bills, decimal bar example sheets—4 sheets per student

Anticipatory Set

Use *number lines, scissors, tape,* and *markers.*

Have students cut out and assemble the number line. They start at 0. Using a marker, they number the first nine *large* ticks 0.01 to 0.09.

Review reading and writing of equivalent decimals. Dictate several decimal amounts, and have students name equivalent decimals.

Procedure 1 ☐ ■

To compare and order decimals to thousandths

Use *pv mats with extensions, decimal bars, number lines from the Anticipatory Set, markers* and *paper.*

Have students place 0.001 on their mats and write 0.001 with pencil at the first *small* tick mark on their number lines. Repeat with another 0.001 bar.

Ask: Which number is more, 0.001 or 0.002?

Students respond: 0.002. They write 0.002 > 0.001 on their paper.

Repeat until students have 0.009 on their mats and number lines.

Say: Add one more 0.001 to your mats. How many thousandths do you have now? (10) What do you need to do?

Students respond: Regroup. They trade 10 thousandths for a hundredth.

How many hundredths? (1) Thousandths? (0)

What do you notice about the number line?

Students respond: The large tick mark is next. It will read 0.01, or 1 hundredth.

How many thousandths is this equivalent to? (10)

Students write 0.01 = 0.010. They write the thousandths numbers in pencil, the hundredths in one color marker, and the tenths in a second color marker.

Repeat the procedure until students have completed their number line to 0.02 = 0.020.

Which is the bigger number, 0.020 or 0.019? (.020)

Write the following numbers: 0.02, 0.020. Which is bigger?

Students respond: They are the same.

Why might you get confused? (They both have a 0 and a 2.) What techniques could you use to decide they were the same?

Have students discuss. They should be able to use the number line, the decimal bars, and write them as equivalent decimals. Discuss how writing them all to the same place value makes comparison easier.

Do you see a pattern on the number line?

Students discuss. For every 10 thousandths, they have another hundredth. Both the thousandths and hundredths increase, but the hundredths increase slowly.

Write the equivalent decimals to thousandths for 0.03 to 0.09 at the correct tick marks.

Now place enough hundredths so that you have 0.09 on your mats.

Write the thousandths that occur between 0.08 and 0.09 on your number lines.

Students do as requested: 0.081, 0.082, 0.083, 0.084, and so on.

Add 0.001 to your mats.

Students add 0.001, regroup for another hundredth, and regroup 10 hundredths for a tenth.

How much do you show on your mats? (Answers may vary from 0.1 to 0.100.)

You have 0.1 on your mats, and you can mark the next tick mark in a new color to show tenths.

Students mark 0.01.

What else could you have on your mats and number lines?

Students respond: 0.010, 0.010. They mark the 0.01 in its color, and 0.010 in pencil: 0.1 = 0.10 = 0.100.

Give students decimals to compare and order, using measurement situations. Example: One snail went 0.030 cm, and the other went 0.04 cm. Which went farther? Vary the number of places. Include some with whole number parts, as well.

Students check bars and number lines as needed, write equivalent decimals to the same number of places, and write in order.

Provide much practice, until students can demonstrate competence in the skill.

Procedure 2 □

To practice comparing and ordering decimals to thousandths

Use *decimal bar example sheets, scissors* and *markers*.

Have students cut out blank decimal bars.

Ask: Each bar is worth how many? (1 whole) If you wanted to color in a tenth, which bar could you use?

Students respond: Any bar.

Yes, you can see the tenth markings on each bar. For decimals to just tenths, we would use the bar to just tenths. We would do the same for numbers to hundredths and thousandths.

Color in 0.1, 0.01, and 0.001 on the appropriate bars.

Students color and compare. They write 0.1 > 0.01 > 0.001.

Add more color until you show 0.2, 0.05, 0.009

Students color and compare.

How many hundredths would you need to color to show 0.2? (20)

How many thousandths would you need to color to show 0.2? (200)

Students next take each bar and color in a number. They write the number on the back. Holding their bars in their laps, they play War with a partner. They first compare the written number and check with the colored bars.

Students then draw three bars at random. They put them in order by their numbers and then check with the colored-bar side. The student with the largest spread between smallest and largest wins.

Practice and Extension

Have students use three *dice* and hold a mini-Olympics. The first throw gives the tenths, the second throw the hundredths, and the third throw the thousandths numbers. The complete number gives their time or distance for events. How far away from actual Olympic results were they? Place results on a class chart.

Use a *deck of cards*. Have students draw three lines on their *papers:* ___. You will draw four cards.

Tens or face cards are zeros. After each card, students decide where to place the number. They may pass once. Winners have the largest/smallest number at the end.

See Measurement 3, 6, and 9 for activities using metric measurement. Measure in thousandths of liters, rather than milliliters, and so on.

Decimals 8

Skill: To add and subtract to thousandths

Time: 2 periods

Materials:

file-folder place value (pv) mats to 1000s with decimal extensions

pv blocks: 10s and 100s

scissors

markers: light-colored; 1 per student

See Reproducibles for: directions for file-folder pv mats and decimal extensions, decimal bars to thousandths—in the same color used for $1 bills, decimal bar example sheets—2 sheets per student

Anticipatory Set

Use *pv mats with extensions, pv blocks,* and *decimal bars to hundredths.*

Have students place 1 hundred flat, 1 ten rod, 1 one bar, 1 tenth bar, and 1 hundredth bar on their mats. Ask how many tens make 1 hundred. (10) Each 10 is $^1/_{10}$ of 1 hundred. Repeat for each place through hundredths. Have students add and subtract several numbers to review regrouping.

Procedure 1 ☐■

To add and subtract to thousandths

Use *pv mats with extensions, pv blocks, decimal bars to thousandths,* and *paper.*

Students should be adept at addition and subtraction at this stage.

Discuss writing equivalent decimals before adding or subtracting; that is, line up the decimal point.

Students will do the work with the decimal bars and blocks first, and then write each step. They will keep a running total.

Refer to Decimals 5 for the type of story to use.

Students could be underwater divers in a cloudy sea. A path only 3 m wide lies between a cliff with sharp rocks rising up on one side and a 1,000-m deep trench on the other. Divers must make their way back to the aquadome where they live.

1 whole bar	= 1 m		
1 tenth bar	= 1 dm	= 0.1 m	
1 hundredth bar	= 1 cm	= 0.01 m	
1 thousandth bar	= 1 mm	= 0.001 m	

Possible deviations from the path with each 10 steps (0 deviation = middle of the path):

Deviation	Total	Skill
0.005	0.005	
0.113	0.118	
0.363	0.481	regroup thousandths

1.54	2.021	regroup hundredths, tenths, add decimals and mixed decimals
−1.01	1.011	subtract non-equivalent decimals
−0.671	0.340	regroup ones, tenths

Continue providing problems to suit students' needs. When students are confident with the process, they can solve the problem on paper first, and then check with the bars and cubes.

Procedure 2 ☐

To practice adding and subtracting decimals to thousandths

Use *decimal bar example sheets, scissors, markers, pv mats,* and *plain paper.*

Have students cut out both sheets and color in one bar of each type.

Students next cut 1 tenth strip from the tenth bar, and an equal amount from the other bars.

Students place colored bars on their mats and turn over the other bars to their totally blank sides.

Say: Using the blank tenth bar, cover all except 0.1 of the colored tenth bar. Using the remaining blank bars, cover all except 0.01 of the hundredth bar and 0.001 of the thousandth bar.

Students cover and write 0.111 on their paper.

Provide numbers for students to add and subtract, as was done in Procedure 1.

Remind students to regroup in addition when they reach 10 in any place. Have them cover the 10 and uncover 1 more in the next larger place.

To regroup for subtraction, students cover 1 in the next larger place and uncover 10 in the desired place before doing subtraction.

Students write problems, do them with bars, and write each step on paper until they are competent in the process.

Practice and Extension

Use *scales* and *masses to milligrams*. Have students measure objects and use the data to construct and solve problems.

Have students bring in *food containers with nutritional values given in milligrams*. Students can figure total amounts of sodium, and so on, in a meal.

Use *materials from Procedure 1, four dice, a bag or can,* and *two counters of different colors*. Divide the class into two diving teams, and continue the story from Procedure 1.

The first die thrown will be the ones amount, the second die will be the tenths amount, the third will be the hundredths, and the fourth thousandths. One color counter will represent addition, and the other subtraction.

Have each team start with 1 m of deviation. Draw a counter from the can. The first team will either add or subtract the subsequent number, depending on the color of the counter.

Students place amounts and do the problem on *paper*. Repeat for the second team. At the end of three rounds the team who has come closest to zero wins, as long as all students on the team have the correct amounts on their mats and papers. Decide ahead of time if falling off the cliff disqualifies a team or not.

Decimals 9

Skill: To round decimals to the nearest tenth, hundredth, and whole number

Time: 3+ periods

Materials:

markers: light- and medium-colored; 1 each per student

file-folder place value (pv) mats to 1000s with decimal extensions

coins: pennies and dimes, or counters to represent them

pv blocks to 10s

See Reproducibles for: Rounding Rhyme, decimal bars to desired place—in the same color used for $1 bills, extra decimal bars to write on, directions for file-folder pv mats and decimal extensions, number lines to 1000 (taped together), bills to 100s—in different colors

Anticipatory Set

Use *Rounding Rhyme.*

Review the Rounding Rhyme. Have students round 5,957 to the nearest ten, hundred, and thousand, rounding up when halfway to the next number.

Procedure 1

To round to the nearest tenth or hundredth

Use *extra decimal bars, markers, pv mats with extensions, decimal bars, Rounding Rhyme,* and *paper.*

Numbers in this Procedure are for rounding to tenths. If rounding to hundredths, substitute thousandths.

Have students color in the amount equal to 1 tenth on an extra hundredth bar with light markers. On a thousandth bar, they color in the amount equal to either a hundredth or tenth. They will use this bar for reference.

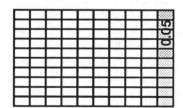

Students use the medium marker to darken the other four hundredths or thousandths in the colored area, and write 0.05 or 0.005 on the darkened part.

Ask: How many hundredths to make 1 tenth? (10) What is half that amount? (5 hundredths)

With 5 hundredths we are halfway to a tenth, closer to 10 hundredths than no hundredths. If we were rounding, we could trade for a tenth and round up.

Have students place 2.66 on their mats.

Find 0.06 on the hundredth bar you shaded. Is it more than half the bar? (yes) Is it closer to 1 tenth or none? (0.1) We can trade for a tenth.

Students trade the 0.06 for 0.1 and have 2.7 on their mats. They write: 2.66 → 2.7.

Have students add 0.02 to the 2.7. They have 2.72.

Say: Find 0.02 on the decimal bar you colored. Is it more than half the bar? (no) Is it closer to a tenth or none? (none) We can't trade for a tenth.

Students pull off the 0.02. They write: 2.72 → 2.7.

We are rounding to the nearest tenth; underline the numbers in the tenths place in 2.66 and 2.72. Does our rounding follow the Rounding Rhyme? (yes)

Dictate numbers with 0.9 to force regrouping. Repeat the procedure for other places as desired. Emphasize that 0.50 = 0.500.

Students use these to make up metric measurement story problems. They practice as before. When ready, they round on paper first before checking with materials.

Procedure 2

To round to the nearest tenth or hundredth, using a number line

Use *number lines to 1000, markers,* and *Rounding Rhyme.*

Have students start with 0.01 at the first small tick mark and label the numbers to 1.0. If rounding to hundredths, use 0.001 as the first number and adapt directions.

Students draw a light line across at all the 0.05 numbers, and a darker line at the tenths, the large tick marks. They discuss patterns they see.

Dictate 0.13, and have students locate on the line and check the nearest light line.

Say: We are rounding to the nearest tenth, the large tick marks with the dark lines. Is the 0.03 "4 or less" or "5 and up"? (4 or less) Which tenth is the 0.13 closer to? (0.1)

Students use Rounding Rhymes and number lines. When they are ready, they write and round numbers first, and then check with the number line.

Discuss how rounding with decimals is like rounding with whole numbers. Can they round large numbers to any place desired, using the same method?

Procedure 3

To round money to the nearest $0.10

Use *pv mats with extensions, bills, decimal bars, coins or counters, Rounding Rhyme, markers,* and *colored copies of decimal bars from Procedure 1.*

Follow Procedure 1 first with bills and bars. Students will place money amounts and estimate to the nearest dime, or tenth of a dollar. Give amounts with nine in the tenths and hundredths places.

Substitute coins for bars, and continue.

Procedure 4

To round to the nearest whole number

Use *pv mats with extensions, pv blocks, decimal bars, extra copies of decimal bars, Rounding Rhyme,* and *paper.*

Have students use extra decimal bars and darken the horizontal line that divides each one in half. They should shade in one half of each one and write 0.5, 0.50, 0.5 on the shaded part, depending on the bars used.

Ask: How many tenths does it take to make a one? (10) What do we need to have before we can round up? (5 tenths)

Students place 12.6 on their mats.

Is 0.6 more than 0.5, half the bar you shaded? (yes) Is it closer to one or none? (1) We can trade for a one. Does this follow the Rounding Rhyme? (yes)

Students trade the 0.6 for a 1 and have 13.0 on their mats. They write: 12.6 → 13.0.

Have students add 0.3 to the 13.0.

Find 0.3 on the extra decimal bar you colored. Is it more than 0.5, half the bar? (no) Is it closer to one or none? (none) We cannot trade for a one.

Students pull off the 0.3. They write: 13.3 → 13.0.

We are rounding to the nearest one. Underline the numbers in the *ones* place in 12.6 and 13.3. Does our rounding follow the Rounding Rhyme rule? (yes)

Students make up story problems and round numbers as above. When ready, they round on paper first.

Repeat for hundredths or thousandths as desired. Emphasize that 0.5 = 0.50 = 0.500.

Procedure 5

To round to the nearest whole number using a number line

Use *number lines to 1000* and *Rounding Rhyme.*

Have students start labeling at the first small tick mark with 0.1. They continue to 5.0. Have them draw a light line across at all the 0.5 numbers, and discuss patterns.

Dictate 1.3, and have students locate it on the line.

Say: Check the nearest light line. Is the 0.3 part of 1.3 "4 or less" or "5 and up"? (0.4 or less) What happens now? (It's out of sight.) Which whole number is the 1.3 closer to? (1)

Students write each new number, and then use the Rounding Rhyme and number lines to practice.

Think of the number line as a measuring line. Example: About how far did the bee fly from home if it went 1.6 miles straight out? About how far was the round trip?

What numbers round to 2 and are over 1.80? (1.81–1.99, 2.01–2.49) Continue the exercise.

Procedure 6

To round money to nearest $1.00

Use *pv mats with extensions, bills, decimals bars, coins or counters, Rounding Rhyme,* and *marked copies of decimal bars from Procedure 4.*

Follow Procedure 4 with bills and bars. Give students money amounts to place, and have them estimate to the nearest dollar. Give amounts with nine and zero in the ones place.

Next substitute coins or counters for the bars, and continue. Example: I only have $10.00, so I need to keep track of purchases at the store. If my items are $2.12, $3.98, and $2.76, will I have enough money?

Practice and Extension

Give students 2 minutes to look through *catalogs* or *menus.* They try to spend as close to $10 as possible without going over. Discuss whether this is easy to do without estimating.

Have students work in pairs. One rounds a list of amounts, while the other adds the list, using a calculator. How close were the totals? Which numbers give the least accurate estimates? Why?

Decimals 10

Skill: To multiply decimals and whole numbers

Time: 2+ periods

Materials:

file-folder place value (pv) mats to 1000s with decimal extensions

pv blocks to 100s

coins: pennies and dimes, or counters to represent them

See Reproducibles for: directions for file-folder pv mats and decimal extensions, decimal bars to desired place—in the same color used for $1 bills, extra decimal bars to write on, bills to 100s—in different colors

Anticipatory Set

Use *pv mats with decimal extensions, pv blocks,* and *paper.*

Tell students we have signed up as a group to bicycle for charity. We need to know the total number of miles bicycled. Have students place 2 ten rods and 4 one cubes on their mats.

Two students each went 24 miles. Write 2×24 on the board. Remind students that the 24 is *the number we start with* and $\times 2$ is *just the directions*.

How many groups of 4 ones do we need? (2) How many groups of 2 tens do we need? (2) Have students place blocks and total them. They write the multiplication problem and solution on paper. Repeat the procedure with 2×25 to review regrouping.

Procedure 1 ■

To multiply decimals and whole numbers with no regrouping; manipulatives only

Use *pv mats with decimal extension* and *decimal bars to desired place.*

Write 0.4 on the board. Ask: What fraction is this? (4 tenths) If we were using graph paper squares of tenths, how many squares would we have? (4)

Write 2×0.4 mi. on the board.

Today we will be walking in groups for charity. What can this equation tell us? (Two students walked 0.4 miles each.)

Circle the $\times 2$, and remind students that $\times 2$ is *just the directions* telling us how many groups of 0.4 we need to place. Ask: Will there be any ones? (no)

Students place bars for a group of 0.4 and then repeat for the second group of 0.4. They state that two groups of 4 tenths is 8 tenths or 0.8.

Finish the problem on the board.

Repeat with 3×0.3 and 4×0.2. Students should do problems with the bars as you do them on the board.

Beside the decimal problems on the board, write and do the same problems without the decimal: $2 \times 4, 3 \times 3, 4 \times 2$.

Do you see a pattern to doing these problems on paper? (If you multiply by tenths, your answer has tenths.)

Continue with other examples. Students work and answer as you write the problems on the board.

Procedure 2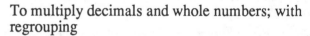

To multiply decimals and whole numbers; with regrouping

Use *pv mats with decimal extensions, decimal bars to desired place,* and *paper.*

It is important in this procedure that students understand that the written form is just a description of what is actually happening.

Have students turn their paper sideways and draw a pv chart for their written problems.

As you dictate several problems *without regrouping,* they write the problem, do the problem with bars on their mats, and write each step on paper after they have done it. They state the problem and solution in terms of how far students walked.

Write 2×0.6 on the board. Have students place bars. Ask: How many tenths? (12) What do we need to do? (regroup) Why can we do this? (10 tenths is equal to 1 ones)

Students do regrouping and solve the problem in writing as you do it on the board.

How does this fit the pattern you saw before?

Students respond: We multiplied tenths, and the answer has tenths in it.

Repeat, giving several more story problems that will require regrouping of both tenths and ones.

Problem situations could be racing times to desired accuracy, measuring the thickness of layers of plastic, or ounces of chocolate to be added to a vat of cookie dough in a bakery.

Students do regrouping and solve problems in writing as you do them on the board.

Have students write each problem in whole numbers next to the decimal problems.

Ask: How many decimal places in the whole number problems? (none) How many decimal places in the whole number products? (none)

How many decimal places in the decimal problems? (1) How many decimal places in the products? (1) Do you see a pattern?

Students respond: The number of decimal places in the product is the same as the number of decimal places in the problem.

Repeat the above procedure for hundredths and thousandths as desired.

Give plenty of practice using manipulatives *and* writing problems so that students understand the concept thoroughly.

Procedure 3 □■

To multiply whole numbers and money amounts

Use *pv mats with decimal extensions, bills, paper,* and *coins or counters.*

Repeat Procedures 1 and 2 with bills and coins or counters. Relate this to multiplying money.

If only working with tenths, tell students they are in a country with no pennies, only tenths of dollars, dimes.

If working with hundredths, then use pennies as well. For thousandths, use decimal bars or colored counters. $.001 is one mil.

Procedure 4 □

To practice multiplying decimals and whole numbers

Use *extra copies of decimal bars.*

Repeat Procedures 1 and 2, but have students color in 0.4 on two bars for 2×0.4. Then have them put the colored amounts next to each other and compare to a single bar to arrive at total. Relate this to adding fraction bars.

Practice and Extension

Play Swimming Race. Use *pv mats with decimal extensions, pv blocks, spinners or die,* and *decimal bars or colored counters.* Students will be in three races. The first race will be three laps.

Each student will throw a die to determine the time each of their laps takes. (First throw for tens place, second throw for ones place, and third throw for tenths place.)

They multiply this time by 3 to see how long it took to swim the first race. The second race will be 4 laps, and the third race 5 laps. Students take turns and follow the same procedure to determine race times. The winner is the one with the least total amount of time.

Decimals 11

Skill: To multiply decimals by decimals

Time: 3–4 periods

Materials:

graph paper: 1/2" squares

scissors

markers: light- and dark-colored; 1 each per student

file-folder place value (pv) mats to 1000s with decimal extensions

pv blocks, or bills to 100s

See Reproducibles for: decimal bars to thousandths—in the same color as for $1 bills, decimal bar example sheets—use several sheets per student, or laminate and have students use washable markers, directions for file-folder pv mats and decimal extensions, bills to $100s—in different colors

Anticipatory Set

Use *graph paper, decimal bars,* and *scissors.*

Have students cut out bars if not already made and then make this chart, labeling 0.1–0.9 and 1–9:

	0.1	0.2	0.3	0.4	0.5	0.6	0.7	0.8	0.9
1	0.1	0.2							
2	0.2	0.4							
3									
4									
5									
6									

Write 1×0.1 on the board. What is one 0.1? (0.1) Students write 0.1 in the chart. Continue down the 0.1 column. Students refer to their bars for help. Continue writing and solving each on the board.

Repeat with the 0.2 column, suggesting students look for patterns that might help them fill out the chart. Students will have to regroup at 5×0.2.

Continue through chart. Students may see that one decimal place in a factor leads to one decimal place in the product, and that the digits themselves act like whole numbers.

Procedure 1   □ ■

To multiply tenths by tenths

Use *graph paper, markers, decimal bar example sheets (to hundredths),* and *scissors.*

Have students cut out blank tenths and hundreds bars, and then make another chart as shown in the next column. Label each axis from 0.1 to 0.9

Write 0.1×0.1 on the board. Say: We don't want to have several groups of 0.1s this time, we want a tenth of 0.1.

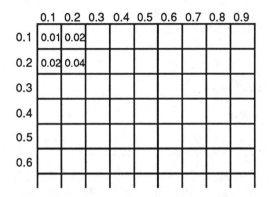

Have students color in 1 tenth on the *tenth* bar. What can they find that would show a tenth of that?

Students use the *hundredth* bar. They shade 1 tenth, and then darken 1 hundredth.

$$\frac{1}{10} \text{ of } \frac{1}{10} = \frac{1}{100}$$
$$0.1 \times 0.1 = 0.01$$

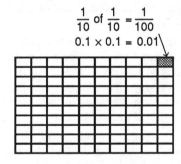

What is 0.1×0.1, or 0.1 *of* 0.1? (0.01) Where should we place the decimal point to have 0.01?

Students discuss that a zero must be written in the tenths place as a place holder. They chart the 0.01 as you finish the problem on the board.

Moving down the 0.1 column, find what would equal 0.2×0.1 or 0.2 *of* 0.1. Write the problem on the board.

Students darken another 0.01 on their hundredth bar and find that equals 0.02. They add 0.02 to the chart.

Continue down the 0.1 column. Can students find a pattern to the products that will help them?

Have students start the 0.2 column by coloring another tenth on *both* bars. What is 0.1×0.2 or 0.1 *of* 0.2?

Students see on their hundred bars that 0.1 of 0.2 is 0.02. They have already colored this in. Each product found is colored in if necessary and charted.

Continue down the column. At 0.5 × 0.2, students should point out that 10 hundredths should be regrouped to 1 tenth. Suggest that they write this as 0.10 so that the pattern will be clearer.

Students begin to see that multiplying tenths and tenths gives hundredths. They finish the chart, using the bars first as long as they feel the need.

Students may think all decimal multiplication results in a product to two decimal places. Caution students that this may not be true. They will need to explore more to find a rule that will work in *all* cases. Go on to Procedure 2.

Procedure 2

To multiply hundredths by tenths

Use *graph paper, markers, blank decimal bar example sheets (to thousandths),* and *scissors.*

Have students cut out blank thousandths and then make another chart with tenths down the left and hundredths across the top.

Use the same procedure as in Procedure 1. Remind students they are looking for a pattern that will work with all decimal multiplication.

Students begin to see the pattern: The number of decimal places in the factors equals the number of decimal places in the products.

Ask *why* this is true. If students need help, remind them that a tenth of one hundreds gives an answer in the tens place, a tenth of ones gives an answer in the tenths place. Each decimal place in the multiplier moves the product over a place on the place value chart.

Give students practice in working problems to various places. They should use the bars as long as they need to, writing each step as they do it.

Procedure 3

To multiply mixed decimals by decimals

Use *graph paper charts from previous procedures, markers, pv bars or bills, blank decimal bars including the one bar,* and *pv mats.*

Write 0.1 × 2.2 on the board. Say: The 0.1 is just the directions and tells us we want a tenth of 2.2. Start with 0.1 × 0.2.

Students work both with bars or bills on their mats, and with the blank bars. They find 0.1 × 0.2 = 0.02 and color this in on a hundredth bar.

Now we want a tenth of two.

Students use their bars to find a tenth of 2 is 0.2. They color this in and read the amounts on the bars: 0.22.

Have students tell you where to place the decimal point in the product on the board. (0.22)

Students may be able to tell you the shortcut for multiplying decimals. They may be able to state that each decimal place in the multiplier moves the product over an extra decimal place

Repeat with other numbers until students are comfortable with the process. Use story problems about distance or measurement when presenting problems. Example: Joe twisted his ankle and finished the race in 11.53 minutes. Jen finished it in a tenth of that time. How long did it take her?

Procedure 4

To multiply mixed decimals by mixed decimals

Use *graph paper charts from previous procedures, decimal bars including the one bar, pv blocks or bills,* and *pv mats.*

Write 4.6 × 3.08 on the board. Remind students that we want 4 of the 3.08s and we also want 6 tenths of it.

Students can use charts, or you can ask such questions as: What is 0.6 of 0.01? (0.006)

We really have 8 of the hundredths in our problem, so we now have? (0.048)

Students work through the problem with you, placing the bars and blocks on the mats as they go.

Remind students as they read their bars that we wanted 4 of the 3.08 and also wanted 6 tenths of 3.08. Have students show with their bars and blocks that this is in fact what we have (partial products).

Provide students with practice until they are competent with the process. Students can then write each step as they complete it. They look for patterns and state the rule, as before.

Practice and Extension

Have students work in pairs. They use four *dice* to generate two 2-digit numbers in the hundredths, and then multiply. The one with the larger product gets 1 point. Vary by allowing students to choose three of the four numbers (one number in tenths, one in hundredths). Have them discuss strategy.

Decimals 12

Skill: To divide decimals by whole numbers

Time: 2 periods

Materials:

graph paper decimals to hundredths (directions in Manipulative Information section and Decimals 3)

pv blocks to 10s

file-folder place value (pv) mats to 1000s with decimal extensions

coins: pennies and dimes, or counters to represent them, or decimal bars to hundredths

See Reproducibles for: directions for pv mats and decimal extensions, bills to 100s—in different colors, decimal bars to hundredths—in the same color used for $1 bills

Anticipatory Set

Use *graph paper decimals* and *pv blocks.*

Have students work in groups of three. One student picks up 2 tens and 4 ones to make 24 and divides the blocks equally between the other two students. Write $2\overline{)24}$ on the board. Did both students receive the same amount?

Have a second student pick up 2 ones and 4 tenths and divide it equally as before. Write $2\overline{)2.4}$. Do both students have an equal amount? Can we divide tenths just as we divide other numbers?

Procedure 1 ☐■

To divide decimals by whole numbers

Use *graph paper decimals, pv blocks, paper,* and *pv mats with decimal extensions.*

Have students fold their paper vertically into thirds, label from left to right: "Tens," "Ones," "Tenths," and place the decimal point between the tenths and ones columns. They will place their decimals on the paper for the first problem.

Next have students place 2.6 with decimals. Ask: How many ones? (2) Tenths? (6)

They write 2.6 below the decimals:

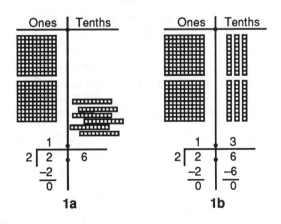

1a   **1b**

Say: A bear brother and sister want to make sure they *always* get the same amount of anything. They have 2 and 6 tenths salmon between them.

Draw a fence around the 2.6, and write a 2 as the divisor (Illustration 1a).

Students copy onto their paper.

Ask: What do the directions tell us to do? (divide the number into two groups) What will our answer show us? (how many are in each group, or how much salmon each bear gets)

Have students start with the whole salmon, the ones. Say: Make two equal groups. How many in each group? (1) What are we dividing? (ones)

The answer needs to show me how many are in each group of ones. Where will I have to write my answer? (above the fence in the ones place)

How many of the ones were we able to put into groups? (2) Any left over? (no) We've taken care of 2 ones.

How do we check? (multiply the number in each group by the number of groups) How do we find leftovers? (subtract this answer from the number of ones we started with) (See Illustration 1a.)

Students copy onto their paper.

The directions say to divide *all* of the salmon into two groups. Divide the 6 tenths of a salmon into two groups.

How many tenths are in each group? (3) What are we dividing? (tenths) Where do I need to write my answer? (in the tenths column)

Students write the three above the fence in the tenths column.

How many of the tenths could we put into groups? (6) Are any left over? (no) To check this, multiply the number in each group by the number of groups. To find leftovers, subtract this product from the number of tenths we started with (Illustration 1b).

Look very carefully at the number you show as your answer. We divided 2 and 6 tenths into two equal groups. Some of you show that 13 are in each group. What happened?

Students respond: Some forgot the decimal point.

If we are dividing tenths, we have to show tenths in the answer. We do this by putting a decimal point in the answer.

The number of ones in each group is shown in the ones column, and the number of tenths in each group is shown in the tenths column. **Where is the decimal point in the answer? (above the decimal point in the number we started with) Why?**

Students should be able to state that the place value columns do not change from the number we started with to the answer.

Have students place and divide 26 by 2 and compare their method and answer with 2.6 ÷ 2. Students should see that the processes are identical. The only difference is in the decimal point.

Next introduce regrouping. Write 3.6 ÷ 2 on the board.

Students now place their decimals on their pv mats and write the problem on their three-column paper. They divide the three ones into two groups and have one left over. They do not finish writing the problem.

How many ones were you able to get into two equal groups? (2) How many left over? (1)

Write the number you were able to get into groups beneath the number of ones we started with. (Demonstrate on the board.) How do you check division? (with multiplication)

Students multiply and subtract to find a remainder of one.

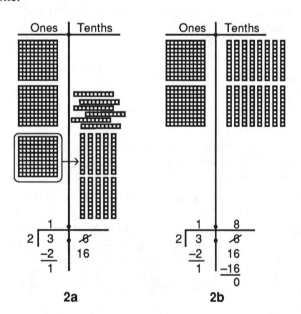

2a   **2b**

What can we do with the last one to be able to divide it? (regroup) Trade the one for 10 tenths on your mat.

Students make the trade and discover they now have 16 tenths.

We don't have 6 tenths any more. Cross out the 6. We have 16 tenths. Write 16 on your paper (Illustration 2a).

Students next divide the 16 tenths into the 2 equal groups that the directions call for. They now have 2 groups of 8.

Where will I write this? (in the tenths place) How many left over? (0) We have taken care of 16 tenths. How can we check this?

Students finish the problem on paper. They check to make sure they have 3.6 instead of 36 in their answer.

Another bear sister comes along. The bears now have ounces of honey and have to divide it three ways.

Repeat the procedure with 33.6 ÷ 3 and 43.08 ÷ 3. Students will need to make new paper pv charts. Have students compare the placement of decimals in dividend and quotient, both when the dividend includes tenths and also when it includes hundredths. Can they state a rule about dividing decimals?

Students respond: Dividing decimals is just like dividing whole numbers, except the decimal point must be in the answer above where it was placed in the original number.

Procedure 2

To divide money amounts by whole numbers

Use *pv mats with decimal extensions, bills, coins or counters or decimal bars,* and *paper.*

Repeat Procedure 1 with bills, and bars or coins. Use a story problem format of dividing money between people or purchases.

Practice and Extension

Have students do problems on *pv mats* and check with *calculators.* Have them speculate on what happens in the case of remainders.

Have students show decimal division with other manipulatives: *pv blocks and counters* or *interlocking cubes.*

Have students write story problems about their families on a trip: use gallons or liters of gas, distance, amounts of food, money amounts, and so on. Have students present their problems to the class.

Skill: To divide by decimals

Time: 3 periods

Materials:

graph paper: ¹/₂" squares

scissors

markers: light-colored; 1 per student

See Reproducibles for: decimal bar example sheets

Anticipatory Set

Use *graph paper, decimal bar example sheets,* and *scissors.*

Have students cut out seven 1 × 10 strips from their graph paper. Each strip will be one unit.

Write 1)‾3 on the board. How many groups of 1 are in the 3? Students divide three strips on their desk.

How many ones go into 3 or, how many ones *are contained in* the 3? (3) Repeat for 2)‾4 and 3)‾6. Have students cut out the decimal bars and set them aside.

Procedure 1

To divide whole numbers by decimals

Use *graph paper strips from the Anticipatory Set, blank decimal bars, markers,* and *paper.*

Have students place three of the graph paper strips on their desk. Write 0.1)‾3 on the board. Ask: What might this mean? (how many 0.1s are contained in 3)

We don't want whole groups, only tenths of groups.

Students count tenths and find 30 tenths in 3.

Write 0.1)‾3 = 30 on the board.

Repeat with 0.2)‾4. Ask: What size group is contained in the 4? (0.2) How many are in 4?

Students count and find 20 groups of 0.2s in 4.

Write 0.2)‾4 = 20 on the board. Say: As written, my answer is too large to go above the 4.

Before, we always divided by a whole number, so maybe the decimal divisor is the problem. There *is* a way to write down division by decimals. See whether you can discover it by looking for patterns.

Have students use markers and blank decimal bars. Write 0.1)‾2 on the board. Have students use their markers to color two *whole* bars.

Say: Now use tenths bars. Color 0.1 at a time until you show how many it would take to equal the 2. You will find how many 0.1 *are contained in* 2.

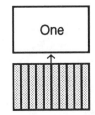

10 0.1s contained in 1   10 0.1s contained in 1

Students discover 20.

Now think of each tenth as a *whole* part. One part is contained in 20 parts 20 times. Write 1)‾20 = 20 on the board.

Repeat with other problems. Students can share or reuse whole bars. Each time, students show the whole number and color the needed groups. Write both versions on the board:

> **0.1)‾2 = 20   1)‾20 = 20**
> **1 part is contained in 20 parts 20 times**
> **.2)‾6 = 30   2)‾60 = 30**
> **a group of 2 parts is contained in 60 parts 30 times**

Ask: Do you see any patterns? What about similarities and differences within pairs of equations? (The quotients and numbers are the same; the equations are equivalent.)

How would we get from 0.1 to 1? (multiply by 10) How would we get from 2 to 20? (multiply by 10)

We changed the place value of *both* numbers in the problem, so we haven't changed the relationship.

If I rewrite 0.2)‾4 as 2)‾40, is the answer the same? (yes)

Which problem is easier to do? (2)‾40) Can you state a rule for dividing easily by decimals?

Students may state that decimal divisors and dividends may be multiplied by 10 to divide easily.

In these cases the rule does work. But will it hold true for other decimals? How could we check?

If students do not suggest dividing by hundredths, ask them to solve 0.02)‾3.

Repeat the procedure with hundredths bars.

$0.02\overline{)3} = 150$ $\quad$ $2\overline{)300} = 150$
a group of 2 parts is contained in 300 parts 150 times

$0.15\overline{)6} = 40$ $\quad$ $15\overline{)600} = 40$
a group of 15 parts is contained in 600 parts 40 times

Students should see that, when dividing by hundredths, both divisor and dividend are multiplied by 100.

Why would we do this?

Students respond: It is easier to divide. We want a whole number divisor.

Yes. Multiply the divisor by what you need to get a whole number. Do the same to the dividend.

Write $0.02\overline{)3} = 2_\wedge\overline{)300_\wedge} = 150$. The quotient's decimal point goes above the new one in the dividend.

Allow students practice with the bars, as well as writing each step on paper, until the concept is understood. They should check the division with multiplication.

Procedure 2 □■

To divide decimals by decimals; whole number quotients

Use *blank decimal bars* and *markers.*

Repeat the general procedure as in Procedure 1. Say: For $0.1\overline{).4}$, we need to know how many groups of 1 tenth are *contained in* 4 tenths.

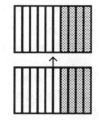

4 0.1s contained in 0.4

Students color 0.4 as shown. Ask: How many tenths were colored? (4) Call attention to thinking of this as a multiplication problem, as well as division: What times the 0.1 will equal 0.4? How many groups of 0.1 will it take? Students then use another bar to color enough 0.1s and find 4 0.1s in 0.4.

Have students now think of each tenth as a whole unit. Write each problem on the board:

$0.1\overline{)0.4} = 4$ $\quad$ $1\overline{)4} = 4$
1 part is contained in 4 parts 4 times

To divide by hundredths, change tenths to equivalent hundredths and use hundredth bars, as well as tenths:

$0.15\overline{)0.3} = 0.15\overline{)0.30} = 2$ $\quad$ $15\overline{)30} = 2$
a group of 15 parts is contained in 30 parts 2 times

Have students look for a pattern.

Students state the rule: Multiply the divisor by what you need to get a whole number. Multiply the dividend by the same amount. Place the decimal point in the quotient right above that in the dividend. Students practice with the bars, as well as on paper, until the concept is understood.

Procedure 3 □■

To divide by decimals; decimal or mixed decimal quotients

Use *blank decimal bars* and *markers.*

Repeat the general procedure as in Procedure 1. The quotient can be expressed as a fraction, and then changed to an equivalent decimal.

For example: $0.3\overline{)0.36} = 0.30\overline{)0.36}$. Students color 0.36. They find how many groups of 0.30 *are contained in* 0.36.

Students may say 0.30 goes into 0.36 one time with 6 hundredths left over.

Remind students that remainders are written as part of the group size they're dividing by. There are 6 of 30 small parts left over; the remainder is $^6/_{30} = ^1/_5 = 0.2$.

$0.3\overline{)0.36} = 0.30\overline{)0.36} = 1.2$ $\quad$ $30\overline{)36} = 1.2$

Provide examples so students see the pattern.

Students should be able to state the rule. They practice with the bars, as well as on paper.

Practice and Extension

Have students gather *track-and-field data.* They can *graph* times versus distance for races and make question *cards.* Example: What was each runner's average time per kilometer in a 10 km race?

A candy company makes 10-kg batches that go into bags that weigh 0.67 g. How many bags? Have students research manufacturers for data.

Have students play in pairs. Each throws four *dice* and uses those numbers to make two numbers in the hundredths. The winner has the largest quotient. What is the best strategy?

Skill: To change fractions and mixed numbers to decimals

coins: pennies and dimes, or counters to represent them

See Reproducibles for: decimal bars to desired place—in the same color used for $1 bills, directions for file-folder pv mats and decimal extensions, bills to 100s—in different colors

Time: 2–3 periods

Materials:

graph paper decimals to hundredths (directions in Manipulative Information section and Decimals 3)

place value (pv) mats to 1000s with decimal extensions

Note: For writing fractions as decimals when the denominator is a power of 10, see Decimals 1.

Anticipatory Set

Write 0.2 on the board, and have students read it. (2 tenths) Write $0.2 = {}^2/_{10}$. Repeat with 0.25, 1.4, 0.05.

Now write ${}^4/_{10}$, and have students write it as a decimal. Repeat with $1{}^6/_{10}$, ${}^4/_{100}$, and so on.

What fractions do we already know how to write as decimals? (fractions that are tenths, hundredths, etc.) Yes, when the denominator is a power, or multiple, of 10 it is easy to write them as decimals. Why? (Our number system is based on 10.)

Procedure 1

To change fractions to decimals by changing the denominator to an equivalent power of ten

Use *decimal bars* or *graph paper decimals*.

Say: You already know how to write many fractions as decimals. Why might we want to be able to write all fractions as decimals?

Students respond: They are easier to work with.

Let's start with ${}^1/_2$. Ask: What does ${}^1/_2$ mean? (1 of 2 parts, 1 divided into 2 parts)

To write ${}^1/_2$ as a decimal, we would need its denominator to be a power of ten.

Can the tenths bar be divided into two even parts?

Students find the tenths bar and respond: Yes.

How many tenths does it take to equal ${}^1/_2$ the bar? (5 tenths) What decimal is that? (0.5)

Write ${}^1/_2 = {}^5/_{10} = 0.5$ on the board.

Try this with ${}^3/_5$. Into how many parts will you divide your tenths bar?

Students respond: 5.

How many tenths in each fifth? (2) We want three of the fifths. How many tenths is that? (6)

Write ${}^3/_5 = {}^6/_{10} = 0.6$.

What about $2{}^1/_2$? What does it mean?

Students respond: Two wholes and ${}^1/_2$ of a whole.

Are the two wholes more than one? (yes) Will I have to change the wholes to decimal fractions?

Students respond: No, decimal fractions are smaller than one.

I only have to change the ${}^1/_2$. What is ${}^1/_2$ as a decimal? (0.5) How would I write $2{}^1/_2$ as a decimal?

Students respond: 2.5.

The next one is a little harder. What does ${}^3/_{25}$ mean?

Students respond: A whole divided into 25 parts, and we want 3 of those parts.

We're looking for an equivalent fraction with a denominator that is a power of ten. Find a decimal bar that can be divided evenly into 25 parts.

Students find the hundredths bar and outline twenty-fifths.

Look at each twenty-fifth. How many hundredths in each? (4) How many hundredths in three of the twenty-fifths? (12)

Can you write ${}^{12}/_{100}$ as a decimal?

Students respond: 0.12.

Write ${}^3/_{25} = {}^{12}/_{100} = 0.12$. Can you state what we know about changing some fractions to decimals?

Students respond: Find an equivalent fraction with a denominator as a power of ten, and then write it as a decimal.

When this will work? Write down all the numbers that will evenly divide 10 or 100.

Students write: 2, 4, 5, 10, 20, 25.

Now factor each number. What patterns do you see?

Students respond: They all have prime factors of only 2 or 5.

Yes, if a number has prime factors of 2 or 5, you can find an equivalent decimal fraction.

Test this. Eight has 2 as its prime factor. What bar is evenly divided by 8?

Students discover the thousandths bar will work.

Have students find equivalent fractions both with the bars and in writing until they are competent in the skill.

Procedure 2

To change fractions to decimals, using division

Use *pv mats with decimal extensions, decimal bars to thousandths,* and *paper.*

Say: You've discovered not all fractions can be changed to decimals by using powers of ten. Let's discover how to change *all* fractions to decimals.

You said $\frac{1}{2}$ was one whole divided into two parts and you want one of those two parts. Place a one bar on your mats, and divide it into two even parts.

Students discover they need to regroup to do this.

Ask: What did you regroup for? (tenths) How many tenths were equal to $\frac{1}{2}$? (5 tenths) I write this as 0.5.

What mathematical operation did you use? (division) Yes. $\frac{1}{2} = 1 \div 2 = 2\overline{)1} = 0.5$. By doing the division on a place value chart, we ended up with a decimal.

Will this work for $\frac{2}{4}$? How many parts is the whole divided into? (4) How many of those parts do we want? (2) Do this on your mats.

Students start with a whole bar. By regrouping until they get to thousandths, they discover $\frac{2}{4} = \frac{357}{1,000}$.

What operation were you using? (division)

We divided 1 into fourths and took 2 of them. What we did was to change the $\frac{2}{4}$ into $\frac{1}{4} \times 2$. By doing the division on a place value chart, we ended up with a decimal. Will this always work?

Students do the division problem on paper for $\frac{1}{2}$, $\frac{2}{4}$. The results are the same as they got earlier.

What is the rule for changing fractions to decimals?

Students respond: Divide the numerator by the denominator.

What do you need to remember to do if you don't have an answer yet and you're still regrouping?

Students respond: Put a zero as a place holder.

What about the number $3\frac{1}{2}$? Can I write the 3 as a decimal? Will I be dividing it?

Students respond: No, decimals are for numbers smaller than 1. You just divide the fraction part.

Have students try changing $\frac{1}{3}$ to a decimal. Since 3 is not a power of ten, students will discover a repeating decimal. Have them explore other fractions to see which result in repeating decimals.

Give students story problems that involve changing fractions to decimals, including improper fractions. They should use the manipulatives until they feel comfortable with the concept.

Procedure 3

To change fractions to decimals using money

Use *pv mats with decimal extensions, bills,* and *coins or counters.*

Repeat Procedure 2 with bills and coins. Have students round any remainders in the hundredths place. This is good practice for estimating.

Practice and Extension

Have students use *calculators* to explore terminating and repeating decimals. What if a pattern doesn't repeat? Will they need to divide further by hand?

Do all decimals change back into the fractions they started as? $1 = \frac{1}{3} + \frac{2}{3}$. Have students change $\frac{1}{3}$ and $\frac{2}{3}$ into decimals, and then back into fractions. What other fractions or decimals can they find that present a problem?

Have students throw four *dice* to get 2-digit numerators and denominators. Change each to a decimal. The largest number gets 1 point. Vary by allowing students to choose three of the four digits to make the fraction. What are the best strategies?

Use *Marvin the Mammoth.* Marvin needs to add up his mixed number amounts of food for his diet. Have students change the amounts to decimals to make his record keeping easier.

Ratio and Percent 1

Skill: To understand ratios and proportions

Time: 4 periods

Materials:

objects: counters, interlocking cubes, or buttons; 3 colors

markers: to match counter colors

geoboards and rubber bands, or geoboard paper

See Reproducibles for: geoboard paper, if needed, multiplication/division tables

Anticipatory Set

Give students the numbers 12 and 24. Ask them to find all the ways they could compare them. Discuss.

Procedure 1

To understand ratio

Use *objects* (3 colors) and *markers*.

Say: We're going to look at one way of comparing two numbers or amounts today, called ratios.

Have students put three yellow counters on their desk with two white ones to the right. On the board write:

yellow	to	white
3	to	2
3	:	2
	$\frac{3}{2}$	

Say: These are all ways of saying that for every three yellow counters, we have two white ones.

Say: Now put the two white ones on the left and the three yellow ones on the right. What would I say and write?

Students respond: 2 to 3, 2 : 3, ²/₃.

Write on the board:

white	to	yellow
2	to	3
2	:	3
	$\frac{2}{3}$	

Are there any other numbers or amounts we can compare here?

Students respond: 2 white to 5 counters in all, 3 yellow to 5 counters in all.

We can compare part of the total to all of the total.

Look around, and see how many ratios you can find in the classroom. What are we comparing? (two numbers or amounts)

Students give examples: girls/class, boys/girls, and so on. They add to the chart on the board, following your format.

Next have students use four red counters as well and find a way of showing a 4 : 1 ratio.

Students discuss the ratios found.

As a final activity, have students work in groups to find, and chart as above, all possible ratios with all nine counters: three yellow, two white, and four red.

Procedure 2

To understand and find equal ratios using multiplication

Use *geoboards and rubber bands, objects* (2 colors), and *multiplication/division tables*.

Have students enclose the top left square of their geoboard and then put two same-color counters in it (Illustration 3a).

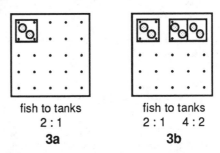

fish to tanks	fish to tanks
2 : 1	2 : 1 4 : 2
3a	**3b**

Say: These are two fish in a tank. We'll call this a unit because in this story, the ratio never changes; there are always two fish per, or for each, tank.

How would I write the ratio of number of fish to number of tanks?

Students respond: 2 to 1, 2 : 1, $^2/_1$, as you write on the board.

In the right corner, make two fish tanks right next to each other with two fish in each. Put a rubber band around each unit, then one around both (Illustration 3b).

What is the ratio of *all* the fish to *all* the tanks on the right side?

Students respond: $^4/_2$.

We have more fish and tanks now, but are the units still the same as for our first ratio?

Students respond: Yes, there are still two fish per tank.

Write $^2/_1 = ^4/_2$, 2 : 1 :: 4 : 2 on the board.

Say: We can call these ratios equal because the units stay the same—even though there may be more units in one of the ratios than the other.

Now use other space on your board and make a different ratio *equal to the first*. What's the rule?

Students respond: The units have to be the same. Students make equal ratios and discuss the results.

Have students write all new ratios: $^2/_1 = ^4/_2 = ^6/_3 = ^8/_4$. Call attention to keeping fish on top and tanks on the bottom, which keeps the basic unit the same.

Ask: What patterns can you find?

Students discuss. They may say they are adding a unit each time.

We are adding a unit each time. Do you know a shortcut for adding the same amount each time? (multiplication)

Let's compare the original ratio with each new one to check. Write:

$^2/_1 = ^4/_2$ we multiplied *each part* of the unit by 2
$^2/_1 = ^6/_3$ we multiplied *each part* of the unit by 3
$^2/_1 = ^8/_4$ we multiplied *each part* of the unit by 4

In each case, every time we multiplied the number of fish, we had to multiply the number of tanks because we couldn't break up our ratio unit of 2 fish per tank.

Are all equal ratios are related this way? Put 1 red counter on your desk with 2 yellows underneath (Illustration 4a).

The red counter is a lollipop, and each yellow counter is 10¢. What is ratio of lollipop to cost?

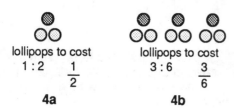

lollipops to cost
1 : 2 $\frac{1}{2}$

4a

lollipops to cost
3 : 6 $\frac{3}{6}$

4b

Students respond: 1 : 2 or $^1/_2$.

Now show the equal ratio for buying three lollipops. Remember to keep the unit the same (Illustration 4b).

Students make a ratio of 3 reds to 6 yellow, or 3 lollipops to 60¢. They tell you to write $^1/_2 = ^3/_6$.

Could we have done this with multiplication? (yes) What would we have to remember?

Students respond: Multiply both parts of the original ratio unit.

Sometimes ratios compare part to all.

Use 2 red counters for red flowers, 3 yellow counters for yellow flowers, and find the ratio of red flowers to all flowers. ($^2/_5$)

Now find and chart three more equal ratios:

	×2	×3	×4
2	4	6	8
5	10	15	20

Look at the multiplication table, and compare twos and fives. What do you notice?

Students notice an equal ratio chart is like the multiplication chart. Equal ratios are sets of multiples.

If both numbers in the ratio are in the same vertical column, as were the 2 and 5, all others in the same rows will have the same relationship.

Provide students with many problem situations to solve with counters and then write on paper.

When students feel comfortable with the concept and skill, have them solve problems first on paper and then check with manipulatives.

Relate equal ratios to equivalent fractions, if you wish. Go on to Procedure 3.

Procedure 3

To find equal ratios using division

Use *geoboards and rubber bands* and *multiplication/division tables*.

Say: Sometimes we want a smaller ratio. Maybe popcorn is 4/$8.00, but we only want 1 box.

Start by enclosing the 4 squares on top for popcorn boxes, and 8 below for dollars (Illustration 6a).

Write $^4/_8$ on the board.

Now use the rubber bands, and enclose what you think is the basic ratio unit that $^4/_8$ was built from. Enclose all the ratio units that you have.

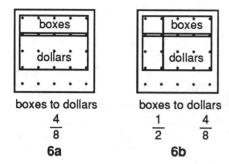

boxes to dollars
$$\frac{4}{8}$$
6a

boxes to dollars
$$\frac{1}{2} \qquad \frac{4}{8}$$
6b

If you have squares left over, try again. The ratio unit stays the same no matter how big the equal ratios.

Students enclose 1 box: 2 dollars (Illustration 6b).

Starting with $^4/_8$, count units and tell me the next smallest ratio—the one for 3 boxes. ($^3/_6$)

The next? ($^2/_4$) And the smallest? ($^1/_2$)

Write $^4/_8 = ^3/_6 = ^2/_4 = ^1/_2$. Say: It's hard to see the process, so I'll compare each ratio to the ratio unit:

$$^4/_8 = ^1/_2$$
$$^3/_6 = ^1/_2$$
$$^2/_4 = ^1/_2$$

How are we getting from each equal ratio to the ratio/unit?

Students respond: Subtraction; some say division.

We could use subtraction, but which is faster? (division)

Remember, we have to keep our basic ratio unit together, so you need to divide *both* parts of any ratio.

You can use your knowledge of ratios to solve problems easily. Can you solve this with counters? Use one color for hours and one for days.

Mali worked on her book for 14 hours in 7 days. Set up this ratio.

Students put 14 counters above and 7 below.

She worked the same amount each day; how many hours for 1 day? Where will your day counter be?

Students respond: Below.

Yes, if you have hours above and days below in the first ratio, it is the same for any other equal ratios.

How do you get from a bigger ratio to a smaller equal ratio? (division) Find the answer, using the counters.

Students find Mali worked 2 hours per day.

Write $^{14}/_7 = ^2/_1$.

How could you do it without your counters?

Students respond: Divide both top and bottom by seven.

Have you noticed that we write ratios like fractions? A fraction is a part/whole ratio. You find equal fractions just as we've been doing for ratios.

Provide students with practice. Have them first try to find the ratio unit by trying to get either the top or bottom equal to one. Then have them make tables of the equal ratios.

Students work with counters and then write the process and results. When they are comfortable with the skill, they can do the problems on paper and then check with the counters.

Show students how to check, using multiplication/division tables. If they can find the ratio in one vertical column, they can work from right to left to find equal ratios with smaller numbers (division) or from left to right to find equal ratios with larger numbers (multiplication).

Procedure 4

To understand the properties of proportions

Use *objects* (2 colors), *paper*, and *objects different from the first set.*

Say: You know how to find equal ratios; two equal ratios together are called a *proportion*. The equal ratios in a proportion are linked in special ways.

Put 2 objects on the left side of your paper with 4 below, a ratio of $^2/_4$.

Now put 3 objects on top with 6 below on the right side of your paper to show $^3/_6$. Draw this on the board or overhead.

$$\frac{2\,\blacksquare\blacksquare}{4\,\blacksquare\blacksquare} = \frac{\blacksquare\blacksquare\blacksquare\,3}{\blacksquare\blacksquare\blacksquare\,6}$$

Students set out the objects. They write $^2/_4 = ^3/_6$.

Now put a red counter between the two top numbers and another between the two bottom ones. Draw this on the board or overhead.

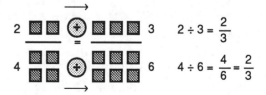

$$2 \div 3 = \frac{2}{3}$$
$$4 \div 6 = \frac{4}{6} = \frac{2}{3}$$

The counters will represent an operation box that tells what to do with the two numbers.

For instance, look at the top numbers. The number 2 is on one side, and 3 is on the other. Ask: If the operation rule is +, addition, what number will result? (5)

Both counters are red because the operation is the same.

Try different operations, and write the answers to the right. *Compare the top answers and the bottom answers.* Look for something interesting.

Students discover that if they *divide*, they have ²/₃ using the top numbers and ⁴/₆ using the bottom ones, which are equal ratios.

In this ratio, dividing one top number by the other and then dividing one bottom number by the other gives equal ratios.

Now put a blue counter in the very middle, on top of the = sign, and draw lines through it. Draw this on the board or overhead.

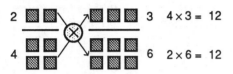

2   4   3   4 × 3 = 12
4   6   2 × 6 = 12

Only one operation box is used this time. It links the numbers at the ends of each line.

See whether you can follow the lines and find the operation that gives an interesting relationship.

Students discover that the operation is multiplication. Cross products are equal: $2 \times 6 = 12$ and $4 \times 3 = 12$.

You used multiplication and found the cross products. The operation lines form a cross.

Ask: Do these two relationships you found work for all proportions? Try the same procedure with ²/₄ and ⁵/₁₀, which are also equal ratios, a proportion.

Students find $^2/_5 = ^4/_{10} = ^2/_5$, and $2 \times 10 = 4 \times 5 = 20$.

These two properties of proportions are not only fascinating, they're handy.

Test ³/₅ and ⁴/₆ to see whether they're equal proportions.

Students discover the properties do not hold, so they are not a proportion.

You can test proportions by multiplying cross products.

Now put out the ratio ²/₆. On the right side I'll only give you the top number, 3. Use the properties to discover the whole equal ratio.

Students put out $^2/_6 = ^3/_?$. They find that $^2/_3 = ^6/_?$ and $2 \times ? = 6 \times 3 = 18$. The missing ratio is ³/₉.

This might be $2 for 6 pens, and $3 for 9 pens.

Provide students with problems, or have them make them up. They should work with the materials until they feel comfortable with the skill, writing down the process as they work. Then they can do the problem first on paper, using the materials as a check.

Practice and Extension

Bring in *grocery store ads,* and *paste* them on *cards.* Students make up proportion questions with the answers on the back of the card and then switch with a partner to solve.

Have students watch the *newspaper* and *television* for ratios. Example: 2 out of 5 people use a certain toothpaste.

Have students gather *data from many classrooms* and look for ratios. Figure the average ratios of brown eyes/blue eyes, boys/girls, and so on, for the school. Do the ratios of any classrooms form a proportion with the average ratios? Try changing ratios to decimals. Are relationships clearer?

Have students create bar *graphs* of equal ratios:

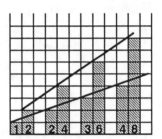

Have students discuss the two different lines. Why does the slope vary? (Multiples will increase faster.)

What happens with different ratios? How can students get the lines to go in a different direction? What would happen if they started with a ratio like 2 : 1?

Explore *body measurements.*

> tibia/height = ¹/₄
> radius/height = ¹/₆
> wingspan/height = ¹/₁
> neck circumference/waist circumference = ¹/₂
> wrist circumference/waist = ¹/₄
> navel-to-floor/height = ¹/₀.₆₁₈₀₃₄ (the golden ratio)

By converting to decimals, comparisons are easier. In what professions would this knowledge be useful? (medical, forensic reconstruction, art, etc.)

Ratio and Percent 2

Skill: To relate fractions, ratios, and decimals to percent

Time: 5+ periods

Materials:

graph paper: ½" squares

markers: in two light colors

place value (pv) blocks to 100s

See Reproducibles for: decimal bars to thousandths to color in

Anticipatory Set

Use *graph paper* and *markers*.

Have students use the back of their paper and make two dots of one color and three dots of the other. They discuss all possible ratio and fraction statements they can make about the dots. Example: ²/₅, ³/₅, 2 : 3, and so on.

Procedure 1 ☐■

To understand the concept of *percent;* to change fractions to percents, using equivalent fractions

Use *graph paper* and *markers*.

Have students outline a 10 × 10 square on their graph paper. Ask: How many squares have we outlined? (100)

Say: Color in 1 of the squares with markers. What fraction have you colored? (¹/₁₀₀)

Because we have a denominator of 100, we have another choice for a name, *percent*. *Percent* means "for each hundred." We write percent as %, which is just a sloppy way of writing /₁₀₀.

How many squares *per hundred* have you colored? (1) You have each colored in 1 percent or 1% of your squares.

Color in two more squares. How many are colored now? (3%) What percent are uncolored? (97%)

Let's interview 100 people. Using the same color as before, color in 17 more squares until you show 20, the people who prefer strawberry ice cream (Illustration 1a).

Use a different color to color another 30, people who prefer chocolate ice cream.

What percent prefer strawberry? (20%) Chocolate? (30%)

The rest prefer vanilla. What percent is that? (50%)

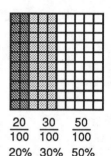

$$\frac{20}{100} \quad \frac{30}{100} \quad \frac{50}{100}$$
20% 30% 50%

1a

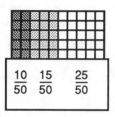

$$\frac{10}{50} \quad \frac{15}{50} \quad \frac{25}{50}$$

1b

Write the *fractions* for these percents.

Students write ²⁰/₁₀₀, ³⁰/₁₀₀ and ⁵⁰/₁₀₀.

Cover the bottom half of the square (Illustration 1b). How many people now? (50)

Find and write the fraction of people for each flavor.

Students write ¹⁰/₅₀, ¹⁵/₅₀ and ²⁵/₅₀.

Compare the fractions for 50 people and 100 people.

Students find ¹⁰/₅₀ = ²⁰/₁₀₀, ¹⁵/₅₀ = ³⁰/₁₀₀; ²⁵/₅₀ = ⁵⁰/₁₀₀.

***Percent* means "per hundred," but if you don't have 100, find the equivalent fraction or ratio with 100 as a denominator.**

Students suggest other data. They color the percent of each and compare the fractions and ratios for more and fewer people.

Procedure 2 ☐

To change fractions to percents, using equivalent fractions

Use *pv blocks* and *paper*.

Say: Put a hundred flat on your desk to represent all the days this winter. *Half* of the days this winter were sunny. Cover half your flat with ten rods to show the sunny days. (See illustration next page.)

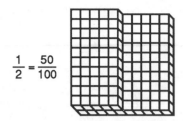

$$\frac{1}{2} = \frac{50}{100}$$

How many sunny days out of 100? (50) What percent is that? (50) What equivalent fractions do we have?

Students respond: $\frac{1}{2} = \frac{50}{100}$.

Repeat for $\frac{1}{4}$.

To have a fraction be percent, what must we do? (change the fraction so that the denominator is 100)

On paper, we can show what we've done with the blocks: $\frac{1}{2} \times \frac{50}{50} = \frac{50}{100} = 50\%$.

Students do examples with blocks and on paper.

Procedure 3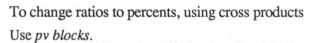

To change ratios to percents, using cross products

Use *pv blocks*.

Have students put a one cube on a ten rod. Say: One of my 10 pencils needs sharpening. Write 1 : 10, $\frac{1}{10}$.

Now have students place a flat separately. Ask: How many pencils do I show with the flat? (100)

Say: For each 10 pencils, one needs sharpening. Put an unsharpened pencil on each 10 pencils in your flat.

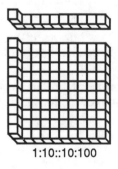

1:10::10:100

Students find there are 10 unsharpened pencils.

Write 1 : 10 :: 10 : 100, $\frac{1}{10} = \frac{10}{100}$ on the board. Ask: Can we write some amounts here as percents?

Students respond: 10 : 100 and $\frac{10}{100}$ are both 10%.

Repeat, using 2 : 5, 3 : 20.

To state a ratio as percent, what do we need to do?

Students respond: Find an equal ratio that has 100 as the bottom number.

Review using cross multiplying with students, using the above examples: $\frac{2}{5} = \frac{?}{100}$.

Students create and solve problems using both blocks and cross multiplication. Eventually they do the problem on paper before checking with the blocks.

Procedure 4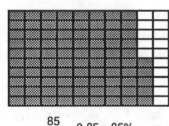

To relate decimals to percent

Use *decimal bars* and *markers*.

Have students color in 25 squares on a hundredth bar. Review that this amount can be written as either $\frac{25}{100}$ or 0.25.

Have students color in more squares and label their total with the appropriate fraction and decimal amounts. The result will be many different amounts.

Review that the special sign for percent is %. It means 5 parts per, or "for each," hundred.

Say: My bar has 85 parts colored. How many ways can I write that amount?

Students respond: $\frac{85}{100}$, 0.85, 85%.

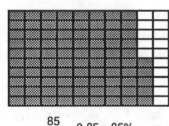

$$\frac{85}{100} = 0.85 = 85\%$$

Students write the percents on their shaded parts.

Look at all the bars. What do you notice about the ways of writing the same amounts?

Students discuss.

Label the colored part of your bar "Shaded." Now write the three ways of showing how much is not shaded, and label them "Not Shaded." What do you notice?

Students respond: The fraction numerators, the decimals, and the percents each add to 100.

Have students take turns showing their bars with one or more of the written equivalent amounts covered. Other students must name the missing amounts.

Ask: Do you know an easy way to convert decimals to percents? Discuss.

Have students now write down the percents and the decimal amounts to test their ideas. If they do not notice it, ask where the decimal point was moved.

Students respond: Moving the decimal point two places to the right gives percent. Moving the decimal point of a percent two places to the left gives the decimal equivalent.

Procedure 5 ▢■

To write tenths and thousandths as percents

Use *decimal bars to thousandths* and *markers*.

Ask: If I give a test with 100 problems and you get 85 right, what percent right is that? (85%)

If the test only had 10 problems and you got 4 right, we can still get a percent score if we remember that *percent* means "for each hundred."

Color in $^4/_{10}$ on a tenth bar. We need to find how much this would be as hundredths. Color an equal amount on your hundredth bar.

Have students color and compare their bars. They find $^4/_{10}$ = 0.4 =.40. If students have trouble, review equivalent decimals.

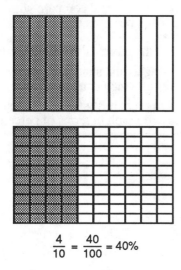

$$\frac{4}{10} = \frac{40}{100} = 40\%$$

What percent is $^{40}/_{100}$ or 0.40? (40%) So if you answered 4 out of 10 questions correctly, what would be the percent you got right? (40%)

Write 0.5, 0.7 and 0.8 on the board.

Students color bars and find the equivalent amount of hundredths. They write 0.5 = 0.50 = 50%, and so on.

What do we know about moving a decimal point to get a percent? (move it two places to the right) Does this work here? (yes, with zeros as place holders)

Repeat with other numbers until students are comfortable converting tenths to percents and back.

Say: Now imagine I took a survey of 1,000 students. I found that 850 wanted school to start later in the morning. How can I show that as a percent?

Students discuss methods to find the percent.

Color 850 of your thousandths bar, and see whether you were right about the percent.

Students color, compare, and find $^{850}/_{1,000} = {}^{85}/_{100} = 85\%$.

You could also think of $^{850}/_{1,000}$ as a decimal, 0.850. What is the equivalent decimal as hundredths? (0.85) That is how many percent? (85%)

Could you have started with 0.850 and moved the decimal point two places to the right and gotten the same answer? (yes)

Now I find some students have changed their minds; 855 want school to start later.

Color in five more thousandths on your bar. What is the equivalent amount on your hundredths bar?

Students compare and find it to be 85½ hundredths.

We can write ½ as 0.5, so $^{85.5}/_{100}$ = 85.5%.

Do you know another way to do this? (Write 0.855, and move the decimal point two places to the right.)

Students color in various amounts on their bars. They cover amounts and quiz each other on the correct percents, checking with other bars if necessary.

When students are competent with bars, have one student give the percent, fraction, or decimal amount orally. Other students write equivalents and then check.

Procedure 6 ▢■

To understand percents larger than 100%

Use *pv blocks*.

Have students put a flat on their desk. Ask: If a one cube represents a question on a test, how many questions does this test have? (100)

If you get all the questions right, what percent of them is that? (100%) Your grade is 100%.

Now I've decided to give extra credit questions. Use one cubes to show that you answered three extra credit questions right, and figure out the percent.

Students put 3 one cubes next to their flat. They report it shows 103%.

Sometimes we have *more* than 100%, more than one whole of something. How would we show our test with a *fraction*?

Students respond: $^{103}/_{100}$.

As a ratio? (103 : 100)

Now what if your goal was to collect 50 pounds of paper. Show that with ten rods (see illustration on the next page).

Students place 5 ten rods.

In fact, you collected 55 pounds. Show that.

Students add 5 cubes to their rods. They report the ratio is 55 : 50.

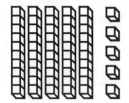

55 collected: 50 expected   110 collected: 100 expected
110%

You collected more than the amount you had planned on. Put a flat on your desk. This is 100, which we will use for figuring the percent.

55 : 50 is our ratio unit. What will the percent be, using 100 as the bottom of our new ratio?

Students place more blocks. They decide that if 50 has 5 extra blocks, 100 needs 10 extra blocks. The percent is 110%:

Repeat with other examples. Students should be encouraged to use the blocks for this type of problem until the concept is understood.

Procedure 7

To understand percents smaller than 1%

Use *graph paper* and *markers*.

Have students outline a 10 × 20 rectangle. Say: Suppose each square represents a car. Color in one square.

This will be a red car. The uncolored squares will be all other colors lumped together. What is the fraction of red cars?

Students respond: $\frac{1}{200}$.

The ratio? (1 : 200) The percent?

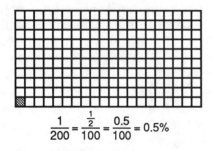

$$\frac{1}{200} = \frac{\frac{1}{2}}{100} = \frac{0.5}{100} = 0.5\%$$

Students complain that there aren't enough red cars to have a percent.

Say: Remember that percent means how many *per hundred*. Sometimes we won't have a whole number if something doesn't occur very often.

Students find ½ car per hundred.

The ratio is ½ : 100. The fraction gets clumsy. Do you know another way to write ½?

Students respond: 0.5.

We can either say ½% or 0.5%. Can you think of examples of other times when we might not get a whole number as a percent?

Students discuss.

Have students show each scenario with graph paper. Remind them they can find the percent, using techniques discussed in other procedures.

Practice and Extension

If you gathered *schoolwide data* (Practice and Extension section of Ratio and Percent 1) have students find the percents represented.

Have students devise and do a survey. Graph the results in terms of percents.

Have students research *weather predictions from the past month's newspapers* and compare with the actual weather. What percents can they find? (accuracy of prediction, amount of rainfall versus expected, percent of the month's expected totals, etc.)

Have students bring in and share *newspaper or magazine articles* in which percent is used.

Do experiments in probability using 100 tosses, flips, and so on. State and graph in terms of percent.

Skill: To calculate percents

Time: 3 periods

Materials:

place value (pv) blocks to 100s

graph paper: $\frac{1}{2}$" squares

markers: light-colored

Anticipatory Set

Review multiplication of fractions and whole numbers with students: $\frac{1}{4}$ of $100 = \frac{1}{4} \times 100$. Remind them that "of" can be read as "times."

Review solving such proportions as 1 : 2 :: ? : 4.

Procedure 1

To find a certain percent of a number

Use *pv blocks* and *paper.*

Write on the board: 5% of 300 = ?. Have students place a flat on their desks. Ask: How many is this? (100)

How can I show 5% of 100?

Students respond: Put 5 one cubes on it. They do this.

5% means $\frac{5}{100}$ or 5 : 100. We know what 5% looks like, but we don't have 100 in our problem, we have 300.

Students put out two more flats to show the 300.

For every 100, we have how many cubes? (5) Show what we will have for 300.

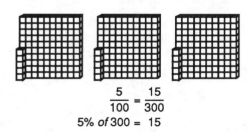

$$\frac{5}{100} = \frac{15}{300}$$
$$5\% \ of \ 300 = 15$$

Students put 5 one cubes on each flat. They find 5% of 300 is 15.

Write $\frac{5}{100} = \frac{?}{300}$. How can we solve this on paper?

Students discuss.

There are several ways:

a. use equivalent fractions:
$$\frac{5}{100} = \frac{n}{300}$$
$$\frac{5}{100} \times \frac{3}{3} = \frac{15}{300}$$
$$n = 15$$

b. use proportions:
$$\frac{5}{100} = \frac{n}{300}$$
$$5 \times 300 = 100 \times n$$
$$\frac{1,500}{100} = n$$
$$n = 15$$

c. multiply by a fraction:
5% *of* 300 means 5% *times* 300
$$\frac{5}{100} \times 300 = \frac{1,500}{100} = 15$$

d. multiply by a decimal:
$$0.05 \times 300 = 15$$

Remind students that these are skills they already have. It will be easier to set up their problems if they read "of" as "times" and rewrite them using /100 instead of %.

Students do other problems first using blocks, setting up the needed number of one cubes on a flat to represent the percent, and then using other blocks to find the answer. They then try each method on paper.

Try: 2% of 50 (4), 10% of 30 (3).

Suggest to students that they use the method that makes the most sense to them.

Procedure 2

To find what percent one number is of another

Use *graph paper* and *markers.*

Write on the board: 5 is what % of 25? Ask: Do we know the percent? (no)

How many in all do we have? (25) And what are we interested in? (5 of them)

Outline a 5 × 5 square on your graph paper to represent the 25. Color in 5 squares.

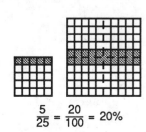

$$\frac{5}{25} = \frac{20}{100} = 20\%$$

Now outline a 10 × 10 square, but don't color any of it because we don't know the percent yet. How could we solve this?

Students discuss. They have used this format working with equivalent fractions and proportions. Some may suggest that 100 is 4 times bigger than 25 and they could multiply. Some may be able to see it as a proportion.

Again, there are several ways:

a. use equivalent fractions:
$$5/25 = n/100$$
$$5/25 \times 4/4 = 20/100$$
$$n = 20/100 = 20\%$$

b. use proportions:
$$5/25 = n/100$$
$$500 = 25 \times n$$
$$500/25 = n$$
$$n = 20$$
$$5/25 = 20/100 = 20\%$$

c. multiply by a fraction:
?% of 25 means ?% times 25
$$5 = n/100 \times 25$$
$$5/25 = n/100$$
$$n = 500/25$$
$$n = 20\%$$

Students color in 20 squares on their 10 × 10 square to show the answer.

Provide other problems for students to work first with the graph paper and then with each of the above methods. Suggest: 20 is what percent of 50? (40) 2 is what % of 10? (20)

Procedure 3

To find a number when the percent of it is known

Use *graph paper* and *markers*.

Write on the board: 20 is 40% of what number?

Ask: Do we know how many we have in all? (no) We do know we have 20 of some mystery number. We can't outline our number, but we can color in the first 20 squares.

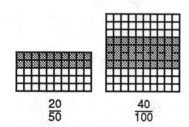

$$\frac{20}{50} \qquad \frac{40}{100}$$

Do we know the percent?

Students respond: We have 40%.

Outline a 10 × 10 square, and color in 40 squares to represent 40%. How could we solve this?

Students discuss. Some may see that the 40 squares are twice the 20 squares, so 100 must be twice the mystery number. Some may see it as a proportion.

Again, there are several ways:

a. use equivalent fractions:
$$40/100 = 20/n$$
$$40/100 \div 2/2 = 20/50$$
$$n = 50$$

b. use proportions:
$$20/n = 40/100$$
$$20 \times 100 = n \times 40$$
$$2{,}000/40 = n$$
$$n = 50$$

c. multiply by a fraction:
40% *of* ? means 40% *times* ?
$$20 = 40/100 \times n$$
$$20 = 4/10 \times n$$
$$20 \times 10/4 = n$$
$$200/4 = n$$
$$n = 50$$

d. multiply by a decimal:
$$20 = 0.40 \times n$$
$$20 \div 0.40 = n$$
$$n = 50$$

Have students outline 50 squares around the 20 colored ones to show the answer.

Provide other problems for students to work first with the graph paper and then with each of the above methods. Suggest: 15 is 75% of what number? (20) 24 = 60% of what number? (40)

Practice and Extension

Have student work in pairs, using *dice, graph paper,* and *markers*. They throw the dice twice to generate two 2-digit numbers. Each decides individually what to call each number: percent, total number, part of total number. They use the graph paper to demonstrate the problem and then solve it. The one with the highest number at the end wins. What are some strategies for winning?

Have students bring in statistics from the *newspaper*. Have them create such problems as: If only 20% of the houses on the market last month sold, how many houses sold if 425 were on the market?

Geometry 1

Skill: To use patterns in geometric shapes: two and three dimensions

cubes: regular or interlocking, in several colors, if possible

pattern blocks

graph paper: any size

tiles

Time: $1/2$–1 period per procedure

Materials:

attribute blocks or paper shapes: 3 shapes, 3 sizes of each shape, 3 colors of each shape and size; 3 of each per group

Note: Procedures are written from easier to more difficult. After identifying the desired level of difficulty, use a previous procedure as an Anticipatory Set.

Anticipatory Set

Use *attribute blocks* or *paper shapes*.

Have students work in small groups. They choose one shape and size and make a single line pattern, varying only the color attribute. Students take turns making patterns for the rest of the group to duplicate.

Procedure 1

To work with attribute patterns

Use *attribute blocks* or *paper shapes*.

Varying two attributes:

Make single line patterns, and have students copy them. Use patterns that vary in two attributes: all squares varying in color and size, all large ones varying in color and shape, etc. Ask: What will come next?

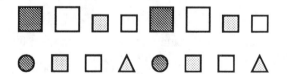

Students copy pattern. They predict the next item and continue the pattern.

Have students work in pairs to devise patterns. Have them copy each other's pattern, predict the next one, and continue the pattern.

Introduce patterns using *combinations,* varying two attributes: all squares—one small blue, a large red and large blue touching, one small blue, a large red and large blue touching, etc.

When students can do this easily, they draw patterns and exchange for their partner to continue.

Varying three attributes:

Follow the same sequence as for two attributes.

Procedure 2

To work with positional change patterns

Use *cubes,* or *paper shapes,* or *attribute blocks*.

Positional changes among pairs:

Start by varying only one attribute: Using paired items, reverse which one is above and which is below, or which is left and which is right.

Example: Using small squares, make a pattern of one blue, a red above a blue, one blue, a blue above a red, etc.

When students can copy, predict, and continue the patterns, they work in pairs as before.

Next vary two attributes.

Example: Using all squares, make a pattern of small red paired with large blue, large red paired with small blue, first pair rotated, second pair rotated.

Advanced students can try varying all three attributes.

Positional changes among the items themselves:

Start by varying only the position. Then vary one attribute. Example: Using small squares, make a pattern of one blue, one red, one blue rotated 45°, one red, etc.

The next level is to vary two attributes, then three.

Procedure 3

To work with building-on patterns

Use *paper shapes, tiles, or pattern blocks* and *graph paper*.

Introduce patterns in which each subsequent item builds on the previous one: one small blue square, two small blue squares, three small blue squares, etc. Start by varying only one attribute at a time as shown in the illustration on the next page.

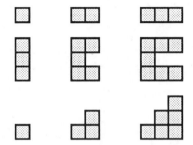

When students are adept at the skill, have them work on graph paper instead of using manipulatives. Challenge them to build and vary with more than one attribute.

Procedure 4 ☐■

To relate numbers to patterns

Use *tiles or cubes* and *graph paper*.

Work first from the patterns in Procedure 3 and then from these:

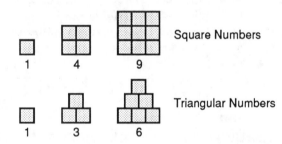

Square Numbers

1   4   9

Triangular Numbers

1   3   6

Have students make charts and look for patterns that will predict the next number in the series. Can they find the 7th? Ask: What rule will work for any number in the series?

	☐	⊞	⊞⊞	?
Position in series	1	2	3	4
# Blocks	1	4	9	
Possible solutions related to number, position	1 + 0 1 × 1	(1 + 1) + 2 2 × 2 2 + 2	(1 + 1) + (2 + 2) + 3 3 × 3 3 + 3 + 3	

Procedure 5 ■

To work with three-dimensional patterns

Use *cubes*.

Start with repeating patterns that vary in height, and then increase in complexity.

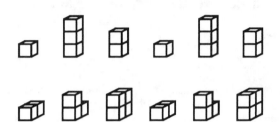

When students can work with repeating patterns, explore three-dimensional patterns in which each subsequent item is built on the previous one.

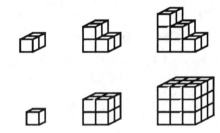

Procedure 6 ☐■

To relate numbers to three-dimensional patterns

Use *cubes* and *graph paper*.

Follow Procedure 4 using the three-dimensional patterns described in Procedure 5.

Student groups make then test their predictions. They try to write a rule for any number in the series.

Practice and Extension

As students become adept at the skills, suggest they try the next level of difficulty. Can they show a pattern using a different manipulative? Can they devise patterns using shoes, books, or other students?

Use *treasure boxes* or *object collections,* and have groups create a series, write down the rule on a piece of *paper,* and put the paper face down. Have the groups rotate and try to figure out the rule for the new series.

Have groups explore the relationships between square and triangular numbers. Can they make pentagonal or hexagonal numbers and figure out the series rules?

Have students use *paper shapes, attribute blocks, pattern blocks,* or *graph paper* to explore tiling patterns using two or more shapes, which fit together in a pattern to completely cover a space.

Geometry 2

Skill: To understand and classify angles

Time: 1 period per procedure

Materials:

tag board cut in ¹/₂" ×3" pieces: 2 per student
scissors

rulers or straightedges
paper fasteners: 1 per student
compasses or round objects for making circles
8"–10" string or yarn: 1 piece per pair of students
pattern blocks or tangrams
graph paper: any size
protractors

Anticipatory Set

Use *tag board pieces, scissors, rulers, paper fasteners, compasses or round objects,* and *plain paper.*

Make angle arrows: Have students mark the center point of each end of their tag board pieces and connect the points with a line. They should cut corners and fasten as shown with a paper fastener.

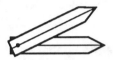

Make clock faces: Have students draw large circles, either with compasses or by tracing around objects. They cut these out, fold in quarters, and mark for clock faces: 3, 6, 9, 12.

Procedure 1 ☐■

To understand angles

Use *pencils, string, angle arrows and clock faces from Anticipatory Set,* and *pattern blocks or tangrams.*

Have students work in pairs to wrap the center of the string around a pencil several times and then place the pencil at the center of the clock face.

Say: Start with both ends of the yarn at 12. Is any space between the lines made of yarn? (no)

Make one end of the yarn point to the three. Use another pencil to trace the space between the two lines, near the center point as shown. This space is called an angle. Ask: Without moving the yarn, can you find another angle?

Students find the 270° angle between 3 and 12.

Which angle is bigger? (the one around to the left)

Now move your yarn from the three to the six. **Ask: How many angles? (2) Which is bigger? (They are the same.)**

Repeat for other combinations of clock times, having students also trace both angles together.

What do you notice about both angles together? (They always add up to a circle.) Angles are always thought of as being part of a circle.

Repeat the procedure with angle arrows, and then have students use angle arrows to identify any angles they can find in the classroom.

Next have them trace pattern block or tangram pieces on paper and indicate the angles. How many angles does each piece have? Which are bigger? Which are the same?

Procedure 2 ☐■

To work with 90° angles

Use *angle arrows and clock faces from Anticipatory Set, pattern blocks or tangrams,* and *graph paper.*

Have students use angle arrows to find and measure several square corners.

Say: Use your angle arrows as clock hands, and show 3 o'clock. What do you notice about the smaller angle you have formed? (It is a square corner.)

We measure the size of an angle in degrees; all around the center point of a circle is 360°. A square corner is 90° and is also called a right angle.

Students find other 90° angles on their clock faces. They identify them as 90°, right angles, and ¼ of a circle.

Now show 4 o'clock. Is this a 90° or right angle?

Students identify this as more than a right angle. They find and identify other clock angles as more or less than a right angle.

If I moved 90° and then another 90°, how far would I have moved? (180°) What's a 180 in skateboarding? (a turn from front to back) That's half a circle: 180°.

What's a 360 in skateboarding? (a turn all the way around) That makes a whole circle: 360°.

Students measure angles on pattern blocks or tangrams. They identify them as 90° or smaller or larger than 90°, using the clock face to check if necessary.

Have students use graph paper to draw polygons. What can they draw with only right angles? No right angles, etc.?

Procedure 3

To work with angles to the nearest 30°, 45°

Use *rulers, clock faces, scissors, angle arrows,* and *pattern blocks or tangrams.*

Have students use the rulers to draw lines on their clock faces from the center to the 12 and the 3. Ask: How big is the angle between 12 and 3? (90°)

Have students cut out clock faces and fold them so that the 3 is on top of the 12. Have them then open then up and draw a line on the fold line.

Say: You folded the 90° angle in half and marked it; how many degrees are the smaller angles you have made? (half of 90°, or 45°)

Students draw lines from the center to the 6, 9, and 12. They then fold the 90° angles in half and mark the 45° angles. They write 45° in each angle.

Repeat the procedure for 30° and 60°, drawing the lines from the center to each number on the clock.

Ask: What combinations of angles could you use to find 120°? (four 30°s, or 90° and 30°, etc.)

Students repeat with other examples that require them to add angles or to subtract angles from 360°.

Have students use angle arrows to measure the angles of pattern blocks or tangrams. They use their marked clock faces to determine the size of each angle and then chart their results.

Students next use graph paper to construct angles and figures of specified angles. How close can they come? They check with their angle arrows and the clocks.

Procedure 4

To measure with protractors

Use *clock faces marked at 30° and 45° increments from Procedure 3, protractors, straightedges,* and *pattern blocks.*

Have students lay protractors over clock faces, with 0° at 12 and 90° at 3. Ask: How many degrees is it from the 12 to the 1? (30°) From the 12 to the 2? (60°) The 0° mark on the protractor lies over the first ray of an angle.

Where would I put the protractor 0° to measure the angle between 2 and 4 on the clock? (at the 2) Where would the center point of the protractor be? (the center of the circle)

Have students place a dot on paper for the vertex of the angle and then center the protractor on that dot. For a 90° angle, where do we put the 0° mark? (at the first ray of the angle) Since we don't have a ray yet, mark a dot at the 0° on your protractor. Do the same at the 90° mark.

Students mark dots. They use straightedges to draw the rays to form the 90° angle.

Repeat until students can construct any desired angles, and then have them measure the angles of their pattern blocks. They chart their results and look for any patterns or matching combinations.

Procedure 5

To understand relationships of angles

Use *pattern blocks* and *graph paper.*

Draw a large × on the board, and label the angles as shown. Have students use two green triangles and two red trapezoids to meet at the center to form an ×.

Students discover and write all the relationships they can find between the angles.

If you wish to treat more complicated angle relationships, have students place pattern blocks to form and explore the figure:

Practice and Extension

Have students use *art paper, angle arrows,* and *rulers* to draw all-over designs incorporating geometric shapes. They can create designs for buildings or skylines in black and white.

Have students research sundials and how they use angles to tell time.

Have students draw a city map with streets at various angles.

Geometry 3

Skill: To understand and find perimeter

Time: 3 periods

Materials:

geoboards and rubber bands or string
scissors

tiles
graph paper: any size
See Reproducibles for: geoboard paper

Anticipatory Set

Have students measure the distance around their desks or tables, using a body part as a unit. Discuss other ways they could measure the distance around.

Procedure 1 □■

To develop the concept of *perimeter*

Use *geoboards, rubber bands, geoboard paper, scissors, tiles,* and *graph paper.*

Have students use the rubber bands to enclose the smallest square possible on their geoboards.

Say: We want to know how far around this square is. We'll call the distance from one peg to the next 1 unit. Start at the bottom left peg and trace the rubber band to the peg at the right.

Ask: How far have we gone?

Students respond: 1 unit.

Write a 1 on the board. Say: Go to the next peg. Now how far have we gone? (2 units)

Write a +1 on the board below the first 1.

Continue until students have gone all the way around. Draw a line under the 1s and write: Perimeter = 4 Units.

$$
\begin{array}{r}
1 \\
+1 \\
+1 \\
\underline{+1} \\
\end{array}
$$
Perimeter = 4 Units

Repeat with a two-peg by three-peg rectangle. Have students identify the length of each of the sides before tracing the perimeter. Write the chart on the board as before. Ask: Can you tell what the word *perimeter* means?

Students respond: It means the distance around.

Repeat with other rectangles, having students chorally count each distance, and continuing to chart perimeter on the board.

Write the following problem on the board.

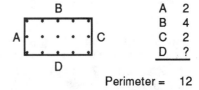

A	2
B	4
C	2
D	?

Perimeter = 12

Discuss with students how to find what's missing.

Ask: What more do we need to add to the distance to get to 12? (4) What is the difference between what we have and what we're supposed to have?

Repeat with other examples.

Students make rectangles with perimeters of 12 units, recording each figure on geoboard paper. They discuss what is the same and different about these.

When students are comfortable with the skill, repeat activities with figures that are not rectangles. *Make sure they do not include slanted lines.*

Students use tiles to make figures with larger perimeters. Each tile must have at least one side touching another tile. They draw and record results on graph paper. They cut out their figures and make a class chart of perimeters.

Procedure 2 □■

To relate perimeter and area

Use *graph paper and tiles* or *geoboards with rubber bands or string.*

Draw the following illustration on the board:

Have students enclose a two-peg by three-peg rectangle on their geoboards, or make a two-tile rectangle.

Ask: How many units around? (6) Each small square covers 1 square unit of space, which is the area. What is the area? (2 square units)

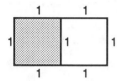

Have students make, and record on graph paper, as many figures as possible with the following perimeters: 4, 6, 8, 10, and 12. For each one, they figure and record the area as well.

Slanted lines are not allowed, and each square must have at least one side adjacent to another square.

Students with geoboards may wish to use string instead of rubber bands.

On the board, set up two perimeter/area charts, one with perimeter first and the other with area.

As students finish, they add their data to both charts, ordering their perimeters and areas from smallest to largest. The class discusses any patterns they see.

Challenge students to discover what figure gives the most area for a given perimeter. (a square) Ask: What is the largest perimeter you can get using a given area? What strategies did you use to figure this out?

Procedure 3

To find the formula for the perimeter of rectangles

Use *graph paper and tiles* or *geoboards with rubber bands or string*.

Have students build rectangles, all with a width of 1 unit but of varying lengths. Make a chart on the board, headed "W, L, W, L, Perimeter."

Students make rectangles and add data to the chart. They repeat with rectangles with a width of 2 units.

Ask: What patterns can you find on the chart?

Students respond: Widths are always alike, and lengths are always alike for a given rectangle.

I could write a rectangle's perimeter as w + l + w + l. Is there another way?

Students respond: 2 w's and 2 l's.

We write this as P = 2 × w + 2 × l, or P = 2w + 2l. Does this work for other four-sided figures?

Students explore, using various materials. They discover that this formula works for some but not all four-sided figures.

Practice and Extension

Have students use *tiles or other squares* as pentominoes. How many different shapes can students make with five of them? (12) How many different perimeters are possible? What strategies did students use to find all the shapes?

Have students use *maps* marked with distances to figure out the perimeter of given areas. Can students find a route for a 100-mile bicycle race that begins and ends at the same place?

Have students use *pattern blocks* to explore figures other than quadrilaterals. Can they find formulas for perimeters? How do the perimeters change when the students use more than one block? Have students chart results and look for patterns.

Geometry 4

Skill: To classify triangles by sides and angles

Time: 2 periods

Materials:

straws: 3 per student

scissors

protractors, or angle arrows (directions in Geometry 2)

geoboards and rubber bands

rulers

pattern blocks

graph paper: any size

See Reproducibles for: geoboard paper

Anticipatory Set

Use *straws* and *scissors*.

Give each student three straws. Have students work in groups of three. One student does not alter his or her straws. One student shortens one of his or her straws. The third student shortens two straws so that all three of his or hers are different lengths.

If students have not made angle arrows previously, have them do so. See Geometry 2.

Name	Sides	Angles	Flipped	Rotated	Symmetrical
equilateral	3 equal	3 equal (60°)	same shape	same shape	yes
isosceles	2 equal	2 equal (varies)	same shape	different shape	yes
scalene	0 equal	0 equal	different shape	different shape	no

Procedure 1

To classify by sides

Use *straws from Anticipatory Set, protractors or angle arrows,* and *paper.*

Have each student make a triangle using the shortest straw as a base. They should set the triangles side by side for easier comparison.

Say: We're going to be comparing these triangles, so we need names. The one with all three sides the same length is called an *equilateral triangle*. If your triangle has only two sides the same length, it is an *isosceles triangle*. No sides the same length is a *scalene triangle*.

Look at the triangles, and write down everything you notice about each kind. Ask: How could you chart your findings so that the data are useful?

Students discuss setting up a chart with categories for comparison.

You may use angle arrows, and you may move or flip over your triangles. Be careful that your statements would be true for all triangles of that kind. You may want to check other groups' triangles, too.

Students compare triangles and write results. They discuss findings and fill in a board chart with the following categories and any other they have devised.

Add the category of Symmetry if students are familiar with the term. Symmetry is covered in Geometry 5.

Students should discuss and discover:

Procedure 2

To construct triangles by name, according to sides

Use *geoboards and rubber bands, geoboard paper, rulers,* and *protractors or angle arrows.*

Have students make triangles of all three types by side length on their geoboards. Tell them to draw each one on their paper as well, labeling by type. Ask: How could you make sure your triangles are correct?

Students respond: Check side lengths with a ruler. Check the number of equal angles with the angle arrow.

Procedure 3

To classify by angles

Use *geoboards and rubber bands,* and *geoboard paper.*

Have students enclose one square around pins 2 and 3 in the bottom two rows (Illustration 2a).

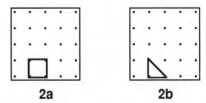

2a   2b

Ask: What do you know about the angles of this square? (They're all right angles.)

Now leave the lower left angle the same but change your square to a triangle (Illustration 2b).

Students make right triangles of various sizes.

How many right angles does your triangle have? (1) Can you make one with two right angles in it?

Students discover this isn't possible. Each right angle is 90°, and triangles have only 180°. They make more examples of right triangles on their boards.

A triangle with one right angle is called a *right triangle*. Make your original square again, and then take the rubber band off the upper right pin so that you have a small right triangle as before.

Now move the top left corner one pin to the left.

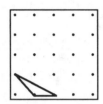

What have you done to the right angle? (made it bigger) This is an obtuse angle, and this kind of triangle is an *obtuse triangle*. How would you know an angle is obtuse? (compare it with a right angle)

Can you make a triangle with two obtuse angles?

Students discover they cannot. They make several more obtuse triangles on their geoboards.

Use three pins as a base, and make a triangle without a right or obtuse angle.

What do you notice about the angles? (They're all less than right angles.) They are all acute angles, and this is called an *acute triangle*. How could you check to make sure which kind of triangle you had? (use an angle arrow or protractor to check the angles)

Students practice making different kinds of triangles. They check the angles.

On the board, set up the following chart, but do not fill in the results:

	Equilateral (3 sides =)	Isosceles (2 sides =)	Scalene (no sides =)
Right triangle	no	yes	yes
Obtuse triangle	no	yes	yes
Acute triangle	yes	yes	yes

Say: Experiment to see whether you can make and draw examples to fill in this chart. Check with a ruler and protractor or angle arrow if necessary.

Students discover the results as shown above and discuss why some types are impossible.

Have students make and draw as many examples of right, obtuse, and acute triangles as possible.

Procedure 4

To construct triangles by name, according to angles

Use *pattern blocks* and *graph paper or geoboard paper*.

Have students make examples of right, obtuse, and acute triangles, using a combination of pattern blocks. Then have them draw results on graph paper or geoboard paper and add their examples to a large class chart.

Discuss which angles were equal and which triangles were symmetrical.

Practice and Extension

Use *thin string, straws,* and *scissors.* Have students construct three-dimensional figures out of specific types of triangles.

To get string through straws: Measure out (but do *not* cut from the ball) a little more string than the length of the straw. Hold the string at the ball end. Insert the free end of the string into a straw, and suck on the other end of the straw. Holding the string prevents too much from going into the mouth.

Cut off the wet part of the string, and pull as much through the straw as is wanted. Fasten three straws together to make desired type of triangle. Connect triangles to construct three-dimensional figures.

Discuss various "building" techniques after figures are built. Have students find examples of triangles in engineering and architecture.

Geometry 5

Skill: To find lines of symmetry

Time: 2 periods

Materials:

pattern blocks
geoboards and rubber bands

scissors
paste
mirrors: if available
See Reproducibles for: geoboard paper

Anticipatory Set

Use *pattern blocks*.

Have students put two squares together. These pieces are equal and meet at a centerline. Have students flip one square on the centerline so that it lies on top of the second square. Repeat with other equal and unequal pieces.

Now have them place shapes other than squares on either side of the original squares. Instruct students to make figures that will flip over to lie exactly on the other half.

Procedure 1

To develop the concept of *symmetry*

Use *geoboards, rubber bands*, and *geoboard paper*.

Have students enclose each of these squares on their geoboards:

Ask: What do you notice about the squares?

Students respond: They are the same size and shape. They share a side.

Say: Put a rubber band around the outside of both squares, making a two-square rectangle.

The line the squares share is called a *line of symmetry*. You will have to find out what this means.

Students draw their rectangles on geoboard paper.

Have students place the original squares on the geoboard and then stretch one square to make the figure shown in the next illustration.

Say: Now enclose the whole figure.

Students enclose the figure and draw their geoboard designs on geoboard paper.

This figure has a line, but it is not a line of symmetry. How is this different from the first rectangle?

Students respond: These parts are unequal.

When can you have a line of symmetry? (when both sides are equal) Let's see if this definition is enough.

Have students make and draw the following figure:

Are both sides equal? (yes) This does not have a line of symmetry. What else do you need to add to your definition?

Students discuss their symmetrical and nonsymmetrical figures.

Suggest they fold the drawn figures on the centerline to see what happens.

Students should discover that the halves are not only equal but are positioned so that one side will flip over, on a line of symmetry, to lie exactly on the other.

Repeat with other shapes, and then give students larger and more complex shapes to subdivide with lines of symmetry.

Students construct, draw, and check the symmetry of more complex figures.

Procedure 2

To work with multiple lines of symmetry

Use *pattern blocks, scissors, paste, mirrors* if available, and *paper*.

Make a table headed: "Symmetrical" and "Non-symmetrical."

Using actual pattern blocks on the overhead, or chalk on the board, construct symmetrical and nonsymmetrical figures under the appropriate heading. Include some nonsymmetrical figures composed of the same parts:

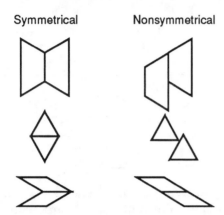

Symmetrical   Nonsymmetrical

Students discuss rules for symmetry: Each half is identical and is positioned so that it can be flipped over the centerline to lie exactly on the other half.

Have students make symmetrical figures with pattern blocks, constructing the figures on paper and then tracing around each part.

Students construct, trace, and fold each figure to check for symmetry. They use mirrors to check, if available.

Have students trace one hexagon. Ask: Is it possible to have more than one line of symmetry?

Students fold hexagons and decide it is possible. They explore multiple lines of symmetry for other pattern block pieces and discuss their findings.

Challenge students to create designs with more than one line of symmetry. What will they have to consider? Is there a pattern to the types of designs that have multiple lines of symmetry?

Students experiment. They trace around, cut out, and paste pattern block shapes to duplicate their design. They mark all lines of symmetry.

Have students explore the relationship between the number of identical parts and the number of lines of symmetry.

Procedure 3

To work further with multiple lines of symmetry

Use *geoboards, rubber bands, geoboard paper,* and *mirrors,* if available.

Repeat Procedure 2 with geoboards. Can students find a large four-sided figure that has four lines of symmetry?

Students construct figures, draw on geoboard paper, and fold to check. They can use mirrors, if available, to check.

Practice and Extension

Challenge students to use *rulers* and *circles* to draw all possible lines of symmetry of a circle. How many can they find? It may take them a while to discover that an infinite number exists.

Have students collect and display *pictures* of examples of symmetry, both in nature and humanmade.

Have students design symmetrical buildings on *graph paper.*

Use *mirrors* and *full-face snapshots* of students. Have students discover that faces are not totally symmetrical.

Geometry 6

Skill: To find the sum of the angles: triangles and polygons

straightedges

scissors

protractors, or angle arrows (directions in Geometry 2)

pattern blocks

Time: varies with level of the procedure

Materials:

geoboards and rubber bands: of several colors

pipe cleaners: 3 per student

Anticipatory Set

Ask students to stand and imagine they are on skateboards. Have them do a 360 turn and relate this to the 360° in a circle. Next relate a 180 turn to 180°, half a circle or a straight line from 12 to 6 on a clock.

Procedure 1

To find the sum of the angles in a right triangle

Use *geoboards and rubber bands.*

Have students make the smallest square possible in the lower left corner of their geoboards.

Ask: Each corner is what kind of angle? (right angle) How many degrees in a right angle? (90°)

How many degrees in all does the square have?

Students respond: $4 \times 90° = 360°$.

Have students make a triangle in the square with a different color rubber band as shown:

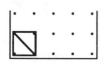

What is the total number of degrees in both triangles?

If students have trouble, ask whether the triangles use the same space as the square. (yes) Same angle total? (yes)

***Each* triangle has how many of those degrees? (180°) Would all right triangles have 180°?**

Students now make identical right triangles two pegs wide and four pegs high. They use another color rubber band to "box in" their triangles.

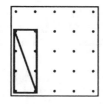

Since triangles are identical, they equally divide the 360° of the square, and each has 180°. Repeat with other right triangles until students are comfortable with the technique.

Procedure 2

To find the sum of the angles in any triangle

Use *pipe cleaners, straightedges, scissors,* and *paper.*

Say: We know that right triangles all have 180°. What about other kinds of triangles?

Have students bend pipe cleaners and fit them together to make a triangle. They may have to adjust. Label a triangle on the board as shown:

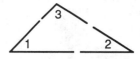

Ask: How can you find the total number of angle degrees in your triangle? (Students discuss.)

Next have students place their angles as shown:

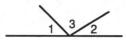

What have you made with all your triangle angles? (A straight line, which is 180°) Does this work for all triangles?

Students compare triangles and decide all triangles have 180°.

To do this with paper and scissors draw triangles with straightedges, and label as below. Cut off each angle with a curved line, and then place them together to make a straight line. The curved lines make it clear which angles were original.

Procedure 3

To measure angles in any triangle

Use *straightedges, scissors,* and *protractors or angle arrows.*

Have students construct and measure a variety of triangles. Students using angle arrows will see the arrow open to 180° after measuring all three angles.

They write angle measurements to arrive at a total of 180° and then compare and discuss the triangles.

Procedure 4 □■

To find the sum of the angles in a quadrilateral

Use *pattern blocks* and *geoboards and rubber bands.*

Review that the sum of the angles in any *triangle* is 180°, and the sum of the angles of a *rectangle* is 360°. Ask: Will all *quadrilaterals* have 360°?

Can you use what you know about triangles to find the sum of the angles in the blue *parallelogram*?

Students discover two green triangles fit over the parallelogram. The triangle angles cover the same space as the parallelogram angles, so a parallelogram has 180° + 180° = 360°.

For the sum of the angles in a *trapezoid,* remember that angles that make a straight line equal 180°.

Students experiment. Three triangles fit over a trapezoid. Three triangle vertices, however, do *not* match a vertex of the trapezoid. Their sum of 180° must be subtracted from the total degrees in the three triangles: $(3 \times 180°) - 180° = 360°$.

Experiment with bigger quadrilaterals. You may have to look for two angles that will add to 180°:

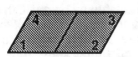

1 + 2 = 180°
3 + 4 = 180°
2 + 3 = 180°
4 + 1 = 180°

Have students use different color rubber bands to make triangles inside quadrilaterals. Can they turn a rhombus into a rectangle, which they know has 360°?

Procedure 5 □■

To find the sum of the angles in any polygon; to find a formula

Use *geoboards and rubber bands.*

On the board write the following chart headings:

Polygon	# of Sides	# of Triangles	Sum of All Angles
triangle	3	1	180°
quadrilateral	4	2	360°

Remind students that they used triangles to find the sum of the angles of a quadrilateral. Ask: Can you use the same technique with a hexagon?

Students make a large hexagon as shown, using different color rubber bands to make triangles:

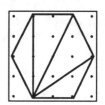

All triangle vertices must be on hexagon vertices.

Students add the number of degrees in each triangle: $4 \times 180° = 720°$.

Have students repeat with a variety of polygons and add the results to the class chart.

Ask: Can you find a formula that would work for all polygons?

If students do not discover the formula, suggest they look for a relationship between the number of triangles and the number of sides of the polygons. The sum of the angles of a polygon is 180 × the number of sides minus 2 or $(S - 2) \times 180°$.

Practice and Extension

Have students use manipulatives to create geometrical designs. They copy onto *graph paper,* label angles by degrees, and add for final totals. Make a class chart.

Have students bring in *magazines pictures* with geometric shapes that can then be measured.

Geometry 7

Skill: To understand area

Time: 5 periods

Materials:

sheets of paper: various sizes
1" tiles or cubes

graph paper: to match tile or cube size
geoboards and rubber bands
pattern blocks or tangrams
See Reproducibles for: geoboard paper

Anticipatory Set

Use *sheets of paper* and *tiles or cubes*.

Have groups of students choose one manipulative and cover their sheet of paper with it. Discuss how many it took to cover each sheet. Can they tell whose sheet was largest? Why not? Discuss the need for all to use the same unit of measurement.

Procedure 1

To establish the concept of *area*

Use *graph paper* and *tiles or cubes (5 per student).*

Tell students they have been measuring area, *a measure of covering*. Discuss when they would need to know a surface's area; e.g., carpeting, paper wrap, paint, grass seed, etc.

Say: We are going to say one tile will cover 1 square unit. Cover 1 square unit of your desks by putting a tile somewhere on it.

Students place tiles.

Now place a second tile next to the first one. Ask: How much area have you covered?

Students respond: 2 square units.

Repeat with a third and fourth tile.

Ask: Are all the shapes alike? (no) How can they all cover the same area?

Students discuss.

Hand out graph paper, and have students make shapes with areas of 1 to 5 square units.

Students place tiles, trace shapes, and label with the area.

Now have students make as many different shapes as they can, using five tiles.

Explain that shapes of five squares are pentominoes. Twelve are possible.

Discuss what constitutes a "different" shape. Be sure shapes that only differ in the amount of rotation are recognized as "same shapes."

Students can color, cut, and display shapes.

Procedure 2

To work with area using whole square units

Use *geoboards, rubber bands,* and *geoboard paper.*

Have students enclose the smallest square possible. This will be 1 square unit.

Have students enclose a rectangle with an area of 2 square units, then 3 square units.

Ask: What other shapes can you make with 3 square units?

Students make a chart: "Area" and "Shapes Possible."

They find shapes of given areas and draw them on geoboard paper.

Discuss students' findings. One discovery they should make is that the larger the area, the more shapes possible.

Procedure 3

To further practice the concept of area

Use *pattern blocks* or *tangrams.*

Have students cover shapes in several different ways. Designate a small block or tangram piece as 1 square unit. Ask: How much area do the others cover?

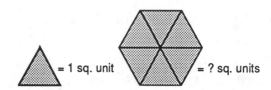

= 1 sq. unit   = ? sq. units

Have students make patterns with the pattern blocks or tangrams.

Students estimate total area and then check with blocks.

Can students make a pattern that covers a specific area? Can they do this without using the unit piece?

It is important for students to use more than one manipulative to establish the concept.

Procedure 4 □ ■

To measure area using half square units

Use *geoboards, rubber bands*, and *geoboard paper*.

Have students enclose the smallest square possible. Then have them use another rubber band to enclose a triangle that is ½ the square.

Ask: What is the area of the square? (1 square unit) Then what is the area of the triangle? (½ square unit)

Have students make a rectangle of 2 square units and then use other rubber bands to show the four ½ square units possible. How many whole square units of area? (2)

How many ½ square units? (4)

Do those four ½ square units add to 2 square units?

Students respond: Yes. They discover sometimes with odd-shaped polygons they have to add the ½ square units to get the whole area.

Have students construct shapes with areas of 2½, 3½, and 4 square units on their geoboards. Make sure ½ square units are actually that; all diagonals must be at a 45° angle.

Draw some polygons. Have students duplicate each, and then see whether they can find the area. How did they find the total area?

Students first predict the area and then find and write the separate areas they measured to get a total. They discuss their strategies with the class.

Advanced students can be given drawings and dimensions of odd floor plans that need carpeting. They can duplicate them proportionally with geoboards or geoboard paper and find the amount of carpet needed.

Procedure 5 □ ■

To find a formula for the area of rectangles

Use *tiles or cubes*.

Tell students you are painting a hall. The walls are each 8 feet high and 20 feet long. A gallon of paint covers 400 square feet.

Ask: How much paint will I need?

Students discuss possible ways of arriving at the answer.

Say: A quick math way exists to find the area of a rectangle, which is the shape of the walls in the hall to be painted, and today you will discover it.

Students make a chart headed: "Number of Rows," "Squares per Row," and "Area in Square Units."

Write the headings on the board. Review rows and number of squares per row to make sure all are charting the same data.

Students make ten rectangles and chart results. They look for a pattern.

When students are finished, suggest it would be easier to see a pattern if the data were organized. Discuss with the students ways to do this.

Number of Rows	Squares per Row	Area in Square Units
1	1	1
1	2	2
1	3	3
1	4	4
2	1	2
2	2	4
2	3	6
2	4	8

Explain that one way is to start with a 1 × 1 rectangle. If nobody made one, what would the area be? (1 square unit) Continue until the chart looks like the illustration.

Again have students look for a pattern.

Students discuss that the first two numbers could be multiplied to find the third.

Ask: When else have we built rectangles from blocks?

Students respond: To show multiplication.

Say: You are adding row after row, with the same number blocks in each row, to make the size rectangle you want.

Ask: What is a shortcut for adding same size groups? (multiplication) When we want to show two groups of three in math language, how do we write it? (2 × 3)

Math language has a way to write directions for finding the area of any rectangle.

General directions are called *formulas* and have letters or symbols to stand for what is happening. When you have a specific rectangle, you put its numbers into the formula and know what to do.

I want to write a formula for area of a rectangle. I start with A =. A stands for what? (area)

We know we are multiplying two things together for any rectangle. Suppose the rectangle is a football field. What do I call one of the sides? (the length)

And the other side? (the width)

What would I multiply to get the area?

Students respond: Length times width.

Add the words "Length" (squares per row) and "Width" (rows) to the chart on the board.

Students add to their charts.

Write A = length × width on the board.

Ask: What letters could I use to stand for the words?

Students respond: l and w.

Write A = l × w.

Suppose I have a rectangle where the length is 5 and the width is 2.

Students build rectangles and find A = 10.

Write on the board to demonstrate form:

A = l × w
A = 5 × 2
A = 10

Explain that math language is just a description of what is really happening. *What we write describes what we can do with manipulatives.*

Give other dimensions, and have students build the rectangles. As students do each step with tiles or cubes, they write the corresponding step on paper. They need much practice at this step.

When students are confident about the process, they can move to doing the problem on paper first and then checking with the manipulatives.

Have students go back and figure the answer to the problem at the beginning of this procedure.

Procedure 6

To find the area of squares

Use *any of the listed materials.*

Have students build squares and chart the dimensions and areas. Discuss patterns: Both factors are the same. These are square numbers.

If you want to introduce A = s², 2² = 4, see Multiplication 10: To understand exponents.

Procedure 7

To understand the area of shapes made of more than one rectangle

Use *any of the listed materials.*

Write A = 12 on the board, and have students find all possible rectangle dimensions for this area.

Have students explore areas and trade findings with partners to make a chart.

Draw an L-shaped floor plan on the board.

Students make the shape and then draw it. They try to devise a way to find the total area.

If students have problems with this task, ask them how this shape differs from the shapes with which they have been working. Can they use their knowledge of area to find at least part of the area of the floor?

Discuss methods students may have used and situations in which they might need to use these methods.

Give other examples. Can students find the areas first with formulas and prove with a manipulative? Repeat until students are competent in the skill.

Practice and Extension

Have student draw four polygons on plain paper and estimate their areas. Which is largest? They then cut them out, trace onto *graph paper*, and figure the area. They need to decide whether a partial square should be counted as ½, 1, or 0 square units. How accurate were their estimates? Did they revise estimates after the first polygon was done?

Give students a *polygon shape with an area of 16 square inches.* Then give them a *4" × 4" piece of graph paper.* Students work in groups to decide how to cover the shapes with the graph paper (without actually cutting it). They mark all lines that will be cut, trying for the fewest possible lines.

Have students bring *supermarket containers from home.* They find the surface area of rectangular sides. How many cereal boxes, cut apart and laid flat, would it take to measure their desks?

Have students interview parents or other adults at home to find how they use the concept of area.

Geometry 8

Skill: To find area: triangles and parallelograms

Time: 1 period per procedure

Materials:

graph paper: any size
straightedges

scissors
geoboards and rubber bands: 2 colors
tangrams or more graph paper
See Reproducibles for: geoboard paper

Anticipatory Set

Use *graph paper, straightedges,* and *scissors.*

Have students draw rectangles and then use a straightedge to draw in a diagonal. They cut out the rectangles and then cut along the diagonals.

Discuss the relationship of the resulting triangles—they are congruent. Each is ½ the area of the rectangle. Review the formula $A = 1 \times w$.

Procedure 1

To find a formula for the area of right triangles

Use *geoboards and rubber bands.*

Have students make the following chart. They will fill in the numbers as they discover them.

▭ Length	▭ Width	▭ Area	◸ Base	◺ Height	◹ Area
2	1	2	2	1	1
3	1	3	3	1	1½
4	1	4	4	1	2
2	2	4	2	2	2
3	2	6	3	2	3
4	2	8	4	2	4
3	3	9	3	3	4½
4	3	12	4	3	6

Review 1 square unit and ½ square unit of area on the geoboard. (See Geometry 7.)

Tell students they will be looking for a formula for the area of a triangle that will work for all triangles.

Have them make a rectangle two squares across and one square high (Illustration 2a). Make sure students are measuring spaces not pegs.

Say: With a different color rubber band, make a triangle using a diagonal as one side of the triangle (Illustration 2b).

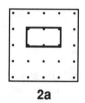 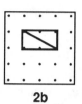

2a   2b

Ask: What is the length of the rectangle? (2) Chart that. What is the width of the rectangle? (1) The area? (2 square units)

Students chart these too.

Our chart asks for the base of the triangle. That is the bottom of the triangle. What is it? (2) The height of a triangle is measured from its top to its base. With a right triangle, it's the same as what?

Students respond: One side of the rectangle. They then chart: base = 2, height = 1.

When we cut the graph paper, what did we find out about area when we drew diagonals?

Students respond: Each triangle was ½ the area of the rectangle.

Our rectangle area is 2 square units. What is the area of this triangle? (1 square unit)

If students do not see this, have them imagine moving the small × part of the triangle up to complete the first square:

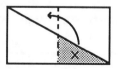

We know data are easier to analyze if the chart is organized. How could we fill in the chart in an organized way?

Have students make and chart 10 rectangle/triangle combinations. Tell them to look for any patterns that would help them find a formula for the area of a triangle.

Discuss with students any patterns they can see. Suggest they compare areas of each rectangle and its triangle. They also should compare dimensions.

Students should see that each triangle area is half of its rectangle's area. They may suggest the formula A = length × width ÷ 2.

Remind students that triangles have bases and heights. Say: We could write A = b × h ÷ 2, but we usually write A = ½bh.

Go directly to Procedure 2.

Procedure 2

To learn a technique for finding the area of triangles

Use *geoboards and rubber bands*.

Say: I've been giving you rectangles. You have made triangles and found half the rectangle's area. Usually you don't have a ready-made rectangle, just a triangle whose area is a mystery.

Make a right triangle with a base of 3 spaces and a height of 2 spaces:

4a   **4b**

If we knew the area of this triangle's rectangle, we would know the triangle's area. Ask: Will the rectangle length be the same as the triangle base? (yes) What about the rectangle's height?

Students respond: It's the same as the triangle's height. They use another color rubber band to "box in" the triangle, to make its rectangle (Illustration 4b).

They find the rectangle's area is 6 square units. The area of the triangle is 3 square units.

Provide practice in this technique, giving triangle dimensions. When students are competent in the skill, they may start writing the formula, using the geoboard and then complete the written problem.

Procedure 3

To find the area of acute and obtuse triangles; to find and validate a formula

Use *geoboards and rubber bands* and *geoboard paper*.

For acute triangles:

Say: We know our formula works for right triangles. Will it work for other triangles?

If it is to work, the area of the acute triangle would have to be ½ the area of what? (the rectangle with the same base and height)

Have students make the acute triangle shown in Illustration 5a.

5a   **5b**

Ask: What is the base? (2)

Remind students the height is measured from the top to the base. What is the height? (2)

Use another color rubber band to box in the triangle (Illustration 5b).

Each side of the earlier triangles was either a side or a diagonal of the corresponding rectangle. Here one triangle side is a rectangle side, but the other sides aren't.

Say: Make a rectangle that has the right side of the triangle as a diagonal (Illustration 6a).

6a   **6b**

Do the same with the other side (Illustration 6b).

Now we've divided our triangle into two sections, A and B. How can we get the total area?

Students respond: Add the two areas together.

Ask: What is the area of triangle A? (1 square unit) What about triangle B?

Students respond: It is the same. The whole big triangle has an area of 1 + 1, or 2 square units.

Have students make many acute triangles, record them on geoboard paper, and find the area using geoboards. Make sure all triangle bases are parallel to the bottom of the geoboard.

Does the formula work for acute triangles? (yes)

For obtuse triangles and triangles not parallel to the bottom:

Box in the whole triangle as in Illustration 7a. Box in one side, making it a diagonal. Find the area outside the diagonal, area A (Illustration 7b).

Rectangle area = 4 sq units   Area A = 1 sq unit

7a   **7b**

Repeat with the other triangle sides.

Ignore this triangle.
It is part of area A
and is already
counted.

Area B = 1 sq unit   Area C = $^1/_2$ sq unit

Total all areas outside the triangle:

Area *outside* triangle = **1 + 1 + $^1/_2$**
= $2^1/_2$ square units

Subtract all outside areas from the large rect-angle area:

Area *inside* triangle = large rectangle area
– area outside triangle
= 4 – 2$^1/_2$
= 1$^1/_2$ square units

Provide practice with a variety of triangles. Relate activities to the formula for triangle area so students see that the formula works with all triangles.

Procedure 4   ⬜⬛

To find the area of parallelograms; to find the formula

Use *graph paper, straightedges, and tangrams or more graph paper.*

If not using tangrams, have students cut out two squares from the graph paper.

Have them cut the second square in half on the diagonal. The resulting square and two triangles match the tangram pieces used in this procedure.

Say: We'll call the side of the square 1 unit long. Experiment to find other measurements, and see how many shapes you can make.

Students find that the triangles have two sides each that are also 1 unit long. They discuss all their findings.

Discuss with students that a parallelogram is a four-sided figure with opposite sides parallel.

Then have students make a parallelogram from their pieces (Illustration 9a).

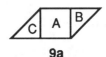
9a   9b

We're looking for a way to find the area of any parallelogram. We know how to find the area of a rectangle.

Ask: Can you make this parallelogram into a rectangle with the same area (Illustration 9b)?

What is the width? (1 square unit) And the length? (2 square units) What is the area of the rectangle?

Students respond: A = l × w. A = 1 × 2 = 2 square units.

Do the rectangle and the parallelogram have the same area? (yes)

Put your parallelogram back together. What is the length of the parallelogram? (2)

What is the height, the measurement from the tallest part straight down to the bottom? (1)

Do you see a relationship between area, length, and height?

Students respond: Yes. The area is l × h.

Because a parallelogram has triangles as part of it, we'll call the formula Area = base × height.

Discuss with students that A = bh is the same formula as a = l × w or A = lw.

Does this work for all parallelograms? Make a parallelogram on graph paper, cut into a rect-angle and two triangles, and find the area. Chart your findings.

Students experiment. They discover A = bh holds true for all parallelograms.

Procedure 5   ⬜

To find the area of parallelograms

Use *geoboards and rubber bands.*

Use the same techniques as were used to find areas of triangles in Procedure 3.

Box in the whole figure. Find the total area.

 .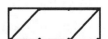

Next find the areas outside the parallelogram, and total them. See the illustration on the next page.

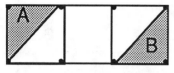

Rectangle area = 3 sq units
Area A = $\frac{1}{2}$ sq unit
Area B = $\frac{1}{2}$ sq unit

Total area outside parallelogram:

A + B = $\frac{1}{2}$ sq unit + $\frac{1}{2}$ sq unit
     1 sq unit

Subtract this total from the whole rectangle area.
Area of the parallelogram = 3 – 1 = 2 square units.

Check findings against the formula A = bh.

Practice and Extension

Have students search for examples that might disprove the formulas.

Have students draw or construct on *geoboards* a rectangle of 6 square units. Can they make a parallelogram of the same area? What about other sizes or figures?

Have students figure the surface area of *solid geometric objects*. If each side of a smooth, square pyramid has a base 200 feet across and is 400 feet high, how much paint is needed to cover the pyramid? Paint covers 400 square feet per gallon. (400 gal)

Geometry 9

Skill: To classify solid figures

Time: 2 periods

Materials:

solid geometric figures (see Manipulative Information section for ideas)

supermarket containers

cubes

geometric solids: rigid plastic foam or clay

graph paper: to match cube size

Anticipatory Set

Use whatever *solid geometric figures* you plan to teach.

Show students the figures, and have them brainstorm examples of these in real life.

Have students list everything they notice about these figures. Discuss lists.

Procedure 1

To learn the concepts of *face, edge,* and *vertex*

Use *geometric figures, supermarket containers,* and *cubes.*

Have students identify and draw the separate sides of each figure or container. Ask: Are they all the same? (not necessarily) Each individual side is called a *face*. How many faces did each figure have?

Students discuss. Did they incude the bottom face?

Have students make a layer of four cubes. On top of these have students build a building three cubes high at its highest point.

Students use various numbers of cubes to build structures.

Discuss the buildings. Some may have made chimneys or smokestacks. How many separate faces does each building have?

Students discuss. Answers will vary.

Have students examine a cube. Tell them to run their fingers over each *edge* and *vertex*. Ask: How many edges does a cube have? (12) Are they straight? (yes)

How many points or vertices? (8) Have students examine their buildings for edges and vertices.

Continue until students have grasped the concepts.

Procedure 2

To practice the concept of face

Use *rigid plastic foam or clay geometric figures.*

Have students predict the shape of the resulting new faces if you cut the figures in half. What clues did they use?

Cut each figure, and discuss which clues worked to help predict correct shapes.

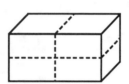

Suggest they label figures with the number of faces and shape of the figure, and set up a display.

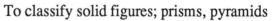

Procedure 3

To classify solid figures; prisms, pyramids

Use whatever *solid geometric figures* you plan to teach.

Have students examine each figure to decide where its base would be.

Have students make charts. As you name each figure, have them fill in the data.

Name	Base Shape	Face Shape
square prism (cube)	square (rectangle)	square
triangular prism	triangle	rectangle
rectangular prism	rectangle	rectangle
square pyramid	square	triangle
triangular pyramid	triangle	triangle
rectangular pyramid	rectangle	triangle

Students fill in data and look for patterns that would help them name any new figures.

Discuss the chart with students. If they do not see patterns, ask what is the same about all pyramids.

Students respond: They come to a point, and they have triangular faces.

Ask: What is the same about all prisms?

Students respond: They all have rectangular faces.

Remind students that squares are one kind of rectangle.

Students see that the shape of a face determines whether a figure is a pyramid or a prism.

Say: One way to remember which is which: A prism looks like a building; a prison is a building. *Prism* sounds like *prison.*

Can students discover how to name each *kind* of pyramid or prism?

Students see that the shape of the base determines this.

Have students find geometric solids within the classroom to identify and classify.

Have students hold a *solid figure* behind their back and give a description: faces, edges, vertices, base. Partners must guess the shape.

Draw a pattern on *tag board* of a square, a rectangle with the width of the square, and an equilateral triangle with the base measurement matching the side of the square. Draw tabs along most of each side.

Have students trace those patterns on tag board, cut them out, and construct the figures of their choice. Tabs are folded under and sides are *pasted* or *taped* together. Students may wish to enlarge patterns to make giant geometric solids. By making hexagons, octagons, etc., many solids are possible.

Procedure 4 □■

To practice three-dimensional visualization

Use *cubes* and *graph paper*.

Give students a base shape and a silhouette. They use cubes to build buildings. Give advanced students several side views of more complex structures.

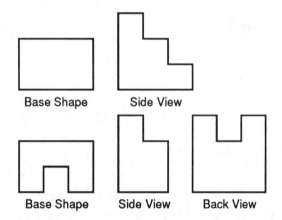

Base Shape   Side View

Base Shape   Side View   Back View

Have students construct their own buildings, draw the base and sides shapes, and give them to partners to construct.

Ask: Are the buildings the same? How many solid figure components can you identify in each building?

Student pairs present their findings to the class.

Practice and Extension

Have students bring in *pictures of their homes* and identify the component solid figure

Students can use *clay* to make and identify different figures.

Geometry 10

Skill: To understand congruence, similarity, and scale

Time: 2 periods

Materials:

attribute blocks or paper shapes: triangles, circles, and rectangles of the same and different sizes

pattern blocks

geoboards and rubber bands

scissors

light source: flashlight, overhead projector, slide projector

rulers or straightedges

graph paper: any size

See Reproducibles for: geoboard paper

Anticipatory Set

Use *attribute blocks* or *paper shapes*.

Have students sort first by shape. Then have students sort each shape into groups of the same size.

Procedure 1

To understand *congruence*

Use *groups of shapes from the Anticipatory Set* and *pattern blocks*.

Say: You have groups of shapes that are exactly the same shape and size. We call shapes *congruent* if they match both shape and size exactly.

Hold up two congruent triangles. Ask: Are these the same shape? (yes) Are these the same size? (yes) Are these congruent? (yes)

Repeat with two triangles different in size from the first.

Have students hold up other congruent figures. Make sure they understand color is not a factor.

Hand out pattern blocks, and instruct students to use three shapes to build a larger shape. Then have them copy their partner's new shapes. Remind them they are trying to make a copy that is congruent.

Next hold up or place on the overhead two congruent shapes. Are these congruent? (yes) Rotate one and ask again.

Students discuss that position isn't a factor for congruence.

Continue until students are responding accurately.

Procedure 2

To practice the concept of congruence

Use *geoboards, rubber bands, geoboard paper,* and *scissors.*

Have students make congruent dot-to-dot shapes on geoboard paper and then cut them out.

Have students set pairs of shapes aside for later to color and display on a class chart.

Have students use different-colored rubber bands to make congruent shapes on the geoboards and then copy a partner's shape.

Ask: How many ways can you find to divide your whole geoboard into two or more congruent parts?

Students chart each on geoboard paper.

Can they make congruent angles? Can they make triangles with only one, two, or three congruent angles?

Students discuss why they cannot make triangles with only two congruent angles.

Procedure 3

To understand *similarity*

Use a *light source* and *attribute blocks or paper shapes.*

Place a triangle in front of a light source or on the overhead, projecting the shadow onto the wall or a screen. Have students compare the original triangle and the large image.

Ask: Are they the exact same shape? (yes) Are they the same size? (no) We call shapes like this *similar.*

What do we call shapes of exactly the same shape *and* size? (congruent)

Tell students to find all the similar shapes they can with their manipulatives.

Students find similar shapes.

Hold up random pairs of shapes, and have students identify them as similar, congruent, or not alike. Repeat until all students are responding accurately.

Procedure 4

To use the concept of similarity to develop understanding of scale

Use *graph paper and rulers* or *geoboards, rubber bands, and geoboard paper.*

Say: Make a 2 × 2 square on your graph paper. We want to make a similar, not congruent square. We'll make it twice as big.

Ask: How many squares long will it be? (4) How many squares wide? (4)

Students construct similar squares.

Discuss how scale is used in maps and how patterns can be enlarged using scale. Have advanced students draw a picture on small graph paper and transfer it to larger scale graph paper or use a different scale.

Students can also do this exercise using geoboards. They would chart the figures on geoboard paper.

Practice and Extension

Have students make a class chart to display the *congruent figures from Procedure 2*. Have students also make and display a chart of *graph paper similar shapes from Procedure 4*.

Gives students squares of *waxed paper*. Use a square on the overhead. Make two intersecting lines by folding the paper and opening it up. The lines will form angles and will show as dark lines on the screen. Ask students to bisect the angle into two congruent parts. Demonstrate on the overhead after they have experimented. Adapt for triangles and rectangles.

Give students five *tiles or construction paper squares*. Have them find and chart on *graph paper* all possible combinations (pentominoes). Caution students that some congruent shapes may appear to be different if one has been rotated. They are still the same shape. Twelve shapes are possible.

Have students take *maps* and measure distance from one place to another using the scale given.

Have students practice making *scale drawings* using simple pictures from *commercial coloring books*.

Measurement 1

Skill: To measure length by inches, feet, and yards; to measure to fractions of inches

scissors

foot rulers: marked to the inch or fraction, as desired

yardsticks

clear tape

Time: 1 period per procedure

Materials:

graph paper: ½" or ¼" squares, depending on the procedure

Anticipatory Set

Have students measure the width of the room in footsteps by placing one foot closely in front of the other and counting the number of steps. Chart and discuss results. Why do results vary?

Procedure 1

To understand and use inches

Use *½" graph paper, scissors,* and *rulers.*

Have students cut out six 1" × 1" squares and label as shown:

Have students find a part of their hand that is close to an inch long. This will help establish the idea of an inch and can be used for estimating without a ruler. Ask: What else can you find that is an inch long?

Students use their body ruler to estimate and measure objects. They check for accuracy with their paper inches.

Have groups of students measure a book all have. If it is not an exact inch measurement, they report which two lengths it is between.

Say: Each arrow point shows us we have measured another inch. Which arrow point is the edge of the book nearer to? We can say the book is about as long as the nearest inch.

Students estimate and then use rulers and paper inches to measure other objects. They chart estimates, actual measurements, and measurements to the nearest inch. See the Practice and Extension for measuring ideas.

Did their estimates improve with practice? Discuss successful strategies.

Have students draw figures to specific lengths.

Procedure 2

To understand and use feet

Use *inch squares from Procedure 1* and *rulers.*

Ask: How many inches long is your ruler? (12) Twelve inches is called a *foot* because one English king's foot was this long. Discuss what is best measured in feet or inches.

Have students estimate and then measure objects. If the objects are more than a foot, will students need another ruler or only some extra inch squares? See the Practice and Extension for measuring ideas.

Have students chart their findings both in feet plus inches, and in inches. How close were their estimates?

Have students construct objects and lines a foot and a certain number of inches long.

Procedure 3

To understand and use yards

Use *yardsticks* and *rulers.*

Repeat Procedure 2 with rulers and yardsticks.

Ask such questions as: If a yard is 3 feet long, how many inches is that? Is 4 feet longer or shorter than a yard? Measurements should be reported in feet and inches, as well as yards.

See the Practice and Extension for ideas.

Procedure 4

To measure to the nearest ½" and ¼"

Use *¼" graph paper, tape, scissors,* and *rulers marked to ¼".*

Have students construct 1" by 12" rulers from the graph paper, taping as necessary. Each inch will

be 4 squares by 4 squares of the graph paper and should be marked as shown:

The small marks are exactly in between the inch marks. Ask: What do these small marks measure? (half inches)

Draw a large replica of their ruler on the board. Below it draw horizontal lines of varying lengths to inches and half inches and have students identify the length of each line.

Draw a line that is almost an inch. Ask students whether it is nearer the ½" or 1" mark. (1") We can call this about 1 inch because it is the closer measurement.

How long is each space on your ruler? (½") To measure to the nearest ½ inch, we look for the nearest mark *whether it is a ½ inch mark or a 1 inch mark,* because each of the units is ½ inch long.

What are some of the possible lengths we could have measuring to the nearest ½ inch?

Students respond: ½", 1", 1½", 2", 2½", and so on.

Have students estimate, measure, and chart the length of objects to the nearest ½ inch, using their graph paper rulers.

Students next use regular rulers to measure, and then construct lines of predetermined length to the ½ inch.

They discuss when they would use measurement to the ½ inch rather than the nearest inch. Example: ordering new windows to fit a window frame.

Repeat the Procedure with ¼ inches if desired. Students mark each ¼" on their graph paper ruler with a vertical line shorter than the ½" inch line. Where is the ²/₄" line? (already marked with ½")

Procedure 5 ⬜◼

To measure to the nearest ⅛" and ¹/₁₆"

Use ¼" *graph paper, rulers marked to* ⅛" *or* ¹/₁₆" *inch, tape,* and *scissors.*

Have students cut out a rectangle 16 × 32 squares and label with *only the inch and half-inch marks.* Ask: What is exactly halfway between the end of the graph paper ruler and the ½" mark? (¼")

Have students draw in and label the ¼" marks. Where is the ²/₄" mark? (already marked with ½", which is equivalent to ²/₄")

Repeat for ⅛" and ¹/₁₆" marks, and discuss all the equivalent relationships.

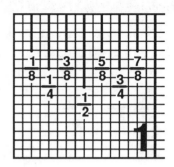

Have students identify where an object would end if it measured 1", 1½", 2³/₈", and so on.

Students measure objects and lines with their replica rulers until all can measure accurately.

Practice and Extension

Have students use *rulers* to draw houses for Inch (or desired unit) City. Houses' heights and widths must be 1 inch each. Cut out and display with trees, and so on to match.

Have students design sports events measured in inches and feet. Who runs the 100-inch race? Write out and illustrate story problems for a class measurement book.

Have students measure distances around school and post signs. Example: 100 feet or yards to the office. How many inches would this be?

Compare and chart lengths of students' feet, hands, pencils, and so on. Results make a good bar graphs.

Have a *paper airplane* contest. Students construct airplanes and throw for longest or specific distance.

Measure and mark a sidewalk or playground every 10 feet or yards. Use it for such physical activities as shuttle runs or relay races.

Have students toss *bean bags,* trying to get them exactly 1, 2, or 3 feet or yards away. Measure after they are thrown or have students estimate the distance they have tossed. Give points for close estimates.

Have students discuss examples of when accurate measurements are needed. Have them measure pencils to the nearest inch and order them. Then repeat to the nearest ½, ¼, ⅛, or ¹/₁₆ inch. Discuss the results.

Draw a starting dot on a piece of paper. Use *counters* as tiddlywinks, with each student shooting them in a different direction. Measure distances to the closest amount possible. Whose went farthest? Whose distances totaled the most? Adapt by drawing a circle around the dot. Who can land closest?

Give students lengths in inches and fractions of inches, and have them construct closed figures of their choice, using only those lengths. What are the perimeters?

Measurement 2

Skill: To change one unit of length to another: inches, feet, and yards

Time: 2 periods

Materials:

clear tape

scissors

rulers

yardsticks

counters: 5 per student

graph paper: 1" or ¹/₂" squares

Anticipatory Set

Use *graph paper, tape, scissors, rulers,* and *yardsticks.*

Have students make 1" × 12" rulers from strips of graph paper, taping extra squares as necessary. Have them mark and number each inch on the graph paper rulers.

Have students practice measuring the same distance in inches, using the graph paper rulers, feet using regular rulers, and yards using yardsticks. Students should make a chart and write in all three measurements.

Procedure 1 ☐■

To change from larger to smaller units using serial addition or multiplication

Use *graph paper rulers from Anticipatory Set, rulers,* and *yardsticks.*

On the board draw three columns and label from left to right: "Yards," "Feet," "Inches." Write only three numbers to start: 1, 2, and then 3 vertically in the Feet column.

Yards	Feet	Inches
	1	12
	2	24
1	3	36
	4	48
	5	60
2	6	72
	7	
	8	
3	9	

Have groups of students lay a yardstick on the floor and line up three regular rulers along it.

Say: Each ruler is 1 foot. How many did it take to make a yard? (3) Each yard is a group of 3 feet.

Write a 1 in the Yard column beside the 3 in the Feet column.

Ask: If I have 2 yards, how many groups of 3 feet is that? (2)

Students put two yardsticks together, with the rulers beneath.

Ask: How do I find two groups of 3? (Multiply 2 × 3, or add 2 groups of 3.) Two yards equals how many feet? (6)

Add a 4, 5, and 6 to the Feet column on the board. Write a 2 in the Yards column next to the 6.

Students put three yardsticks together, with the rulers beneath. They find that 3 yards is three groups of 3 feet, or 9 feet. This is added to the chart, continuing the pattern.

Do you see a pattern to the yards and feet on the board?

Students respond: Each time the number of yards increases by one, the feet increase by three.

If I have a certain number of yards, what's the rule for finding how many feet? (Multiply the number of yards by 3 feet, or add groups of 3 feet.)

Students next lay out one regular ruler and place a paper ruler beneath.

Each foot is a group of how many inches? (12)

Add this to the chart.

Students lay another regular ruler beside the first, placing another paper ruler beneath.

Ask: How many feet do we have? (2) How many groups of 12 inches? (2) How do we find how many inches in all?

Students respond: Multiply 2 × 12 inches, or add groups of 12 inches.

Add the 24 to the chart.

Students place another regular and paper ruler, multiply 3 × 12 or add 12 + 12 + 12, and find that 3 feet equals 36 inches. This is added to the chart. They next lay a yardstick above the sets of rulers.

What can you tell me about yards and inches? (1 yard is a group of 36 inches) How many groups of 36 is 2 yards? (2) Two groups of 36 is how many inches? (72)

What is the rule for finding out how many inches are in any number of yards?

Students respond: Multiply the number of yards times 36 inches, or add groups of 36 inches.

Is the yard a big or small measurement? (big) If I measured the door with it, would I have many yards? (no) Is a foot bigger or smaller than a yard? (smaller)

If I measured the door in feet, would I have more or fewer than the number of yards? Why? (It would take more feet because feet are smaller.)

What can you say about measuring the door in inches? (It would be the biggest number because inches are smaller than feet.)

Have students measure out 2 yards 5 inches with their yardsticks and paper rulers.

A yard is a group of 36 inches. Do we have extra inches? (yes, 5) How can we find the total number of inches? (add the extra 5 to the 36) Repeat with other mixed measurements.

Students estimate and then measure the height of the classroom door in yards, feet, and inches. Which estimate was the closest? What strategies did those students use?

As you dictate lengths in yards or feet, students estimate the length and then use rulers and yardsticks to measure and convert to feet and inches. When they feel comfortable with the process, they do the addition or multiplication on paper and then check with the rulers.

See Practice and Extension of this lesson or Measurement 1 for measuring ideas.

Procedure 2

To change from smaller to larger units using division or repeated subtraction

Use *graph paper rulers from Anticipatory Set, rulers,* and *yardsticks.*

Make another chart as in Procedure 1. Write 12 in the Inches column.

Students work in groups. They set out one paper ruler, with a regular ruler above it.

Say: Your paper rulers are 12 inches. How many feet is that? (1) Write 1 in the Feet column next to the 12.

Students add another graph paper and regular ruler. They find that 24 inches equals 2 feet.

Repeat once more.

Students find that 36 inches equals 3 feet. They add each new result to the chart.

Ask: Do you see a pattern? (Inches increase by 12s, and the feet increase one at a time.)

Each time I have a group of 12 inches, what can I do with it? (change it for 1 foot) Does that fit the rest of the chart? (yes)

We are dividing the inches into groups of 12 and calling each group 1 foot. How could I explain this in math language?

Students respond: Subtract 12s from the inches, or divide by 12.

Students continue placing rulers and adding to the chart until they have 72 inches = 6 feet. Each time they convert to feet, they repeat they are dividing the inches into groups of 12 and then subtracting the groups to find the feet.

Have students lay a yardstick above the first three rulers. How many inches measure the same length? (36) Thirty-six inches makes how many groups of 12 to find feet? (3)

Ask: How many feet do we need for each yard? (3)

Add 1 in the Yards column.

Students repeat with a second yardstick and chart 2 in the Yards column by the 72 inches.

Ask: Do you see a pattern for the yards on the chart?

Students again look for patterns, looking this time at feet divided into groups of three and called yards. They see that every 3 feet or 36 inches, the yards increase one at a time.

Each time I have a group of 36 inches, what can I do with it? (change it for 1 yard) Does that fit the rest of the chart? (yes)

We are dividing the inches into groups of 36 and calling each group 1 yard. How could I explain this in math language?

Students respond: Subtract 36s from the inches, or divide by 36.

Is an inch a big or small measurement? (small) If I measured the door with inches, would I have many of them? (yes) Is a foot bigger or smaller than an inch? (bigger)

If I measured the door in feet, would I have more or fewer than the number of inches? Why? (It would take fewer feet because feet take up more distance.)

What can you say about measuring the door in yards? (It would be the smallest number because yards are the biggest measurement.)

Have students measure out 15 inches with their paper rulers.

Ask: How many groups of 12 can we get? (1) How many inches are left over? (3) We call this length 1 foot 3 inches. Repeat with other lengths.

As you dictate lengths in inches, students estimate the length and then use rulers and yardsticks to measure and convert to feet and yards. When they feel comfortable with the skill, they do the subtraction or division on paper and then check with the rulers.

Procedure 3

☐■

To compute using mixed measurements

Use *graph paper rulers from Anticipatory Set, graph paper, scissors, tape,* and *counters.*

Have students cut 20 1" × 1" squares, and three more 1" × 12" rulers, which need not be labeled with inches. Then have them make a place value type chart headed "Yards," "Feet," "Inches." Counters will represent yards.

Say: I need to measure a package to wrap it. One side is 1 foot 8 inches wide.

Students put 1 ruler and 8 inch-squares on their charts.

The next side is 4 inches.

Students place and report they have 1 foot 12 inches.

Ask: How can I make this simpler? (change the 12 inches for 1 foot) What is another word for making this kind of exchange? (regrouping) How is this like or unlike our usual regrouping?

Students discuss. This regrouping is done at 12 instead of 10. They now show 2 feet.

Say: The next side is again 1 foot 8 inches. Place the amount and make your total as simple as possible.

Students place and have 3 feet 8 inches. They exchange the 3 feet for 1 yard-counter and show 1 yard 8 inches. They discuss that the regrouping is at three, different from the exchange at 12.

The last side is 4 inches, but why am I not done?

Students allow another 4 inches for overlap. They place 8 inches and show 1 yard 16 inches, which is regrouped to 1 yard 1 foot 4 inches.

Summary:	Yards	Feet	Inches
Place:		1	8
Place:			4
Show:		1	12
Regroup:		2	0
Place:		1	8
Show:		3	8
Regroup:	1	0	8
Place:			8
Show:	1		16
Regroup:	1	1	4

Repeat with other measurements.

Students place and write each new measurement as an addition problem. They write each step after doing it on their charts.

When they "carry" what will they do? (They will carry 1 to the feet column for every 12 inches regrouped, and 1 to the yard column for every 3 feet regrouped.)

Repeat the procedure for subtraction, starting with a roll of paper 3 yards 2 feet 10 inches long. Subtract 8 inches at a time.

Students write each problem as they are doing it. They discuss the need to show an extra 12 in the inches column when they "borrow" from the feet, and an extra 3 in the feet column when they "borrow" from yards.

Have students make up mixed measurement problems for the class to do.

Practice and Extension

Have students research lengths of sharks, whales, or other animals. They measure and mark these with *tape* along the wall and label the distance in yards, feet, and inches.

Students estimate, measure, and chart each other's heights. They add all the heights together to find the total in yards, feet, and inches. Next they measure this distance down a hall. By lying down in a line, they can check for accuracy. What is the average height of the students in the class?

Students can estimate and then measure the distance between classrooms in yards and then convert. How many yards do they walk each day between classes? How many feet or inches? Post signs with arrows giving the distances to various points in several units.

Measurement 3

Skill: To measure length by centimeters, meters, and millimeters; to use decimal notation

scissors

metersticks

See Reproducibles for: graph paper with 1 cm squares, Metric Reference Chart

Time: 1 period per procedure

Materials:

place value (pv) blocks or Cuisenaire® rods: 1s and 10s

rulers: with cm or mm markings

Anticipatory Set

Have student groups measure the width of their desks, using a body part as a unit. Chart and discuss results. Do we need a better way to measure an item? Discuss why people internationally need to be able to arrive at standard measurement terms.

Procedure 1 □■

To understand and use centimeters

Use *pv one cubes or Cuisenaire® rods (1s only), cm graph paper, scissors,* and *rulers.*

Give students cubes or rods, and explain that these are 1 cm long. Have students find a part of their hand that is close to 1 cm long. This will help establish the idea of a cm and can be used for estimating without a ruler.

Ask: What standard objects can you find that are 1 centimeter long? Example: A raisin.

Students use their hand ruler to estimate and measure objects and then check for accuracy with their blocks.

Have students cut out 1 cm × 10 cm strips of graph paper and label as shown:

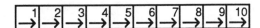

They use their paper rulers to estimate and measure objects to the nearest cm. How close were their estimates? Did they get more accurate with practice? Can they use the cm hand part to help estimate?

Have students measure with real rulers. See the Practice and Extension for ideas. Students can draw lines and figures to specific lengths. Continue the procedure until all students are competent in the skill.

Procedure 2 □■

To understand and use meters

Use *pv blocks or Cuisenaire® rods to 10s* and *metersticks.*

Have students work in groups and place 10 one cubes or rods next to 1 ten rod. Have students then place 10 ten rods in a line next to a meterstick.

Ask: *About* how long is this line? (a yard) It is a little longer than a yard and is called a *meter.* How many one cubes would it take to equal this? (100) If a meter were a dollar, what would a centimeter be? (cents or pennies)

Students estimate and then measure and chart lengths with their metersticks and ten rods. See the Practice and Extension for ideas. They report lengths in m and extra cm, as well as in cm only. Students can chart or graph how close their estimates were.

Discuss with students what they would measure with a meter. A centimeter.

Students use metersticks to answer such questions as: How many cm are 2 m? Half a m?

Procedure 3 □■

To understand and use millimeters; to use decimal notation with centimeters and millimeters

Use *cm graph paper, scissors, rulers with millimeters,* and *Metric Reference Chart.*

Metric measurement is based on what number? (10) Ask: For a measurement smaller than centimeters, into how many parts will we have to divide each centimeter? (10)

Have students cut a 2 cm × 20 cm strip from graph paper and label as shown:

Say: Each of these *small* distances is a millimeter; how many to a centimeter? (10) If a meter were a dollar, centimeters would be cents, and millimeters would be a tenths of cents, or mils.

Can you think of anything else in mathematics in which ten is important? Introduce the Metric Reference Chart to reinforce the base ten relationships.

We have divided each centimeter into 10 parts. What do we call each part? (1 mm) How can we write millimeters, or tenths of centimeters? ($^1/_{10}$ or 0.1) Because metric measurement is based on tens, we use the decimal form.

Draw a large replica of the illustration on the board. Draw a line 1.5 cm long, and ask how we would label it.

Students respond: 1.5 cm. If students answer $1^1/_2$ cm, repeat that we use the decimal form, even though $^1/_2$ is the same as 0.5.

Repeat with other examples, including lengths of less than 1 cm.

Encourage students to see the advantage of decimals: I want to put two books end to end. One measures $10^7/_8$ inches and the other $9^1/_4$ inches. What must I do to know how much space I need?

Students respond: Find equivalent fractions before you can add.

What if one of the books is 10.7 centimeters and the other is 9.3 centimeters? (add decimals) Do you see an advantage to using the metric system?

Students use graph paper rulers to estimate and measure objects and lengths. They find perimeters of objects by adding decimal lengths. Can they find shortcuts to measuring objects with regular dimensions?

Have students repeat the measuring activities with regular centimeter rulers.

Procedure 4

To use decimal notation with meters and centimeters

Use *metersticks marked to centimeters.*

Ask: How many centimeters are in each meter? (100) What fraction of a meter is one centimeter? ($^1/_{100}$) How do we write this in decimal form? (0.01)

Have students find 34 cm on their metersticks. 34 centimeters is $^{34}/_{100}$ of a meter. What is this in decimal form? (0.34) Repeat with other numbers.

Student groups estimate and measure distances with their metersticks. They write both the m-plus-cm amount and the m amount in decimal form. They compare results with other groups.

Have students measure perimeters, total distances from room to room, and other distances for which they will have to add shorter distances to find total distance.

Practice and Extension

Have students bring in lightweight *objects 1 cm long.* Glue these to tag board for a display.

Have students use *rulers* to draw houses for Centimeter City. Object dimensions must be multiples of exact cm.

Have students research *track-and-field records* for metric measurements using decimals. Students can measure the lengths of long jumps, high jumps, and so on.

Have students design sports events measured in cm and m. Who or what runs the 100-cm race? Illustrate story problems for a class measurement book.

Have students measure distances around school and post signs. Example: 100 m to the Office. How many cm would this be?

Have a *paper airplane* contest. Students construct airplanes and throw for distance. Flight length is measured in m and cm.

Measure and mark a sidewalk every 10 m. Use it for such physical activities as shuttle runs.

Have students toss *bean bags,* trying to get them exactly 1, 2, or 3 m away. Measure after they are thrown. Or, have students estimate the distance they have tossed. Give points for close estimates.

Tell students they have a board 3 m, or 300 cm long, by 30 cm wide. They can make any cuts they wish. They are to make a bookcase with three shelves. Students draw the plans, marking all lengths, then they construct their bookcases from *tag board* and *tape.*

Have students use *1 cm graph paper* to construct figures with given dimensions or perimeters. Discuss the limits of a figure with a 20-cm perimeter: What is the maximum height possible with two sides? Three sides? How many sides are possible?

Measurement 4

Skill: To change one unit to another:
centimeters, meters, and millimeters

Time: 2 periods

Materials:

cm rulers

metersticks

place value (pv) blocks to 100s

See Reproducibles for: Metric Reference Chart

Anticipatory Set

Use *rulers* and *metersticks*.

Have pairs of students measure several distances.
One uses a ruler and measures in cm. The other uses
a meterstick and measures in m. They compare
measurements and look for patterns.

Procedure 1 □ ■

To change from one unit to another

Use *pv blocks, metersticks, rulers, Metric Reference
Chart,* and *paper.*

**Directions are for m and cm. Adapt as needed if
you wish to include mm.**

**On the board draw desired columns and label as
shown. Students should copy. Put 1 under Meters.**

Meters	Centimeters	Millimeters
		1
	1	10
	2	20
	3	30
1	100	1,000
2	200	2,000
3	300	3,000

**Have groups lay a meterstick on the floor and
make a line below it of 10 one cubes and 9 ten
rods.**

**Say: Check the centimeter markings on the ten
rods. How many did it take to make a meter? (100)**

Students write a 100 in the Centimeter column.

**If I have 2 meters, how many groups of 100
centimeters is that?**

Students add another meterstick and 10 ten rods.
2 m = 200 cm. Students add to chart.

How could I find two groups of 100?

Students respond: Add together, or multiply 2 × 100.

**Repeat for 3 meters. Ask: Do you see a pattern on
the chart?**

Students respond: Each time the number of m
increases by 1, the cm increase by 100.

**If I have a certain number of meters, what's the
rule for finding how many centimeters?**

Students respond: Add 100 cm for each m, multiply
the number of m by 100 cm.

**Is the meter a big or small measurement? (big) If I
measured the door with it, would I have many
meters? (no)**

**Is a centimeter bigger or smaller than a meter?
(smaller) If I measured the door in centimeters,
would I have more or less than the number of
meters? (more) Why?**

Students discuss why they would need more cm.

Students find this pattern on the chart. They measure
as you dictate lengths in meters, using rulers or rods,
and metersticks to convert measurements. When they
feel comfortable with this skill, they do the addition
or multiplication on paper and then check with rulers.

**Have students measure out 2 meters and
5 centimeters with their metersticks and rulers.**

**Say: A meter is a group of 100 centimeters. Do
we have extra centimeters? (yes, 5) How can we
find the total number of centimeters? (add the
extra 5 to the 200 we already have) Repeat with
other mixed measurements.**

Students estimate and then measure the width of the
classroom board in m, then cm. Which estimates
were closer? What strategies did those students use?

**Introduce the Metric Reference Chart. Have
students relate it to a place value chart. Ask: How
could this help you remember what to do?**

**Now introduce changing from smaller to larger
measurements. Say: If all I had were centimeters,
how would I know how many meters they would
equal? Can you state a rule?**

Students respond: Each group of 100 cm makes a m.
You can subtract 100 cm at a time for each m; you
divide the cm into groups of 100 to find m.

If I start with centimeters and want to change to meters, will I get a larger or smaller number? (smaller)

Students practice measuring as you dictate lengths in cm. They use rulers or rods, and metersticks to convert measurements. When they feel comfortable with the skill, they do the subtraction or division on paper and then check with the rulers.

Have students measure out 115 cm. Say: To find out how many meters this is, think how many groups of 100? (1)

How many centimeters are left over? (15) We call this length 1 meter 15 centimeters.

Repeat with other mixed-unit measurements until students are competent in the skill.

Procedure 2 □■

To compute using mixed measurements

Use *Metric Reference Charts, metersticks,* and *rulers.*

Introduce the Metric Reference Chart. Point out that it is similar to a place value chart, as metric measurement is base ten.

Say: Since we usually don't use decimeters, we commonly wait until we have enough centimeters (ones) to regroup all the way to the meters (hundreds) place.

Students draw the following chart as you draw it on the board without the numbers.

Meters	Decimeters	Centimeters
1		30
+ 2		40

Students will lay out measurements on the floor, using rulers and metersticks, and then chart the numbers.

I love licorice. My first piece is 1 meter 30 centimeters long.

Students measure this on the floor. They write 1 in the Meters place and 30 in the Centimeters place on the chart.

My second piece is 2 meters 40 centimeters long. What is the total?

Students extend the measurement on the floor. They write and find the total length is 3 m 70 cm.

Add 30 more centimeters. How many centimeters now? (100) What do you have to do? (regroup) Since we are using only centimeters and meters, we wait until we have 100 centimeters to regroup.

Repeat with examples until the class is competent in the skill.

Introduce subtraction, as well. This is a good time to assess whether the students know what they are doing when they "borrow" in subtraction.

Ask: How does computing with measurement units compare with the computing you're used to?

Practice and Extension

Have students research lengths of sharks, whales, or other animals. They measure and mark these with *tape* along the wall, writing the measurement in m and cm.

Students can estimate and then measure and chart each other's heights. They add all the heights together to find the total in m and cm. They measure this distance down a hall. How many students does it take to equal a whale?

Students can measure the distance between classrooms in m and then convert. How many m, and so on, do they walk each day between classes?

Research lengths in the *Guiness Book of World Records.* Convert as desired.

Measurement 5

Skill: To understand capacity: cups, pints, quarts, and gallons

Time: 1 period per procedure

Materials:

materials to measure: water, unpopped popcorn, rice, or beans

containers: small and large (see Manipulative Information section)

measuring sets to desired capacity (see Manipulative Information section for suggestions)

counters: separate colors for each desired capacity

Anticipatory Set

Use *materials to measure* and *two containers of similar but different sizes.*

Pour beans into one container. Have students decide whether this container holds more or less than the second container. How could they tell? (pour the same beans into the second container) Have them predict results with other containers.

Procedure 1 □■

To understand and use cups, pints, quarts, and gallons

Use *measuring sets to desired capacity, materials to measure,* and *containers of different sizes.*

Directions are written for understanding cups. Follow the same procedure for other measures. As students measure, have them work with any previously learned units, as well as the new one.

Have students use cup measures to estimate, measure, and chart the capacity of a few of the containers.

Ask: What will you decide to do if a container doesn't hold an exact amount?

After measuring, discuss the problems they had estimating.

Discuss what strategies students used for estimating.

Ask: Does the shape of some containers make estimation more difficult? Did your estimates get better as you practiced?

Identify the unit they have been using as 1 cup. Explain they have been measuring *capacity,* or the amount a container will hold.

Students use their data to arrange containers in order according to capacity.

Students discuss examples of when using estimates would be appropriate. They practice estimating, measuring, and charting amounts to the nearest cup. Are their estimates getting more accurate? They discuss what they could measure using a cup.

Procedure 2 □■

To change from one unit of capacity to another

Use *cup, pint, quart, and gallon measures, materials to measure,* and *counters.*

Designate counter colors for units. On the board draw four columns and label as shown. Do not add numbers yet.

Gallons	Quarts	Pints	Cups
			1
		1	2
			3
	1	2	4
			5
		3	6

Students copy the chart and add to it during the lesson.

Fill one cup with beans and put a 1 under Cups.

Students put one cup-counter on their chart and mark a 1 next to it.

Repeat the process for a second cup. Ask: What can I do with 2 cups? (trade for a pint)

Pour the 2 cups into the pint measure and mark 1 in the Pints column.

Students trade two cup-counters for a pint-counter and mark a 1 in the Pints column.

Continue the procedure until the desired capacity is reached.

Discuss the relationships among the measures; e.g., how many cups to make a gallon, what's the smallest number of containers you could use to hold 7 cups.

A cup is a small measurement. If I filled one large container with *cups* of beans, and an equal size container with *quarts* of beans, would I have used a larger number of cups or quarts? (cups)

Students demonstrate with counters.

Repeat for other measures.

If I only know *pints,* how can I find the number of *cups*? (Trade a pint for 2 cups; add together 2 cups for each pint.)

If I am adding the same number each time, what shortcut could I use? (multiplication)

I could multiply the number of pints by the 2 cups I know are in each pint, or I could add 2 cups to the total for each pint I have.

Students practice converting from a large measure to a small measure. They use actual measurements, as well as counters, to check their calculations. They write each step of the process as they do it.

Say: Remember when we go from a large unit like quarts to a small unit like cups, we end up with a larger number of cups.

What if we knew only how many *cups* we had but needed to know the number of *pints* we could fill? Are we going to end up with a larger or smaller amount of pints than cups? (smaller) How could we actually measure?

Students respond: Pour the cups into the pints.

We would put all the cups into groups of two to trade for pints, subtracting groups of two from the total cups we have. What's another way to it?

Students respond: Divide the cups into groups of two; each group means another pint.

Students practice converting from a small measure to a large one. They use actual measurements and counters to check their calculations. They write each step of the process as they do it.

Procedure 3

To compute using mixed capacities

Use *cup, pint, quart, and gallon measures, materials to measure,* and *counters.*

Have students make charts as shown in the illustrations. Designate counter colors for capacity.

Say: I'm collecting rainwater to test for acid rain. I need a gallon, but I only have unusual-sized containers. How can I see how much water I've collected?

Students respond: Pour the water into a measuring container, and add the amounts.

Say: The first one holds 1 pint and 1 cup. Measure out 1 pint and 1 cup.

Students place one pint-counter and one cup-counter. On a separate paper they write: 1 pint 1 cup.

Say: The second holds 1 pint. Measure out 1 pint. Write on the board:

$$\begin{array}{rl} 1\ \text{pint} & 1\ \text{cup} \\ +\ 1\ \text{pint} & \\ \hline \end{array}$$

Students place pint-counter and copy the problem. They check their counters: 2 pints 1 cup.

Quarts	Pints	Cups
	⬤	⬤
	⬤	

Ask: Can I do anything else?

Students respond: Trade 2 pints for a quart. They trade counters and regroup on paper.

Quarts	Pints	Cups
	1	1
	1	
1	2̶	1

The next holds 2 cups. Repeat the process, discussing the regrouping at 2 cups and adding to the total. How is this similar or different from regular adding?

Students discuss. The cups are regrouped at 2, not 10.

Continue adding and regrouping, discussing and writing.

Repeat for subtraction. This is a good time to assess whether students really understand what they are doing when they "borrow" in subtraction. Do students see patterns? How is this related to other subtraction we've done?

When students are comfortable with the skill, they make up measurement problems with partners and then exchange with other pairs.

Practice and Extension

Have students bring in *containers from home* to measure. Make a class chart, and order the containers by capacity.

Have students find out the gasoline capacity of their families' cars in gallons. How many quarts, pints, or cups is that?

Use *self-sealing plastic bags of different sizes* and *rice* as a display. Have students use these to help estimate the capacity of their *shoes, desks, paper bags,* etc.

Have students research the capacity of nearby lakes, reservoirs, water towers, etc. Have them then figure the equivalent cups, pints, and quarts. How much water is used for a bath? A shower? A bath a day for a week, month, or year? A faucet that leaks a cup an hour?

Have students bring in *recipes* from home and rewrite them, increasing ingredients to serve 3×, 4×, 5× the number of people. Can they change measurements to use the least number of measuring devices possible?

Skill: To understand capacity: liters and milliliters

Time: 1 period per procedure

Materials:

materials to measure: water, unpopped popcorn, rice, beans

containers: small and large; of different sizes (see Manipulative Information section for suggestions)

liter measures: marked with milliliters

containers: small; of identical size and less than 1 liter, such as paper cups

measures smaller than 1 liter: marked with milliliters, if possible

See Reproducibles for: Metric Reference Charts

Anticipatory Set

Use *materials to measure* and *two containers of similar but different sizes.*

Pour beans into one container. Have students decide whether this container holds more or less than the second container. How could they tell? Do the measurement.

Procedure 1

To understand and use liters

Use *liter measures, materials to measure, identical small containers of less than a liter,* and *containers of different sizes.*

Have students use liter measures to estimate, measure, and chart the capacity of a few of the containers. Ask: What if a container doesn't hold an exact amount?

After measuring, discuss the problems they had estimating. Does container shape make estimation more difficult? Did they improve with practice?

Identify the unit they have been using as 1 liter. Explain that they have been measuring *capacity,* or the amount a container will hold.

Students use their data to arrange containers in order according to capacity.

Have students find containers that hold exactly 1 and 2 L. You have a liter of beans, but you need to use the liter to measure something else. Ask: How many of the small containers will you need for the beans?

Students discover how many small cups or containers it takes to total 1 L of capacity.

Discuss instances when it would be appropriate to have only an approximate measurement of capacity.

Students practice estimating and then measuring to the nearest liter. See Practice and Extension for suggestions.

Discuss with students what they could measure using a liter. Is a liter the only measure of capacity they will need? What's a better way to measure the amount of water an eyedropper will hold?

Procedure 2

To understand and use milliliters

Use *liter measures, materials to measure, identical small containers of less than a liter, containers of different sizes,* and *measures smaller than a liter.*

If you would like to use a weighing activity as well, see the Practice and Extension.

Have students examine the liter measures to discover how many milliliters are in 1 L. (1,000) Ask: When would you be more likely to use milliliters than liters? (medicine amounts, cooking, science experiments, small amounts)

Have students fill their small identical containers with beans. How many milliliters of beans do they think they have? Write all amounts on the board.

Students measure the amount in milliliters.

Repeat with other containers, charting all estimates and then having a student do the actual measurement. Are their estimates becoming more accurate?

Set up measuring stations with containers of different sizes at each stations. Have students make a chart: "Container," "Liters and Milliliters," "Milliliters."

Students work in groups to estimate, measure, and chart the results at each station. For each container, they should have both estimates and actual measurements. They compare their results with those from other groups.

Procedure 3

To change from one unit of capacity to another

Use *liter measures* and *materials to measure.*

On the board draw the following chart headings.

Liters	Deciliters	Centiliters	Milliliters
1			1,000

Point out that this is like a place value chart, since metric measurement is base ten. However, since we usually use only liters and milliliters we have to regroup across three places.

Have one group of students measure 1 liter and another measure 1,000 milliliters. Compare.

Write 1 in the Liter column. Ask: How many go in the Milliliter column? (1,000) Repeat for 2 liters.

Students predict the next figures will be 3 liters and 3,000 milliliters. They confirm by measuring.

Every time I added another liter, it was equal to another group of how many milliliters? (1,000) Ask: If I had something that contained 8 liters, how would I find the number of milliliters? (add 8 groups of 1,000)

If I'm adding same-size groups, what's a shortcut? (multiply) I can multiply the number of liters I have by 1,000, or I can add that many 1,000s together. How many milliliters in 8 liters? (8,000)

Repeat with more examples until students are comfortable with the concept.

Next show students 2,000 mL of beans. I only know how many milliliters this is, 2,000. How can I find how many liters?

Students respond: Separate the milliliters into piles of 1,000.

Write 2,000 mL on the board. Pour beans into a liter measure. Write –1,000 under the 2,000. Ask: How many liters do I have so far? (1)

Repeat for the second liter.

I can subtract 1,000 milliliters at a time. I'm separating them into groups of the same size—1,000. Ask: What's a shorter way of doing this? (dividing)

I can divide by 1,000 to find the number of groups or liters that size, or I can subtract 1,000 at a time to make liters. Relate to the chart on the board.

Is liter a large or small measure? (large) If I measure an amount in both liters and milliliters, which will I measure more of, liters or milliliters?

Students respond: Milliliters. They are smaller; it takes more of them.

Repeat with examples until students are comfortable with the concept.

Procedure 4

To compute using mixed capacities

Use copies of the *Metric Reference Chart* and *paper*.

Introduce the Metric Reference Chart. Point out to students that it is similar to a place value chart but that we usually use only liters (thousands) and milliliters (ones).

Students next draw a place value chart to 1,000, labeled with mL and L instead of ones and thousands. They write 1 in the thousands place and 550 in the ones place.

I have something containing 1 liters 550 milliliters. I add 2 more liters and 400 more milliliters. What's the total?

Students write and find: 3 liters 950 milliliters.

Add 50 more milliliters. How many milliliters now? (1,000) What do you have to do? (regroup) Since we are using only milliliters and liters, we wait until we have 1,000 milliliters to regroup.

Repeat with examples until the class is comfortable with the concept. Introduce subtraction as well, starting with 3 liters of ice cream and dipping out various amounts. How much is left each time?

Practice and Extension

Have students bring in *containers from home*. They estimate and then measure the capacity. Make a class chart and order the containers by capacity.

Have students find out the gasoline capacity of their families' cars in liters. How many milliliters is that?

Fill *self-sealing plastic bags* with 1 L, 500 mL, and 250 mL of *rice*. Mark amounts on the bags with marker. Students use the bags to help estimate the capacity of their *shoes, small containers,* etc. They then fill the objects with rice and measure the capacities accurately.

Have students add capacities of *snack drink containers*. How much would they drink if they finished an apple drink and an orange drink? Which add up to a liter?

Have students bring in *recipes* from home and measure the amounts in liters and milliliters. Are any amounts similar to standard measurement?

Add a weighing activity to Procedure 2. Add *scales* and *metric masses* to each station. Have students include mass as one of their chart headings. Do not tell students that a L of water has a mass of a kilogram. Discuss how they will measure only the mass of the beans or water and not the mass of the container as well. Have them look for any patterns. If you use water, call it Water Math and include *large pitchers* for pouring water, and *rags*. Introduce the *Metric Reference Chart* for discussion after the activity.

Measurement 7

Skill: To measure temperature and read thermometers

Time: 1–2 periods

Materials:

containers of hot and cold water: 2 per group

thermometers: Fahrenheit or Celsius; 1 per container

large demonstration thermometer: made from tag board with ribbon loop running through it to represent the alcohol—mark half of ribbon red with marker

scissors

clear tape

red crayons or markers: 1 per student

See Reproducibles for: number lines to 1000

Anticipatory Set

Use *containers of hot and cold water.*

Work in small groups. Give each group two containers of water, one cold and one warm or hot. Have students decide which water is warmer. Explain that *temperature* means how hot or cold something is.

Ask each group to describe the temperature of their warm or hot water. Then ask which group has the warmest water. How could they tell? (feel each one and compare)

Have groups try to order the warm water containers from least warm to most warm. Is this difficult? (Some are very close.) Do they need a way of measuring temperature more accurately? (yes)

Procedure 1 ☐■

To measure temperature

Use *containers of hot and cold water, thermometers, number lines, tag board thermometer, scissors, tape,* and *crayons or markers.*

Say: When we measured weight and capacity, we used numbers to tell how many pounds or quarts we had. We measure temperature with numbers, too. The more heat we have, the higher the temperature numbers.

For temperature our unit is degrees instead of pounds or quarts. Which would be the higher or warmer temperature, 30° or 10°? (30°)

Students put thermometers in their containers of water.

Move the ribbon on the tag board thermometer to demonstrate a variety of temperatures. Have students practice reading temperatures until they can read them accurately.

Relate warm and cool temperatures to the bowls of water and to air temperature. Heat makes the alcohol inside the thermometer expand, or take up more space.

Students draw thermometer bulbs around one end of the number line. They cut out the line, tape it together, and turn it vertically. They label the large tick

marks 10°, 20°, etc. As they measure temperatures, they will fill in the exact degrees.

Have groups decide on the thermometer reading of their bowls.

Students use red crayons or markers to duplicate the readings on both their thermometers. They mark one "Cool" and one "Warm" or "Hot."

Before, we couldn't tell for sure which group had the warmest water. Can we tell now? (Yes, check the temperature.) Ask each group their temperatures, and discuss which groups have the coldest and warmest water.

Students decide which of their thermometers shows the colder temperature and which is the warmer.

Holding their number line thermometers, students order themselves from coldest to warmest. They check the order by calling off their temperatures in degrees.

Procedure 2 ☐

To estimate and measure temperature

Use *containers of hot and cold water, thermometers,* and *number line thermometers from Procedure 1.*

Replace the water in the bowls, and put thermometers into the water. Turn the thermometers so they cannot be read.

Have each group make a chart headed "Guess" and "Temperature." If you wish, they can also make a column headed "Degrees Off." Down the left have them list the station numbers as they come to them.

Students go from station to station. They first decide on and chart an estimate for the warm temperature.

Then they read and record the actual temperature, both on their number line and on their chart. Next they subtract to find how many degrees off they were. They repeat for the cold water.

Discuss with groups how close they were able to come with their estimates. Ask: Did you get more accurate as you practiced? How can you tell?

Students respond: They weren't so many degrees off.

Ask: Was it easier to estimate cold or warm water? How could they figure this out using their data?

Students respond: Compare the degrees off for the cold versus the warm.

Have students compare first and last readings for several containers. Why might they not agree? Was the water getting cooler or warmer? Why?

Procedure 3   □■

To find changes in temperature above and below zero

Use *number lines, markers, scissors, tape, tag board thermometer showing above and below zero,* and *paper.*

Use a tag board thermometer or a thermometer drawn on the board to review the reading of temperatures with students. Then set the temperature at 40° and explain that this was a morning temperature. As the day warmed, the temperature rose to 50°.

Students count the number of degrees as you change the reading to 50°.

Ask: How many degrees difference between 40° and 50°? (10°) How do we find the difference between two numbers? (subtract) Does this work with temperature? (yes)

Repeat with several other temperature changes, using such examples as temperature in the shade, in the sun, a sudden rain shower dropping the temperature, etc.

Students cut out and tape number lines together and then turn them vertically. Using the left number line, they label the lower large tick mark "0." They mark each smaller tick mark below 0°: −1° through −9°. Above 0° they mark from 1° to 19°, using a different color marker. The upper large tick mark is ignored.

Give students several temperature changes, all above 0°. Have them figure the change in temperature on paper and then check with their number lines.

Next have them put their finger on −5°. This was a very cold morning. It started at −5° but rose to 0°. How many degrees is that? (5)

It got warmer in the afternoon and rose to 10° above zero. How much did it rise in the afternoon? (10°) How can I figure out how much it rose in all that day? (Add the morning rise to the afternoon rise; 15°.)

Student repeat the procedure several times as you give temperature changes and different degree readings.

Write −5° on your paper. Now write a new reading of 15°. This is above zero, so it doesn't need a

minus sign. If I asked you how much the temperature changed, you might just subtract the numbers and get a result of 10°. What is the problem with this?

Students respond: The change is from −5° to 0° and then from 0° to 15° for a total of 20° change.

What will I have to do? (figure out how much from the minus number to 0°, then how much from 0° up, then add the two)

Students practice with their thermometers and on paper as you give temperature changes and different degree readings.

Practice and Extension

Have students leave *thermometers* in various places around the room, school, and outdoors. Record temperatures at various times of the day and discuss.

Have students experiment with *thermometers* left in the sun on white versus black paper, in and out of boxes, etc.

Provide *ice cubes,* and have students design experiments using *thermometers.*

Use two *dice, number line thermometers,* and two *paper clips* per student to play Degree Derby. Students make two columns on paper: "Degrees," "Total." They start with 100 in the Total column.

First a student throws the dice and chooses which 2-digit temperature to make from the numbers. The temperature is marked with a paper clip on the thermometer and is written in the Degrees column.

For the second round, the second temperature thrown is marked with a paper clip and in the Degrees column. The difference between the two temperatures is added to or subtracted from the 100 in the Total column, depending on the rise or fall in temperature. The winner is the student with the highest total. If the winner is then changed to be the student with the lowest total, the students will need to change their strategy.

Measurement 8

Skill: To understand pounds and ounces

Time: 1 period per procedure

Materials:

objects: weighing a pound, such as a loaf of bread, boxes of sugar

measurement sets: pounds and ounces

scales: balance, kitchen, bathroom

collections of objects: weighing under and over a pound, such as pencils, boxes of crayons

objects: weighing an ounce, such as several pencils held with a rubber band, small bags of paper clips, buttons

collections of objects: weighing under an ounce, such as paper clips, beans

counters: 32 per group

Note: *Mass* is a measure of the amount of material an object contains. *Weight* is the force with which an object, or mass, is attracted toward the earth (or other body) by gravitation. Balance scales measure mass; kitchen scales measure weight. However, when a kitchen scale's unit of measurement is kilograms, it is commonly accepted that, at sea level, the reading is interchangeable with that of the mass of the object. For everyday purposes, the distinction between mass and weight is not critical. Scientists and engineers, however, appreciate the difference.

Anticipatory Set

Use *1-pound objects or weights, balance scales,* and *collections of objects weighing over and under a pound.*

Set up balance scales several days ahead, and ask students to find objects and groups of items that weigh the same as the weights or objects weighing 1 pound. Let students experiment with the equipment without introducing pounds as a label.

Procedure 1

To understand and use pounds

Use *1-pound objects or weights, collections of objects weighing under and over a pound,* and *scales.*

Identify objects as weighing 1 pound. Have students lift each one and compare two at the same time. Objects in their dominant hand often will feel lighter; have them switch hands several times.

Weigh the 1-pound object on a kitchen scale. Identify the pound markings, and add objects to make 2 and 3 pounds of weight.

Ask: Do you see a pattern? (The heavier an object is, the higher the number on the scale.)

Ask students to compare the weight of a pencil to a pound. Does the pencil weigh more or less than a pound? (less)

Have them use a balance scale to check. Then have them use a kitchen scale. Was the reading closer to 0 or to 1 pound? (0)

Have students make a chart labeled: "Object," "Estimate," "Result."

Students then measure a variety of classroom objects. They estimate the objects as more or less than a pound and then check with the balance scale. Next they check with the kitchen scale.

Ask: How did the information you got from scale to scale differ? Were your estimates more accurate as you practiced? Why?

Discuss strategies students used for estimating.

Next have the class find several different objects that together will weigh 1 pound. Encourage them to use their findings from before to predict the results.

Ask: How many pencils weighed 1 pound? How many crayon boxes? Can you find a mix of pencils and crayon boxes that will weigh 1 pound?

Students weigh and chart their estimated and actual results. They can add any combinations that weigh 1 pound to a large class chart. They repeat with weight of 2 pounds.

Next have student volunteers weigh themselves on a bathroom scale.

Ask: How many 1-pound weights do you equal? How much will two students weigh? How much will they weigh holding two 1-pound weights?

Introduce estimation by measuring an object on the balance scale that is obviously closer to 1 pound than 2 pounds. What do the students observe?

Students respond: The scales almost balanced with the 1-pound weight but were not balanced at all with the 2-pound weight.

Students practice estimating and then measuring to the nearest pound. They note the position of the pointer on the kitchen scale to help them decide the nearest pound.

Procedure 2 ■

To understand and use ounces

Use *1-ounce objects or weights, collections of objects weighing over an ounce, balance scales,* and *kitchen scales.*

Use activities from Procedure 1 with ounce weights instead of pounds. Have students discover how many 1-ounce objects are needed for 1 pound.

After charting an activity for 1 ounce, students repeat for groups weighing 8 ounces, or half a pound.

Introduce approximation by weighing an object on the kitchen scale that is closer to 1 ounce than 2 ounces. Ask: Where is the pointer? (closer to the 1) We can call this *about* 1 ounce.

Continue to add objects, having the class name both the nearest ounce and the nearest pound.

Say: In our number system, we've learned to round up at the halfway mark. What number is halfway between one place and another on a place value chart? (5) What is the halfway number for ounces and pounds? (8 ounces—half a pound)

Students practice estimating and weighing as they complete a class chart: What weighs 1 ounce, 2 ounces, 3 ounces, etc., up to several pounds.

Procedure 3 ■

To change from one unit of weight to another

Use *counters* and *larger objects such as pencils.*

Have student groups make a chart labeled "Pounds" on the left and "Ounces" on the right. Draw the same chart on the board; in the Ounces column, write the numbers vertically 1 through 16.

Students add counters representing 1 ounce each to their charts as you write.

Say: When I have 16 ounces of anything, can I call that amount something else? (1 pound)

I can exchange, or regroup, 16 ounces for a pound. Ask: What is this like in our number system? (regrouping)

On the chart write 1 in the Pounds column next to the 16 Ounces.

Students exchange 16 ounce-counters for 1 object to represent 1 pound.

Repeat to 2 pounds. Ask: Do you see a pattern? (For every 16 ounces, there is another 1 pound.)

What if we had 64 ounces and needed to know the number of pounds? (change groups of 16 for pounds) We could subtract out groups of 16 to find the number of pounds. What is another way

to divide something into same-size groups? (divide) We can divide the number of ounces into groups of 16 to find pounds.

Repeat with other examples until students are competent with the concept.

Ask: What if we start with pounds? Clear your charts and place 2 pound-objects.

Regroup to find how many groups of 16 would be in 2 pounds. (2) How else could I find how many ounces? (add or multiply 2 groups of 16)

Repeat with other examples. Have students write conversions on paper as they do them with objects until students are competent in the skill.

Procedure 4 □

To compute using mixed weights

Use *counters* and *larger objects such as pencils.*

Counters will be ounces, larger objects will be pounds. Have students make a place value type chart labeled "Pounds" and "Ounces."

Say: I raise pigeons and can only carry 10 pounds of pigeons at once. I'll have to add up their weights to know which pigeons to take.

The first pigeon weighs 1 pound 5 ounces. The second one weighs 2 pounds 10 ounces.

Students place counters and objects. They report the total so far is 3 pounds 15 ounces.

Does this look familiar? (It is like adding on a regular place value chart.) The next pigeon weighs 1 pound 1 ounce.

Students place additional objects and counters. They regroup the ounces and have a total of 5 pounds.

Continue adding and then subtracting weights until students are comfortable with the concept. Then have students do the addition and subtraction on paper as they move the counters and objects. This is a good time to assess whether students understand what they are doing when they "borrow" in subtraction.

Practice and Extension

Have students weigh and chart their *snacks or lunches* for a week. Compile a class chart. How could they sort these data: by day of the week, sex, type of snack, etc. What was the average snack weight?

Have students research the weights of various animals and make a bar chart showing relative weight.

Have students estimate and weigh various *articles of clothing.* How much would a whole outfit weigh? Do winter outfits weigh more or less than spring outfits?

Measurement 9

Skill: To understand kilograms and grams

Time: 1 period per procedure

Materials:

measurement set: grams, kilograms

objects: with a mass of 1 kilogram (2.2 pounds)

collections of objects: under and over 1 kilogram

scales: balance, metric kitchen

objects: with a mass of 1 gram, such as raisins

collections of objects: under and over 1 gram

See Reproducibles for: Metric Reference Chart

Note: *Mass* is a measure of the amount of material an object contains. *Weight* is the force with which an object, or mass, is attracted toward the earth (or other body) by gravitation. Balance scales measure mass; kitchen scales measure weight. However, when a kitchen scale's unit of measurement is kilograms, it is commonly accepted that, at sea level, the reading is interchangeable with that of the mass of the object. For everyday purposes, the distinction between mass and weight is not critical. Scientists and engineers, however, appreciate the difference.

Anticipatory Set

Use *1-kilogram objects or weights, collections of objects under and over 1 kilogram,* and *scales.*

Do this the day before. Refer to the exercises in measuring pounds and ounces. Then let students explore measuring the mass of the objects in kilograms and grams.

Procedure 1

To understand and use kilograms

Use *1-kilogram objects or masses, collections of objects under and over 1 kilogram, and scales.*

Identify objects as having a mass of 1 kilogram. Have students lift each one and compare two at the same time. Objects in their dominant hand often will feel lighter; have them switch hands several times.

Weigh the 1-kilogram object using a kitchen scale. Identify the kilogram markings, and add objects to make 2 and 3 kilograms. Have students predict the scale readings as you add objects.

Ask students to compare the mass of a pencil to a kilogram. Does the pencil have more or less mass than a kilogram? (less) Have them first use a balance scale to check, then a kitchen scale.

Students make a chart labeled: "Object," "Estimate," "Result." They estimate the mass of classroom objects as more or less than 1 kilogram and then check with the balance scale and kitchen scale. Were their estimates more accurate as they practiced?

Next have the class find several different objects that together will have a mass of 1 kilogram. Encourage them to use their findings from before to predict the results. How many shoes together

had a mass of 1 kilogram? Can they find a mix that will measure exactly 1 kilogram?

Students use scales to measure and chart their estimated and actual results. They can add any combinations that have a mass of 1 kilogram to a large class chart. Repeat with mass of 2 kilograms.

Introduce approximation by finding the mass of an object that is obviously closer to 1 kilogram than 2 kilograms. Is the mass closer to 1 or 2 kilograms? (1 kilogram) We call this measuring to the nearest kilogram.

Students practice estimating and then measuring to the nearest kilogram.

Procedure 2

To understand and use grams

Use *1-gram objects or masses, collections of objects under and over 1 gram,* and *scales.*

Identify objects as having a mass of 1 gram. Have students lift each one and compare two at the same time. Weigh the 1–gram object using a kitchen scale. Identify the gram markings, and add objects to make several grams.

Have students predict the scale readings as you add objects. How many grams to a kilogram? (1,000)

Ask students to compare the mass of a paper clip or pencil to a gram. Ask: Is the pencil's mass more or less than 1 gram? Have them use a balance scale and then a kitchen scale to check. Which is the better scale to use? Why? Repeat with 10 grams. Why is this more accurate?

Students make a chart labeled "Object," "Estimate," "Result." They estimate and find the mass of objects. Were their estimates more accurate as they practiced?

Next have students find objects that have a mass of exactly I gram, 5 grams, 10 grams, and 500 grams. How many pencils? How many paper clips? Make a class collection of objects or groups of objects that have a mass of exactly these amounts.

Introduce approximation by weighing an object that is closer to I kilogram than 2 kilograms using the kitchen scale. How many grams over 1 kilogram? Where is the pointer? (closer to the 1) We can call this about 1 kilogram.

Continue to add objects, having the class name both the nearest gram and the nearest kilogram. In our number system, what number is halfway between one place and another on a place value chart? (5) We've learned to round up at the half-way mark. What is the halfway number for grams and kilograms? (500 grams or 0.5 kilogram)

Have students practice estimating, weighing, and rounding to the nearest kilogram or 0.5 kilogram.

Procedure 3 □■

To change from one unit of mass to another

Use *1 kilogram masses, 3,000 grams of objects or masses, balance scales*, and *Metric Reference Charts*.

Introduce the Metric Reference Chart and on the board draw the chart shown below. Point out that it is similar to a place value chart, as metric measurement is base ten.

1000s kilograms	100s hectograms	10s decagrams	1s grams
1			1000

Say: Since we usually use only grams and kilograms, we wait until we have enough grams to regroup all the way to the kilograms place.

Have students balance 1 kilogram against 1,000 grams. Write 1 in the Kilogram column and 1,000 in the Gram column. Repeat for 2 kilograms = 2,000 grams.

Students predict the next figures will be 3 kilograms and 3,000 grams. They confirm this with the scale.

Every time I added another kilogram, it was equal to another group of how many grams? (1,000) If I had something that had a mass of 8 *kilograms,* how would I find the number of *grams?* (add 8 groups of 1,000) Is there a shortcut for adding same-size groups? (multiplication) I could multiply 8 kilograms by the 1,000 grams in each kilogram.

Repeat until students are competent in the skill.

Students make up and solve problems. They write the process as they are measuring. Later they can do the problem on paper first and then check by measuring.

If I only knew how many *grams* I had, how could I find how many *kilograms?* (separate the grams into piles of 1,000) I can subtract out 1,000 grams at a time. If I'm separating them into same-size groups of 1,000, is there a shortcut? (divide by 1,000)

Repeat with examples until students are competent with the concept.

Students make up and solve problems. They write the process as they are measuring. Later they can do the problem on paper first and then check with the objects and scales.

Procedure 4 □

To compute using mixed masses

Use *1 kilogram masses, 3,000 grams of objects or masses, balance scales*, and *Metric Reference Charts*.

On the board draw the chart shown in Procedure 3. Remind students that the chart is like a place value chart, but we only use grams and kilograms.

Students copy the chart and write 1 in the thousands place and 550 in the ones place.

I have something with a mass of 1 kilogram 550 grams. I add 2 more kilograms and 400 grams. What is the total?

Students find the total is 3 kilograms 950 grams.

Use the objects and scales to demonstrate.

Add 50 more grams. How many grams now? (1,000) What do you have to do? (regroup) If we are using only grams and kilograms, we wait until we have 1,000 grams to regroup.

Repeat with examples until the class is competent with the concept. Introduce subtraction as well. This is a good time to assess whether the students know what they are doing when they "borrow" in subtraction. How does computing with weight units compare with the computing they're used to?

Practice and Extension

Have students find the mass in grams of their *snacks* for a week and chart the results. Compile a class chart. How could they sort these data: by day of the week, sex, type of snack, etc. What mass did the average snack have in grams? The total mass in both grams and kilograms? Are there patterns? How would these results be helpful to a grocer?

Have student bring in *food packages with nutritional information marked in grams*. How many grams of protein in each one? Have students choose a food and figure out how much they would need to eat a kilogram of protein. Repeat for other nutrients.

Measurement 10

Skill: To measure volume

Time: 2–3 periods

Materials:

boxes: of different small sizes, such as pencil boxes, milk containers, jewelry gift boxes; 1 per group

cubes: small, enough to fill one of the boxes; 30 or more per group

graph paper: any size; several sheets per student

Anticipatory Set

Use *boxes* and *cubes*.

Have students work in groups to find how many cubes their box holds. What will they do if they have space left over too small to measure with a block? Is this an accurate way of finding out how many cubes a container will hold?

Procedure 1

To understand volume

Use *cubes* and *graph paper*.

Tell students they have been finding *cubic volume,* the number of real or imaginary cubes that will fit into a space. We measure volume in cubic units because it is the number of same-size cubes it takes to fill a space. Ask: When might they want to find the volume of something? (classroom air, desks, cars)

Have each group hold up its box and report their findings. Ask: Were any the same volume? Were they the same shape? Which had the larger volumes? (the bigger boxes) Did you discover any shortcuts to finding the total?

Have groups use 30 cubes to build a building of 30 cubic units. Building shapes will vary.

Discuss the variety of shapes. How could they all have the same volume?

Students respond: They hold the same number of cubes.

Have pairs of students make rectangular prism buildings of different numbers of cubes. Have them exchange positions with another pair and estimate the volume of the new buildings.

Have pairs then show their building to the whole class for an estimate.

Did anyone find ways to make a close estimate?

Have students look for patterns. Some may begin to see that layers repeat themselves.

If students are capable, have them draw side, top, and back views of their building. They should mark the volume on the back. Have them switch drawings with other groups and try to construct buildings from the drawings. Have them use the measurement on the back as a check.

Procedure 2

To measure volume

Use *cubes* and *graph paper*.

Have students build a 2×3 rectangle, the first layer of a building. What's the volume so far? (6 cubic units) Write a chart on the board headed:

Layers	Cubes in Each Layer	Volume
1	6	6

Say: Add another 2×3 layer on top of the first. Now what is the volume?

Students respond: 12 cubic units. Chart: 2, 6, 12.

Repeat with another layer. The chart now reads 3, 6, 18. Ask: Do you see any patterns?

Students who can multiply may see that they can multiply the number of layers by the number of cubes in each layer. Others may see it as serial addition.

Repeat with another layer. Can students predict the next result before building it?

Give students dimensions of buildings to build, and have them chart the volume after each layer. Can they predict the total before finishing?

If students start with 36 or 48 cubes, can they chart several different buildings *before* they build them?

Relate this to state requirements of a certain number of cubic feet of air per classroom. If they built for ants some classrooms that conform to the regulations, should they consider other things as well? Have students list these and sketch several views of their classrooms on graph paper.

Have students write a rule for finding the volume of a rectangular solid.

Explore volume and numbers. See Practice and Extension for suggestions.

Procedure 3 □ ■

To develop the concept of volume; to find the formula for the volume of a rectangular prism

Use *cubes*.

Review the concept of volume. Before, they filled the space and then counted all the cubes. Ask: What's the problem with this technique?

Students respond: You can't always fill a space with cubes; it takes a lot of time.

We'll build a building with a volume of 30 cubes. On the board write and have students copy the following chart, headings only:

l Length of Row	w # Rows Wide	# Blocks per Layer	h Height	V Volume
3	2	6	1	6
3	2	6	2	12

Have students make a row of three cubes. Say: Our first row is a group of three cubes. Now make another identical row next to the first one. What shall we put on our charts?

Students respond: Length is 3; width or number of rows is 2.

This is our first layer. How many cubes?

Students respond: 6. They add this to their charts. They write 1 as the height and 6 as the volume so far.

How could you get that total without actually using cubes? (Add two rows together; multiply the number in each row by the number of rows.) We can call this length times width, and write it: l × w.

Students build a second layer on top of the first.

How many cubes have we used so far? (12) How did you get that number? (added six and six) Since we're adding same-size groups, what is a shortcut? (multiply 2 groups × 6 in each group)

What is the height so far? (2) The volume is the number of cubes used in all. Add these numbers to your chart.

Student groups finish the buildings, using 30 cubes. They add the data from each layer to their charts.

We are looking for a way to find V, or volume. Do you see any patterns?

Students respond: You can multiply the number of cubes in each layer by the number of layers.

We could add each layer, but multiplication is faster. We multiplied the length times the width and then we multiplied by the height to get volume. I've used letters on the chart.

Can you come up with a description of the math we did, *using only letters*?

Students respond: Multiply l × w × h.

Yes, V = l × w × h. Now predict what the volume in cubic blocks will be of a building 10 blocks long, 1 block wide, and 3 layers high. (30 cubic blocks) Can you find another shape building that has a volume of 30 cubic blocks?

Students build more buildings. They add each set of data to the chart and check that the formula would work.

Repeat the building activities. Give dimensions or volumes. Have students use the formula to predict results and then check with the cubes.

Say: In the real world, we can't measure with real cubes, so we use imaginary ones. If we measure a small volume, we could use cubes 1 centimeter long, wide, and high. Our volume would be in cubic centimeters or cm³. Your place value one cubes have a volume of 1 cubic centimeter each.

What size cubes would we use to measure the volume of your desks? (cubic inches or feet) What about the volume of air in the classroom? (cubic feet, yards, meters)

Students discuss possible volumes and appropriate choices of measurements. They imagine cubes of those sizes.

Practice and Extension

Use *tag board or construction paper, rulers, yardsticks or metersticks,* and *tape.* Have students build cubes for each different unit of measurement in which you are interested.

On one side of the cubes have them write (for example) Volume = 1" × 1" × 1"= 1 cu. in. On another side of the cube have them list instances in which their unit of volume would be used.

Have students put several cubes together to make a building. How will they find the volume? (find the volume of separate sections and add together) What should they do if one section is in feet and one is in inches? (change one unit to the other)

Explore cubic numbers. Have students construct shapes using *place value blocks*. How can they quickly make a building of 48 cu. cm? If they have 27 one cubes, can they build a building that has equal dimensions? (3 × 3 × 3) What other numbers make cubes?

Ones Bills

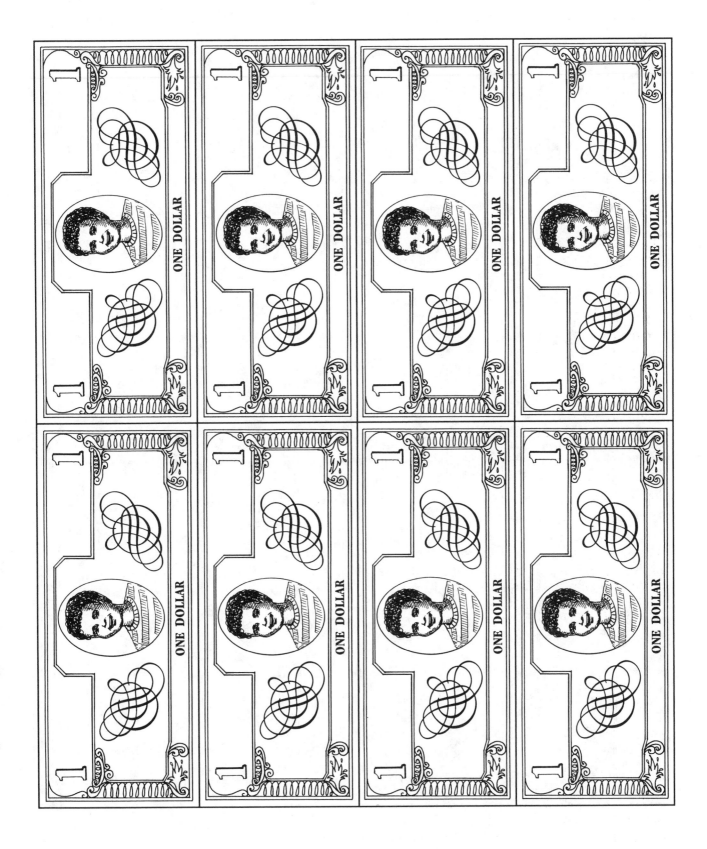

Hundreds Bills

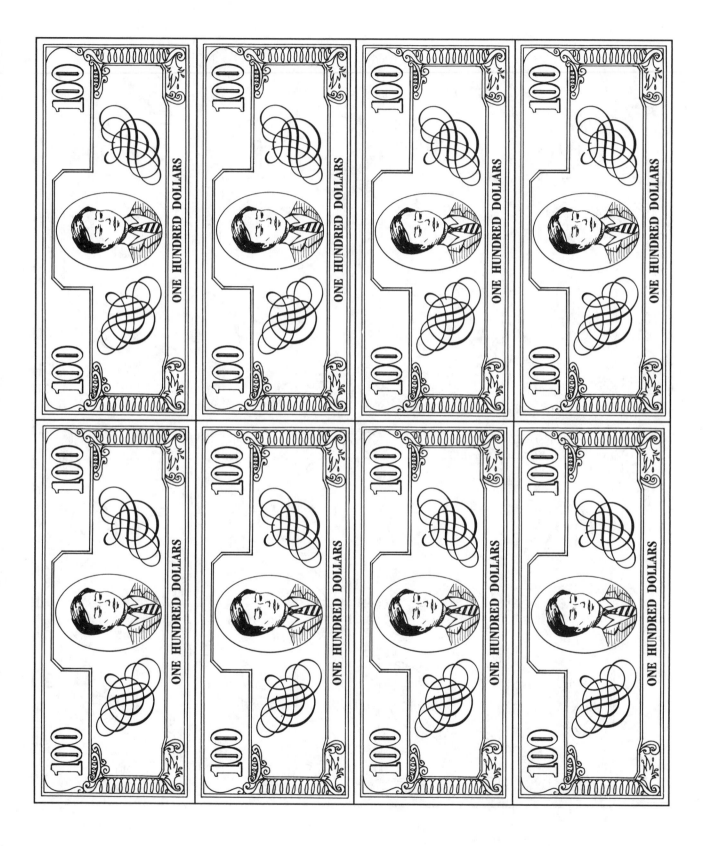

Thousands Bills

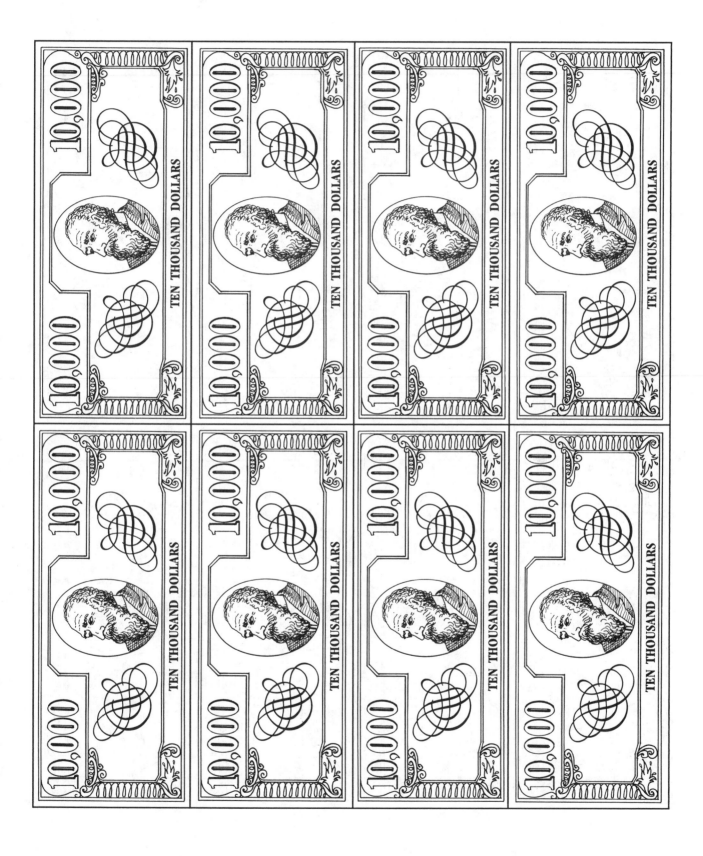

Hundred-Thousands Bills

Counter-Trading Board

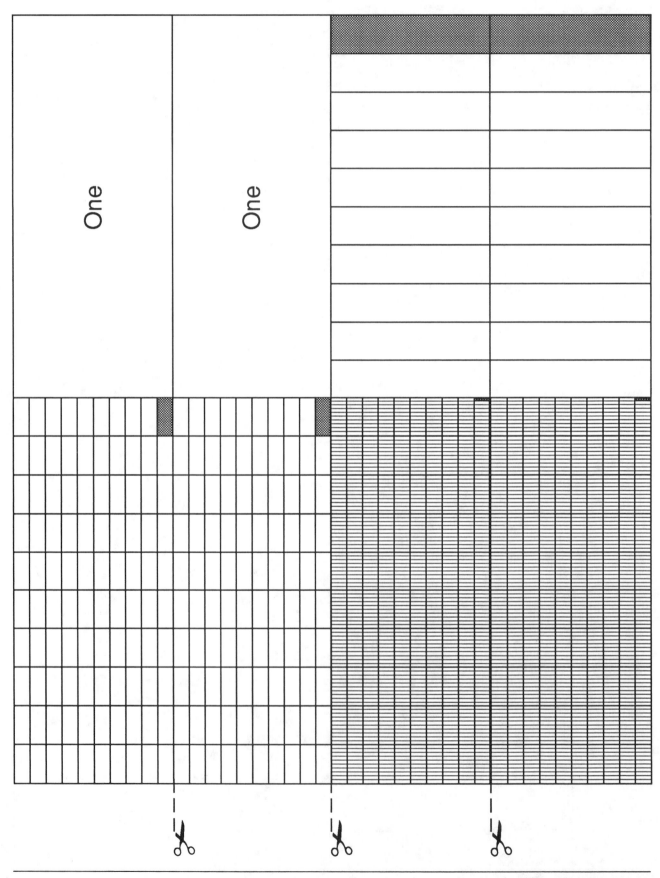

One

One

One	One	One	One
One	One	One	One

Decimal Bars—Tenths

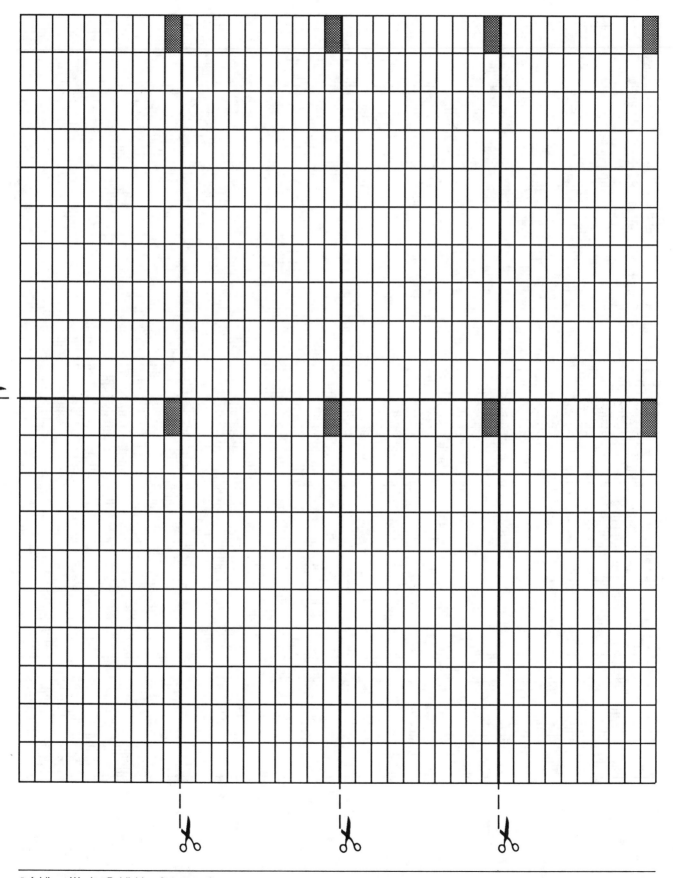

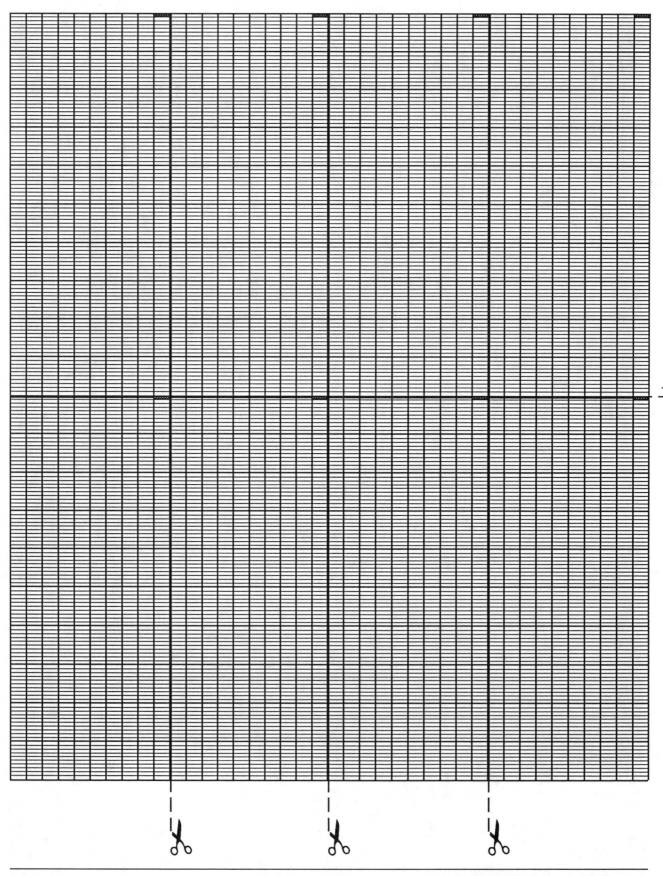

Division Paper

Hundreds	Tens	Ones	Check	Hundreds	Tens	Ones	Check
5 ⌐ 1	3	5					

Equivalency Chart

1 Unit											
	$\frac{1}{2}$	$\frac{1}{3}$	$\frac{1}{4}$	$\frac{1}{5}$	$\frac{1}{6}$	$\frac{1}{7}$	$\frac{1}{8}$	$\frac{1}{9}$	$\frac{1}{10}$	$\frac{1}{11}$	$\frac{1}{12}$
											$\frac{1}{12}$
			$\frac{1}{4}$	$\frac{1}{5}$	$\frac{1}{6}$	$\frac{1}{7}$	$\frac{1}{8}$	$\frac{1}{9}$	$\frac{1}{10}$	$\frac{1}{11}$	$\frac{1}{12}$
		$\frac{1}{3}$				$\frac{1}{7}$	$\frac{1}{8}$	$\frac{1}{9}$	$\frac{1}{10}$	$\frac{1}{11}$	$\frac{1}{12}$
				$\frac{1}{5}$	$\frac{1}{6}$				$\frac{1}{10}$	$\frac{1}{11}$	$\frac{1}{12}$
			$\frac{1}{4}$			$\frac{1}{7}$	$\frac{1}{8}$	$\frac{1}{9}$	$\frac{1}{10}$	$\frac{1}{11}$	$\frac{1}{12}$
					$\frac{1}{6}$						
	$\frac{1}{2}$	$\frac{1}{3}$		$\frac{1}{5}$		$\frac{1}{7}$	$\frac{1}{8}$	$\frac{1}{9}$	$\frac{1}{10}$	$\frac{1}{11}$	$\frac{1}{12}$
									$\frac{1}{10}$	$\frac{1}{11}$	$\frac{1}{12}$
								$\frac{1}{9}$			

File-Folder Place Value Mat to Thousands

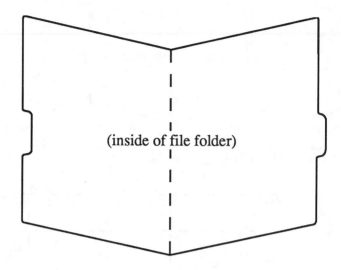

(inside of file folder)

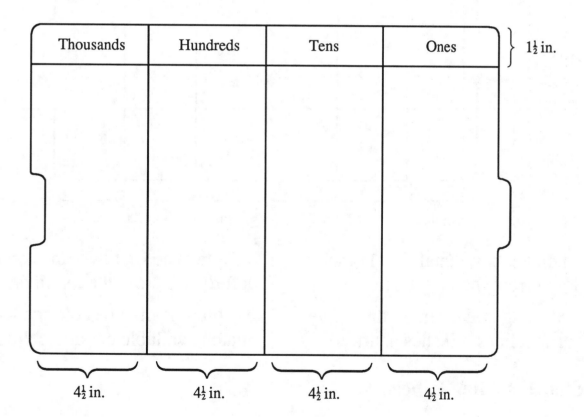

Thousands	Hundreds	Tens	Ones

$1\frac{1}{2}$ in.

$4\frac{1}{2}$ in.　　$4\frac{1}{2}$ in.　　$4\frac{1}{2}$ in.　　$4\frac{1}{2}$ in.

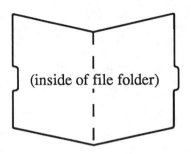

(inside of file folder)

Step 1. Setting up File Folder

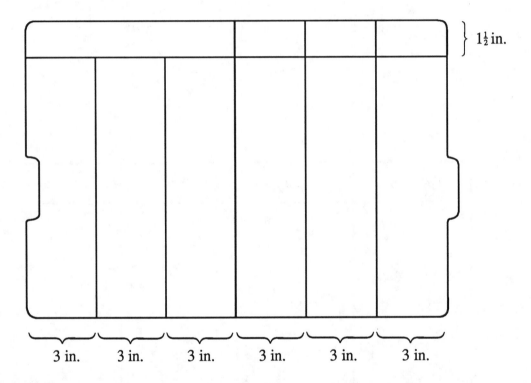

$1\frac{1}{2}$ in.

3 in. 3 in. 3 in. 3 in. 3 in. 3 in.

- Draw a horizontal line $1\frac{1}{2}$ inches down from the long edge.

- Starting at the center, draw five vertical lines 3 inches apart.

- Note: The first two lines on the left *do not* cross the top line.

- Columns may be color coded to match available counter colors.

Step 2. Adding Labels

Thousands					
Hundreds	Tens	Ones	Hundreds	Tens	Ones

Geoboard Paper

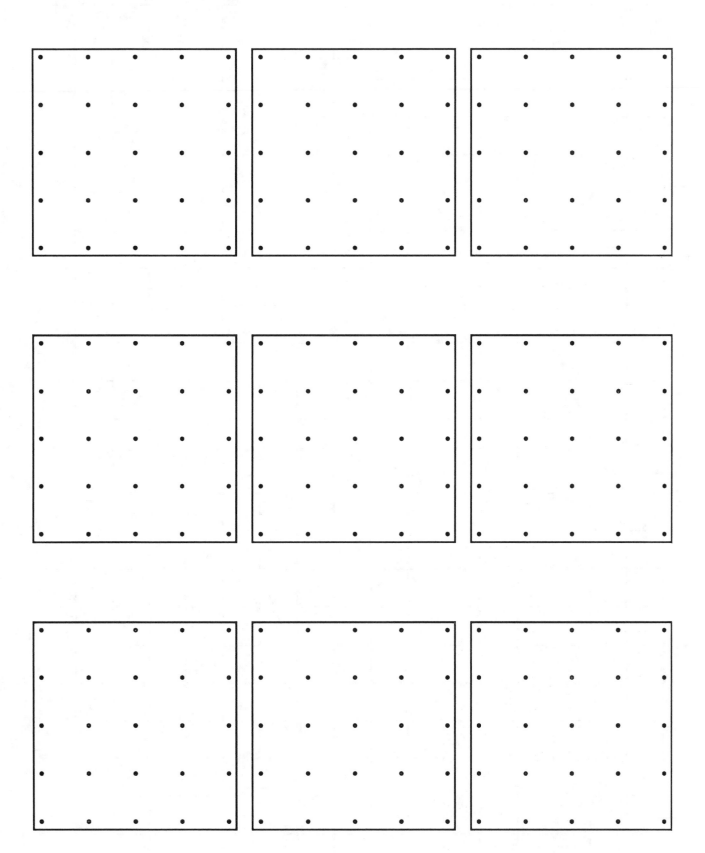

Hundred Board

1	2	3	4	5	6	7	8	9	10
11	12	13	14	15	16	17	18	19	20
21	22	23	24	25	26	27	28	29	30
31	32	33	34	35	36	37	38	39	40
41	42	43	44	45	46	47	48	49	50
51	52	53	54	55	56	57	58	59	60
61	62	63	64	65	66	67	68	69	70
71	72	73	74	75	76	77	78	79	80
81	82	83	84	85	86	87	88	89	90
91	92	93	94	95	96	97	98	99	100

	10^3	10^2	10^1	10^0 (Base Units)	10^{-1}	10^{-2}	10^{-3}
Hindu Arabic	1000	100	10	1	$\frac{1}{10}$ or 0.1	$\frac{1}{100}$ or 0.01	$\frac{1}{1000}$ or 0.001
Money	$1000	$100	$10	$1	$0.10	$0.01	$0.001 (mil)
Metric prefix	kilo	hecto	deca		deci	centi	milli
Length	**kilometer**	hectometer	decameter	**meter**	decimeter	**centimeter**	**millimeter**
Volume (capacity)	kiloliter	hectoliter	decaliter	**liter**	deciliter	centiliter	**milliliter**
Weight (mass)	**kilogram**	hectogram	decagram	**gram**	decigram	centigram	**milligram**

Bold print indicates most commonly used units.

Volume: 1 cubic decimeter (1 dm³) holds 1 liter (1 L)

Mass: 1 cubic decimeter (1 dm³) of water at 4° C has a mass of 1 kilogram (1 kg)

Multiplication Aids 1

Garden Glove Multiplication

Materials:

permanent markers

old or new garden gloves: 1 pair per student

For Help with Facts

This activity can be done without gloves by writing the numbers on the finger tips with washable markers. It can also be copied and sent home for parents to use to help students after they master the process.

Anticipatory Set

Review, saying answers to facts with products up to 16. We will be doing garden glove multiplication today. Have students wear the gloves and put the numbers 6 to 10 on their fingertips, as shown in the illustration. (Numbers go on the palm side of fingertips.)

Ask: How can we use these to do multiplication facts? Let the students work in pairs to make some guesses about how this could work.

Procedure

With the numbers facing them and their thumbs pointed up, instruct the students to touch a 7 to an 8. Count the touching fingers and all fingers of lower numerical value, counting by tens. Students may find it easier to remember to count the touching numbers and all other fingers closer to the floor. All count chorally: 10, 20, 30, 40, 50.

Then, multiply the number of fingers remaining on each hand, rather than counting by tens. In this case there are 2 fingers left on one hand and 3 left on the other; $2 \times 3 = 6$. Add this product to the sum of the tens ($50 + 6 = 56$).

Do the same activity with 6 and 7. (This is slightly harder, as the students must add 30 plus 12.) Give the students about 5 to 10 minutes to experiment with other pairs and to write down their results.

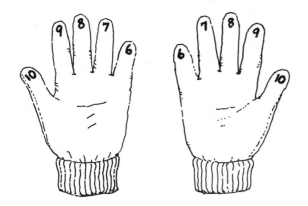

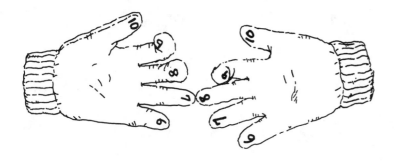

This is a hands-on way to multiply by nine.

Procedure

Have students place their hands on their desks with the backs of the hands up. To do 3×9, each student tucks under the third finger from the left, starting as they do when they read. See illustration below.

The answer is displayed with their fingers. The tens are to the left of the tucked finger, and the ones are to the right of the tucked finger. The number is read, as usual, from left to right.

Repeat with 4×9. This time the students tuck under the fourth finger from the left before reading the untucked fingers to the left and the right.

Have the students practice other nines facts, writing down the results and checking with each other to make sure they understand the procedure.

Practice and Extension

Use garden glove multiplication to discover and write down lists of $\times 6$, $\times 7$, and $\times 8$ facts. Use finger nines to write down $\times 9$ facts. Have the students work in small groups and check each other.

Have students look for patterns in their lists of $\times 9$ products. For each product, the tens digit is always one less than the number which was multiplied by nine, and the sum of the tens digit and the ones digit is always nine. Example: $7 \times 9 = 63$. Six is one less than the seven; $6 + 3 = 9$.

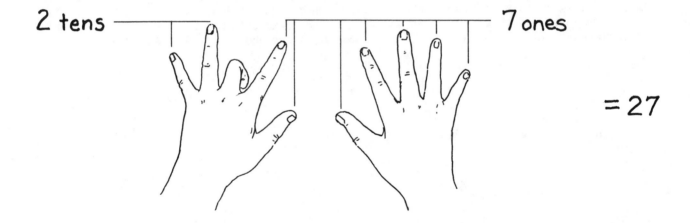

2 tens   7 ones   = 27

3 and 7 played cards;
Lenny won.
They played the game of 21.

3 and 6 are legal teens;
See them now,
They are 18.

3 and 8; 4 and 6; 2 and 12;
All stand at Denny's door,
Let them in . . . all 24.

4 and 7 stand at the gate,
Plenty old to make a date;
They are 28.

4 and 8 lost dirty shoe(s),
Help them find all 32.

Multiplication Clue Rhymes

6 and 7 are sort of blue,
What an age to be—
It's 42!

6 and 6 play
Pick up sticks,
They pick up all 36.

6 and 8 hurry
So they won't be late;
They equal 48.

Clue for 7 and 8—COUNT
1 2 3 4 5 6 7 8
Strike out 1 to 4 and
$56 = 7 \times 8$.

7 and 7 stand in a football line;
See them play;
They're the 49(ers).

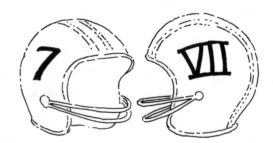

8 and 8 fell on the floor,
Pick them up;
They're 64.

Multiplication/Division Table

	0	1	2	3	4	5	6	7	8	9	10
0	0	0	0	0	0	0	0	0	0	0	0
1	0	1	2	3	4	5	6	7	8	9	10
2	0	2	4	6	8	10	12	14	16	18	20
3	0	3	6	9	12	15	18	21	24	27	30
4	0	4	8	12	16	20	24	28	32	36	40
5	0	5	10	15	20	25	30	35	40	45	50
6	0	6	12	18	24	30	36	42	48	54	60
7	0	7	14	21	28	35	42	49	56	63	70
8	0	8	16	24	32	40	48	56	64	72	80
9	0	9	18	27	36	45	54	63	72	81	90
10	0	10	20	30	40	50	60	70	80	90	100

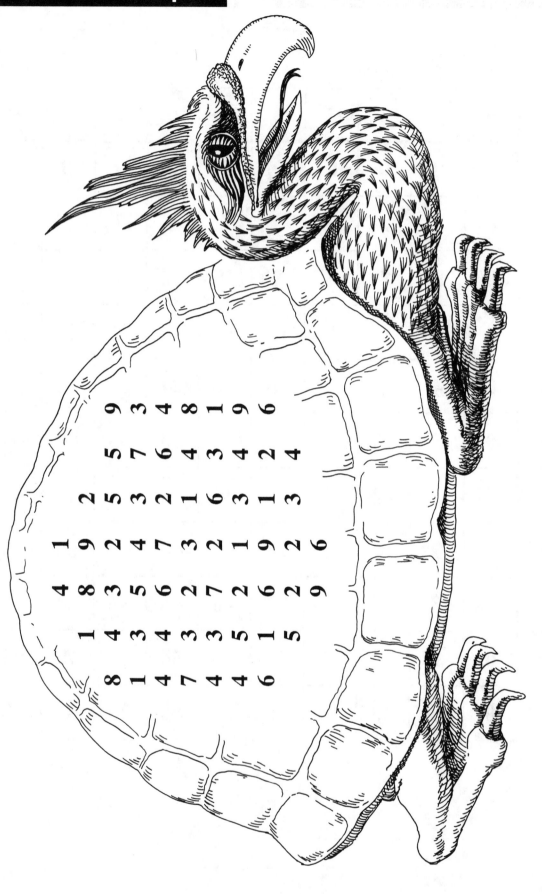

Circle all pairs of numbers whose product equals 25 or more. Can you find 32 pairs?

8	1	4	1	2	5	9
1	4	8	9	5	7	3
4	3	3	2	3	6	4
7	4	5	4	2	4	8
4	3	6	7	1	3	1
4	3	2	3	6	4	9
4	7	7	2	3	3	9
4	5	2	1	2	4	9
6	1	6	9	1	2	6
5	5	2	2	3	4	9
6	9	6				

This animal is a _____

Circle all pairs of numbers whose product is less than 26.

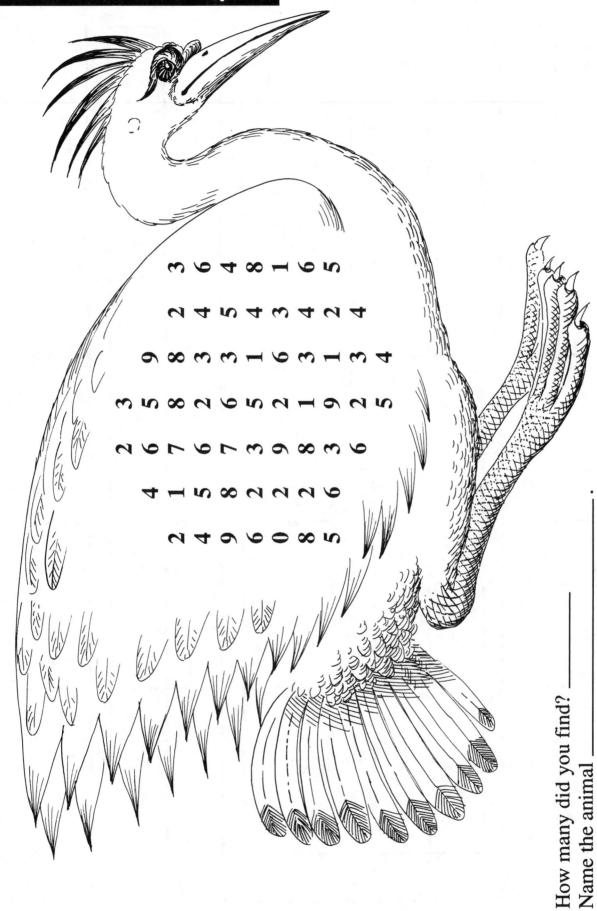

How many did you find? _____

Name the animal _____ .

Write a story about it on the back of this sheet.

Number Line 0 to 25

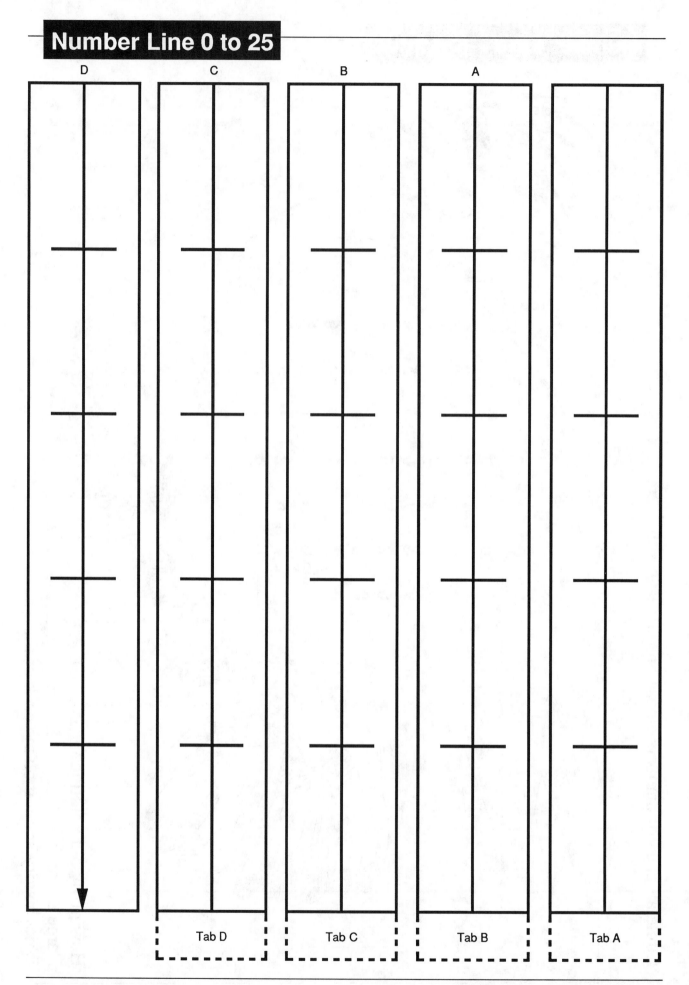

D   C   B   A

Tab D   Tab C   Tab B   Tab A

Number Line 0 to 100

D   C   B   A

Tab D   Tab C   Tab B   Tab A

Number Line 0 to 1000

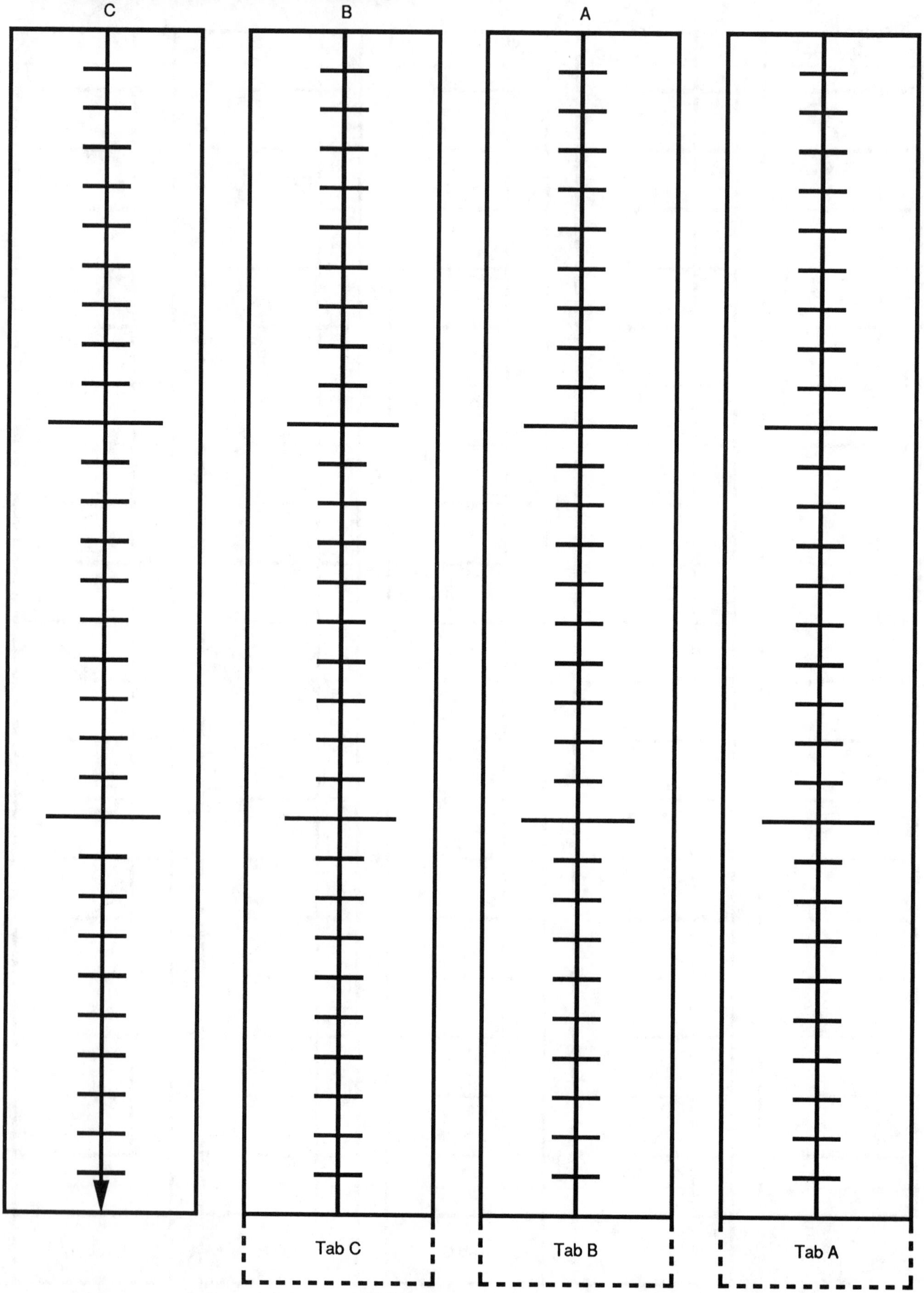

C

B

A

Tab C

Tab B

Tab A

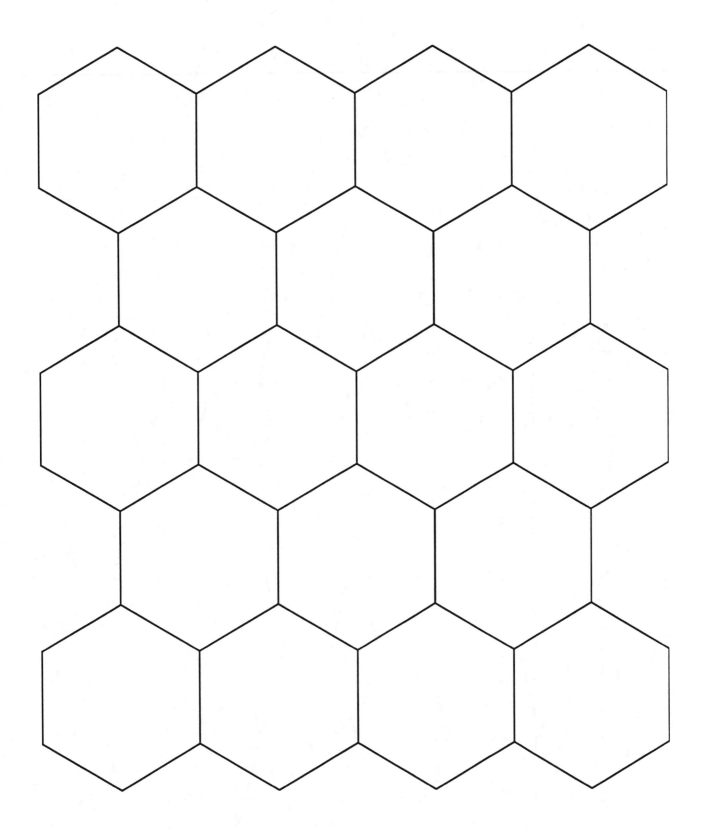

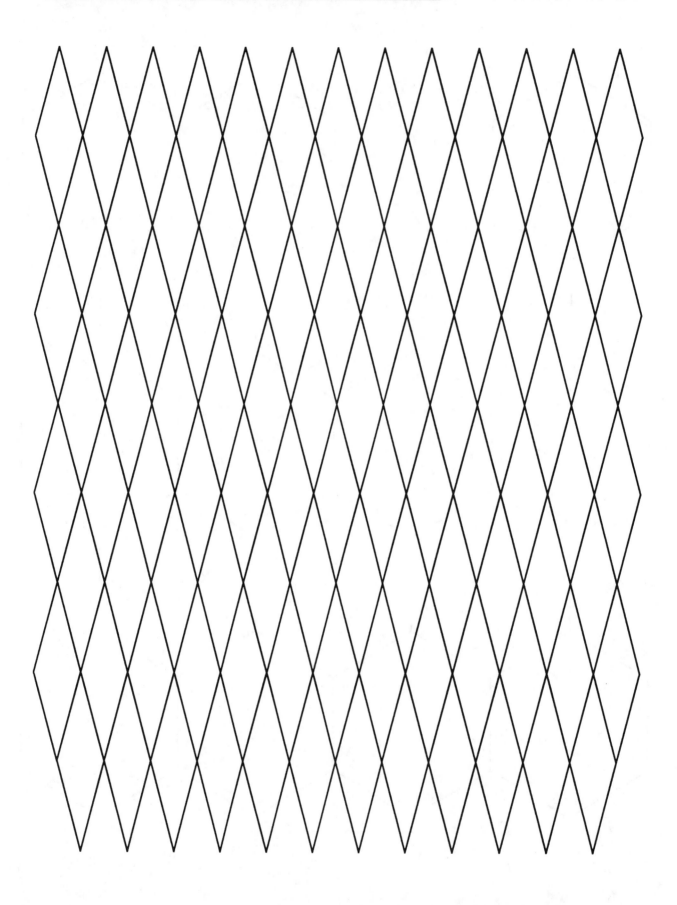

Pattern Blocks: Blue Rhombuses

Pattern Blocks: Orange Squares

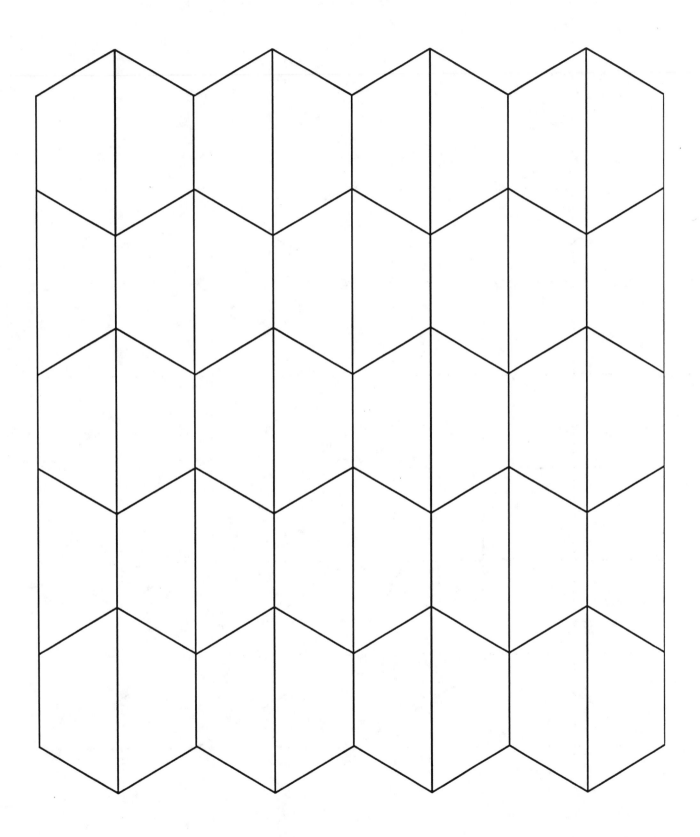

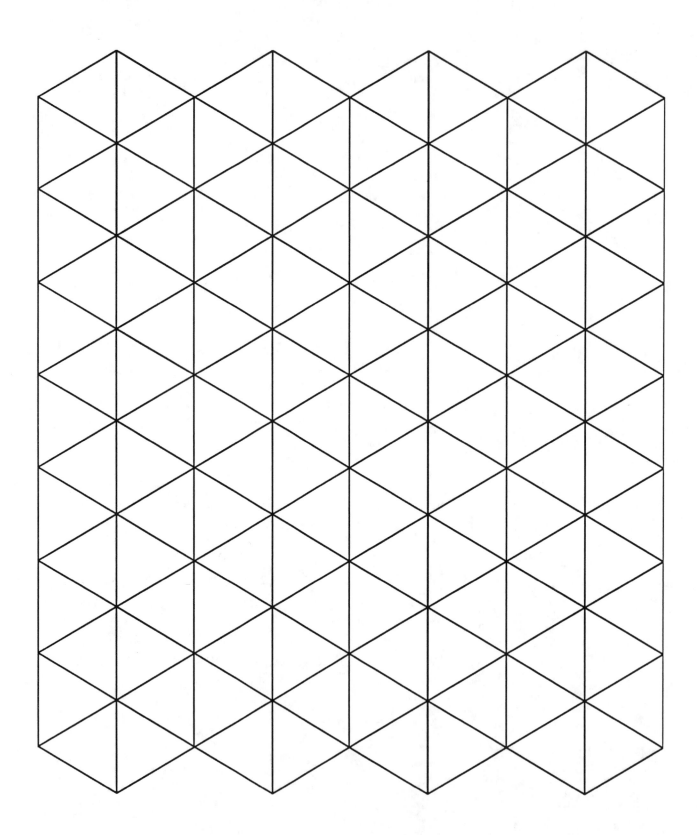

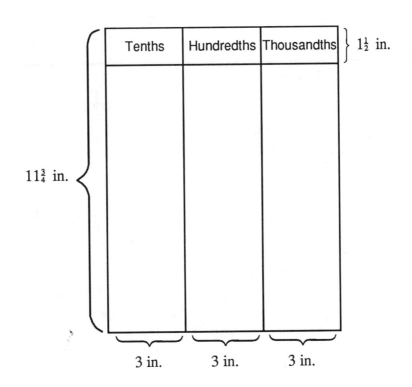

Use 12" × 18" tag board, cut to 11¾" × 18".

Adjust directions according to need:

Decimals to tenths:
3" × 11¾" per student

Decimals to hundredths:
6" × 11¾" per student

Decimals to thousandths:
9" × 11¾" per student

- Draw a line 11½" down from the long edge.

- Starting at the left, draw two vertical lines 3" apart.

- Tape to right side of file-folder place value mat. Extension will fold inside mat.

- Place a large adhesive dot on label line between ones and tenths as a decimal point.

Place Value Mat to Hundreds

Ones

Tens

Hundreds

Place Value Mat to Thousands

Thousands	Hundreds	Tens	Ones

Rounding Rhyme

(Read using a RAP rhythm)

Mark the place,
Look to the right.
Four or less are out of sight.

Five and up
Will buy one more
Before they, too, are out the door.

In those empty
Right-hand spaces,
Zeros keep the proper places.

3 4 2

3 4 2 ↗ ↗

+1
3 6 2

4 6 2 ↗ ↗

3 0 0

4 0 0

Rounding Rhyme

(Read using a RAP rhythm)

Mark the place,
Look to the right.
Four or less are out of sight.

Five and up
Will buy one more
Before they, too, are out the door.

In those empty
Right-hand spaces,
Zeros keep the proper places.

3 4 2

3 4 2 ↗ ↗

+1
3 6 2

4 6 2 ↗ ↗

3 0 0

4 0 0